CAKES &
CAKE DECORATING

THE PRACTICAL ENCYCLOPEDIA OF

CAKES &
CAKE
DECORATING

CLASSIC, CELEBRATION, NOVELTY

AND PARTY CAKES

HERMES
HOUSE.

First published in 1999 by Hermes House

HERMES HOUSE books are available for bulk purchase for sales promotion and for premium use.
For details, write or call the sales director, Hermes House, 27 West 20th Street,
New York, NY 10011; (800) 354-9657

© Anness Publishing Limited 1999

Hermes House is an imprint of Anness Publishing Inc.

ISBN 1 84038 232 5

Publisher: Joanna Lorenz
Project Editor: Felicity Forster
Recipes by: Catherine Atkinson, Carla Capalbo, Carole Clements, Christine France, Sarah Gates,
Carole Handslip, Patricia Lousada, Sue Maggs, Sarah Maxwell, Janice Murfitt, Angela Nilsen,
Louise Pickford, Laura Washburn, Elizabeth Wolf-Cohen
Photographers: Karl Adamson, Edward Allwright, David Armstrong, Steve Baxter,
James Duncan, Amanda Heywood, Tim Hill, Don Last
Editor: Beverley Jollands
Typesetter: Diane Pullen
Designer: Axis Design
Jacket Designer: Mabel Chan
Indexer: Dawn Butcher
Editorial Reader: Jan Cutler
Production Controller: Jessica Arendt

Previously published as two separate titles, *The Cake Decorator's Bible* and *The Ultimate Cake Decorator*

Printed and bound in China

1 3 5 7 9 10 8 6 4 2

ontents

Introduction

This book is not only an invaluable foundation course in cake decorating techniques, but also a wonderful reference book for a host of tried-and-tested recipes for classic cake bases and icings, as well as inspirational cake projects, which you will use again and again.

Clearly structured, the decorating course leads you through all the different decorating techniques that can be applied to marzipan, sugar paste (fondant), royal icing, chocolate and other icings. There are basic recipes for sponge cakes, jelly rolls, Madeira cakes, fruit cakes and truffle cakes, with step-by-step instructions and photographs for piping, crimping, embossing, frills, plaques, coloring, run-outs, modeling, stenciling and flowers, as well as using purchased decorations such as candies, ribbons and fresh flowers.

The wonderful decorated cakes featured in this book are a feast for the eye and palate. Follow the detailed illustrated step-by-step guides to perfect cake making and decorating to create a host of varied finishes, from the simple to the lavish.

Using this book

For best results, use large eggs at room temperature. Always use unsalted butter. Sift flour from a fair height, to give it a chance to aerate and lighten.

No two ovens are alike. If possible, buy a reliable oven thermometer and test the temperature of your oven. Bake in the center of the oven, where the heat is more likely to be constant. For convection ovens, follow the manufacturer's guidelines. Good-quality cake pans will also improve results, as they conduct heat more efficiently.

There are some current health concerns about the use of raw eggs in uncooked recipes. Homemade royal icing, marzipan and sugar paste icing (fondant) do include raw egg. An alternative recipe for royal icing, using pure albumen (egg white) powder, has been provided in light of this. If you prefer to avoid raw egg, buy ready-made marzipan and sugar paste (fondant).

Follow these simple guidelines, and baking success is yours.

Basic Cake Recipes

Cakes are the highlight of many celebrations. What birthday would be complete without a cake with candles to blow out, or a wedding without a beautiful cake to cut? Some of the most traditional cake recipes provide the best bases for decorating. Recipes can be found in this chapter, and are used as bases for the decorated cakes later in the book. None of the cakes involve complicated techniques, and several are as simple as putting the ingredients into a bowl, and mixing them together.

Fruit cake is one of the most popular special occasion cakes. Among its advantages is that it keeps really well and in fact improves with storage, so it can be baked well ahead of time and decorated in easy stages. It also provides a wonderfully firm base for all sorts of elegant or novelty decorations. There are other ideas, too, for those who prefer a less rich tasting cake, such as the Madeira or a light fruit cake, as well as a quick-mix sponge for those last-minute, spontaneous celebrations.

Baking Equipment

A selection of basic equipment is needed for successful cake making. The following are a few of the more necessary items:

Scales For good, consistent results, ingredients for cake making require precise measuring. An accurate set of scales is therefore essential.
Bowls Various sizes of glass or china heatproof bowls with rounded sides make mixing easier and are useful when baking.
Measuring Cup A glass measuring cup is easy to read and means liquids are calculated accurately.
Measuring Spoons These are available in a standard size, making the measuring of small amounts more accurate.
Sifters These are used to aerate flour before baking, making cakes lighter in texture, and to remove lumps from confectioners' sugar or cocoa powder.
Electric Beaters These are particularly useful for whisking egg whites for jelly rolls.
Balloon Whisks Useful for beating smaller amounts of either egg or cream mixtures.
Waxed Paper Used to line cake pans to prevent cakes from sticking.
Wooden and Metal Spoons Wooden

spoons in various sizes are essential for beating mixtures together when not using electric beaters, while metal spoons are necessary for folding in ingredients and for smoothing over mixtures to give a flat surface before baking.

Spatulas Because they are so pliable, plastic spatulas are particularly useful for scraping all the cake mixture from a bowl.

Cake Pans These are available in all shapes and sizes, and the thicker the metal the less likely the cake will be to overcook. Most cake icing specialists rent cake pans, useful when very large or unusual shaped pans are required.

Oven Gloves Essential when removing anything hot from the oven. It is worth choosing a good

quality, well lined pair of gloves.

Wire Racks Made from wire mesh, these are available in different sizes and shapes and allow cakes to "breathe" as they cool.

Cake Boards Choose the shape and size to fit the cake. Thick boards are for large, heavy cakes, royal iced cakes and any other fruit cake coated in icing. The board should be 2 inches larger than the size of the cake. Thinner boards are for small Madeira cakes and other lighter cakes covered with icings such as butter, glacé or fudge. These can be about 1 inch larger than the cake size.

1 *glass mixing bowls*
2 *balloon whisk*
3 *large round cake pan*
4 *electric beaters*
5 *small round cake pan*
6 *scales*
7 *large square cake pan*
8 *measuring cup*
9 *measuring spoons*
10 *cake boards*
11 *pastry brush*
12 *pre-cut waxed paper pan liners*
13 *scissors*
14 *wooden mixing spoons*
15 *wire rack*
16 *sifter*
17 *oven gloves*
18 *plastic spatula*

LINING CAKE PANS

Waxed paper is normally used for lining cake pans. The paper lining prevents the cakes from sticking to the pans and makes them easier to turn out. Different cake recipes require slightly different techniques of lining, depending on the shape of the pan, the type of cake mixture, and how long the cake needs to cook. Quick-mix sponge cakes require only one layer of paper to line the base, for example, whereas rich fruit cakes that often bake for several hours if they are large need to be lined with a double layer of paper on the base and sides. This extra protection also helps cakes to cook evenly.

Lining a shallow round pan

This technique is used for a quick-mix sponge cake.

1 Put the pan on a piece of waxed paper and draw around the base of the pan. Cut out the circle just inside the marked line.

2 ▲ Lightly brush the inside of the pan with a little vegetable oil and position the paper circle in the base of the pan. Brush the paper with a little more vegetable oil.

Tip

Softened butter or margarine can be used as a greasing agent in place of vegetable oil, if wished.

Lining a jelly roll pan

1 Put the pan on a piece of waxed paper and draw around the base. Increase the rectangle by 1 inch on all sides. Cut out this rectangle and snip each corner diagonally down to the original rectangle.

2 ▲ Lightly brush the inside of the pan with a little vegetable oil and fit the paper into the pan, overlapping the corners slightly so that they fit neatly. Brush the paper with a little more vegetable oil.

Lining a deep round cake pan

This technique should be used for all rich or light fruit cakes and Madeira cakes. Use this method for a square pan, but cut out the sides separately.

1 Put the pan on a double thickness of waxed paper and draw around the base. Cut out just inside the line.

2 For the sides of the pan, cut out a double thickness strip of waxed paper that will wrap around the outside of the pan, allowing a slight overlap, and which is 1 inch taller than the depth of the pan.

3 Fold over 1 inch along the length of the side lining. Snip the paper along its length, inside the fold, at short, evenly spaced intervals.

4 Brush the inside of the pan with vegetable oil. Slip the side lining into the pan so the snipped edge fits into the curve of the base and sits flat.

5 ▲ Position the base lining in the pan and brush the paper with a little more vegetable oil.

Testing cakes

• Always check the cake 5–10 minutes before the given cooking time is completed, just in case the oven is a little fast. It is always better to undercook a cake slightly, since the mixture continues to cook in the pan after it is removed from the oven.

• Always test the cake immediately before removing it from the oven, just in case it is not ready at the advised time. This could be due to a slow oven.

• For all cakes, other than fruit cakes, test by pressing very lightly on the center of the cake with the fingers; if it springs back, the cake is cooked. Otherwise your fingers will leave a slight depression, indicating that the cake needs extra cooking time. Retest at 5-minute intervals.

• Fruit cakes are best tested using a warmed skewer inserted into the center of the cake. If the skewer comes out clean, the cake is ready. Otherwise, return the cake to the oven and retest at 10-minute intervals.

Storing cakes

Everyday cakes, sponges and meringues may be kept in an airtight container or simply wrapped in plastic wrap or foil; this will ensure that they keep moist and fresh with the exclusion of the air. Store the cakes in a cool, dry place for up to a week; meringues will store for up to a month. Avoid warm, moist conditions, as this will encourage mold growth.

To store fruit cakes, leave the lining paper on the cakes. This seals onto the surface during cooking and keeps the cakes moist and fresh. Wrap the cakes in a double layer of foil and keep in a cool place. Never seal a fruit cake in an airtight container for long periods of time, as this may encourage mold growth.

Rich, heavy fruit cakes keep well because of their high fruit content; although they stay moist and full of flavor, they are at their best when they are first made. Such cakes mature with keeping, but most should be consumed within three months. If you are going to keep a fruit cake for several months before marzipanning or icing it, pour alcohol (such as brandy or sherry) over it a little at a time at monthly intervals, turning the cake each time.

Light fruit cakes are stored in the same way as their rich cousins, but since they have less fruit in them, their keeping qualities are not so good. These cakes are at their best when first made, or eaten within a month of making.

For long-term storage, fruit cakes are better frozen in their double wrapping and foil.

Once the cakes have been marzipanned and iced, they will keep longer. But iced cakes must be stored in cardboard boxes in a warm, dry atmosphere, to keep them dust-free and in good condition. Damp and cold are the worst conditions, causing the icing to stain and colorings to run.

Freeze a decorated celebration cake in a cake box, making sure the lid is sealed with tape. To defrost, take the cake out of its box and defrost it slowly in a cool, dry place. When the cake has thawed, transfer to a warm, dry place to ensure that the icing dries completely. Wedding cakes that have been kept for a long time may need re-icing and decorating.

Calculating quantities and cutting cakes

To work out the number of servings from a round or square cake is extremely simple; the final total depends on whether you require just a small sliver of cake or a more substantial slice.

Whether the cake is round or square, cut across the cake from edge to edge into about 1 inch slices, thinner if desired. Cut each slice into approximately 2 inch pieces.

Using these guidelines, it should be easy to calculate the number of cake slices you can cut from any given size cake. A square cake is larger than a round cake of the same proportions and will yield more slices. On a round cake the slices become smaller at the curved edges, and the first and last slice of the cake is mainly marzipan and icing. Always keep this in mind when calculating the servings.

Example
According to the measurements above an 8-inch square cake will yield about 40 slices and an 8-inch round cake will yield about 35 slices.

Quick-mix Sponge Cake

Here's a no-fuss, foolproof all-in-one cake, where the ingredients are quickly mixed together. The following quantities and baking instructions are for a deep 8 inch round cake pan or an 8 inch ring mold. For other quantities and pan sizes, follow the baking instructions given in the decorated cake recipes.

INGREDIENTS
1 cup self-rising flour
1 tsp baking powder
½ cup soft margarine
½ cup superfine sugar
2 large eggs

STORING AND FREEZING
The cake can be made up to two days in advance, wrapped in plastic wrap or foil and stored in an airtight container. The cake can be frozen for up to three months.

FLAVORINGS
The following amounts are for a 2-egg, single quantity cake, as above. Increase the amounts proportionally for larger cakes.
Chocolate *Fold 1 tbsp cocoa powder blended with 1 tbsp boiling water into the cake mixture.*
Citrus *Fold 2 tsp of finely grated lemon, orange or lime zest into the cake mixture.*

1 Preheat the oven to 325°F. Grease the round cake pan, line the base with waxed paper and then grease the paper, or grease and flour the ring mold.

2 ▲ Sift the flour and baking powder into a bowl. Add the margarine, sugar and eggs.

3 ▲ Beat with a wooden spoon for 2–3 minutes. The mixture should be pale in color and slightly glossy.

4 Spoon the cake mixture into the prepared pan and then smooth the surface. Bake for 20–30 minutes. To test if cooked, press the cake lightly in the center. If firm, the cake is done, if soft, cook for a little longer. Alternatively, insert a skewer into the center of the cake. If it comes out clean the cake is ready. Turn out on to a wire rack, remove the lining paper and leave to cool completely.

This quick-mix sponge cake can be filled and simply decorated with icing for a special occasion.

Whisked Sponge Cake

This delicious light-textured sponge can be used to make jelly rolls or cakes.
As it contains no fat it does not keep well, so it is best baked on the day it will be eaten.
The following quantities are for a 13 x 9-inch jelly roll pan or an 8-inch round cake pan.

INGREDIENTS
4 large eggs
½ cup superfine sugar
1 cup all-purpose flour

1 Preheat the oven to 350°F. Grease the jelly roll pan or round cake pan, line with waxed or parchment paper and grease the paper.

2 ▲ Whisk together the eggs and sugar in a heatproof bowl until thoroughly blended. Place the bowl over a saucepan of simmering water and whisk until thick and pale. Remove the bowl from the saucepan and continue whisking until the mixture is cool and leaves a thick trail when the beaters are lifted.

3 ▲ Sift the flour onto the surface and, using a metal spoon or plastic spatula, carefully fold the flour into the mixture until smooth.

4 ▲ Pour the cake batter into the prepared pan and tilt to level. Bake in the center of the oven for 12–15 minutes for the jelly roll or 25–30 minutes for the round cake. To test if cooked, press lightly in the center: if the cake springs back, it is done.

5 Turn the jelly roll out onto a piece of waxed paper sprinkled with superfine sugar. Peel off the lining paper, fill as required and roll up. Leave the round cake in the pan for 5 minutes, then turn out onto a wire rack, peel off the lining paper and allow to cool completely.

Airy whisked sponge cake is the classic base for jelly rolls; here, one incorporating a cream and raspberry filling.

Jelly Roll

Jelly rolls are traditionally made without fat, so they don't keep as long as most other cakes. However, they have a deliciously light texture and provide the cook with the potential for all sorts of luscious fillings and tasty toppings.

INGREDIENTS
4 large eggs, separated
½ cup superfine sugar
1 cup flour
1 tsp baking powder

STORING AND FREEZING
Jelly rolls and other fat-free sponges do not keep well, so if possible bake on the day of eating. Otherwise, wrap in plastic wrap or foil and store in an airtight container overnight or freeze for up to three months.

1 Preheat the oven to 350°F. Grease a 13 x 9 inch jelly roll pan, line with waxed paper and grease the paper.

2 Whisk the egg whites in a clean, dry bowl until stiff. Beat in 2 tbsp of the sugar.

3 ▲ Place the egg yolks, remaining sugar and 1 tbsp water in a bowl and beat for about 2 minutes until the mixture is pale and leaves a thick trail when the beaters are lifted.

4 ▼ Carefully fold the beaten egg yolks into the egg white mixture with a metal spoon.

5 Sift together the flour and baking powder. Carefully fold the flour mixture into the egg mixture with a metal spoon.

6 ▲ Pour the cake mixture into the prepared pan and then smooth the surface, being careful not to press out any air.

7 Bake in the center of the oven for 12 –15 minutes. To test if cooked, press lightly in the center. If the cake springs back it is done. It will also start to come away from the edges of the pan.

8 Turn the cake out on to a piece of waxed paper lightly sprinkled with superfine sugar. Peel off the lining paper and cut off any crisp edges of the cake with a sharp knife. Spread with jam or jelly, if wished, and roll up, using the waxed paper as a guide. Leave to cool on a wire rack.

Vary the flavor of a traditional jelly roll by adding a little grated orange, lime or lemon rind to the basic mixture.

ruffle Cake Mix

This is a no-cook recipe, using leftover pieces of sponge cake or plain store-bought sponge to make a moist, rich cake mixture, which is used in several of the novelty cakes.

INGREDIENTS
6 oz plain sponge cake pieces
2 cups ground almonds
scant ⅓ cup dark brown
sugar, firmly packed
1 tsp ground allspice
pinch of ground cinnamon
finely grated zest of 1 orange
3 tbsp freshly squeezed orange juice
5 tbsp honey

STORING AND FREEZING
The mixture can be made up to two days in advance, wrapped in plastic wrap and stored in an airtight container. Not suitable for freezing.

1 Place the sponge cake pieces into the bowl of a food processor or blender and process for a few seconds to form fine crumbs.

2 Place the cake crumbs, ground almonds, sugar, spices, orange zest, orange juice and honey in a large mixing bowl. Stir well to combine into a thick, smooth mixture.

3 ▲ Use the mixture as directed in the novelty cake recipes. The truffle mixture can be made and molded into any simple shape, such as a log or round balls. The molded mixture can be covered either with marzipan or with sugarpaste icing.

Tip

Dampen your hands slightly before handling the truffle mixture, as it is very sticky.

Here the truffle mixture has been rolled into a log shape to form the sausage in this sweet-tasting novelty Hot Dog cake.

Madeira Cake

This fine-textured cake makes a good base for decorating and is therefore a useful alternative to fruit cake, although it will not keep as long. It provides a firmer, longer-lasting base than a Victoria sponge, and can be covered with butter icing, fudge frosting, a thin layer of marzipan or sugarpaste icing. For the ingredients, decide what size and shape of cake you wish to make and then follow the chart shown opposite.

STORING AND FREEZING
The cake can be made up to a week in advance, wrapped in plastic wrap or foil and stored in an airtight container. The cake can be frozen for up to three months.

Madeira cake provides a firmer base for icing than a Victoria sponge. It can be covered with a thin layer of sugarpaste, as here, or marzipan, and is a great alternative for anyone who does not like fruit cake.

1 Preheat the oven to 325°F. Grease a deep cake pan, line the base and sides with a double thickness of waxed paper and then lightly grease the paper.

2 ▲ Sift together the flour and baking powder into a mixing bowl. Add the margarine, sugar, eggs and lemon juice.

3 ▲ Stir the ingredients together with a wooden spoon until they are all well combined.

4 ▲ Beat the mixture for about 2 minutes until smooth and glossy.

5 Spoon the mixture into the prepared pan and smooth the top. Bake in the center of the oven, following the chart opposite as a guide for baking times. If the cake browns too quickly, cover the top loosely with foil. To test if baked, press lightly in the center. If the cake springs back it is done. Alternatively, test by inserting a skewer into the center of the cake. If it comes out clean the cake is done. Leave the cake to cool in the pan for 5 minutes and then turn out on to a wire rack. Remove the lining paper and leave to cool.

MADEIRA CAKE CHART

Cake pan sizes	7 in round	8 in round	9 in round	10 in round	12 in round
	6 in square	7 in square	8 in square	9 in square	11 in square
Flour	2 cups	3 cups	4 cups	4½ cups	6 cups
Baking powder	1½ tsp	2 tsp	2½ tsp	1 tbsp	4 tsp
Soft margarine	¾ cup	1¼ cups	1½ cups	1¾ cups	2¼ cups
Superfine sugar	¾ cup	1¼ cups	1½ cups	1¾ cups	2½ cups
Eggs, large, beaten	3	4	6	7	10
Lemon juice	1 tbsp	1½ tbsp	2 tbsp	2½ tbsp	4 tbsp
Approx. baking time	1¼ – 1½ hours	1½ – 1¾ hours	1¾ – 2 hours	1¾ – 2 hours	2¼ – 2½ hours

A traditional Madeira cake peaks and cracks slightly on the top. For a flat surface on which to ice, simply level the top with a sharp knife.

$\mathcal{R}$ich Fruit Cake

This is the traditional cake mixture for many cakes made for special occasions such as weddings, Christmas, anniversaries and christenings. Make the cake a few weeks before icing, keep it well wrapped and stored in an airtight container and it should mature beautifully. Because of all its rich ingredients, this fruit cake will keep moist and fresh for several months. Follow the ingredients guide in the chart opposite for the size of cake you wish to make.

STORING
When the cake is cold, wrap in a double thickness of waxed paper or foil. Store in an airtight container in a cool dry place where it will keep for several months. During storage, the cake can be unwrapped and the bottom brushed with brandy (about half the amount used in the recipe). Re-wrap before storing again. As the cake keeps so well, there is no need to freeze.

A long-lasting cake which is full of rich flavors.

1 Preheat the oven to 275°F. Grease a deep cake pan, line the base and sides with a double thickness of waxed paper and then lightly grease the paper.

2 ▲ Place all the ingredients in a large mixing bowl.

3 ▲ Stir to combine, then beat thoroughly with a wooden spoon for 3–6 minutes (depending on size), until well mixed.

4 ▲ Spoon the mixture into the prepared pan and smooth the surface with the back of a wet metal spoon. Make a slight impression in the center to help prevent the cake from doming.

5 Bake in the center of the oven. Use the chart opposite as a guide for timing the cake you are baking. Test the cake about 30 minutes before the end of the baking time. If the cake browns too quickly, cover the top loosely with foil. To test if baked, press lightly in the center. If the cake feels firm and when a skewer inserted in the center comes out clean, it is done. Test again at intervals if necessary.

6 Leave the cake to cool in the pan. When completely cool, turn out of the pan. The lining paper can be left on to help keep the cake moist.

RICH FRUIT CAKE CHART

Cake pan sizes	6 in round	7 in round	8 in round	9 in round	10 in round	11 in round	12 in round	13 in round
	5 in square	6 in square	7 in square	8 in square	9 in square	10 in square	11 in square	12 in square
Currants	1¼ cups	1¾ cups	2¼ cups	3 cups	3½ cups	4½ cups	5¼ cups	6 cups
Sultanas	⅔ cup	1 cup	1½ cups	1¾ cups	2 cups	2½ cups	3 cups	3½ cups
Raisins	⅓ cup	⅔ cup	¾ cup	1 cup	1 cup	1⅓ cups	1½ cups	1½ cups
Glacé cherries, halved	¼ cup	⅓ cup	½ cup	½ cup	⅔ cup	¾ cup	1 cup	1¼ cups
Almonds, chopped	⅓ cup	½ cup	¾ cup	1 cup	1¼ cups	1½ cups	1⅔ cups	2 cups
Mixed citrus peel	¼ cup	½ cup	½ cup	⅔ cup	¾ cup	1 cup	1 cup	1⅓ cups
Lemon, grated rind	½	1	1	2	2	2	3	3
Brandy	1½ tbsp	2 tbsp	2½ tbsp	3 tbsp	3½ tbsp	4 tbsp	4½ tbsp	5 tbsp
Flour	1⅓ cups	1¾ cups	2 cups	2¾ cups	3½ cups	4 cups	4½ cups	5½ cups
Ground allspice	1 tsp	1 tsp	1¼ tsp	1½ tsp	1½ tsp	2 tsp	2½ tsp	1 tbsp
Ground nutmeg	¼ tsp	½ tsp	½ tsp	1 tsp	1 tsp	1 tsp	1½ tsp	2 tsp
Ground almonds	½ cup	⅔ cup	¾ cup	1 cup	1¼ cups	1⅓ cups	1½ cups	1⅔ cups
Soft margarine or butter	½ cup	⅔ cup	scant 1 cup	scant 1¼ cups	scant 1½ cups	scant 1¾ cups	scant 2 cups	2¼ cups
Soft brown sugar	⅔ cup	¾ cup	1 cup	1⅓ cups	1½ cups	scant 2 cups	2 cups	2¼ cups
Black molasses	1 tbsp	1 tbsp	1 tbsp	1½ tbsp	2 tbsp	2 tbsp	2 tbsp	2½ tbsp
Eggs, large, beaten	3	4	5	6	7	8	9	10
Approx. baking time	2¼–2½ hours	2½–2¾ hours	3–3½ hours	3¼–3¾ hours	3¾–4¼ hours	4–4½ hours	4½–5¼ hours	5¼–5¾ hours

Light Fruit Cake

For those who prefer a lighter fruit cake, here is a less rich version, still ideal for marzipanning and covering with sugarpaste or royal icing. Follow the ingredients guide in the chart opposite according to the size of cake you wish to make.

STORING AND FREEZING
When the cake is cold, wrap well in waxed paper, plastic wrap or foil. It will keep for several weeks, stored in an airtight container. As the cake keeps so well, there is no need to freeze, but, if wished, freeze for up to three months.

1 Preheat the oven to 300°F. Grease a deep cake pan, line the sides and base with a double thickness of waxed paper and lightly grease the paper.

2 ▲ Measure and prepare all the ingredients, then place them all together in a large mixing bowl.

3 ▲ Stir to combine, then beat thoroughly with a wooden spoon for 3–4 minutes, depending on the size, until well mixed.

4 ▲ Spoon the mixture into the prepared pan and smooth the surface with the back of a wet metal spoon. Make a slight impression in the center to help prevent the cake from doming.

5 Bake in the center of the oven. Use the chart opposite as a guide according to the size of cake you are baking. Test the cake about 15 minutes before the end of the baking time. If the cake browns too quickly, cover the top loosely with foil. To test if baked, press lightly in the center. If the cake feels firm, and when a skewer inserted in the center comes out clean, it is done. Test again at intervals if necessary.

6 Leave the cake to cool in the pan. When completely cool, turn out of the pan. The lining paper can be left on to help keep the cake moist.

Round, square, ring or heart-shaped – the shape of this light fruit cake can be varied to suit the occasion.

LIGHT FRUIT CAKE CHART

Cake pan sizes	6 in round	7 in round	8 in round	9 in round
	5 in square	6 in square	7 in square	8 in square
Soft margarine or butter	½ cup	¾ cup	1 cup	1⅓ cups
Superfine sugar	½ cup	¾ cup	1 cup	1⅓ cups
Orange, grated rind	½	½	1	1
Eggs, large, beaten	3	4	5	6
Flour	1½ cups	1¾ cups	2¾ cups	3½ cups
Baking powder	¼ tsp	½ tsp	½ tsp	1 tsp
Ground allspice	1 tsp	1½ tsp	2 tsp	2½ tsp
Currants	⅓ cup	⅔ cup	1 cup	1½ cups
Sultanas	⅓ cup	⅔ cup	1 cup	1⅓ cups
Raisins	⅓ cup	⅔ cup	1 cup	1⅓ cups
Dried apricots, chopped	7	14	14	21
Mixed cut citrus peel	scant ½ cup	good ½ cup	¾ cup	1 cup
Approx. baking time	2¼ – 2½ hours	2½ – 2¾ hours	2¾ – 3¼ hours	3¼ – 3¾ hours

Basic Icing Recipes

Cakes can take on many guises, and nothing enhances their appearance more for that extra special occasion than a little icing. This chapter offers a range of simple classic icing recipes to suit the type of cake you have made and which can be adapted according to the occasion. Ideas range from quick-mix icings, such as butter icing and satin chocolate icing, which may be instantly poured, spread, swirled or piped on to sponge and Madeira cakes or jelly rolls, to the more regal icings, such as royal icing and sugarpaste icing. These are ideal for covering and decorating fruit cakes intended for more formal occasions, such as anniversaries, christenings and weddings.

The icings in this section are all fairly traditional. However, if you want to substitute any of them with a favorite icing recipe when decorating, make sure that it suits the cake on which you are working.

Decorating Equipment

With a few simple tools, it is possible to create the most stunning of cake decorations. Thick swirls of butter icing formed with a spatula, or stark white confectioners' sugar dusted over a contrastingly dark chocolate icing, instantly provide an impressive effect. As your skills develop, however, you will probably want to invest in some specialized pieces of icing equipment, such as those listed here.

Icing Turntable This is one of the most expensive but useful items for either the novice or more advanced cake decorator. Because it revolves, it is particularly handy for piping, or for icing the sides of a round cake with royal icing.

Straight-edge Ruler Choose one made of stainless steel so that it will not bend as you pull it across a layer of royal icing, to give a smooth, flat surface to a cake.

Icing Scrapers These can have straight or serrated edges for giving a smooth or patterned surface to the sides or tops of cakes coated with royal, butter or fudge icing.

Small Rolling Pin Made in a handy size for rolling out small amounts of marzipan or sugarpaste icing for decorations.

Nozzles There are numerous shapes and sizes to choose from, but it is best to start off with some of the basic shapes. Small straight-sided nozzles fit homemade waxed paper piping bags. Larger ones are more suitable for the commercially-made fabric bags when piping large amounts of icing.

Nozzle Brush A small wire brush which makes the job of cleaning out nozzles a lot easier.

Flower Nail Used as a support when piping flowers.

Crimping Tools These are available with different end-shapes which produce varied patterns and offer a quick way of giving a professional finish to a cake.

Paintbrushes Brushes for painting designs on to cakes, adding highlights to flowers or modeled shapes, or for making run-outs are available at cake icing specialists, stationers or art supply shops.

Florists' Wire, Tape and Stamens All available from cake icing specialists. The wire, available in different gauges, is handy for wiring small sugarpaste flowers together to form floral sprays. The tape is used to neaten the stems, and the stamens, available in many colors, form the centers of the flowers.

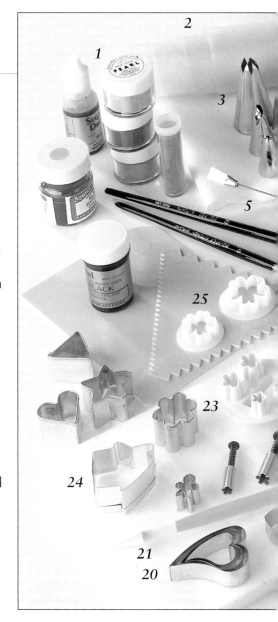

Papers There are two types of papers used in cake decorating. Waxed paper is used for making piping bags and for drying sugar-frosted flowers and fruits, while parchment paper is used for spreading melted chocolate and for icing run-outs.

Cutters Small cocktail cutters are useful for making cut-out shapes from chocolate, sugarpaste and marzipan. Blossom cutters, available in different shapes and sizes, are good for making small flowers, while a special frill cutter can be used to cut out quick-and-easy frills.

1 food colorings
2 waxed paper and parchment paper
3 piping nozzles
4 fabric piping bag
5 nozzle brush
6 paintbrushes
7 icing turntable
8 florists' wire
9 stamens
10 florists' tape
11 straight-edge ruler
12 cake pillars

13 cake pillar supports
14 crimping tools
15 food coloring pens
16 flower nail
17 frill cutter
18 textured rolling pin
19 foam pad
20 shaped cutters
21 modeling tool
22 plunger cutters
23 dual blossom cutter
24 cocktail cutters
25 plain and serrated side scrapers

*M*arzipan

With its smooth, pliable texture, marzipan has been popular for centuries in cake making, especially for large cakes such as wedding and christening cakes. It is also excellent for making a variety of cake decorations. The following recipe is sufficient to cover the top and sides of a 7 inch round or a 6 inch square cake. Make half the amount if only the top is to be covered.

INGREDIENTS
Makes 1 lb
2¼ cups ground almonds
1 cup confectioners' sugar, sifted
½ cup superfine sugar
1 tsp lemon juice
2 drops almond extract
1 medium egg, beaten

STORING
The marzipan will keep for up to four days, wrapped in plastic wrap in an airtight container, and stored in the refrigerator.

1 ▲ Put the ground almonds, confectioners' and superfine sugars into a bowl and mix together.

2 ▲ Add the lemon juice, almond extract and enough beaten egg to mix to a soft but firm dough. Gather together with your fingers to form a ball.

3 ▲ Knead the marzipan on a work surface lightly dusted with sifted confectioners' sugar until smooth.

Using Marzipan

Marzipan is applied to the sides and top of a cake, particularly rich fruit cakes, to prevent moisture seeping through the cake and to provide a smooth undercoat for the top covering of royal icing or sugarpaste icing.

Once the marzipan has been applied, leave it to dry for a day or two before applying the icing. For a richer taste you can mix up your own marzipan. However, if you have any concerns about using raw eggs in uncooked recipes, especially in light of current health warnings, do buy ready-made marzipan. It is very good quality, does not contain raw egg and is available in two colors, white and yellow. White is the best choice if you want to add your own colors and create different molded shapes.

Marzipan can be used as an attractive cake coating in its own right as well as providing a base for other icings.

*S*ugarpaste Icing

Sugarpaste icing has opened up a whole new concept in cake decorating. It is wonderfully pliable, easy to make and use, and can be colored, molded and shaped in the most imaginative fashion. Though quick to make at home, store-bought sugarpaste, also known as easy-roll or ready-to-roll icing, is very good quality and handy to use. This recipe makes sufficient to cover the top and sides of a 7 inch round or a 6 inch square cake.

INGREDIENTS
Makes 12 oz
1 large egg white
1 tbsp liquid glucose, warmed
3 cups confectioners' sugar, sifted

STORING
The icing will keep for up to a week, wrapped in plastic wrap or a plastic bag and stored in the refrigerator. Bring to room temperature before using. If a thin crust forms, trim off before using or it will make the icing lumpy. Also, if the icing dries out or hardens, knead in a little boiled water to make it smooth and pliable again.

1 Put the egg white and glucose in a bowl. Stir together with a wooden spoon to break up the egg white.

2 ▲ Add the confectioners' sugar and mix together with a spatula or knife, using a chopping action, until well blended and the icing begins to bind together.

3 Knead the mixture with your fingers until it forms a ball.

4 ▲ Knead the sugarpaste on a work surface lightly dusted with sifted confectioners' sugar until smooth, soft and pliable. If the icing is too soft, knead in more sifted confectioners' sugar until it is firm and pliable.

*T*ip

Ready-made store-bought sugarpaste does not contain raw egg, so do use this if you prefer to avoid uncooked egg in recipes in light of current health warnings.

Tinted or left pure white, sugarpaste icing can be used to cover cakes, and molded to make decorations to suit any shape of cake.

Royal Icing

Royal icing has gained a regal position in the world of icing. Any special occasion cake which demands a classical, professional finish uses this smooth, satin-like icing. The following recipe makes sufficient to cover the top and sides of a 7 inch round or a 6 inch square cake.

INGREDIENTS
Makes 1½ lb
3 large egg whites
about 6 cups confectioners' sugar, sifted
1½ tsp glycerine
few drops lemon juice
food coloring (optional)

STORING
Royal icing will keep for up to three days in an airtight container, stored in the refrigerator. Stir the icing well before using.

ips

• Always sift confectioners' sugar before using, to get rid of any lumps.
• Never add more than the stated amount of glycerine. Too much will make the icing crumbly and too fragile to use.
• A little lemon juice is added to prevent the icing from discoloring, but too much will make the icing become hard.

1 ▲ Put the egg whites in a bowl and stir lightly with a wooden spoon to break them up.

2 ▲ Add the confectioners' sugar gradually in small quantities, beating well with a wooden spoon between each addition. Add sufficient sugar to make a smooth, white, shiny icing with the consistency of very stiff meringue. It should be thin enough to spread, but thick enough to hold its shape.

3 ▲ Beat in the glycerine, lemon juice and food coloring, if using.

4 It is best to let the icing sit for about 1 hour before using. Cover the surface with a piece of damp plastic wrap or a lid so the icing does not dry out. Before using, stir the icing to burst any air bubbles. Even when working with royal icing, always keep it covered.

Royal Icing Using Pure Albumen Powder

If you are concerned about current health warnings advising against the use of raw eggs in uncooked recipes, try the following recipe.

INGREDIENTS
Makes 1 lb
4 cups confectioners' sugar, sifted
6 tbsp water
7 tsp pure albumen powder

STORING
This royal icing will keep for up to a week in an airtight container, stored in a cool place.

1 Mix the pure albumen powder with the water. Leave to stand for 15 minutes, then stir until the powder dissolves.

2 Sieve the albumen solution into a mixing bowl. Add half the confectioners' sugar and beat until smooth. Add the remaining sugar and beat again for 12–14 minutes or until smooth.

3 Adjust the consistency as needed, adding a little more confectioners' sugar for a stiffer icing or a little water for a thinner one. If storing, transfer to an airtight container, cover the surface of the royal icing with plastic wrap and then close the lid.

ICING CONSISTENCIES

For flat icing

▲ The recipes on the opposite page are for a consistency of icing suitable for flat icing a rich fruit cake covered in marzipan. When the spoon is lifted out of the icing, it should form a sharp point, with a slight curve at the end, known as a "soft peak."

For peaking

▲ Make the royal icing as before, but to a stiffer consistency so that when the spoon is lifted out of the bowl the icing stands in straight peaks.

For piping

For piping purposes, the icing needs to be slightly stiffer than for peaked icing so that it forms a fine, sharp peak when the spoon is lifted out. This allows the icing to flow easily for piping, at the same time enabling it to keep its definition.

For run-outs

For elegant and more elaborate cakes, you may want to pipe outlines of shapes and then fill these in with different colored icing. These are known as run-outs. For the outlines, you need to make the icing to a piping consistency, while for the insides you need a slightly thinner icing with a consistency of thick cream, so that with a little help it will flow within the shapes. Ideally the icing should hold its shape and be slightly rounded after filling the outlines.

The right consistency

If you need to change the consistency of your icing, add a little sifted confectioners' sugar to make it stiffer, or beat in a little egg white for a thinner icing. Be sure to do this carefully, as a little of one or the other will change the consistency quickly.

A traditional look for a classic royal icing. This square rich fruit cake has been marzipanned and then flat iced with three, ultra-smooth layers of royal icing. It is simply, but elegantly, decorated with piped borders, a crisp, white ribbon and fresh roses.

Butter Icing

The creamy, rich flavor and silky smoothness of butter icing are popular with both children and adults. The icing can be varied in color and flavor and makes a decorative filling and coating for sponge and Madeira cakes or jelly rolls. Simply swirled, or more elaborately piped, butter icing gives a delicious and attractive finish. The following quantity makes enough to fill and coat the sides and top of an 8 inch sponge cake.

INGREDIENTS
Makes 12 oz
6 tbsp butter, softened,
or soft margarine
2 cups confectioners' sugar, sifted
1 tsp vanilla extract
2–3 tsp milk

STORING
The icing will keep for up to three days, in an airtight container stored in the refrigerator.

1 ▲ Put the butter or margarine, confectioners' sugar, vanilla extract and 1 tsp of the milk in a bowl.

2 ▲ Beat with a wooden spoon or electric beaters adding sufficient extra milk to give a light, smooth and fluffy consistency.

FLAVORINGS
The following amounts are for a single quantity of icing. Increase or decrease the amounts proportionally as needed.
Chocolate *Blend 1 tbsp cocoa powder with 1 tbsp hot water. Allow to cool before beating into the icing.*
Coffee *Blend 2 tsp instant coffee powder or granules with 1 tbsp boiling water. Allow to cool before beating into the icing.*
Lemon, orange or lime *Substitute the vanilla extract and milk with lemon, orange or lime juice and 2 tsp of finely grated citrus zest. Omit the zest if using the icing for piping. Lightly color the icing with the appropriate shade of food coloring, if wished.*

Generous swirls of butter icing give a mouth-watering effect to a cake.

*C*lassic Buttercream

This icing takes a little more time to make, but it is well worth it. The rich, smooth, light texture makes it suitable for spreading, filling or piping onto special cakes. Use it as soon as it is made for best results, or keep it at room temperature for a few hours. Do not reheat or it will curdle. The following amount will fill and decorate the top and sides of an 8-inch round cake.

INGREDIENTS
Makes 12 ounces
4 tablespoons water
6 tablespoons superfine sugar
2 egg yolks
10 tablespoons (²/₃ cup) butter, softened

FLAVORINGS
The following amounts are for a single quantity of icing.
Orange, lemon or lime *Replace the water with orange, lemon or lime juice and 2 teaspoons finely grated orange, lemon or lime zest.*
Chocolate *Add 2 ounces semisweet chocolate, melted.*
Coffee *Blend 2 teaspoons instant coffee powder or granules with 1 tablespoon boiling water. Cool before folding into the icing.*

1 Place the water in a small saucepan, bring to a boil, remove the saucepan from the heat and stir in the sugar. Heat gently until the sugar has completely dissolved. Remove the spoon.

2 ▲ Boil rapidly until the mixture becomes syrupy. To test, remove the pan from the heat and place a little syrup on the back of a dry teaspoon. Press a second teaspoon onto the syrup and gently pull apart. The syrup should form a fine thread. If it doesn't, return the saucepan to the heat.

3 ▲ Beat the egg yolks together in a bowl. Continue beating while slowly adding the sugar syrup in a steady stream. Beat until the mixture becomes thick, pale and cool, and leaves a trail on the surface when the beaters are lifted.

4 ▲ Beat the butter in a separate bowl until light and fluffy. Add the egg mixture gradually, beating well after each addition, until thick and fluffy. Fold in the chosen flavoring, using a spatula, until evenly blended.

Seven-Minute Frosting

A traditional American light marshmallow icing that hardens on the outside when left to dry, this versatile frosting may be swirled or peaked into a soft coating. It looks perfect as a snowy landscape for a Christmas cake. The following amount is sufficient to cover an 8-inch round cake.

INGREDIENTS
Makes 12 ounces
1 egg white
2 tablespoons water
1 tablespoon golden or
light corn syrup
1 teaspoon cream of tartar
1½ cups confectioners'
sugar, sifted

This frosting makes a light, fluffy yet crisp topping, its soft white contrasting well with chocolate curls.

1 ▲ Place the egg white, water, syrup and cream of tartar in a heatproof bowl. Beat until thoroughly blended.

2 ▲ Stir the confectioners' sugar into the mixture and place the bowl over a saucepan of simmering water. Beat until the mixture becomes thick and white and holds soft peaks.

3 Remove the bowl from the saucepan and continue to beat the frosting until it is cool and thick, and stands up in soft peaks.

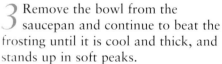

4 ▲ Use immediately to fill or cover the cake. Once iced, the cake can be decorated in any way you like, such as with chocolate curls, as shown here.

Glacé Icing

This icing can be made in just a few minutes and can be varied by adding a few drops of food coloring or flavoring. The following quantity makes enough to cover the top and decorate an 8 inch round sponge cake.

INGREDIENTS
Makes 8 oz
2 cups confectioners' sugar
2–3 tbsp warm water or fruit juice
food coloring, optional

STORING
Not suitable for storing. The icing must be used immediately after making.

1 ▲ Sift the confectioners' sugar into a bowl to get rid of any lumps.

2 ▲ Using a wooden spoon, gradually stir in enough water to make an icing with the consistency of thick cream. Beat until the icing is smooth. It should be thick enough to coat the back of the spoon. If it is too runny, beat in a little more sifted confectioners' sugar.

3 To color the icing, beat in a few drops of food coloring. Use the icing immediately for coating or piping.

Drizzled or spread, glacé icing can quickly turn a plain cake into something special.

$\mathcal{B}$utterscotch Frosting

This is a richly flavored frosting, made with brown sugar and molasses. It is useful for coating any sponge cake to impart a smooth or swirled finish.

INGREDIENTS
Makes 1 pound
6 tablespoons unsalted butter
3 tablespoons milk
2 tablespoons light brown sugar
1 tablespoon molasses
2¼ cups confectioners'
sugar, sifted

Butterscotch frosting is deliciously caramel-flavored and an unusual alternative for coating a cake.

FLAVORINGS
The following amounts are for a single quantity of icing. Increase or decrease the amounts proportionally as needed.
Orange, lemon or lime *Replace the molasses with golden or light corn syrup and add 2 teaspoons of finely grated orange, lemon or lime zest.*
Chocolate *Sift 1 tablespoon cocoa powder with the confectioners' sugar.*
Coffee *Replace the molasses with 1 tablespoon instant coffee powder or granules.*

1 ▲ Place the butter, milk, brown sugar and molasses in a heatproof bowl over a saucepan of simmering water. Stir occasionally, using a wooden spoon, until the butter and sugar have melted.

2 ▲ Remove the bowl from the saucepan. Stir in the confectioners' sugar, then beat until smooth and glossy.

3 ▲ Pour immediately over the cake for a smooth finish, or allow to cool for a thicker spreading consistency.

*F*udge Frosting

*A rich, darkly delicious frosting, this can transform a simple sponge cake into
one worthy of a very special occasion. Spread fudge frosting smoothly over the cake or swirl it.
Or be even more elaborate with a little piping - it is very versatile. The following amount
will fill and coat the top and sides of an 8 inch or 9 inch round sponge cake.*

INGREDIENTS
Makes 12 oz
2 x 1 oz squares plain chocolate
2 cups confectioners' sugar, sifted
4 tbsp butter or margarine
3 tbsp milk or light cream
1 tsp vanilla extract

STORING
*Not suitable for storing. The icing
must be used immediately after
making.*

1 ▲ Break the chocolate into small pieces. Put the chocolate, confectioners' sugar, butter or margarine, milk and vanilla extract in a heavy-based saucepan.

2 ▲ Stir over a very low heat until the chocolate and butter or margarine melt. Remove from the heat and stir until evenly blended.

3 ▲ Beat the icing frequently as it cools until it thickens sufficiently to use for spreading or piping. Use immediately and work quickly once it has reached the right consistency.

*Thick glossy swirls of fudge icing
almost make a decoration in
themselves on this cake.*

Satin Chocolate Icing

Shiny as satin and smooth as silk, this dark chocolate icing can be poured over a sponge cake. A few fresh flowers, pieces of fresh fruit, simple chocolate shapes or white chocolate piping add the finishing touch. Use this recipe to cover an 8 inch square or a 9 inch round quick-mix sponge or Madeira cake.

INGREDIENTS
Makes 8 oz
6 x 1oz squares plain chocolate
⅔ cup light cream
½ tsp instant coffee powder

STORING
Not suitable for storing. The icing must be used immediately after making.

Tip

Before using the icing, place the cake on a wire rack positioned over a baking sheet or a piece of waxed paper. This will avoid unnecessary mess on the work surface.

1 ▲ Break the chocolate into small pieces. Put the chocolate, cream and coffee in a small heavy-based saucepan. Place the cake to be iced on a wire rack.

2 ▲ Stir over a very low heat until the chocolate melts and the mixture is smooth and evenly blended.

3 Remove from the heat and then immediately pour the icing over the cake, letting it slowly run down the sides to coat it completely. Spread the icing with a spatula as necessary, working quickly before the icing has time to thicken.

Satin chocolate icing brings a real touch of sophistication to the most humble of cakes.

Meringue Frosting

A lightly whisked meringue cooked over hot water and combined with softly beaten butter, this icing may be varied with the suggested flavorings, and should be used as soon as it is made. The following amount will fill and coat the top and sides of an 8-inch sponge cake.

INGREDIENTS
Makes 12 ounces
2 egg whites
1 cup confectioners' sugar, sifted
10 tablespoons (⅔ cup) butter, softened

1 Beat the egg whites in a clean, ovenproof bowl, add the confectioners' sugar and gently beat to mix well.

2 Place the bowl over a saucepan of simmering water and beat until thick and white. Remove the bowl from the saucepan, continue to beat until it is cool and the meringue stands up in soft peaks.

3 ▲ Beat the butter in a separate bowl until light and fluffy. Add the meringue gradually, beating well after each addition, until thick and fluffy. Fold in the chosen flavoring, using a spatula, until evenly blended. Use immediately for coating, filling and piping on cakes.

FLAVORINGS
The following amounts are for a single quantity of icing. Increase or decrease the amounts proportionally as needed.
Orange, lemon or lime *Fold in 2 teaspoons finely grated orange, lemon or lime zest.*
Chocolate *Fold in 2 ounces melted semisweet chocolate.*
Coffee *Blend 2 teaspoons instant coffee powder or granules with 1 tablespoon boiling water. Allow to cool before folding into the icing.*

Meringue frosting creates a fluffy coating for cakes that can be spread or peaked to create a variety of effects.

Petal Paste

Petal paste, or gum paste, is used only for making cake decorations. It is exceptionally strong and can be molded into very fine flowers or cut into individual sugar pieces that dry very quickly. Liquid glucose and gum tragacanth are available at drugstores and cake-decorating supply stores. Petal paste can also be bought in a powdered form ready to mix. This is very convenient for small quantities but can be rather expensive if using large amounts.

INGREDIENTS
Makes 1¼ pounds
2 teaspoons powdered gelatin
5 teaspoons cold water
2 teaspoons liquid glucose
2 teaspoons solid white vegetable
shortening
4 cups confectioners' sugar, sifted
1 teaspoon gum tragacanth
1 egg white

2 ▲ Sift the confectioners' sugar and gum tragacanth into a bowl. Make a well in the center and add the egg white and gelatin mixture. Mix together with a wooden spoon to form a soft paste.

1 ▲ Heat the gelatin, water, liquid glucose and shortening in a heatproof bowl over a saucepan of hot water until melted, stirring occasionally. Remove the bowl from the heat.

3 ▲ Knead on a surface dusted with confectioners' sugar until smooth, white and free from cracks.

4 ▲ Place in a plastic bag or wrap in plastic wrap and seal well to exclude all the air. Let stand for 2 hours before use, then re-knead and use a few small pieces at a time, leaving the remaining petal paste well sealed.

Petal paste can be used to make tiny flowers for a special celebratory or formal birthday cake.

Covering Cakes

Covering cakes with icing – whether marzipan, royal or sugarpaste – not only provides a wonderful surface for decorating but also helps to keep the cakes moist. The icings need to be applied with care to ensure that the finish is beautifully smooth. Always plan ahead; it will take several days to marzipan and royal ice a cake, allowing for the drying out times.

Marzipanning a Cake for Sugarpaste Icing

Marzipan can be applied as an icing in its own right, but is mainly used as a base for sugarpaste or royal icing. Unlike a cake covered in royal icing which traditionally has sharp, well defined corners, a cake covered in sugarpaste has much smoother lines with rounded corners and edges. There are therefore two different techniques depending on how you wish to ice the cake.

1 If the cake is not absolutely flat, fill any hollows or build up the top edge (if it is lower than the top of the cake) with a little marzipan. Brush the top of the cake with a little warmed and sieved apricot jam.

3 ▲ Lift the marzipan using your hands, or place it over a rolling pin to support it, and position over the top of the cake. Drape the marzipan over the cake to cover it evenly.

5 ▲ With a sharp knife, trim the excess marzipan, cutting it flush with the base of the cake.

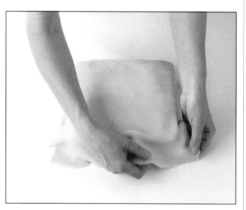

2 ▲ Lightly dust a work surface with confectioners' sugar. Knead the marzipan into a smooth ball. Roll out to a ¼ inch thickness and large enough to cover the top and sides of the cake, allowing about an extra 3 inches all around for trimming. Make sure the marzipan does not stick to the work surface and moves freely.

4 ▲ Smooth the top with the palm of your hand to eliminate any air bubbles. Then carefully lift up the edges of the marzipan and let them fall against the sides of the cake, being careful not to stretch the marzipan. Ensure the marzipanned sides are flat and there are no creases - all the excess marzipan should fall on to the work surface. Use the palms of your hands to smooth the sides and eliminate air bubbles.

6 ▲ With your hands, work in a circular motion over the surface of the marzipan to give it a smooth finish. Spread a little royal icing over the middle of a cake board and place the cake in the center to secure. Lay a piece of waxed paper over the top to protect the surface, then leave the cake for at least 12 hours to dry before covering with icing.

Marzipanning a Round Cake for Royal Icing

1 ▲ If the cake is not absolutely flat, fill any hollows or build up the top edge (if it is lower than the top of the cake) with a little marzipan.

2 Brush the top of the cake with warmed and sieved apricot jam.

3 Lightly dust a work surface with confectioners' sugar. Using one-third of the marzipan, knead it into a ball. Roll out to a round ¼ inch thickness and ½ inch larger than the top of the cake. Make sure that the marzipan does not stick to the work surface and moves freely.

4 ▲ Invert the top of the cake on to the marzipan. Trim the marzipan almost to the edge of the cake. With a small metal spatula, press the marzipan inwards so it is flush with the edge of the cake.

▶ The method for marzipanning a square cake for royal icing is the same as for a round one, except for the sides. Measure the length and height of the sides with string and roll out the marzipan in four separate pieces, using the string measurements as a guide.

5 Carefully turn the cake the right way up. Check the sides of the cake. If there are any holes, fill them with marzipan to make a flat surface. Brush the sides with apricot jam.

6 Knead the remaining marzipan and any trimmings (making sure there are no cake crumbs on the work surface) to form a ball. For the sides of the cake, measure the circumference with a piece of string, and the height of the sides with another piece.

7 ▲ Roll out a strip of marzipan to the same thickness as the top, matching the length and width to the measured string. Hold the cake on its side, being careful to touch the marzipanned top as lightly as possible. Roll the cake along the marzipan strip, pressing the marzipan into position to cover the sides. Trim if necessary to fit.

8 ▲ Smooth the joins together with a spatula. Spread a little royal icing into the middle of a cake board and place the cake in the center to secure. Lay a piece of waxed paper very loosely over the top to protect the surface, then leave for at least 24 hours to dry before covering with icing.

Tip

When buying marzipan, it is best to choose the white kind for covering a cake, as the bright yellow marzipan may discolor pale colored sugarpaste or royal icing.

Covering a Round Cake with Royal Icing

A cake which is coated with royal icing is always covered with marzipan first. The marzipan should be applied one to two days before the royal icing so it has time to dry out slightly, giving a firm surface on which to work. The royal icing is then built up in two or three layers, each one being allowed to dry out before covering with the next. The final coat should be perfectly flat and smooth, with no air bubbles.

Tip

It is difficult to calculate the exact amount of icing required, but if you work with 1 lb/⅔ quantity batches, it should always be fresh. While working, keep the royal icing in a bowl and cover tightly with a clean, damp cloth or plastic wrap so it does not dry out.

1 The icing should be of "soft peak" consistency. Put about 2 tbsp of icing in the center of the marzipanned cake (the exact amount will depend on the size of cake you are icing).

2 ▲ Using a small spatula, spread the icing over the top of the cake, working back and forth with the flat of the blade to eliminate any air bubbles. Keep working the icing in this way until the top of the cake is completely covered. Carefully trim any icing that extends over the edge of the cake with the spatula.

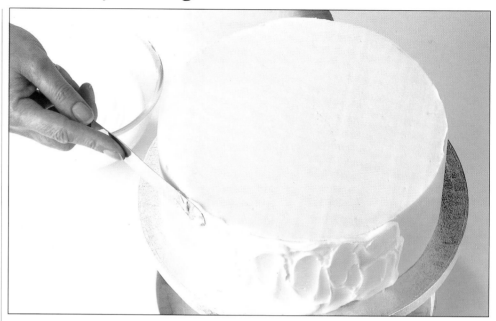

3 ▲ Position a straight-edge ruler on the top edge of the cake furthest away from you. Slowly and smoothly pull the ruler across the surface of the icing, holding it at a slight angle. Do this without stopping to prevent ridges forming. You may need several attempts to get a smooth layer, in which case simply re-spread the top of the cake with icing and try again.

4 ▲ Trim any excess icing from the top edges of the cake with the spatula to give a straight, neat edge. Leave the icing to dry for several hours, or preferably overnight, in a dry place before continuing.

5 ▲ Place the cake on a turntable. To cover the sides, spread some icing on to the side of the cake with a spatula. Rock the spatula back and forth as you spread the icing to eliminate air bubbles. Rotate the turntable as you work your way around the cake.

6 ▲ Using a plain side-scraper, hold it firmly in one hand against the side of the cake at a slight angle. Turn the turntable round in a continuous motion and in one direction with the other hand, while pulling the scraper smoothly in the opposite direction to give a smooth surface to the iced sides. When you have completed the full turn, carefully lift off the scraper to leave a neat join. Trim off any excess icing from the top edge and the cake board.

7 Leave the cake to dry, uncovered, then apply the icing in the same way to give the cake two or three more coats of icing. For a really smooth final layer, use a slightly softer consistency of icing.

Covering a Square Cake Rough Icing a Cake

The method is essentially the same as for icing a round cake.

1 Cover the top with icing as for the round cake. Leave to dry.

2 ▲ Cover the sides as for the round cake, but work on one side at a time and allow the icing to dry out before continuing with the next side. You will not need a turntable. Simply pull the scraper firmly and smoothly across each side in a single movement, repeating if necessary, for a really smooth finish.

3 ▲ Trim off any excess icing from the cake board with a knife.

4 Leave the cake to dry, uncovered, then apply the icing in the same way to give the cake two or three more coats of icing. For a really smooth final layer, use a slightly softer consistency.

This colorful Christmas Tree cake shows an interesting version of peaked, or rough, icing. The fruit cake is first covered with colored marzipan and left to dry for 12 hours, then royal icing is peaked around the lower half of the sides. The decorations are also made of colored marzipan.

Peaking the icing to give it a rough appearance, like that of snow, is a much quicker and simpler way of applying royal icing to a cake. It is also much quicker to apply as you only need one covering of icing.

1 ▲ Spread the icing evenly over the cake, bringing the icing right to the edges so the cake is completely covered.

2 ▲ Starting at the bottom of the cake, press the flat side of a spatula into the icing, then pull away sharply to form a peak. Repeat until the whole cake is covered with icing peaks. Alternatively, flat ice the top of the cake and rough ice the sides – or vice versa.

Covering with Sugarpaste Icing

Sugarpaste icing is a quick, professional way to cover a cake. Although fruit cakes are usually covered with marzipan first, this is not necessary if you are using a sponge base. The sugarpaste can be applied in one coating, unlike royal icing which requires several coats for a really smooth finish. Keep the icing white or knead in a little food coloring to tint. Ready-made sugarpaste is extremely good quality and is available in various colors for fast and professional results.

1 Carefully brush a little water or sherry over the marzipanned surface to help the icing stick to the marzipan. (If you miss a patch, unsightly air bubbles may form.)

2 ▲ Lightly dust a work surface with confectioners' sugar. Roll out the sugarpaste to a ¼ inch thickness and large enough to cover the top and sides of the cake plus a little extra for trimming. Make sure the icing does not stick to the surface and moves freely.

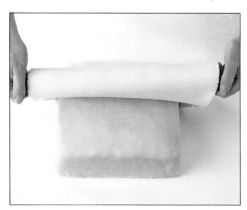

3 ▲ Lift the sugarpaste using your hands, or place it over a rolling pin to support it, and position over the top of the cake. Drape the sugarpaste over the cake to cover it evenly.

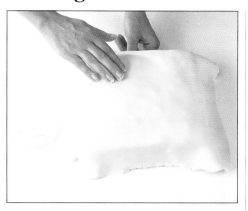

4 ▲ Dust your hands with a little cornstarch. Smooth the top and sides of the cake with your hands, working from top to bottom, to eliminate any air bubbles.

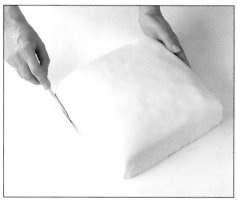

5 ▲ With a sharp knife, trim off the excess sugarpaste, cutting flush with the base of the cake.

6 Spread a little royal icing into the middle of a cake board and place the cake in the center to secure.

Tip

To avoid damaging the surface of the cake while you move it, slide the cake to the edge of the work surface and support it underneath with your hand. Lift it and place on the cake board.

Covering Awkward Shapes

Although most shapes of cake can be covered smoothly with one piece of sugarpaste icing, there are some which need to be covered in sections. A cake baked in a ring mold is one example. The top and outer side of the cake are covered with two identical pieces of sugarpaste, and the inner side with a third piece.

1 ▲ Measure half of the outer circumference of the cake with a piece of string, then measure the side and rounded top with another piece of string.

2 ▲ Take three-quarters of the sugarpaste icing and cut in half. Keep the remaining icing well wrapped until needed. Brush the marzipan lightly with water. Roll out each half of the icing into a rectangle, matching the string measurements. Cover the top and side of the cake in two halves.

3 Measure the circumference and the height of the inner side with two pieces of string. Roll out the reserved sugarpaste icing into a rectangle matching the string measurements, and use to cover the inside of the ring. Trim the sugarpaste to fit and press the joins together securely.

FOOD COLORINGS & TINTS

Food colorings and tints for cake making are available today in almost as large a range as those found on an artist's palette. This has opened up endless possibilities for the cake decorator to create the most imaginative and colorful designs. Liquid colors are only suitable for marzipan and sugarpaste icing if a few drops are required to tint the icing a very pale shade. If used in large amounts they will soften the icings too much. So for vibrant, stronger colors, as well as for subtle sparkling tints, use pastes or powders, available from cake icing specialists. When choosing colors for icings, ensure that they are harmonious, and complement your design.

Coloring icings

How you apply the color to an icing depends on whether it is in liquid form, a paste or powder. While working with the colorings it is best to stand them on a plate or washable board so they do not mark your work surface. When using toothpicks for transferring the color to the icing, select a fresh stick for each color so the colors do not become mixed together.

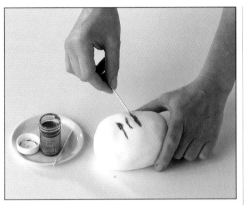

2 ▲ To color firmer icings, such as sugarpaste and marzipan, use paste colorings. Dip a toothpick into the coloring and streak it on to the surface of a ball of the icing.

4 ▲ To create subtle pants in specific areas, brush powdered colorings on to the surface of the icing.

1 ▲ Add liquid color to the icing a few drops at a time until the required shade is reached. Stir into softer icings, such as butter, royal or glacé.

3 ▲ Knead thoroughly until the color is evenly worked in and there is no streaking. Add sparingly at first, remembering that the color becomes more intense as the icing stands, then leave for about 10 minutes to see if it is the shade you need.

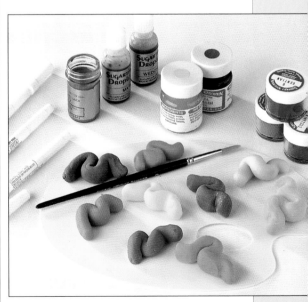

A cake decorator's palette – a vivid array of food colorings to help bring out the artist in you.

ecorating with Royal Icing

Of all the icings, royal icing is probably the most complex and hardest to work with. But once the techniques are mastered, it provides a classic backdrop for both traditional as well as more contemporary cake designs. Traditionally it is used for decorating white wedding and Christmas cakes, but, as color is being introduced more and more into cake decorating, royal icing can now be used in many imaginative ways. This chapter demonstrates how to introduce a modern look using a wide variety of classic techniques.

Making and Using Piping Bags

A piping bag is an essential tool when working with royal icing. You can buy piping bags made of washable fabric and icing syringes, which are ideal for the beginner or for piping butter icing in bold designs. However, for more intricate piping, particularly if using several icing colors and nozzles, homemade waxed paper or parchment paper piping bags are more practical and flexible to handle. Make up several ahead of time, following the instructions given here, then fit them with straight-sided nozzles. Do not use nozzles with ridges as they do not have such a tight fit in the bag. To prevent the icing drying out when working with several bags, cover the nozzle ends with a damp cloth when they are not in use.

2 ▶ With the point of the triangle facing away from you, hold the triangle with your thumb in the middle of the longest edge. Take the left corner and bring it over to meet the point of the triangle, as shown.

3 ▼ Hold in position and bring the remaining corner round and back over to meet the other two points, forming a cone shape. Holding all the points together, position them to make the cone tight and the point of it sharp, as shown.

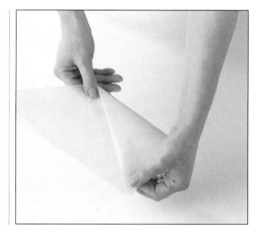

1 ▲ Cut out a 10 inch square of waxed paper or parchment paper, then fold this in half diagonally to make a triangle.

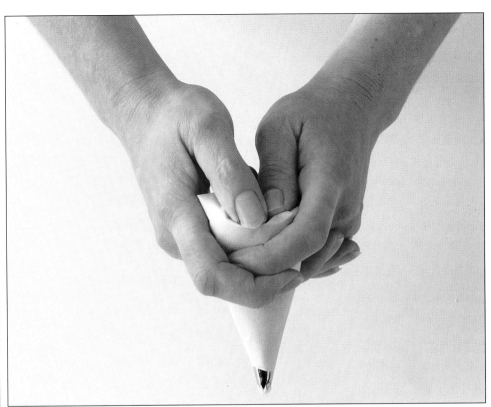

4 ▲ With the cone open, turn the points neatly inside the top edge, creasing firmly down. Secure the cone with a staple.

5 For using with a nozzle, cut off the pointed end of the bag and position the nozzle so it fits snugly into the point. Half-fill the bag with icing and fold over the top to seal. To use without a nozzle, add the icing, seal, then cut a small straight piece off the end of the bag to pipe lines.

6 For ease and control, it is important to hold the bag in a relaxed position. You may find it easier to hold it with one or both hands. For one hand, hold the bag between your middle and index fingers and push out the icing with your thumb.

7 ▲ If using both hands, simply wrap the other hand around the bag in the same manner, so both thumbs can push the icing out.

8 ▲ To pipe, hold the bag so the nozzle is directly over the area you want to pipe on. The bag will be held straight or at an angle, depending on the shape you are piping. Gently press down with your thumb on the top of the bag to release the icing, and lift your thumb to stop the flow of icing. Use a small spatula to cut off any excess icing from the tip of the nozzle as you lift the bag from each piped shape, to keep the shapes neat.

Royal icing is the perfect icing for piping. This cake shows how you can achieve pretty effects with shells, stars, lines and beads. Piped roses in full bloom complement the color chosen for the top of the cake, and the petal tips have been highlighted with food coloring. Carry the design on to the cake board for a classic celebratory cake.

Piping Shapes

Royal icing gives cakes a professional finish, and is often used in decorating to give a formal and ornate character to a cake. However, simple piping skills can easily be achieved given a little practice. This section shows you how, with just a few piping nozzles, you can enhance the look of your cakes. Remember that the icing must be of the correct consistency – not too firm or it will be difficult to squeeze out of the piping bag, and not too soft or the piping will not hold its shape. Small nozzles are used for the delicate designs made with royal icing. Larger ones are more suitable for butter icing and frostings.

PIPING TWISTED ROPES AND LEAVES

For the ropes, fit nozzles Nos 43 or 44, or a writing nozzle, into a waxed paper piping bag and half-fill with icing. Hold the bag at a slight angle and pipe in a continuous line with even pressure, twisting the bag as you pipe. For leaves, you can use a No 18 petal nozzle or simply cut off the point of the bag in the shape of an arrow. Place the tip of the bag on the cake, holding the bag at a slight angle. Pipe out the icing, then pull away quickly to make the tapering end of a leaf.

Twisted ropes and leaves

Stars, swirls and scrolls

PIPING STARS

For a simple star shape, choose a star-shaped nozzle in a size to suit your design. Hold the piping bag upright directly over the area to be iced. Gently squeeze the bag to release the icing and to form a star. Pull off quickly and sharply, keeping the bag straight, to give a neat point to the star.

PIPING SWIRLS

Choose a star-shaped nozzle in a size to suit your design. Hold the piping bag directly over the area to be iced. Pipe a swirl in a circular movement, then pull off quickly and sharply, keeping the bag straight to leave a neat point.

PIPING SCROLLS

Choose star or rope nozzles in a size to suit your design. Hold the piping bag at a slight angle and place the tip of the nozzle on the cake. Pipe the icing lightly upwards and outwards, then come down in a circular movement, tailing off the icing so the end rests on the cake to make a scroll. The action is a little like piping a large "comma." For a reverse scroll, repeat as before, but pipe in the opposite direction, going inwards to reverse the shape. A scroll border can be particularly effective if you alternate two colors of icing.

PIPING CORNELLI

Cornelli is a fun technique which can be carried out in one or more colors. It is a little like doodling. Use writing nozzles Nos 1 or 2 and pipe a continuous flow of icing, squiggling the lines in the shape of W's and M's.

PIPING SIMPLE EMBROIDERY

Piped embroidery is very fine work, requiring writing nozzles Nos 0 or 1. Keep the design simple and work in one or several colors. Pipe little circles, lines and dots to make a delicate pattern for your cake. Look at textile embroidery designs for some ideas.

Cornelli and simple embroidery

PIPING DOTS OR BEADS

Use writing nozzles Nos 1, 2 or 3. Hold the piping bag directly over the area you wish to pipe. Press out the icing so it forms a bead, then release the pressure on the bag and take it off gently to one side. The smaller size nozzle will make simple dots. Neither dots nor beads should end in a sharp point. If this happens, lightly press any sharp points back into the bead with a small damp brush, or try making the icing a little softer.

PIPING SHELLS

Use star nozzles Nos 5 or 8. Rest the tip of the nozzle on the cake and pipe out a little icing to secure it to the surface. Gently squeeze out the icing while lifting the bag slightly up and then down, ending with the nozzle back on the surface of the cake. Pull off to release the icing. Repeat, allowing the beginning of the next shell to touch the end of the first one and carry on in this way until you have completed a continuous line of shells.

PIPING LINES

Use a writing nozzle, remembering that the smaller the hole, the finer the line. Hold the bag at an angle, rest the nozzle on the cake and pipe out a little icing to secure it to the surface. Pipe the icing, lifting the bag slightly as you work, so it is just above the surface of the cake. Continue to pipe, allowing the line of piping to fall in a straight line. Do not pull or the line will break. At the end of the line, release the pressure, rest the nozzle on the surface of the cake and pull off to break the icing. The line can be varied by curving or looping it.

PIPING TRELLISES

To pipe trellises, use the same technique as above to pipe a set of parallel lines. Then overpipe a set in the opposite direction for squares, or horizontally across the lines for diamonds. You can also get different effects by using different widths of writing nozzles.

PIPING ZIGZAGS

Use a No 2 or 3 writing nozzle and pipe either one continuous zigzag, or stop and start at the end of each point to make them sharper.

Dots and beads

Lines, trellises and zigzags

Shells

Piped Sugar Pieces

These little piped sugar pieces are very fragile and have the appearance of fine lace. They must be made ahead of time, and left to dry. The sugar pieces need to be handled carefully, and it is a good idea to make plenty in case of breakages.

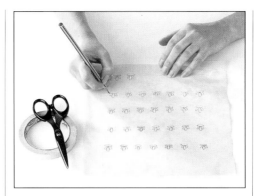

1 ▲ On a piece of waxed paper, draw your chosen design several times with pencil. The designs should be kept fairly small.

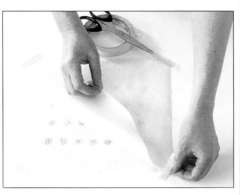

2 ▲ Tape the paper to the work surface or a flat board and secure a piece of waxed paper or parchment paper over the top. Tape the paper down at the corners with masking tape.

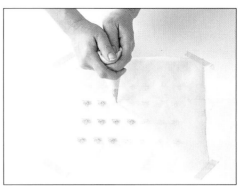

3 ▲ Fit a piping bag with a No 1 writing nozzle. Half-fill with royal icing, and fold over the top to seal. Pipe over each design, carefully following the penciled lines with a continuous thread of icing. Repeat, piping as many pieces as you need plus a few extra in case of any breakages.

4 Leave to dry for at least two hours. Remove from the paper by carefully turning it back and lifting off each piece with a spatula. When dry, store in a box between layers of tissue paper.

Shapely forms – delicate piped sugar pieces can be made in all kinds of designs and colors and attached to the sides, tops or edges of cakes with a dab of royal icing.

Simple Piped Flowers

To make these pretty piped flowers, you will need a petal nozzle – either small, medium or large depending on how big you want the flowers to be – a paper piping bag, a toothpick and a flower nail. Make the flowers ahead of time and, when dry, store in a box between layers of tissue paper.

ROSE

1 For a tightly formed rose, make a fairly firm icing. Color the icing, or leave it white. Fit the petal nozzle into a paper piping bag, half-fill with royal icing and fold over the top to seal.

2 Hold the piping bag so the wider end of the nozzle is pointing into what will be the base of the flower, and hold a toothpick in the other hand. Carefully pipe a small cone shape around the tip of a toothpick. Pipe a petal half way around the cone, lifting it so that it is at an angle and curling outwards, not flat, and turning the toothpick at the same time.

3 ▲ Repeat with more petals so they overlap each other slightly. The last petals can lie flatter and be more open. Remove the rose from the toothpick by threading the toothpick through a large hole on a grater. The rose will rest on the grater. Leave until dry and firm.

PANSY

1 Color the icing. Fit the petal nozzle into a paper piping bag, half-fill with royal icing and fold over the top to seal. Cut out a small square of waxed paper and secure to the flower nail with a little icing.

2 ▲ Holding the nozzle flat, pipe the petal shape in a curve, turning the flower nail at the same time. Pipe five petals in all. Pipe beads of yellow icing in the center with a small writing nozzle, or use florists' stamens.

3 Remove the paper from the flower nail, but leave the pansy on the paper until it is dry and firm. Colored details can be added by painting with food coloring, or using food coloring pens, once the flower has dried. Lift the pansy from the paper by carefully slipping a spatula underneath the base of the flower.

COLORED SUMMER FLOWERS

1 Color the icing. Make up the flowers in a variety of shades for a colorful arrangement. Fit the petal nozzle into a paper piping bag, half-fill with royal icing and fold over the top to seal. Cut out a small square of waxed paper and secure to the flower nail with a little icing.

2 ▲ Pipe five flat petals in a circle so they slightly overlap each other. Pipe beads of yellow icing in the center of each flower or sprinkle with hundreds and thousands. Leave to dry and add colored details as for the pansy.

Bouquet of iced blossoms, including roses, pansies and bright summer flowers – arrangements of piped flowers make colorful cake decorations.

Run-outs

Designs for run-outs can be as complicated or as simple as you like. It is best to start off with a fairly solid shape for your first attempt, as these decorations can be quite fragile to handle. Always make a few more run-outs than you think you will need in case of breakages.

1 Make up the royal icings to the correct consistencies: a stiffer one for the outline, and a softer one for filling in (see the basic recipe for Royal Icing). Leave the icing to stand, preferably overnight, to allow any air bubbles to come to the surface. Stir the icing before using. On a piece of waxed paper, draw your chosen design several times.

2 ▲ Tape the paper to the work surface or a flat board and lay a piece of parchment paper over the top. Tape the paper down at the corners with masking tape.

3 ▲ Fit a paper piping bag with a No 1 writing nozzle, and half-fill with the stiffer icing for piping the outline. Carefully pipe over the outline of your design with a continuous thread of icing.

4 ▲ Add the softer icing for filling in into a second paper piping bag. Cut the pointed end off the bag in a straight line. Do not make it too big, or the icing will flow out too quickly. Pipe the icing into the outlines to fill, working from the outline into the center, being careful not to touch the outline or it may break. To prevent air bubbles forming, keep the end of the bag in the icing. The icing should look overfilled and rounded, as it will shrink slightly as it dries.

5 ▲ You now need to work quickly while the icing is still soft. Move a paintbrush carefully through the icing to fill in any gaps and to ensure it goes right to the edge of the outline, keeping the icing smooth. If any air bubbles do appear, smooth them out with the brush or burst with a pin.

6 ▲ Leave the run-outs on the paper to dry; the drying time will vary depending on their size, but leave for at least one day and preferably longer. When completely dry, remove by carefully slipping a spatula under the shapes and easing them off the paper. Decorative details can then be piped on to the dried run-outs. Allow these to dry before using or storing.

7 Store the run-outs in a box between layers of waxed paper.

When royal icing is presented in bright colors it takes on a lively new look. The hearts and brilliant butterflies are made using the run-out technique. The wings are made separately, then joined with a line of piping to form the body of each butterfly. This also secures them to the cake. Piped sugar pieces, scroll borders and polka dots complete the design.

ecorating with Sugarpaste Icing

As a covering, sugarpaste icing gives a softer look to a cake than royal icing. It is much quicker to work with, requiring only one rolled out layer. This is then placed in position so it curves itself over the edges of the cake. Because it is so pliable, sugarpaste can also be used for a wide range of decorative effects. When making sugarpaste decorations, always wrap any icing you are not using immediately in plastic wrap to stop it drying out.

Marbling

As an alternative to covering a cake in a single color, sugarpaste icing can be marbled for a multi-colored effect. Use several colors and keep them quite vibrant, or use one or two delicate tones. Marbled sugarpaste icing can also be used to make effective molded flowers and other modeled decorations.

1 ▲ Form the sugarpaste icing into a smooth roll or ball. Dip the end of a toothpick into the food coloring and dab a few drops on to the icing. Repeat with more colors if wished.

2 ▲ Knead the sugarpaste icing just a few times. The coloring should look very patchy.

3 ▲ On a work surface lightly sprinkled with confectioners' sugar, roll out the sugarpaste icing to reveal the marbled effect.

4 ▲ Alternatively, for a very bold interweaving of colors, use the following technique. Divide the sugarpaste icing into three or four equal portions, depending on how many colors you want to use. Color with food coloring. Divide each color into four or five portions and roll out with your hands into sausage shapes. You could even put two colors together for an instant marbled sausage. Place the different-colored sausages side-by-side on the work surface.

5 ▲ Twist the colors together and knead for several seconds until the strips of color are fused together but retain their individual colors.

6 ▲ Roll out the marbled icing on a work surface lightly dusted with confectioners' sugar.

Crimping

Crimping tools are similar to large tweezers with patterned ends and are available in a good variety of styles. Crimping is a very quick and efficient way of giving decorative edges and borders to sugarpaste-coated cakes – the effect is similar to the embroidery technique of smocking. For a simple finish to the crimped cake, top with a small posy of edible flowers, a ribbon, or other bought decorations.

3 ▲ Slowly release the crimper so as not to tear the icing. Repeat the pattern, either touching the last one or spacing them evenly apart. The pattern can be varied by using different crimping tools.

1 ▲ Cover the cake with sugarpaste icing. For crimping, the icing must still be soft, so do not allow it to dry out before decorating. Dip the crimping tool in a little cornstarch.

2 ▼ Position the crimping tool on the cake in the place you wish to start the design and squeeze the teeth together to make the pattern.

4 ▲ The same technique can be used to crimp decorative designs down the sides of a cake. If applying sugarpaste frills to a cake, crimp the edges for a neat and pretty finish.

Embossing

Special embossing tools can be purchased from cake icing specialists, but you can also use any other patterned items such as cookie cutters or piping nozzles.

1 ▲ Cover the cake with sugarpaste icing. For embossing, the icing must still be soft, so do not allow it to dry out. Brush a little cornstarch on to the embossing tool and press firmly on to the soft icing. Repeat, brushing with cornstarch each time.

2 ▲ To add color, brush a little powdered food coloring on to the embossing tool instead of the cornstarch and press on to the icing as before. Highlights can also be added with food coloring pens, as shown.

3 ▲ Textured rolling pins are also available from cake icing specialists. Cover the cake with sugarpaste icing as before and smooth over with your hand. Roll over the surface of the icing with the textured rolling pin. This rolling pin gives a basketweave effect.

Modeling

Sugarpaste is wonderfully adaptable, and can be used to model almost any shape you can think of. Choose small objects, such as flowers, fruits, vegetables, animals, or whatever is going to suit your cake. Using this technique, every cake you make will be unique. Remember to dust the work surface lightly with confectioners' sugar before you start, to prevent sticking. Leave the modeled shapes to dry on waxed paper, before applying to the cake.

SMART TEDDY BEAR

▲ Mold each part of the bear's body separately in cream-colored sugarpaste icing. Roll out the waistcoat to fit the body and cut out the bow tie in purple icing. Mold the buttons and eyes in black icing. Attach the head to the body with a little water, pressing together to secure. Brush the body lightly with water and wrap the waistcoat round, folding back the top two corners. Attach the arms, legs and ears with a little water, pressing to secure, then bend into shape. Attach the bow tie, buttons and eyes with a little water, then paint on any details such as nose and mouth with brown food coloring.

FROSTY SNOWMAN

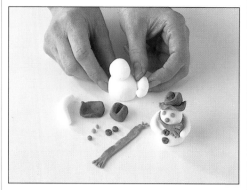

▲ Mold the snowman's body, head and arms in white sugarpaste icing. Roll out the scarf in red icing, cutting the ends with a sharp knife to represent the tassels. Shape two small balls of blue icing for the eyes, one of red for the nose and two of black for buttons. Using black icing, shape the hat in two pieces, as shown. Attach the head to the body with a little water, then the arms, pressing lightly to secure. Attach the scarf, eyes, nose, buttons and hat in the same way.

HUNGRY RABBIT

▼ Mold the rabbit's body and head, legs, tail and ears in light brown sugarpaste icing. Shape two small balls of blue icing for the eyes. Attach the tail, legs and ears to the rabbit's body with a little water, pressing lightly to secure. Paint the nose and details on the eyes with brown food coloring. For the carrots, shape long ovals out of orange icing, tapering at one end, then make markings on them with the back of a knife. Attach small pieces of green icing on to the ends.

CAT ON A MAT

▲ Mold and shape the cat's body, head, legs, tail and ears in gray marbled sugarpaste icing. Shape two small ovals in black for the eyes and a small pink ball for the nose. Roll out a piece of green icing for the mat. Attach the head to the body with a little water, then the legs, tail, ears, eyes and nose, pressing lightly to secure and bending into shape where necessary. Press four short lengths of florists' wire into the head to represent whiskers (these must be removed before serving the cake). Paint the mouth with black food coloring and place the cat on the mat.

Let your imagination run riot when it comes to using sugarpaste icing. All the inhabitants of this water-lily pond are molded or cut out of sugarpaste. The water lilies are formed with a small petal-shaped cocktail cutter, then bent into shape. The lily pads are formed with a small round cutter, and then snipped with a knife to make them more lifelike. A blossom cutter creates the flowers on the grassy bank, and the irises, bulrushes, frog and goldfish are modeled by hand.

Cut-out Shapes

Cut-out Borders

Using a variety of shaped cutters, sugarpaste icing can be stamped out to make all kinds of colorful shapes for decorating cakes.

1 Color the sugarpaste icing to the desired shade, then roll out evenly on a work surface lightly dusted with confectioners' sugar.

2 ▲ Dip the ends of the cutter in cornstarch and cut out the shapes. Leave to dry flat on waxed paper, then attach the shapes to the cake with a little royal icing.

The sky's the limit – use cutters or make your own templates for creating a variety of cut-out images.

Borders on the cutting edge – cut-out shapes can also be positioned around the edge of a cake to add a decorative border. Make the borders in bold or delicate designs so that they fit the character of the cake.

1 ▲ Roll out the sugarpaste icing thinly and cut out with a medium-sized cutter - a round, fluted cookie cutter has been used here. Leave whole or cut in half, depending on the shape.

2 ▲ Use smaller cutters to cut out inside shapes for a filigree effect, or make up your own shapes and use templates cut out of card.

3 Leave the shapes to dry flat on waxed paper, then attach them around the top edges of the cake with a little royal icing.

Plunger Blossoms

A special plunger blossom cutter, available in different sizes, is used to make these dainty flowers. The cutter contains a plunger for ejecting the delicate shapes once they have been cut out.

1 ▲ Roll out the icing thinly on a work surface lightly dusted with confectioners' sugar. Dip the cutter in cornstarch and cut out the flower shapes.

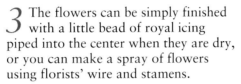

2 ▲ The flower should remain on the end of the cutter. To remove the flower, hold the cutter on a foam pad and depress the plunger. As it goes into the foam it will bend the flower into shape and release it.

3 The flowers can be simply finished with a little bead of royal icing piped into the center when they are dry, or you can make a spray of flowers using florists' wire and stamens.

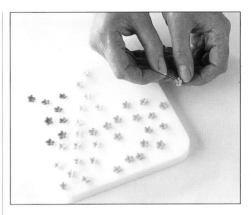

4 ▲ To make a spray, push a pin through the center of each flower. Leave the flowers to dry on the foam.

5 ▲ When dry, pipe a little royal icing on to a stamen and thread it through the hole. This will hold it in position. Repeat with all the flowers.

6 ▲ When the individual flowers are completely dry, twist a piece of florists' wire on to the end of each stamen. Group the flowers and twist the wires together to make a spray.

This pretty Teddy Bear Christening cake is simply decorated with a modeled bear and some delicate plunger blossoms.

Frills

Sugarpaste frills give a particularly elaborate finish to a cake and are especially appropriate for decorating wedding, christening and anniversary cakes. Try layering two different colored frills together for a very special occasion.

1 ▲ Roll out the sugarpaste icing thinly on a work surface lightly dusted with confectioners' sugar. Use a special frill cutter to cut out the rings for the frills. One ring will make one large or two smaller frills.

2 ▲ Position the end of a wooden toothpick over about ¼ inch of the outer edge of the ring. Roll the toothpick back and forth firmly around the edge with your finger. The edge will become thinner and start to frill. Continue in this way until the ring is completely frilled.

3 ▲ Using a sharp knife, cut through the ring once to open it up. Gently ease it open. For shorter frills, cut the ring in half to make two frills.

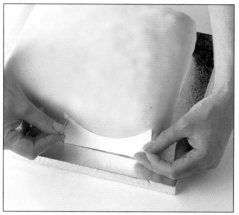

4 ▲ Cut out a template the size of the opened frill and hold against the side of a covered cake. Mark with a pin to show where to attach the frill, and repeat all around the cake.

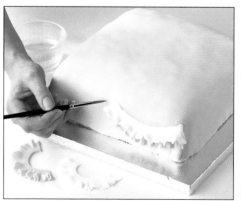

5 ▲ To attach the frill, either pipe a line of royal icing on to the cake or brush a line of water. Carefully secure the frill on to the line of royal icing or water. Overlay with a second frill in the same or a different colored icing if wished. Repeat around the cake. The top edge of each frill can be decorated with piping or with a crimping tool.

Tip

If you do not have a special frill cutter at home you can easily use individual pastry cutters instead. Use a 3–4 inch plain or fluted cutter to cut out the outer circle and a 1½–2 inch plain cutter to cut out the inner circle.

Design Variations

1 ▲ Looped frills look very pretty attached to the cake "upside-down" as shown here. They are made and attached in the same way as described for looped frills, except that you need to cut out a larger hole from the middle of the ring to make the frills thinner. They will drape more effectively this way.

2 ▲ Frills look equally attractive applied diagonally to the cake sides at regular intervals. They are made and attached to the cake in exactly the same way as described for looped frills, although each ring will probably be large enough to make two frills.

Plaques

A plaque can simply be a plain cut-out shape, or it can be more decorative with, for example, a frilled edge and delicate piping work. Use a plaque as a focal point on a cake to dedicate it to someone special, for a wedding, christening, anniversary or birthday, or as a base on which to paint a picture with food colorings.

2 ▲ Using royal or glacé icing, pipe on a decoration or name. Alternatively, carefully write or draw on the plaque with a food coloring pen, or with food colorings and a fine paintbrush.

3 ▲ For a frilled plaque, cut out the shape as described above. While the icing is still soft, position the end of a wooden toothpick over about ¼ inch of the outer edge of the plaque. Roll the toothpick back and forth firmly around the edge with your finger. The edge will become thinner and start to frill. Continue until the edge of the plaque is completely frilled.

1 ▲ To make a plain plaque, roll out the sugarpaste thinly on a work surface lightly dusted with confectioners' sugar. Dip a cutter (round, oval, heart-shaped or fluted) in a little cornstarch. Cut out the shape and leave it to dry flat on waxed paper.

Endlessly versatile, sugarpaste icing can be embossed, crimped, cut out and marbled, techniques which are all displayed on this unusual diamond-shaped cake. Small cutters have been used for the embossed pattern on the sides, and different crimping tools for the designs at the corners. "Paprika" food coloring has been used for the sugarpaste covering for a contemporary terracotta shade, and the trimmings have been marbled with a little blue icing both for the unusual cut-out edging and the star decorations.

ecorating with Marzipan

Marzipan can be a decorative icing in its own right, or it can provide a firm undercoat for a royal icing or sugarpaste icing covering. It is extremely pliable, and the white variety in particular takes color well.

Marzipan can be molded and shaped, crimped and embossed, and cut out or modeled into all kinds of animal shapes, figures, flowers, fruits, and even edible Christmas decorations, to name just a few possibilities.

Embossing

A "pattern in relief" can be created on cakes by using special embossing tools, or any piece of kitchen equipment that will leave a patterned indentation on the marzipan. To make the embossed picture more interesting, paint on highlights with food coloring.

1 Cover the cake with marzipan, then emboss straight away before the icing dries. Dust the embossing tool with a little cornstarch, press firmly into the marzipan, then lift off carefully to reveal the pattern. Alternatively, for a colored design, brush a little powdered food coloring on to the embossing tool instead of the cornstarch and press on to the marzipan as before.

2 ▼ Paint on colored highlights with food coloring, if you wish.

Very simple versions of crimping and embossing have been applied to the marzipan top of this Simnel cake. The edges are crimped – or fluted – with the fingers and the top is embossed using the back of the fork.

Crimping

As with sugarpaste icing, marzipan can be crimped to give simple, pretty edgings and patterns to cakes.

1 Cover a cake with marzipan, but do not allow it to dry out. To prevent the crimping tool from sticking, dip it in a little cornstarch.

2 Place the crimping tool on the edge of the cake where it is to be decorated and then squeeze the teeth together to make the design. Slowly release the crimping tool, being careful not to let it open quickly or it will tear the marzipan.

3 ▲ Re-position the crimper and repeat to complete the design. You can decorate both the top and base edges of the cake, or the whole side, if you wish. The crimper can also be used to make a pattern on top of the cake.

Marzipan Cut-outs

Small flower and other shaped cutters can be purchased from cake icing specialists for cutting out marzipan shapes. Aspic, cocktail or cookie cutters can also be used. Once you have cut out the basic shapes, you can decorate them with different colored marzipan trims, small sweets or piping. Here are some ideas for cut-out marzipan flowers.

COLORFUL BLOSSOMS

▲ Color the marzipan to the desired shades, then roll it out evenly on a work surface lightly dusted with confectioners' sugar. Dip the ends of a leaf cutter or a small round cutter in cornstarch, and cut out five petals for each flower. Overlap the petals in a circle, securing with a little water. Shape small balls of yellow or orange marzipan and place one in the center of each flower.

FRILLY BLOSSOMS AND LEAVES

▲ Color and roll out the marzipan as for the Colorful Blossoms. For each flower, cut out two circles using two fluted cutters, one slightly smaller than the other. (The sizes will depend on the size of flower you are making.) To frill the edges, position the end of a wooden toothpick over 1/8 inch of the outer edge of each circle. Roll the toothpick firmly back and forth around the edges with your finger so the edges become thinner and begin to frill. Continue until the circles are completely frilled.

Place the smaller frill on top of the larger, and lightly press together to secure. Take a small ball of the deeper shade of marzipan and press through a fine sifter. Cut off the marzipan which has been pushed through the sifter and place in the center of the flower.

Cut out leaves from green marzipan with a leaf cutter. Bend the leaves slightly to make them look more lifelike. Larger leaves can be left to bend over the handle of a wooden spoon until firm.

VIOLETS

▲ Color the marzipan purple and roll out as for the Colorful Blossoms. Cut out each flower with a four-petal cocktail cutter. With a little yellow marzipan, shape small balls and then position in the center of each flower.

Creative cut-outs – marzipan can be used in unusual ways to make imaginative shapes and borders.

Modeling

Marzipan is a wonderful icing to use for modeling. Either work with colored marzipan, or use white and highlight it with color after shaping. If coloring your own marzipan, pant it to the required shade, then paint on extra tones and details when the model is assembled to make the objects more life-like. Here are just a few suggestions for shaping fruits and vegetables.

RED-HOT CHILI PEPPERS

▲ Color equal portions of marzipan red and green. Mold the chili shapes, tapering them to a point towards the ends. Shape the stems from green marzipan and attach to the chilies, pressing together lightly to secure.

BUNCH OF GRAPES

▲ Color the marzipan purple. Shape a cone for the main body of the grape bunch, then mold small individual balls for the grapes. Mold the stem, using a little brown marzipan. Arrange the grapes until the cone is completely covered. Use a little water if necessary to make them stick and press lightly to secure. Make a small indentation in the top of the cone and then press in the stem to secure.

RIPE BANANAS

▲ Color the marzipan yellow or use yellow marzipan. Mold and bend small pieces of the icing into the shapes of bananas. Paint on highlights with brown food coloring.

ROSY APPLES

▲ Color the marzipan green for the apples and brown for the stems. Shape the green marzipan into rounds and make an indent at one end with a modeling tool. Shape small pieces of brown icing for the stems. Paint a rosy bloom on the apples with red food coloring and press the stems into the indents.

More familiar as an undercoat for a cake, marzipan should not be neglected as a decoration in itself. It takes color well, and when used to coat this light fruit ring cake, it should certainly not be covered up. Marzipan's plasticity also makes it ideal for molding flowers, such as this colorful collection of roses, and for twisting into ropes to make a colorful edging.

Braiding and Weaving

Use these techniques with marzipan to make colorful edgings and decorations for cakes.

CANDY-STRIPE ROPE

1 Take two pieces of different colored marzipan. On a work surface dusted with confectioners' sugar, roll out two or three ropes of even length and width with your fingers.

2 ▲ Pinch the ends together at the top, then twist into a rope. Pinch the other ends to seal neatly.

BRAID

1 Take three pieces of different colored marzipan. On a work surface dusted with confectioners' sugar, roll out three ropes of even length and width with your fingers.

2 ▲ Pinch the ends together at the top, then braid the ropes neatly and pinch the other ends to seal.

MARZIPAN TWIST

1 Color the marzipan (working with one or two colors). On a work surface dusted with confectioners' sugar, roll out each piece of marzipan to a ¼ inch thickness, then cut each piece into ½ inch wide strips.

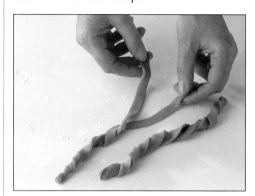

2 ▲ Take two different colored strips and pinch the ends together at the top. Twist the strips together, joining on more strips with water, if needed.

BASKET-WEAVE

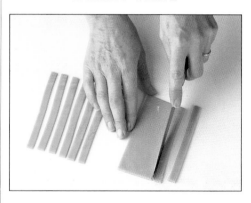

1 ▲ On a work surface lightly dusted with confectioners' sugar, roll out a piece of marzipan (or work with two colors and roll out each one separately) to a ¼ inch thickness. Cut into ¼ inch wide strips.

2 ◄ Arrange the strips, evenly spaced, in parallel lines, then weave the strips in and out. Alternate the colors if using two, as shown. This decoration looks stunning on top of a cake. The edges can be trimmed to fit the shape of the cake.

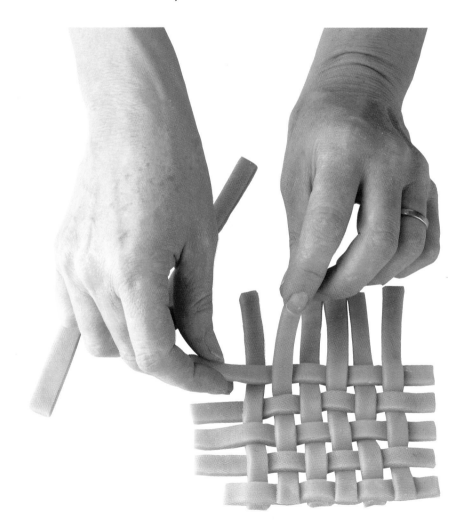

Marzipan Roses

Not only do these roses smell sweet, they taste good too. Though they may look difficult to make, marzipan roses are quite simple to mold. For a formally decorated cake, shape the roses in a variety of colors and sizes, then arrange flamboyantly on top.

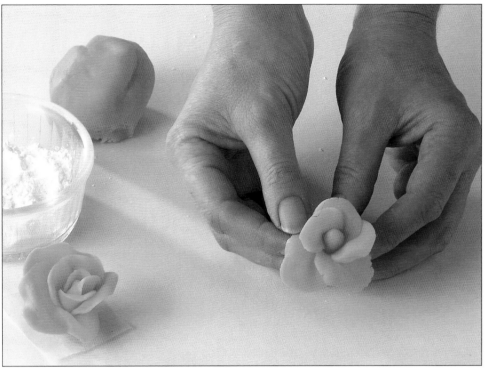

1 ▲ Take a small ball of colored marzipan and form it into a cone shape. This forms the central core which supports the petals.

2 ▲ To make each petal, take a piece of marzipan about the size of a large pea, and work it with your fingers to a petal shape which is slightly thicker at the base. If the marzipan sticks, dust your fingers with cornstarch.

3 ▲ Wrap the petal around the cone as shown. Press the petal to the cone to secure. Bend the ends of the petal back slightly, to curl.

4 ▲ Mold the next petal in the same way and attach as before, so it just overlaps the first one. Curl the ends back slightly. Repeat with several more petals, making them slightly bigger until you have the size of rose you want. Overlap each petal and curl the ends back as before. Make sure all the petals are securely attached, then cut off the base of the cone. This provides a flat surface so the rose will stand on the cake.

5 For rosebuds, make just a few smaller petals and do not curl the ends back.

6 To add more detail to the rose, paint pants on to the petals using a paintbrush and food coloring. Leave to stand on waxed paper until firm.

Blooming roses – molded roses can add glamor to any cake.

ecorating with Butter Icing

Butter icing is very quick to make up and is easy to use for quick and simple decorations. It can be used to sandwich cakes together, or to coat the top and sides with a thick, creamy layer of icing. To make your butter-iced cakes a little more individual, texture the icing on the tops or sides – or both if you wish. To finish, you can pipe the icing in swirls.

Cake Sides

For decorating cake sides, all you need is a plain or serrated scraper, depending on whether you want a smooth or a textured finish to the icing. If you have an icing turntable, it will make icing cake sides a much simpler task, but it is not essential.

Here a chocolate-flavored and green-colored butter icing have been realistically swirled to imitate tree bark and leaves in this delightful novelty cake idea.

1 ▲ Secure the cake to a cake board with a little icing. Cover the top and sides of the cake with icing and put it on an icing turntable. Using a plain or serrated scraper, hold it with one hand firmly against the side of the cake at a slight angle.

2 ▲ Turn the turntable round in a steady continuous motion and in one direction with the other hand, while pulling the scraper smoothly in the opposite direction to give a smooth or serrated surface to the iced sides. When you have completed the full turn, stop the turntable and carefully lift off the scraper to leave a neat join. Trim off any excess icing from the top edge and the cake board.

Cake Tops

More intricate patterns can be made on the tops of cakes with a few simple tools. Use a small spatula, a plain or serrated scraper or a fork to give a silky smooth finish to the cake, or to make a variety of patterned ridges or some deep, generous swirls.

SWIRLS

1 ▲ Spread the icing smoothly over the top of the cake, and then work over the icing with the tip of a spatula from side to side to create a series of swirled grooves.

2 For a more formal appearance, draw the tip of a spatula carefully through the swirled grooves in evenly spaced lines.

RIDGED SPIRAL

1 Spread the icing smoothly over the top of the cake, then place the cake on a turntable.

2 ▲ Hold a serrated scraper at a slight angle, pointing it towards the center of the cake. Rotate the cake with your other hand, while moving the scraper sideways to make undulations and a ridged spiral pattern.

FEATHERED SPIRAL

1 Spread the icing smoothly over the top of the cake and place the cake on a turntable. Rotate the turntable slowly, drawing the flat tip of a spatula in a continuous curved line, starting from the edge of the cake and working in a spiral into the center.

2 ▲ Pull out lines with the tip of the spatula, radiating out from a central point to the edge of the cake.

RIDGED SQUARES

1 Spread the icing smoothly over the top of the cake. Pull a fork across the cake four or five times, depending on the size of the cake, to produce groupings of evenly spaced lines.

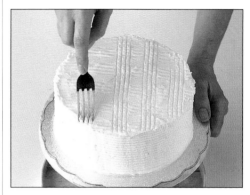

2 ▲ Pull the fork across the cake four or five times as before, but at right angles to the first lines, to give a series of large squares.

DIAMONDS

1 Spread the icing smoothly over the top of the cake. Then lightly dredge with cocoa powder, if using white or lightly tinted butter icing, or confectioners' sugar if using chocolate icing.

2 ▲ Draw a series of lines with the flat side of a spatula to expose the butter icing and to make a diamond pattern over the top.

Piping with Butter Icing

The butter icing needs to be of the correct consistency for piping. To check, dip a spatula and then lift out – the icing should form a sharp point. If too stiff, the icing will be difficult to pipe; if too soft, it will not hold its shape. Add a little extra milk or fruit juice if the consistency is too stiff, or more confectioners' sugar if it is too thin.

DRAMATIC TOUCHES

Piping butter icing in bold, swirling designs with large nozzles can produce dramatic effects.

1 ▲ Cover the top of the cake with a smooth, thin layer of butter icing and smooth the sides with a plain scraper. Using a No 13 plain piping nozzle fitted in a fabric piping bag, pipe large overlapping spirals to cover the top of the cake. For each spiral, start in the center and work outwards, until they are the required size.

2 ▼ Pipe large beads of icing around the edges of the cake, using a large writing nozzle. Lightly sprinkle the spirals with either a little sifted cocoa powder or confectioners' sugar, depending on the color of the butter icing.

DAINTY DESIGNS

For a more delicate effect, use small nozzles to pipe shapes such as dots and beads, stars or scrolls, as demonstrated for royal icing.

1 Cover the top of the cake with a smooth, thin layer of butter icing. Make a ridged pattern with a serrated scraper around the sides of the cake and then a swirled spiral with a spatula over the top.

2 Using a writing nozzle fitted in a paper piping bag, pipe loops and beads of icing in a contrasting color.

3 ▲ Pipe beads of icing at the ends of each loop in the same color as used to cover the cake.

BASKET-WEAVE DESIGN

Butter icing can be piped very effectively with a ribbon nozzle to make a basket-weave design. You can use different colors for the vertical and horizontal lines.

1 Fit a ribbon nozzle into a paper piping bag. Add the icing and fold over the top of the bag to secure. Pipe a vertical line the length of the area you wish to cover with basket weave.

2 Pipe ¾ inch horizontal lines over the vertical line (slightly longer each side than the width of the vertical line) at ½ inch intervals.

3 ▲ Pipe another vertical line so that it just covers one end of all the horizontal lines.

4 ▲ Fill in the spaces between the horizontal lines with an alternating row of horizontal lines to make the basket-weave design. Repeat until the area you wish to cover is completed.

Few can resist the glossy smoothness of butter icing. If you add flavoring and food coloring, the color of the icing should reflect the taste, as with this tangy lemon-iced cake. Use a serrated scraper to create ridges in the icing on the sides and a spatula to make the swirled and feathered effect on the top of the cake. Finish off with generous swirls of piped white butter icing.

Decorating with Glacé Icing

Using white and colored glacé icing, simple but effective patterns can be created for decorating sponges, Madeira cakes or jelly rolls. To vary the ideas shown here using one color of icing, make up two colors of icing and pipe them alternately. Glacé icing sets quickly but needs to be very soft to create the following designs, so make a batch just before you want to decorate the cake and work quickly before it hardens.

Cobweb, Feather and Fan Icing

Cobweb, feather and fan effects are created using the same basic technique. For the cobweb, the colored lines are piped in circles. For the fan, the color is applied in straight lines and the skewer is pulled across in radiating lines. For feather icing the skewer is pulled at right angles through them.

COBWEB ICING

1 Make the glacé icing, color a portion and put in a paper piping bag, as for feather icing. Coat the top of the cake evenly and smoothly with the remaining white icing.

2 ▲ Work quickly before the icing has a chance to set. Pipe evenly spaced circles on top of the icing, starting from the center of the cake and moving towards the edge.

3 ▲ Using a skewer, pull it in straight lines from the edge of the cake to the center so that it is evenly divided into four sections.

4 ▲ Working from the center of the cake to the edge, pull the skewer between the four lines to divide the cake evenly into eight. Leave to set.

For an effective Spider's web cake, use the cobweb icing technique. First cover the cake with yellow glacé icing. Pipe a continuous spiral of black glacé icing, then draw a skewer down from the top at regular intervals.

FEATHER ICING

1 Make the glacé icing (see Basic Icing Recipes). Put 2 tbsp of the icing in a small bowl and color it with a little food coloring.

2 Fit a paper piping bag with a No 2 writing nozzle, then spoon in the colored icing and fold over the top of the bag to secure.

3 ▼ Coat the top of the cake evenly with the remaining white icing. Working quickly so the icing does not set, pipe the colored icing in straight lines across the cake. You may find it easier to work from the center outwards when doing this.

4 ▲ Using a skewer, pull it at right angles through the colored lines in one direction, leaving an even spacing between the lines.

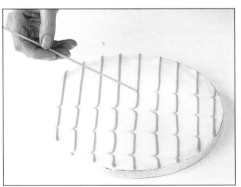

5 ▲ Working in the space between the lines, pull the skewer in the opposite direction, to give a feather pattern. Leave to set.

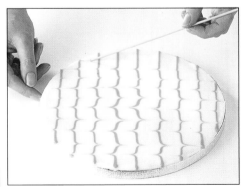

FAN ICING

1 Make the glacé icing, color a portion and put in a paper piping bag. Ice the top of the cake as for the Feather and Cobweb techniques.

2 Working quickly so the icing does not set, pipe the colored icing in evenly spaced straight lines across the cake. You may find it easier to work from the center outwards.

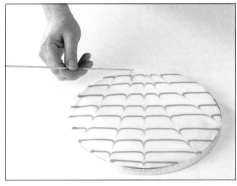

3 ▲ Using a skewer, pull it through the colored lines, starting from a point at one edge of the cake and radiating the lines out from it.

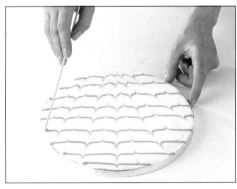

4 ▲ Working in the space between the lines, pull the skewer through the piped lines in the opposite direction to give a fan pattern. Leave to set.

Squiggle Icing

Here a random patterning of icing, similar to cornelli (see Decorating with Royal Icing), is lightly feathered or marbled. The technique is shown here using white icing on a chocolate-tinted background, but would be equally effective using one or two colors on a white icing background.

1 Make the glacé icing. Put 2 tbsp of the icing into a paper piping bag fitted with a No 2 writing nozzle, and color the rest with cocoa mixed with a little water. Coat the top of the cake evenly with the chocolate icing.

2 ▲ Working quickly before the icing has a chance to set, pipe haphazard squiggles all over the top of the cake in a continuous line.

3 ▼ Using a toothpick, carefully pull it through the lines in short, swirling movements and in different directions, to create a random feathered effect.

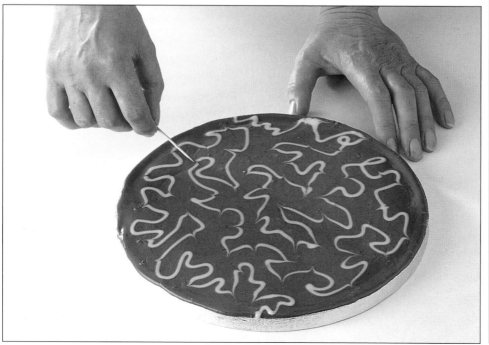

Marbling Flowers and Leaves

The feathering technique can also be used to give a marbled effect to piped decorations. The technique has been used here for a pretty flower and leaf design. The method is also effective for holly leaves, with the lines being pulled outwards to create the spiky points on the leaves.

1 Make the glacé icing, color a small portion green and a portion red and put each in a paper piping bag fitted with a No 2 writing nozzle. Coat the top of the cake evenly with the remaining white icing.

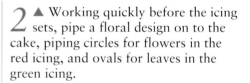

2 ▲ Working quickly before the icing sets, pipe a floral design on to the cake, piping circles for flowers in the red icing, and ovals for leaves in the green icing.

3 ▲ To marble the flowers, pull a skewer through the lines from the outer edge almost to the middle. The number of petals will be determined by the number of lines you pull. Do the same for the leaves.

Tip

If the top of the cake is not perfectly flat for piping on, simply turn the cake upside down and use the flat base as the top.

Piping with Glacé Icing

All kinds of imaginative designs can be created, using the following method, to decorate the tops and edges of cakes.

This cake is covered with white glacé icing and the side is then coated with green-tinted shredded coconut. The bold, exotic flowers are piped in red and green glacé icing and then marbled with a small toothpick, before the white or colored icings have time to set, for a delicate finish.

1 Make the glacé icing, reserving a few tablespoons for piping. Coat the top of the cake evenly with the remaining icing (either colored or white) and leave to set.

2 Divide the reserved icing into two equal portions and color each in contrasting but complementary shades. Spoon the icings into two separate paper piping bags, each fitted with a No 2 writing nozzle. Use one color to pipe geometric shapes or other simple designs over the icing.

3 ▲ Pipe a border around the edge of the cake with the other color.

ecorating with Chocolate

Nothing adds a luxurious touch to a cake quite like chocolate, whether it is poured over to form a glossy icing, or piped, shaved, dipped or curled. There are several types of chocolate to choose from, and all should be used with care. Couverture is the best and used for professional chocolate work, but it is expensive and requires particularly careful handling. For the following techniques, baking chocolate or eating chocolate are suitable. Chocolate-flavored cake covering is easy to use but is inferior both in taste and texture.

Chocolate decorations can look particularly interesting if different kinds of chocolate – plain, milk and white – are used in combination. White chocolate can be colored, but make sure you use powdered food coloring for this as liquid colorings will thicken it. Store chocolate decorations in the refrigerator in a plastic container between layers of waxed paper until ready to use. Also, handle the decorations as little as possible with your fingers, as they will leave dull marks on the shiny surface of the chocolate and spoil the finished effect.

Melting

For most of the decorations described in this section, the chocolate must be melted first.

1 ▼ Break the chocolate into small pieces and place in a bowl set over a pan of hot water. Do not allow the bowl to touch the water and do not let the water boil; the chocolate will spoil if overheated. Melt the chocolate slowly and stir occasionally. Be careful not to let water or steam near the chocolate or it will become too thick.

2 ▲ When the chocolate is completely melted, remove the pan from the heat and stir.

Coating Cakes

1 ▲ Stand the cake on a wire rack. It is a good idea to place a sheet of waxed paper or a baking sheet underneath the rack to catch any chocolate drips. Pour the chocolate over the cake quickly, in one smooth motion, to coat the top and sides.

2 Use a spatula to smooth the chocolate over the sides, if necessary. Allow the chocolate to set, then coat with another layer, if wished.

Piping with Chocolate

Chocolate can be piped directly on to a cake, or it can be piped on to parchment paper to make run-outs, small outlined shapes or irregular designs. After melting the chocolate, allow it to cool slightly so it just coats the back of a spoon. If it still flows freely it will be too runny to hold its shape when piped. When it is the right consistency, you then need to work fast as the chocolate will set quickly.

CHOCOLATE OUTLINES

Pipe the chocolate in small, delicate shapes to use as elegant decorations on cakes. Or pipe random squiggles and loosely drizzle a contrasting chocolate over the top.

1 Melt 4 oz chocolate and allow to cool slightly. Tape a piece of parchment paper to a baking sheet or flat board.

2 ▼ Fill a paper piping bag with the chocolate. Cut a small piece off the pointed end of the bag in a straight line. Pipe your chosen shape in a continuous line, and repeat or vary. Leave to set in a cool place, then carefully lift off the paper with a spatula.

PIPING ON TO CAKES

This looks effective on top of a cake iced with coffee glacé icing.

1 Melt 2 oz each of white and plain chocolate in separate bowls and allow to cool slightly. Place the chocolates in separate paper piping bags. Cut a small piece off the pointed end of each bag in a straight line.

2 ▲ Hold each piping bag in turn above the surface of the cake and pipe the chocolates all over. Here, the chocolates have been piped in overlapping semi-circles of different sizes. Try your own designs, too.

CHOCOLATE LACE CURLS

Make lots of these curly shapes and store them in a cool place ready for using as cake decorations. Try piping the lines in contrasting colors of chocolate to vary the effect.

1 ▲ Melt 4 oz chocolate and allow to cool slightly. Cover a rolling pin with parchment paper and attach it with tape. Fill a paper piping bag with the chocolate and cut a small piece off the pointed end in a straight line.

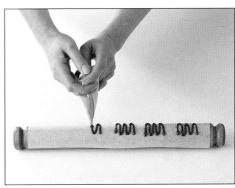

2 ▲ Pipe lines of chocolate backwards and forwards over the parchment paper, as shown.

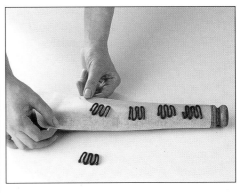

3 ▲ Leave the chocolate lace curls to set in a cool place, then carefully peel off the paper.

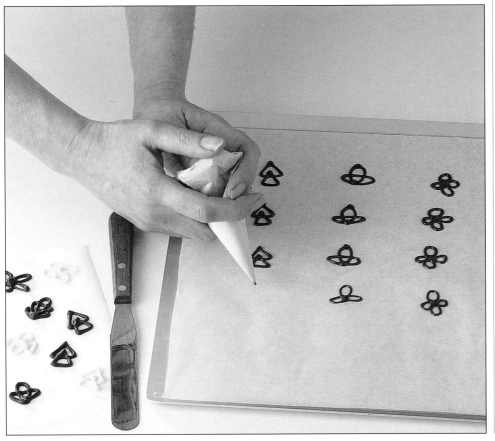

Marbling Chocolate

Here, plain chocolate is swirled over a white glacé-iced cake for a stunningly simple effect. Before melting the chocolate, make the icing, then work very quickly while both the chocolate and the icing are still soft.

1 Melt 2 oz plain chocolate. Coat the top of the cake evenly and smoothly with white glacé icing.

2 ▲ Spoon the chocolate into a paper piping bag, cut a small piece off the pointed end in a straight line and then quickly pipe the chocolate in large, loose loops.

3 ▼ Pull a toothpick through the chocolate in short, swirling movements and in different directions, to create a random marbled effect.

Chocolate Run-outs

The same basic method used for making royal icing run-outs is used here with chocolate. Try piping the outline in one color of chocolate and then filling in the middle with another.

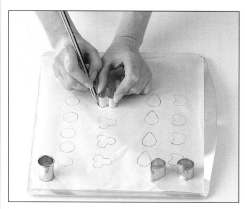

1 ▲ Tape a piece of waxed paper to a baking sheet or flat board. Draw around a shaped cookie cutter on to the paper, or trace or draw a shape of your choice freehand. Repeat the design several times.

2 Secure a piece of parchment paper over the top of the penciled design. Tape it down securely at the corners with masking tape.

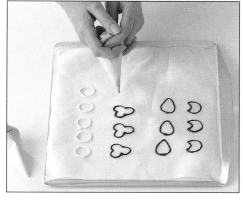

3 ▲ Fill two paper piping bags with melted chocolate. Cut a small piece off the pointed end of one of the bags in a straight line and pipe over the outline of your design in a continuous thread.

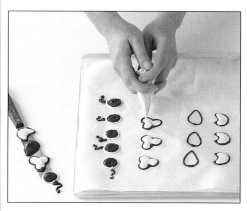

4 ▲ Cut the end off the other bag, slightly wider than before, and pipe the chocolate to fill in the outline so it looks slightly rounded. Leave to set in a cool place, then carefully lift off the paper with a spatula.

Chocolate icing and decorating techniques are demonstrated in all their glory on this sumptuous chocolate gâteau. The cake is covered with fudge frosting. A neat ring of cocoa is then dusted around the edge, using a round stencil to protect the center of the cake. The cake is decorated with mottled white and plain chocolate leaves. Chocolate curls adorn the top, and haphazardly piped white chocolate shapes, loosely overpiped with plain chocolate, complete the ultimate chocoholic extravaganza.

Chocolate Leaves

Chocolate Cut-outs

Chocolate leaves are made by coating real leaves with plain, white or milk chocolate or any combination of the three. Choose small freshly-picked leaves with simple shapes and well-defined veins, such as rose leaves. Leave a short stem on the leaves so you have something to hold.

You can make abstract shapes, or circles, squares and diamonds, by cutting them out freehand with a sharp knife. Alternatively, use a large cookie cutter or ruler as a guide, or cut out the shapes with small cookie or cocktail cutters. These shapes look equally attractive whether evenly positioned around the sides of the cake, spaced apart or over-lapping each other, or simply arranged haphazardly.

3 ▲ Press the cutter firmly through the chocolate and lift off the paper with a spatula. Try not to touch the surface of the chocolate or you will leave marks on it.

1 ▲ Wash and dry the leaves well on paper towels. Melt 4 oz chocolate. Using a paintbrush, brush the underside of each leaf with chocolate. Take care not to go over the edge of the leaf or the chocolate will be difficult to peel off.

1 ▲ Cover a baking sheet with parchment paper and tape down at each corner. Melt 4 oz plain, milk or white chocolate. Pour the chocolate on to the parchment paper.

4 ▲ The finished shapes can be left plain or piped with a contrasting chocolate if you wish.

2 ▲ Using different chocolates for a mottled effect, brush the leaves in the same way, partly with plain or milk and partly with white chocolate.

3 Place the leaves chocolate-side up on parchment paper. Leave to set.

2 ▲ Spread the chocolate evenly with a spatula. Allow to stand until the surface is firm enough to cut, but not so hard that it will break. It should no longer feel sticky when touched with your finger.

5 ▲ Abstract shapes can be cut with a sharp knife freehand. They look particularly effective pressed on to the sides of a butter iced cake.

4 ▲ Carefully peel the leaf from the chocolate, handling the chocolate as little as possible. If the chocolate seems too thin, re-coat with more melted chocolate. Leave to set.

Chocolate-dipped Fruit and Nuts

Use small, fresh fruit such as strawberries, grapes and kumquats for dipping, and whole nuts such as almonds, cashews, brazils or macadamias. Make sure that the fruit and nuts are at room temperature, or the chocolate will set too quickly.

1 Line a baking sheet with parchment paper. Wash the fruit and dry well on paper towels. Hold the fruit by its stem, then dip into the chocolate. You can either coat the piece of fruit completely, or just dip half of it, leaving the line of chocolate straight or at a slight angle. Remove the fruit, shake it gently and let any excess chocolate fall back into the bowl. Place on parchment paper and leave to set.

2 ▲ For nuts, place a nut on the end of a long kitchen fork or dipping fork. Lower into the chocolate and coat completely. Lift out of the chocolate and shake off any excess, then leave to set as for fruit. To coat just half of the nut, hold it between your fingers and dip part way into the chocolate.

3 For a two-tone effect, melt plain and white chocolate in separate bowls. Dip the fruit or nuts into one color to coat completely, then, when set, half-dip into the other color.

Chocolate Curls

1 Melt 4 oz chocolate. Pour the chocolate on to a firm, smooth surface such as a marble, wood or formica, set on a slightly damp cloth to prevent slipping. Spread the chocolate evenly and smoothly over the surface with a large spatula.

2 ▲ Leave the chocolate to cool slightly. It should feel just set, but not hard. Hold a large sharp knife at a 45° angle to the chocolate and push it along the chocolate in short sawing movements from right to left and left to right to make curls.

3 ▲ Remove the curls by sliding the point of the knife underneath each one and lifting off. Leave until firm.

Chocolate Shavings

The quickest way to turn chocolate into a decoration is simply to grate or shave it. The chocolate should be at room temperature for this.

1 ▲ For fine shavings, grate the chocolate on the coarse side of a grater. For coarser shavings, peel off curls with a vegetable peeler.

This sophisticated heart-shaped cake is a wonderful idea for Valentine's Day or to celebrate an engagement. It is completely covered with rich, plain chocolate curls.

COLOR EFFECTS

*If you think of the surface of a cake as an artist's canvas, it opens up
all sorts of decorating ideas using painting and drawing techniques.
This is made possible by the wide range of colors available in the form
of food colorings and food coloring pens.*

Using Stencils

Cards with stencil patterns on them can be found at cake icing specialists or at stationers, or you can make your own stencils out of thin cardboard.

1 Coat the cake with sugarpaste, royal or marzipan icing and leave to dry.

2 ▲ Lay the stencil over the surface of the cake. Dip a completely dry, clean paintbrush into some powdered food coloring and dab into the stencil. Lift off the stencil to reveal the design. You could also fill in the color with a food coloring pen.

Flicking

Use one color or several. This is almost a decoration in itself.

1 Cover the cake with sugarpaste, royal or marzipan icing and leave to dry. Place the cake on a fairly large sheet of waxed paper to protect the work surface.

2 ▲ Water down the food coloring, and then load up the end of the paintbrush with the color. Position the brush over the area you wish to color, then flick your wrist in the direction of the cake, so the color falls on to it in small beads.

Linework

Food coloring pens are a quick way to add simple line designs to the tops and sides of cakes. Use a ruler to achieve straight lines, and a pair of compasses for large curved lines.

1 Cover the cake and leave to dry. Royal icing gives the firmest surface for the pens. Work out the design.

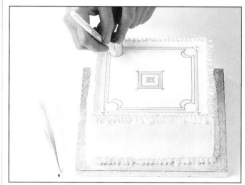

2 ▲ For small circles, curves or semi-circles, draw around the edge of a plain round cutter.

3 ▼ Add details to the design with small dots.

Painting and Drawing

Food colorings can be used like water-colors and food coloring pens like crayons or felt-tip pens on iced cakes. Let the icing dry before applying the design. Before working on the cake, you might find it easier to practice on a spare piece of icing. When painting different colors next to each other, allow the first color to dry before applying the second to prevent colors running into each other – unless that is the effect you wish to achieve.

1 ▲ Dilute food colorings with a little water or use straight from the bottle. A small plastic palette is useful for mixing the colors. Work out the design and either paint it straight on to the cake, or draw it out first with a food coloring pen.

2 ▲ Food coloring pens look like felt-tip pens, but are filled with edible food colorings. They are a speedy way to add lively highlights to designs. They can also be used to color in patterned borders, to draw personalized pictures or to write messages.

3 ▶ Look to the great artists, such as Matisse and Picasso, for inspiration, either for a painting style or theme.

Stippling

This is normally used as a background decoration, so it is best to keep the colors delicate. Try blending two soft shades together.

1 Cover the cake with sugarpaste, royal or marzipan icing and leave until the icing is dry.

2 ▲ Water down the food coloring and apply with a dry, clean piece of sponge or paper towel, by dabbing it on to the surface of the cake.

Powdered Tints

These can be brushed on dry, either with a paintbrush for detail, or with a clean, dry piece of sponge when you wish to cover larger areas.

1 Cover the cake with sugarpaste, royal or marzipan icing and leave until the icing is dry.

2 ▲ Draw on the design with different colored food coloring pens, and then brush in the colors with powdered tints.

Using Bought Decorations

When you want to put a cake together in a hurry for a last-minute celebration, or even if you do not have much time to spend on decorating cakes, remember there are all kinds of easy-to-use edible items and ready-to-use decorations that can be found in supermarkets, health food shops, and in confectionery and specialist cake icing shops.

Edible Decorations

Here are just some of the delicious edible decorations which can be used for quick-and-easy cake decorating. Keep a few of these in your cupboard, ready for an impromptu celebration cake.

Candies Choose small, colorful, simple shapes such as jelly babies, jellybeans, colored chocolate beans, chocolate buttons, liquorice gum drops, chocolate-coated espresso beans, yogurt-coated nuts and raisins, small molded chocolate shapes or sugared almonds. These are just a few of the candies which, used with imagination and flair, turn a cake into something special.

Jellied Shapes Packaged jellied orange and lemon slices are also useful, either whole or cut into wedges, as are jelly diamonds, available in several colors.

Nuts Use these chopped or whole, plain or toasted, for decorating the tops and to coat the sides of cakes.

Glacé and Crystallized Fruits Glacé cherries and angelica are probably the most familiar of these popular quick cake decorations, but there are many other tasty varieties to choose from, such as pineapple and ginger – even diced papaya. Depending on their size, the fruits can be halved, sliced, chopped or cut into shapes ready for arranging on the cake.

Coconut Shredded coconut is another useful cake decoration, particularly as it can also be panted with a few drops of food coloring to give an attractive coating for the sides of a cake. Other more unusual kinds of coconut are also available, such as coconut threads, coconut chips and coconut slices. All can be used raw or toasted.

Marzipan Fruits and Sugar Flowers Both can be bought ready-made if you do not wish to shape your own.

Citrus Fruits Fresh lemon, lime and orange zest can be transformed into attractive cake decorations. Cut off thin, curly strips of rind with a sharp knife or zester. Alternatively, use pany aspic cutters to cut out shapes from the rinds, but be careful not to include the white pith. The shapes can be grouped together or linked to form a border around the cake.

MAKING PATTERNS WITH EDIBLE DECORATIONS

1 ▲ Arrange jelly diamonds and jellied orange slices on a square or round cake to form a pretty stylized design such as the one shown.

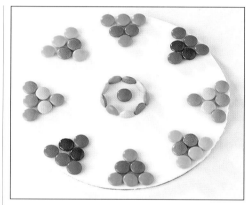

2 ▲ This jazzy design is ideal for a child's cake. It is made from whole and halved colored chocolate beans.

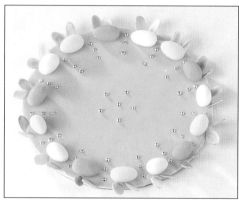

3 ▲ Sugared almonds, flaked toasted almonds and silver balls add life to any cake iced in pastel shades, and are ideal for Easter.

Decorative edibles help to make cake decorating fun as well as easy.

Candy Flowers

Edible decorations can be used in different combinations to make attractive floral designs for cakes.

1 ▲ Use jelly diamonds for the petals and leaves, slices of colored candies for the centers and strips of angelica for the stems.

2 ▲ Arrange halved colored chocolate beans, cut-side down, to form a flower. Use different colors, with a silver ball for the center.

3 ▲ Dip blanched whole almonds in melted chocolate to form the petals of a flower, then arrange with a chocolate button or chocolate bean for the center.

Stenciling

For this technique you can use confectioners' sugar, cocoa or finely ground nuts to create the stenciling effect.

1 ▲ For a quick stenciled pattern, lay a patterned doiley on the cake and sift confectioners' sugar over it, then lift off the doiley. The center can be cut out of the doiley to create another stenciled area. For maximum color contrast, use confectioners' sugar on a chocolate cake and cocoa on a plain cake.

2 ▼ Another stenciling method is to lay strips of paper over the cake, either in straight lines, diagonally or in a lattice pattern. Use fairly thick paper so it lies flat. For more dramatic effects, cut out strips of paper in wavy, zigzag or other geometric patterns.

It's time to have fun. Load up a paintbrush with orange food coloring and then flick it over a sugarpaste-iced cake. Cut out bears with the icing and paint on their features. Line up jelly teddy bears, jellybeans and other colorful candies, paint a bright design on the iced board and you have a cake that is surprisingly easy to decorate.

Ribbon Decorations

Stripy ones, dotty ones, sparkly ones, wide and pencil-thin ones – ribbons are a lovely way to add height, color and a special celebratory look to a cake. They can be wrapped around the cake, using varying widths and colors for different effects, made into simple shapes, or threaded into the icing. Tiny colored bows can be purchased from cake icing specialists, or you can make your own decorations as suggested here.

RIBBON LOOPS

These look pretty if one or several loops are attached to florists' wire, or if alternating colors are looped together.

1 Use a length of thin ribbon, about ¼ inch wide. Make two or three small loops of ribbon.

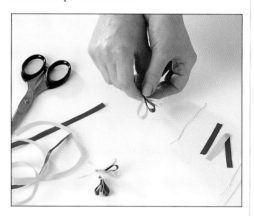

2 ▲ Using a piece of florists' wire, twist it around the ends of the ribbon to secure the loops together. Trim the ends of the ribbon. The wire will form a stem for the loops, so cut it to the required length and use it to put the loops in position on the cake. The loops must be removed from the cake before serving.

RIBBON CURLS

▲ Use a thin piece of gift wrapping ribbon, about ¼ inch wide, and cut into the chosen lengths. Run the blade of a pair of scissors or a sharp knife down the length of the ribbons to make them curl.

MULTIPLE CURLS

▲ Use a thick piece of gift wrapping ribbon, about ¾ inch wide, and cut into the chosen lengths. Tear the ribbon into four or five thin strips, almost to the end. Run the blade of a pair of scissors or a sharp knife down the length of each strip to curl.

OVALS

▲ Hold both ends of a thin piece of ribbon. With your left hand bring the end up and twist it over to cross and form an oval with two straight ends hanging down. Where the ribbon crosses, secure with a little royal icing. Cut the ends diagonally to neaten.

RIBBON DESIGNS

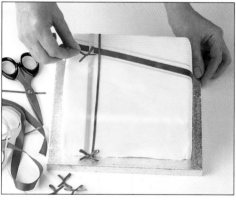

▲ Use combinations of colors and widths of ribbons and bows to create special patterns on the tops and sides of cakes. Secure with a little royal icing.

A riot of ribbons – let the colors or patterns of ribbon you choose complement the shade and design of the cake without dominating it.

RIBBON INSERTION

This technique looks much more difficult than it actually is. A cake covered with sugarpaste icing provides the best surface for this decoration. Leave the icing to dry until it is soft underneath and just firm on the top.

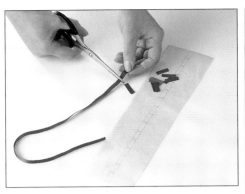

2 ▲ Cut pieces of ribbon which are fractionally longer than the size of each slit.

4 ▲ With the aid of a pointed tool, insert one end of the ribbon into the first slit and the other end into the second slit.

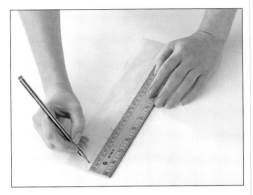

1 ▲ Work out your design for the number and size of slits, and whether the design is to be straight or curved. Draw the design on a piece of waxed paper.

3 ▲ Secure the template to the cake with pins. Cut through the drawn lines to make the slits in the icing using a scalpel. Remove the template.

5 ▲ Leave a space and repeat, filling all the slits with the pieces of ribbon in the same way.

Sugar-frosting Flowers and Fruit

Something as simple as a spray of fresh sugar-frosted flowers or a grouping of small fruits is often all that is needed to decorate a cake. When frosting flowers choose ones that are edible, such as pansies, primroses, violets, roses, freesias, pany daffodils or nasturtiums.

FLOWERS

Sugar-frosted flowers keep surprisingly well, and you may want to make the most of springtime primroses and violets to liven up cakes later in the year. Once the flowers are dry, store them in a single layer between sheets of tissue paper in a small box. Keep the box in a cool, dry place.

1 ▲ Lightly whisk an egg white in a small bowl, and sprinkle some superfine sugar on to a plate. Dry the flower on paper towels. If possible, leave some stem attached. Evenly brush both sides of the petals with egg white.

2 ▲ Holding the flower by its stem over a plate lined with paper towels, sprinkle it evenly with the sugar, then shake off any excess.

Frosty florals – whole flowers or individual petals can be frosted in the same way.

3 ▲ Place on a flat board or wire rack covered with paper towels and leave to dry in a warm place.

FRUITS

When frosting fruits, choose really fresh ones which are small and firm such as kumquats, cherries, grapes or strawberries. Frosted fruits will only keep as long as the fruits themselves stay fresh. Place on a lined tray and keep in the refrigerator. Eat within two days.

1 Wash the fruit and then pat dry on paper towels.

2 ▲ Lightly whisk an egg white in a small bowl, and sprinkle some superfine sugar on to a plate. Hold the fruit by the stem if possible and evenly brush all over with the egg white.

Sometimes the simplest cakes can be the most elegant. The stark white background of sugarpaste icing is all that is needed to show off a sweeping spray of frosted flowers, an interlocking design of ribbons and a few ribbon curls and bows.

3 ▲ Holding the fruit over a plate lined with paper towels, sprinkle it evenly with the sugar, then shake off any excess.

4 Place on a flat board or wire rack covered with paper towels and leave to dry in a warm place.

Frosty fruits – make a pile of these luscious fruits for a stunning centerpiece on a cake.

Classic Cakes

This chapter features new takes on the perennial favorites that form an essential part of every good cake maker's repertoire. Ranging from the ever-popular apple crumble to the sheer luxury of a Black Forest Cake, this is the ultimate collection of family favorites that will continue to entice generation after generation.

Simple Chocolate Cake

An easy, everyday chocolate cake that can be simply filled with chocolate butter icing, or pepped up with a rich chocolate ganache for a special occasion.

INGREDIENTS
Serves 6–8
4 ounces semisweet chocolate
3 tablespoons milk
10 tablespoons (²⁄₃ cup) butter or margarine, softened
¼ cup light brown sugar
3 eggs
1¾ cups self-rising flour
1 tablespoon cocoa powder

For the Filling
1 quantity chocolate-flavor Butter Icing

To Decorate
confectioners' sugar and cocoa powder, for dusting

1 Preheat the oven to 350°F. Grease two 7-inch round cake pans and line the bottom of each with baking parchment. Melt the chocolate with the milk in a heatproof bowl set over a pan of simmering water.

2 ▲ Cream the butter or margarine with the sugar in a mixing bowl until pale and fluffy. Add the eggs one at a time, beating well after each addition. Stir in the chocolate mixture and mix until thoroughly combined.

3 ▲ Sift the flour and cocoa over the mixture and fold in with a metal spoon until evenly mixed. Divide the mixture between the prepared pans, smooth level and bake for 35–40 minutes, or until well risen and springy to the touch. Turn out onto wire racks, peel off the lining paper and let cool.

4 ▲ Sandwich the cake layers together with the butter icing. Dust with a mixture of confectioners' sugar and cocoa just before serving.

Tip

For a richer finish, make a double quantity of butter icing and spread or pipe over the top of the cake as well as using for the filling.

Spiced Apple Cake

Grated apple and chopped dates give this cake a natural sweetness—omit 2 tablespoons of the sugar if the fruit is very sweet.

INGREDIENTS
Serves 8
2 cups whole-wheat flour
2 teaspoons baking powder
1 teaspoon salt
2 teaspoons ground cinnamon
1 cup chopped dates
⅓ cup light brown sugar
1 tablespoon pear and apple spread
or fruit concentrate
½ cup apple juice
2 eggs
6 tablespoons sunflower oil
2 apples, cored and grated
1 tablespoon chopped walnuts

1 ▲ Preheat the oven to 350°F. Grease a deep 8-inch round cake pan, line the bottom with waxed or parchment paper and grease the paper. Sift the flour, baking powder and cinnamon into a mixing bowl, then mix in the dates and make a well in the center.

Tip

It is not necessary to peel the apples—the skin adds extra fiber and softens on cooking.

2 ▲ Mix the sugar with the pear and apple spread or fruit concentrate in a small bowl. Gradually stir in the apple juice. Add to the dry ingredients with the eggs, oil and apples. Mix thoroughly.

3 ▲ Spoon the mixture into the pan, sprinkle with the walnuts and bake for 60–65 minutes, or until a skewer inserted into the center of the cake comes out clean. Transfer to a wire rack, peel off the lining paper and allow to cool.

Black Forest Gâteau

*A perfect gâteau for a special occasion tea party, or for serving
as a sumptuous dessert at a dinner party.*

INGREDIENTS
Serves 10–12
5 large eggs
¾ cup superfine sugar
½ cup flour, sifted
⅓ cup cocoa powder, sifted
6 tbsp butter, melted

For the Filling
5–6 tbsp Kirsch
2½ cups heavy cream
*1 x 15 oz can black cherries,
drained, pitted and chopped*

To Decorate
8 x 1 oz squares plain chocolate
*15–20 fresh cherries, preferably
with stems*
sifted confectioners' sugar (optional)

1 Preheat the oven to 350°F. Grease two deep 8 inch round cake pans, line the bases with waxed paper and grease the paper.

2 ▲ Place the eggs and sugar in a large mixing bowl and beat with electric beaters for about 10 minutes or until the mixture is thick and pale.

3 Sift together the flour and cocoa powder, then sift again into the whisked mixture. Fold in very gently, then slowly trickle in the melted butter and continue to fold in gently.

4 Divide the mixture between the pans and smooth the surfaces. Bake in the center of the oven for about 30 minutes, or until springy to the touch. Leave in the pans for about 5 minutes, then turn out on to a wire rack, peel off the lining paper and leave to cool.

5 ▲ Cut each cake in half horizontally and lay on a work surface. Sprinkle the four layers with the Kirsch.

6 ▲ In a large bowl, whip the cream until it holds soft peaks. Transfer two-thirds of the cream to another bowl and stir in the chopped cherries. Place a layer of cake on a serving plate or cake board and spread over one-third of the filling. Top with another layer of cake and continue layering, finishing with a layer of cake.

7 Use the remaining whipped cream to cover the top and sides of the gâteau, spreading it evenly with a knife.

8 To decorate the gâteau, melt the chocolate in a bowl over a pan of hot water, or in a double boiler. Spread the chocolate out on to a plastic chopping board and allow to set.

9 ▲ Using a long, sharp knife, scrape along the surface of the melted chocolate to make thin shavings and use these to cover the sides of the cake and to decorate the top. Finish by arranging the cherries on top of the gâteau. Dust with confectioners' sugar, if wished.

Tip

If liked, the cherries can be coated or half-coated in chocolate before arranging on the cake. To do this, reserve 2–3 tbsp of the melted chocolate and dip the cherries into it. Allow the dipped cherries to set on waxed paper.

Mocha-hazelnut Battenberg

The traditional Battenberg cake originated in Germany when the Prince of Battenberg married Queen Victoria's daughter, Beatrice. This recipe is a variation of the original theme.

INGREDIENTS

Serves 6–8
$\frac{1}{2}$ *cup butter, softened*
$\frac{1}{2}$ *cup sugar*
2 large eggs
1 cup self-rising flour, sifted
$\frac{2}{3}$ *cup ground hazelnuts*
2 tsp coffee extract
1 tbsp cocoa powder

To Finish
7 tbsp apricot jam, warmed and sieved
8 oz yellow marzipan
$\frac{2}{3}$ *cup ground hazelnuts*
sifted confectioners' sugar, for rolling out
ground hazelnuts, to decorate

1 Preheat the oven to 350°F. Meanwhile, grease a 7 inch square cake pan, line the base with waxed paper and grease

2 ▲ Place the butter and sugar in a bowl and beat until fluffy. Gradually beat in the eggs, then fold in the flour. Transfer half the mixture to another bowl.

3 ▲ Stir the ground hazelnuts into one half of the cake mixture and the coffee extract and cocoa powder into the other half.

4 ▲ Prepare a strip of foil to fit the width and height of the cake pan, then place the mocha-flavored cake mixture in one half of the pan. Position the strip of foil down the center, then spoon the hazelnut-flavored cake mixture into the other half of the pan. Smooth the surface of both mixtures.

5 Bake for 30–35 minutes or until a skewer inserted into the center of both halves comes out clean. Leave the cakes to cool in the pan for about 5 minutes, then turn out on to a wire rack, peel off the lining paper and leave to cool completely.

6 ▲ Separate the cakes and cut each one in half lengthwise. Take one portion of the mocha-flavored cake and brush along one long side with a little apricot jam. Sandwich this surface with a portion of the hazelnut-flavored cake. Brush the top of the cakes with apricot jam and position the other portion of mocha-flavored cake on top of the hazelnut base. Brush along the inner long side with apricot jam and sandwich with the final portion of hazelnut-flavored cake. Set aside.

7 Knead the marzipan on the work surface to soften, then knead in the ground hazelnuts until evenly blended. On the work surface lightly dusted with confectioners' sugar, roll out the marzipan into a rectangle large enough to wrap around the cake, but excluding the ends.

8 Brush the long sides of the cake with apricot jam, then lay the cake on top of the marzipan. Wrap the marzipan around the cake, sealing the edge neatly. Place the cake on a serving plate, seal-side down, and pinch the edges of the marzipan to give an attractive finish. Score the top surface with a knife and sprinkle with ground hazelnuts.

*A*pple Crumble Cake

In the autumn use windfall apples. Served warm with heavy cream or custard this cake doubles as a dessert.

INGREDIENTS
Serves 8-10
For the Topping
³/₄ cup self-rising flour
½ tsp ground cinnamon
3 tbsp butter
2 tbsp sugar

For the Base
4 tbsp butter, softened
6 tbsp sugar
1 large egg, beaten
1 cup self-rising flour,
sifted
2 cooking apples, peeled, cored
and sliced
¹/₃ cup sultanas

To Decorate
1 red dessert apple, cored,.thinly
sliced and tossed in lemon juice
2 tbsp sugar, sifted
pinch of ground cinnamon

1 Preheat the oven 350°F. Grease a deep 7 inch springform pan, line the base with waxed paper and grease the paper.

2 ▲ To make the topping, sift the flour and cinnamon into a mixing bowl. Rub the butter into the flour until it resembles breadcrumbs, then stir in the sugar. Set aside.

3 ▲ To make the base, put the butter, sugar, egg and flour into a bowl and beat for 1–2 minutes until smooth . Spoon into the prepared pan.

4 ▲ Mix together the apple slices and sultanas and spread them evenly over the top. Sprinkle with the topping.

5 Bake in the center of the oven for about 1 hour. Cool in the pan for 10 minutes before turning out on to a wire rack and peeling off the lining paper. Serve warm or cool, decorated with slices of red dessert apple, and with sugar and cinnamon sprinkled over.

Marbled Spice Cake

This cake is baked in a fluted ring-shaped tin called a kugelhupf, or gugelhupf, mold from Germany and Austria to give it a pretty shape.

INGREDIENTS
Serves 8–10
6 tbsp butter, softened
½ cup sugar
2 large eggs, lightly beaten
few drops of vanilla extract
⅞ cup flour
1½ tsp baking powder
3 tbsp milk
3 tbsp molasses
1 tsp ground cinnamon
½ tsp ground ginger
1⅛ cups confectioners' sugar, sifted, to decorate

1 Preheat the oven to 350°F. Grease and flour a 2 lb kugelhupf mold or ring-shaped cake pan.

2 Cream the butter and sugar together in a bowl until light and fluffy. Beat in the egg and vanilla extract.

3 ▲ Sift together the flour and baking powder, then fold into the mixture, alternating with the milk, until the ingredients are evenly combined.

4 Spoon about one-third of the mixture into a small bowl and stir in the molasses and spices.

5 ▲ Drop alternating spoonfuls of the light and dark mixtures into the tin. Run a knife or skewer through them to give a marbled effect.

6 ▲ Bake in the center of the oven for about 50 minutes or until a skewer inserted into the center comes out clean. Leave in the pan for 10 minutes before turning out on to a wire rack to cool.

7 ▲ To decorate, stir enough warm water into the confectioners' sugar to make a smooth icing. Spoon quickly over the cake. Allow to set before serving.

Tip
If you do not have a kugelhupf mold or a ring-shaped cake pan, use an 8 inch round cake pan.

Best-Ever Chocolate Cake

This classic layer cake is a crowd-pleaser whatever the occasion. Three extra-chocolatey layers of sponge cake are sandwiched together with an irresistible chocolate icing. It looks magnificent left unadorned, but could be embellished with chocolate curls, leaves or other decorations.

INGREDIENTS
Serves 12–14
8 tablespoons (½ cup) unsalted butter
1 cup all-purpose flour
½ cup unsweetened cocoa powder
1 teaspoon baking powder
⅛ teaspoon salt
6 eggs
1 cup sugar
2 teaspoons vanilla extract

For the Icing
8 × 1-ounce squares semisweet chocolate, chopped
6 tablespoons unsalted butter
3 eggs, separated
1 cup heavy cream
3 tablespoons sugar

1 Preheat the oven to 350°F. Line three 8 x 1½-inch round cake pans with waxed or parchment paper and grease.

2 ▲ Dust evenly with flour and spread with a brush. Set aside.

3 ▲ Melt the butter over low heat. With a spoon, skim off any foam that rises to the surface. Set aside.

4 ▲ Sift the flour, cocoa, baking powder and salt together three times and set aside.

5 Place the eggs and sugar in a large heatproof bowl set over a pan of hot water. With an electric mixer, beat until the mixture doubles in volume and is thick enough to leave a ribbon trail when the beaters are lifted, about 10 minutes. Add the vanilla.

6 ▲ Sift the dry ingredients over in three batches, folding in carefully after each addition. Fold in the butter.

7 Divide the batter between the pans and bake until the cakes pull away from the sides of the pan, about 25 minutes. Transfer to a rack.

8 For the icing, melt the chopped chocolate in the top of a double boiler, or in a heatproof bowl set over hot water.

9 ▲ Off the heat, stir in the butter and egg yolks. Return to low heat and stir until thick. Remove from the heat and set aside. Whip the cream until firm; set aside. In another bowl, beat the egg whites until stiff. Add the sugar and beat until glossy.

10 Fold the cream into the chocolate mixture, then carefully fold in the egg whites. Refrigerate for 20 minutes to thicken the icing.

11 ▶ Sandwich the cake layers with icing, stacking them carefully. Spread the remaining icing evenly over the top and sides of the cake.

 Tip

For a simpler icing, combine 1 cup whipping cream with 8 ounces finely chopped semisweet chocolate in a saucepan. Stir over low heat until the chocolate has melted. Let cool and whisk to spreading consistency.

Angel Food Cake

This is a true American classic. Although similar to a whisked sponge cake, it differs in that it contains no egg yolks. This results in a snowy white cake with a delicate texture. The cream of tartar helps to stiffen the egg whites, and the addition of the sugar forms a light meringue mixture. The cake is baked in a nonstick ungreased tube pan. This enables the mixture to cling to the sides of the pan as it rises. The traditional whipped frosting is a basic Italian meringue, which has a hot sugar syrup whisked into it.

INGREDIENTS
Serves 20
5 tablespoons all-purpose flour
1 tablespoon cornstarch
1 cup superfine sugar
10 egg whites
1 teaspoon cream of tartar
1 teaspoon vanilla extract

For the Frosting
½ cup superfine sugar
4 tablespoons water
2 egg whites
2 teaspoons golden or light corn syrup
½ teaspoon vanilla extract

To Decorate
2 teaspoons each dried coconut, chopped pistachio nuts and chopped candied orange peel gold and silver dragées

1 Preheat the oven to 350°F. Sift the flour, cornstarch and ¼ cup of the sugar together three times.

2 ▲ Whisk 10 of the egg whites with the cream of tartar until stiff, and gradually whisk in the remaining sugar, a tablespoon at a time, until the mixture is thick and glossy.

3 ▲ Fold in the sifted flours and sugar and vanilla until combined, and transfer to a 10-inch nonstick tube pan. Bake for 35–40 minutes, until risen and golden. Remove from the oven, invert the cake in its pan, and let cool. To make the frosting, heat the sugar and water in a small pan until the sugar dissolves. Increase the heat and boil until the temperature reaches 240°F on a candy thermometer (or the thread stage).

4 ▲ As soon as the mixture boils, whisk the egg whites until very stiff and dry. Pour the syrup in a steady stream into the center of the egg whites, whisking continually, until thick and glossy. Beat in the syrup and vanilla and continue beating for 5 minutes, until the frosting is cooled.

5 ▲ Carefully remove the cooled cake from its pan, place on a turntable and coat with the frosting, using a baking spatula to make a swirling pattern and peak effect.

6 ▲ To decorate, sprinkle the coconut, pistachios and orange peel over the top, and stud with gold and silver dragées.

Savarin with Fresh Berries

This classic French yeast cake is soaked with a rum syrup and glazed, then served with fresh cream and a mixture of fresh berries. Choose your favorite fruits in season.

INGREDIENTS
Serves 8
1 tablespoon dried
(not rapid-rise) yeast
2½ tablespoons superfine sugar
6 tablespoons tepid milk
2 cups bread flour
pinch of salt
4 eggs, beaten
8 tablespoons (½ cup) butter, softened

For the Syrup
½ cup honey
4 tablespoons water
2 tablespoons lemon juice
2 tablespoons dark rum or
Grand Marnier

To Decorate
3 tablespoons apricot jam,
warmed and sieved
⅔ cup heavy cream
¼ pound summer fruits
lemon balm leaves

1 Grease and flour a 6¼-cup-capacity ring mold. Blend the yeast, 1½ teaspoons sugar, milk and 1 tablespoon flour together. Cover and let stand in a warm place for 15 minutes, until frothy.

2 ▲ Sift the remaining flour and salt into a bowl and stir in the remaining sugar. Make a well in the center and beat in the yeast mixture, eggs and butter until glossy.

3 Heat the oven to 400°F. Transfer the batter to the prepared pan, cover and let it sit in a warm place for 30 minutes, or until the batter almost reaches the top of the pan. Bake for 35 minutes, until risen and golden. Remove from the oven and let cool in the pan for 5 minutes before turning out onto a wire rack. Prick the cake all over with a skewer.

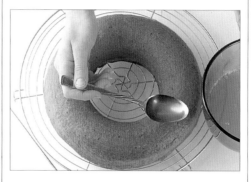

4 ▲ To make the syrup, heat the honey, water and lemon juice together and boil for 3 minutes, until thick and syrupy. Remove from the heat. Stir in the rum or Grand Marnier and spoon over the cooling cake. Allow to cool completely.

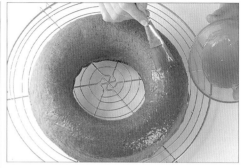

5 ▲ Heat the apricot jam until it just boils, remove from the heat and brush over the cooled cake.

6 ▲ Whip the cream until thick and transfer to a piping bag. Pipe swirls all around the top of the cake and decorate with the fruits and lemon balm leaves.

*D*undee Cake

This is the perfect fruit cake for those who prefer a lighter style than the traditional sticky fruit cake. It has a wonderful fruit and nut flavor and a light, slightly crumbly texture.

INGREDIENTS
Serves 16–20
12 tablespoons (¾ cup)
unsalted butter
¾ cup light brown sugar
3 eggs
2 cups all-purpose flour
2 teaspoons baking powder
1 teaspoon ground cinnamon
½ teaspoon ground cloves
¼ teaspoon ground nutmeg
1⅓ cups golden raisins
1 cup raisins
¾ cup candied cherries, halved
¾ cup chopped mixed peel
½ cup blanched
almonds, chopped
grated zest of 1 lemon
2 tablespoons brandy

To Decorate
⅔ cup whole
blanched almonds

1 Preheat the oven to 350°F. Grease a deep 8-inch round cake pan, line the base and sides with waxed or parchment paper and grease the paper.

2 Cream the butter and sugar together until pale and light. Add the eggs, one at a time, beating well after each addition.

3 ▲ Sift the flour, baking powder and spices together and fold into the creamed mixture alternately with the remaining ingredients until all the ingredients are evenly incorporated.

4 ▲ Spoon into the prepared pan and smooth the surface, making a small dip in the center. Begin decorating the top of the cake with almonds.

5 ▲ Continue decorating the cake by pressing almonds in decreasing circles over the entire surface. Bake for 2–2¼ hours, until a skewer inserted in the center comes out clean.

6 Remove the cake from the oven, allow to cool in the pan for 30 minutes, then transfer to a wire rack to cool completely.

Carrot Cake

So easy to make, this is a wonderfully moist and tasty cake, enriched with grated carrots and vegetable oil—a classic "all-in-one" cake. The chopped nuts impart an even fuller flavor. Although often served with a simple dusting of confectioners' sugar, the cream cheese icing and marzipan carrots make the cake a little more special.

INGREDIENTS
Serves 8
1 cup superfine sugar
3 eggs
1 scant cup vegetable oil
grated zest and juice of 1 orange
2 cups whole-wheat flour
3 teaspoons baking powder
1 teaspoon ground cinnamon
½ teaspoon ground nutmeg
1½ teaspoons salt
3–4 carrots, finely grated and
squeezed dry
1 cup walnuts, ground

For the Filling
1 cup cream cheese
2 tablespoons honey
1 tablespoon orange juice

To Decorate
2 ounces marzipan
orange food coloring
angelica
2 walnut halves (optional)

1 Preheat the oven to 350°F. Grease an 8-inch round cake pan, line the bottom with waxed or parchment paper and grease the paper.

2 Beat the sugar, eggs, oil, orange zest and juice together until light and frothy. Sift in the flour, baking powder, salt and spices and beat for another minute. Stir in the carrots and nuts and spoon the batter into the prepared pan.

3 Bake for 1½–1¾ hours, until risen and a skewer inserted into the center of the cake comes out clean.

4 ▲ To make the icing, beat the cheese, honey and 1 tablespoon orange juice together until smooth. Chill for 30 minutes to firm up.

5 ▲ Tint the marzipan with the food coloring to resemble the color of carrots.

6 Break off small pieces and roll between your palms to form small carrot shapes.

7 ▲ Using a small knife, press marks around the sides and stick a small piece of angelica in the top of each one to resemble the stalk.

8 ▲ Spread the icing over the top of the cooled cake. Arrange the carrots, in a bunch, in the center of the cake and decorate with the walnut halves, if using.

Panforte

*This rich, spicy nougat-type cake is a speciality of Siena in Italy, where
it is traditionally baked at Christmas. It is a combination of chopped candied
peel and nuts, which are mixed with a sugar syrup before baking.
It will keep well for several weeks in an airtight container.
Keep on hand over the Christmas season to serve with morning coffee.*

INGREDIENTS
Serves 8
*2 cups mixed candied exotic peel,
to include: papaya, pineapple,
orange, lemon and citron*
²⁄₃ cup unblanched almonds
½ cup walnut halves
½ cup all-purpose flour
1 teaspoon ground cinnamon
*¼ teaspoon each ground nutmeg,
cloves and coriander*
¾ cup superfine sugar
4 tablespoons water

To Decorate
confectioners' sugar

1 Preheat the oven to 350°F. Grease an 8-inch round loose-bottomed cake pan and line the bottom with a sheet of rice or parchment paper.

2 Combine the mixed candied peel and nuts in a bowl. Sift in the flour and spices and mix well.

3 Heat the sugar and water in a small pan until the sugar dissolves. Increase the heat and boil until the mixture reaches 240°F on a sugar thermometer, or until it reaches the thread stage.

4 ▲ Remove from the heat and pour onto the fruit mixture, stirring with a wooden spoon until well coated. Transfer to the prepared pan, pressing the batter firmly into the sides with a metal spoon.

5 ▲ Bake for 25–30 minutes, until the batter is bubbling all over. Remove from the oven and let stand in the pan to cool for 5 minutes.

6 ▲ With a lightly oiled baking spatula, work around the edges of the cake to loosen and remove the side of the pan, leaving the base in place. Allow to cool completely.

7 ▲ Remove from the base of the pan and decorate with a generous dusting of confectioners' sugar.

Cassata Siciliana

This is a chilled cake from Sicily, where it is traditional to cover the cake with a layer of almond paste and to decorate the top with an exotic selection of candied fruits.

INGREDIENTS
Serves 12
1 quantity Whisked Sponge Cake baked in a 9-inch round pan
scant ½ cup Marsala

For the Filling
1½ cups ricotta cheese
2 tablespoons honey
¼ teaspoon vanilla extract
grated zest and juice of ½ lemon
¾ cup mixed candied peel, finely chopped
½ cup semisweet chocolate chips

For the Icing
1½ cups ground almonds
6 tablespoons superfine sugar
¾ cup confectioners' sugar, sifted
1 egg white, lightly whisked
1 teaspoon lemon juice
2 drops almond extract
green food coloring
3 tablespoons apricot jam, warmed and sieved

To Decorate
8 ounces mixed candied fruits

1 Line an 8-inch round springform pan with plastic wrap.

2 ▲ Cut the cake into three layers. Trim one to fit into the bottom of the pan. Cut the second into strips to line the sides. Brush with a little Marsala.

3 ▲ To make the filling, beat the ricotta, honey, 1 tablespoon Marsala, vanilla and lemon zest and juice together until very smooth. Chop the sponge trimmings and stir into the cheese mixture, with the peel and chocolate chips. Spoon into the sponge cake shell, pressing the mixture into the sides.

4 ▲ Smooth the surface and trim the reserved layer of sponge cake to fit tightly over the filling. Pour the remaining Marsala over and cover with plastic wrap. Place a weight on top of the cake and chill for several hours, until firm.

5 Meanwhile, make the icing. Combine the almonds, superfine sugar and confectioners' sugar together. Make a well in the center and work in the egg white, lemon juice and almond extract to form a soft, pliable paste. Add a few drops of food coloring and knead on a clean surface dusted with a little confectioners' sugar until smooth and evenly colored. Wrap the icing and keep cool until required.

6 ▲ Remove the cake from the refrigerator and turn out of the pan. Remove the plastic wrap and brush the cake with warmed apricot jam. Roll out the almond paste to a circle a little larger than the cake and use to cover, pressing gently to the top and sides. Smooth on the icing with a baking spatula or small rolling pin. Transfer to a cake board.

7 ▲ Make an attractive arrangement of mixed candied fruits in the center of the cake.

Kulich

This Russian yeast cake is known under other names throughout Eastern Europe, where it is traditionally made at Easter. The delicious spiced cake is baked in special molds that can be purchased at some specialty shops, but for convenience the recipe has been converted for use in either clay flowerpots or coffee cans. The cake is best eaten on the day it is made.

INGREDIENTS
Makes 2 cakes
1 tablespoon dried yeast
6 tablespoons tepid milk
6 tablespoons superfine sugar
4½ cups all-purpose flour
pinch of saffron strands
2 tablespoons dark rum
½ teaspoon ground cardamom
½ teaspoon ground cumin
4 tablespoons butter
2 eggs plus 2 egg yolks
½ vanilla bean, finely chopped
2 tablespoons each chopped
mixed candied peel, chopped
crystallized ginger, chopped
almonds and currants

To Decorate
¾ cup confectioners' sugar, sifted
1½–2 teaspoons warm water
1 drop almond extract
blanched almonds
mixed candied peel
2 candles

1 Blend the yeast, milk, 2 tablespoons sugar and ½ cup flour together until smooth. Let sit in a warm place for 15 minutes, until frothy. Soak the saffron in the rum for 15 minutes.

2 ▲ Sift the remaining flour and spices into a bowl and rub in the butter. Stir in the remaining sugar, make a well in the center and work in the frothed yeast mixture, the saffron liquid and the remaining ingredients to form a fine dough.

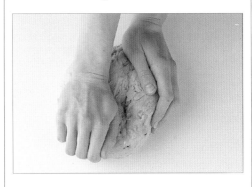

3 ▲ Knead on a lightly floured surface for 5 minutes, until smooth and pliable. Place in an oiled bowl, cover and let rise in a warm place for 1–1½ hours, until doubled in size.

4 ▲ Preheat the oven to 375°F. Grease two clean 6-inch clay flowerpots or two 1¼-pound coffee cans. Line the bottoms with waxed or parchment paper and flour the sides.

5 ▲ Knock back the dough. Divide in two and form each lump into a round. Press into the prepared pots or cans, cover and let sit in a warm place for another 30 minutes, until the dough comes two-thirds of the way up the sides. Bake for 35 minutes if using the coffee cans or 50 minutes if using the clay pots. Test with a skewer and remove from the oven. Turn out onto a wire rack and allow to cool.

6 Blend the confectioners' sugar, water and almond together until smooth to form a thick glacé icing. Drizzle over the top of each cake and decorate with the nuts, peel and candles.

Baked Cheesecake with Fresh Fruits

A rich, creamy cheesecake, baked on a sweet crumb crust. It is topped with a selection of exotic fresh fruit; vary the decoration to suit the season.

INGREDIENTS
Serves 12
6 ounces graham crackers or
digestive biscuits, crushed
4 tablespoons unsalted butter, melted
1 pound curd cheese
⅔ cup sour cream
½ cup superfine sugar
3 eggs, separated
grated zest of 1 lemon
2 tablespoons Marsala
½ teaspoon almond extract
½ cup ground almonds
⅓ cup golden raisins

To Decorate
1 pound prepared mixed fruits
(figs, cherries, peaches, strawberries,
hulled, halved and pitted,
as necessary)

1 ▲ Preheat the oven to 350°F. Grease the sides of a 10-inch round springform pan and line with baking parchment.

2 ▲ Mix the crushed crackers with the butter until well combined and press into the bottom of the prepared pan. Smooth the surface with a metal spoon and chill for 20 minutes.

3 ▲ Meanwhile prepare the cake mixture. Beat the cheese, cream, sugar, egg yolks, lemon zest, Marsala and almond extract together until smooth and creamy.

4 ▲ Whisk the egg whites until stiff and fold into the creamed mixture with the remaining ingredients until evenly combined. Pour over the chilled crust and bake for 45 minutes, until risen and just set in the center.

5 Remove from the oven and let sit in the pan in a warm, draft-free place until completely cool. Carefully remove the pan and peel away the lining paper.

6 ▲ Chill the cheesecake for at least an hour before decorating with the prepared fruits, just before serving.

Chilled Grape Cheesecake

An attractive and unusual topping decorates this classic chilled cheesecake. Use green grapes and white grape juice if you like, for an equally attractive cheesecake.

INGREDIENTS
Serves 12
6 ounces ginger snaps (1⅓ cups), crushed
4 tablespoons butter, melted
12 ounces (1½ cups) cream cheese
7 ounces (scant 1 cup) fromage frais
6 tablespoons honey
2 eggs, separated
1 teaspoon grated lemon zest
1 tablespoon lemon juice
4 tablespoons Muscat de Beaumes de Venise (or other sweet white dessert wine)
1 tablespoon powdered gelatin

For the Topping
4 ounces red or green seedless grapes, halved
small piece of angelica
2 tablespoons Muscat de Beaumes de Venise (or other sweet white dessert wine)
1½ teaspoons powdered gelatin
1¼ cups red or white grape juice

1 Grease the sides of a 9-inch round springform pan and line with baking parchment.

2 Mix the crushed ginger snaps with the butter until well combined. Press into the bottom of the prepared pan. Smooth the surface with a metal spoon and chill for 20 minutes.

3 To prepare the cake mixture, beat together the cream cheese, fromage frais, honey, egg yolks and lemon zest and juice until smooth and creamy.

4 ▲ Heat the wine and gelatin together in a small pan over low heat until the gelatin dissolves. Remove from the heat, stir in a little of the creamed mixture and pour back into the remaining creamed mixture, stirring until combined.

5 Whisk the egg whites until stiff and fold into the creamed mixture until evenly incorporated. Pour over the chilled crust and return to the refrigerator to set.

6 ▲ When the cheesecake is just setting, arrange the grapes over the top in the shape of a bunch of grapes, and make a stem from the angelica. Chill until completely set.

7 To complete the topping, heat the wine and gelatin together as before, until dissolved. Pour in the grape juice and allow to cool.

8 ▲ Using a small paintbrush, carefully dampen the edges of the lined pan, directly above the set level of the cheesecake.

9 ▲ Carefully pour the cooled grape juice over to cover the grapes. Chill again until set.

10 ▲ Just before serving, remove the pan and carefully peel away the lining paper, using a baking spatula to help the process.

Sticky Gingerbread Loaf

Moist and sticky, this classic gingerbread is made even more delicious with a tart lemon glacé icing, or glaze, drizzled over the top. The icing is simple, but looks extremely effective.

INGREDIENTS
Makes 1 loaf
1½ *cups all-purpose flour*
2 *teaspoons ground ginger*
½ *teaspoon ground pumpkin*
pie spice
½ *teaspoon baking soda*
2 *tablespoons molasses*
2 *tablespoons golden or light*
corn syrup
½ *cup dark brown sugar*
6 *tablespoons butter*
1 *egg*
1 *tablespoon milk*
1 *tablespoon orange juice*
2 *pieces of crystallized ginger,*
finely chopped
⅓ *cup golden raisins*
5 *dried apricots, finely chopped*

For the Icing
3 *tablespoons confectioners' sugar*
2 *teaspoons lemon juice*

1 Preheat the oven to 325°F. Grease a 9 x 5 x 3-inch loaf pan, line with waxed or parchment paper and grease the paper. Sift the flour, spices and baking soda into a bowl.

2 ▲ Place the molasses, syrup, sugar and butter in a pan and heat gently until the butter has melted.

3 ▲ In a separate bowl, beat the egg, milk and orange juice together. Add the syrup mixture, egg mixture, chopped ginger, golden raisins and apricots to the dry ingredients and stir to combine thoroughly.

4 ▲ Spoon into the prepared pan and level with the back of a metal spoon. Bake in the center of the oven for about 50 minutes, or until the gingerbread is well risen, firm when touched gently in the center and cooked through.

5 ▲ Allow the loaf to cool in the pan, then turn out onto a wire rack. Mix the confectioners' sugar with the lemon juice in a bowl and beat until smooth. Drizzle the icing back and forth over the top of the gingerbread, allow to set, then cut into thick slices to serve.

Irish Whiskey Cake

This moist, rich fruit cake is drizzled with whiskey as soon as it comes out of the oven.

INGREDIENTS
Serves 12
½ cup candied cherries
1 cup dark brown sugar
⅔ cup golden raisins
⅔ cup raisins
⅔ cup currants
1¼ cups cold tea
2¾ cups self-rising flour, sifted
1 egg
3 tablespoons Irish whiskey

1 ▲ Mix the cherries, sugar, dried fruit and tea in a large bowl. Soak overnight, or until all the tea has been absorbed by the fruit. If time is short, use hot tea and soak the fruit for just 2 hours.

2 ▲ Preheat the oven to 350°F. Grease a 9 x 5 x 3-inch loaf pan, line with waxed or parchment paper and grease the paper. Add the flour, then the egg to the fruit mixture and beat thoroughly.

3 ▲ Pour the batter into the prepared pan and bake for 1½ hours, or until a skewer inserted into the center of the cake comes out clean.

4 ▲ Prick the top of the cake with a skewer and drizzle the whiskey over while the cake is still hot. Let stand for about 5 minutes, then remove from the pan and cool on a wire rack.

Banana-Lemon Layer Cake

Banana loaf is a favorite tea bread or snack; here is its more sophisticated cousin. This moist banana and walnut cake is deliciously complemented by a tangy lemon butter icing.

INGREDIENTS
Serves 8–10
2 cups all-purpose flour
1½ teaspoons baking powder
½ teaspoon salt
8 tablespoons (½ cup) unsalted
butter, softened
1 cup granulated sugar
½ cup light brown sugar
2 eggs
½ teaspoon grated lemon zest
2 very ripe bananas, mashed
1 teaspoon vanilla extract
¼ cup milk
¾ cup chopped walnuts
pared lemon zest, to decorate

For the Icing
8 tablespoons (½ cup) unsalted
butter, softened
5 cups confectioners' sugar
1 teaspoon grated lemon zest

1 Preheat the oven to 350°F. Grease two 9-inch round cake pans, line the bottoms with waxed or parchment paper and grease the paper. Sift the flour with the baking powder and salt.

2 ▲ Cream the butter with the sugars until light and fluffy. Beat in the eggs, then stir in the grated lemon zest.

3 ▲ In a small bowl mix the mashed bananas with the vanilla and milk. Add the banana mixture and the dry ingredients to the butter mixture alternately in two or three batches and stir until just blended. Fold in the nuts.

4 Divide the batter between the cake pans. Bake for 30–35 minutes, let stand for 5 minutes, then turn out onto a wire rack.

5 Make the icing. Cream the butter until smooth, then gradually beat in the confectioners' sugar. Stir in the lemon zest and enough juice to make a spreadable consistency.

6 ▲ Put one of the cake layers on a serving plate. Cover with about one-third of the icing. Top with the second cake layer. Spread the remaining icing evenly over the cake and decorate with the pared lemon zest.

Génoise with Fruit and Cream

Génoise is a classic sponge cake that can be used as the base for both simple and elaborate creations. In this version a little butter is added to make a moister cake. You could simply dust it with confectioners' sugar, or layer it with seasonal fruits.

INGREDIENTS
Serves 6
1 cup all-purpose flour
pinch of salt
4 eggs, at room temperature
½ cup superfine sugar
½ teaspoon vanilla extract
4 tablespoons butter, melted or
clarified and cooled

For the Filling
1 pound fresh strawberries
2–4 tablespoons superfine sugar
2 cups whipping cream
1 teaspoon vanilla extract

1 Preheat the oven to 350°F. Lightly butter a 9-inch springform pan or deep cake pan. Line the bottom with baking parchment and dust lightly with flour. Sift the flour and salt together twice.

2 ▲ Half-fill a medium saucepan with hot water and set over low heat (do not allow the water to boil). Break the eggs into a heatproof bowl that just fits into the pan without touching the water. Using an electric mixer, beat the eggs, gradually adding the sugar, for 8–10 minutes, until the mixture is very thick and pale and leaves a ribbon trail. Remove the bowl from the pan, add the vanilla and continue beating until cool.

3 ▲ Fold in the flour mixture in three batches, using a balloon whisk or metal spoon. Before the third addition of flour, stir a large spoonful of the cake mixture into the melted or clarified butter, then fold the butter mixture into the remaining mixture with the last addition of flour. Work quickly, but gently, so the mixture does not deflate. Pour into the prepared pan, smoothing the top so the sides are slightly higher than the center.

4 ▲ Bake for 25–30 minutes, until the top of the cake springs back when touched and the edge begins to shrink away from the side of the pan. Place the cake in its pan on a wire rack to cool for 5–10 minutes, then invert the cake onto the rack and allow to cool completely. Peel off the lining paper.

5 ▲ To make the filling, slice the strawberries, place in a bowl, sprinkle with 1–2 tablespoons of the sugar and set aside. Beat the cream with enough of the remaining sugar to sweeten it to your taste. Beat in the vanilla until the cream holds soft peaks: do not overbeat.

6 ▲ To assemble the cake, split the sponge in half horizontally, using a serrated knife. Place the top, cut side up, on a serving plate. Spread with a third of the cream and cover with a layer of sliced strawberries. Place the bottom half of the cake, cut side down, on top of the filling and press lightly. Spread the remaining cream over the top and sides of the cake. Chill and serve with the remaining strawberries.

$\mathcal{P}$each Jelly Roll

*A featherlight sponge enclosing peach jam, this would be delicious at teatime.
It needs to be baked on the day you are going to serve it.*

INGREDIENTS
Serves 6–8
3 eggs
*$^1/_2$ cup superfine sugar,
plus extra for dusting*
$^3/_4$ cup all-purpose flour, sifted
6 tablespoons peach jam
confectioners' sugar, for dusting

1▲ Preheat the oven to 400°F. Grease a 12 x 8-inch jelly roll pan and line with baking parchment. Combine the eggs and sugar in a bowl. Beat with a handheld electric mixer until the batter is thick and pale and leaves a trail on the surface when the beaters are lifted.

2▲ Carefully fold in the flour with a large metal spoon, then add 1 tablespoon boiling water in the same way.

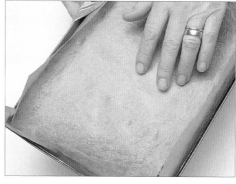

3▲ Spoon into the prepared pan, spread evenly to the edge and bake for 10–12 minutes, until the cake springs back when lightly pressed in the center.

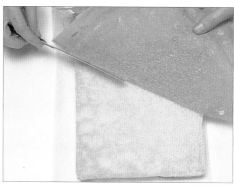

4▲ Spread a sheet of waxed or parchment paper on a flat surface, sprinkle superfine sugar over it, then invert the cake on top. Peel off the lining paper.

5▲ Neatly trim the edges of the cake. Make a neat cut two-thirds of the way through the cake, about $^1/_2$ inch from the short edge nearest you.

6▲ Spread the cake with the peach jam and roll up quickly from the partially cut end. Hold in position for a minute, making sure the seam is underneath. Cool on a wire rack. Dust with confectioners' sugar before serving, or decorate with Glacé Icing (see Tip).

$\mathcal{T}$ip

To decorate the jelly roll, put 4 ounces Glacé Icing (glaze) in a piping bag fitted with a small writing nozzle and pipe lines over the top of the cake.

Queen of Sheba Cake

This rich chocolate and almond cake is so moist it needs no filling. It is wonderful for entertaining, as it can be made in advance and stored, well wrapped, in the refrigerator for up to three days.

INGREDIENTS
Serves 8–10
⅔ cup whole blanched almonds, lightly toasted
½ cup superfine sugar
¼ cup all-purpose flour
8 tablespoons (½ cup) unsalted butter, softened
5 ounces semisweet chocolate, melted
3 eggs, separated
2 tablespoons almond liqueur (optional)

For the Chocolate Glaze
¾ cup heavy cream
8 ounces semisweet chocolate, chopped
2 tablespoons unsalted butter
2 tablespoons almond liqueur (optional)
chopped toasted almonds, to decorate

3 ▲ In a medium bowl, beat the butter with an electric mixer until creamy, then add half of the remaining sugar and beat for 1–2 minutes, until very light and creamy. Gradually beat in the melted chocolate until well blended, then add the egg yolks one at a time, beating well after each addition, and beat in the liqueur, if using.

5 Bake for 30–35 minutes, until the edges are puffed but the center is still soft and wobbly (a skewer inserted about 2 inches from the edge should come out clean). Transfer the cake in its pan to a wire rack to cool for about 15 minutes, then remove the sides of the cake pan and let cool completely. Invert the cake onto an 8-inch cake board and remove the bottom of the pan and the paper.

6 To make the chocolate glaze, bring the cream to a boil in a saucepan. Remove from the heat and add the chocolate. Stir gently until the chocolate has melted and is smooth, then beat in the butter and liqueur, if using. Cool for 20–30 minutes, until slightly thickened, stirring the mixture occasionally.

1 ▲ Preheat the oven to 350°F. Lightly butter an 8- or 9-inch springform pan or deep loose-bottomed cake pan. Line the bottom with baking parchment and dust the pan lightly with flour.

2 In the bowl of a food processor fitted with the metal blade, process the almonds and 2 tablespoons of the sugar until very fine. Transfer to a bowl and sift the flour over. Stir to mix, then set aside.

4 ▲ In another bowl, beat the egg whites until soft peaks form. Add the remaining sugar and beat until the whites are stiff and glossy, but not dry. Fold a quarter of the whites into the chocolate mixture to lighten it, then alternately fold in the almond mixture and the remaining whites in three batches. Spoon the batter into the prepared pan and spread evenly. Tap the pan gently to release any air bubbles.

7 ▲ Place the cake on a wire rack over a baking sheet and pour the warm chocolate glaze over to cover the top completely. Using a baking spatula, smooth the glaze around the sides of the cake. Spoon a little of the glaze into a piping bag fitted with a writing nozzle and use to write the name of the cake, if you like. Let stand for 5 minutes to set slightly, then carefully press the nuts onto the sides of the cake. Using two long baking spatulas, transfer the cake to a serving plate and chill until ready to serve.

Sacher Torte

One of the world's finest—and most famous—cakes, Sacher Torte is a dark and delectable chocolate cake. Serve in tiny slices.

INGREDIENTS
Serves 8–10
2 ounces semisweet chocolate
2 ounces bittersweet chocolate
6 tablespoons unsalted butter, softened
½ cup sugar
4 eggs, separated, plus 1 egg white
¼ teaspoon salt
½ cup all-purpose flour

For the Topping
5 tablespoons apricot jam
1 cup plus 1 tablespoon water
1 tablespoon unsalted butter
6 ounces bittersweet chocolate
¾ cup sugar
ready-made chocolate icing (optional)

1 ▲ Preheat the oven to 325°F. Grease a 9-inch round cake pan. Line the pan with waxed or parchment paper and grease the paper. Melt both chocolates in the top of a double boiler or in a heatproof bowl set over hot water. Set aside.

2 ▲ Cream the butter and sugar until fluffy. Stir in the chocolate, then beat in the 4 egg yolks, one at a time.

3 ▲ In a grease-free bowl, beat the 5 egg whites with the salt until stiff. Fold a dollop of whites into the chocolate mixture to lighten it. Fold in the remaining whites in three batches, alternating with the sifted flour.

4 ▲ Pour into the pan and bake for about 45 minutes, until a skewer inserted into the center of the cake comes out clean. Cool on a wire rack.

5 ▲ Make the topping. Melt the jam with 1 tablespoon of the water over low heat, then strain for a smooth consistency. In the top of a double boiler or in a heatproof bowl set over hot water, melt the butter and the chocolate together.

6 ▲ In a heavy saucepan, dissolve the sugar in the remaining 1 cup water over low heat. Raise the heat and boil until the mixture reaches 230°F on a candy thermometer. Immediately plunge the bottom of the pan into cold water and leave for 1 minute. Pour into the chocolate mixture and stir to blend. Let the icing cool for a few minutes. Meanwhile, brush the warm jam over the cake. Starting in the center, pour the chocolate icing over and work outward in a circular movement. Tilt the rack to spread; use a spatula only for the sides of the cake. Allow to set overnight. If you like, decorate with chocolate icing.

Mississippi Mud Cake

There are many versions of this cake, but all of them are based on a dark cocoa-based chocolate cake that is meant to be reminiscent of the muddy shores of the Mississippi River.

INGREDIENTS
Serves 8–10
cocoa powder for dusting
2½ cups all-purpose flour
1 teaspoon baking powder
5 ounces unsweetened chocolate
2 sticks (1 cup) unsalted butter
1¼ cups strong coffee or espresso
pinch of salt
2 cups granulated sugar
4 tablespoons bourbon or whisky
2 eggs, lightly beaten
2 teaspoons vanilla extract
2 cups sweetened dried coconut

For the Filling
1 cup evaporated milk
½ cup (packed) light brown sugar
8 tablespoons (½ cup) unsalted butter
3 ounces semisweet chocolate
3 egg yolks, lightly beaten
1 teaspoon vanilla extract
2 cups pecans, chopped
1 cup miniature marshmallows

For the Topping
1½ cups double cream
1 teaspoon vanilla extract

To Decorate
fresh coconut

1 ▲ Preheat the oven to 350°F. Grease two 9-inch cake pans and dust bottoms and sides with cocoa. Sift the flour and baking powder into a bowl. In a saucepan over low heat, melt the chocolate, butter, coffee, salt and sugar, stirring occasionally until the mixture is smooth and the sugar has dissolved. Stir in the bourbon or whisky. Pour the chocolate mixture into a bowl and cool slightly. With an electric mixer on medium speed, beat in the eggs and vanilla. Decrease the speed and beat in the flour. Stir in the coconut. Pour into the prepared pans.

2 ▲ Bake for 25–30 minutes, until a skewer inserted in the center comes out with just a few crumbs attached; do not overbake or the cake will be too dry. Let cool on a wire rack for 10 minutes. Remove the cakes from the pans and place on a wire rack to cool completely.

3 ▲ For the filling, combine the evaporated milk, sugar, butter, chocolate, egg yolks and vanilla in a large heavy-bottomed saucepan. Cook over medium heat, stirring frequently, for 8–10 minutes, until the chocolate is melted and smooth and the batter is thick enough to coat the back of a wooden spoon; do not boil or the mixture will curdle. Remove from the heat and stir in the nuts and marshmallows, stirring until melted. Refrigerate until thick enough to spread, stirring occasionally to prevent a skin from forming.

4 ▲ Assemble the cake. With a serrated knife, slice both cake layers in half horizontally, making four layers. Spread each of the bottom cake layers with half the chocolate nut filling and cover each bottom half with its respective top layer.

6 Using a heavy hammer and nail, puncture the eyes of a fresh coconut. Drain off the liquid and reserve if desired. Place the coconut in a thick plastic bag and hit the shell very hard with the hammer to crack the coconut open.

5 ▲ In a medium bowl, whip the cream and the vanilla until firm peaks form. Place one filled cake layer on a serving plate and spread with half the whipped cream. Top with the second filled cake layer and spread with the remaining cream, swirling it to form an attractive pattern.

Tip

If fresh coconut is unavailable, you can decorate the cake with unsweetened dried coconut.

7 ▲ With a sturdy blunt-bladed knife, separate the flesh from the shell; it will break into medium-sized pieces. Rinse the pieces under cold running water and store in cold water. With a swivel-bladed peeler, draw the blade along the curved edge of a coconut piece to make thin wide curls with a brown edge. Use these to decorate the top of the cake.

Strawberry Cake

It is hard to believe that this delicious cake is low in fat, but the sponge base contains no fat and the filling is made of low-fat soft cheese and fromage frais. Enjoy it with a clear conscience.

INGREDIENTS
Serves 6
2 eggs
6 tablespoons superfine sugar
grated zest of ½ orange
½ cup all-purpose flour

For the Filling
1¼ cups low-fat soft cheese
grated zest of ½ orange
2 tablespoons superfine sugar
4 tablespoons low-fat fromage frais
¼ cup chopped almonds, toasted

To Decorate
8 ounces strawberries, halved
strawberry leaves
confectioners' sugar

1 Preheat the oven to 375°F. Grease a 12 x 8-inch jelly roll pan and line with baking parchment.

2 ▲ In a bowl, beat the eggs, sugar and orange zest together for about 2 minutes, until the mixture is pale and leaves a thick trail when the beaters are lifted.

3 ▲ Fold in the flour with a metal spoon, being careful not to knock out any air. Turn into the prepared pan. Bake for 15–20 minutes, or until the cake springs back when lightly pressed. Turn the cake out onto a wire rack, remove the lining paper and allow to cool completely.

4 ▲ Meanwhile, make the filling. In a bowl, mix the soft cheese with the orange rind, sugar and fromage frais until smooth. Divide between two bowls. Chop half the strawberry halves and add to one bowl of filling.

5 ▲ Cut the sponge widthwise into three equal pieces and sandwich them together with the strawberry filling. Spread two-thirds of the plain filling over the sides of the cake and press on the toasted almonds.

6 ▲ Spread the rest of the filling over the top of the cake and decorate with the remaining strawberry halves and strawberry leaves. Dust with confectioners' sugar and transfer to a serving plate.

Tip

Use other soft fruits in season, such as currants, raspberries, blackberries or blueberries, or try a mixture of different berries.

Kugelhopf

Guaranteed to rise to the occasion, this fruit-and-nut bread looks as good as it tastes.

INGREDIENTS
Makes 1 loaf
⅔ cup raisins
1 tablespoon kirsch or brandy
1 tablespoon dried (not rapid-rise) yeast
4 tablespoons lukewarm water
8 tablespoons (½ cup) unsalted butter
½ cup superfine sugar
3 eggs
grated zest of 1 lemon
1 teaspoon salt
½ teaspoon vanilla extract
3 cups flour
½ cup milk
¼ cup slivered almonds
½ cup blanched almonds, chopped
confectioners' sugar, for dusting

1 ▲ In a bowl, combine the raisins and kirsch or brandy. Set aside. Combine the yeast and water, stir and let sit for 5 minutes, until frothy.

2 With an electric mixer, cream the butter and sugar until thick and fluffy. Beat in the eggs, one at a time. Add the lemon zest, salt and vanilla. Stir in the yeast mixture.

3 ▲ Add the flour, alternating with the milk, until the mixture is well blended. Cover and allow to rise in a warm place until doubled in volume, about 2 hours.

4 ▲ Grease a 10-cup kugelhopf pan, then sprinkle the slivered almonds evenly over the bottom of the pan.

5 Work the raisins and blanched almonds into the dough, then spoon into the pan. Cover with a plastic bag and let rise in a warm place for about 1 hour, until the dough almost reaches the top of the pan. Preheat the oven to 350°F.

6 Bake for 45 minutes, or until golden brown. If the top browns too quickly, cover it with foil. Allow to cool in the pan for 15 minutes, then turn out onto a rack. Dust the top lightly with confectioners' sugar before serving.

Fruit and Nut Cake

This fruit cake is made without saturated fat, yet retains the rich, familiar flavor of traditional fruit cakes. It improves with keeping.

INGREDIENTS
Serves 12–14

1½ cups whole-wheat flour
1½ cups self-rising white flour
2 teaspoons baking powder
1 teaspoon salt
2 teaspoons pumpkin pie spice
1 tablespoon fruit concentrate
3 tablespoons honey
1 tablespoon molasses
6 tablespoons sunflower oil
¾ cup orange juice
2 eggs, beaten
4 cups deluxe mixed dried fruit
3 tablespoons split almonds
¼ cup candied cherries, halved

3 ▲ Put the fruit concentrate in a small bowl. Gradually stir in the honey and molasses. Add to the dry ingredients with the oil, orange juice, eggs and mixed fruit. Mix together thoroughly.

4 ▲ Turn the mixture into the prepared pan and smooth the surface. Arrange the almonds and cherries in a pattern over the top. Stand the pan on newspaper and bake for 2 hours, or until a skewer inserted into the center of the cake comes out clean. Let stand on a wire rack until cool, then lift out of the pan and remove the paper.

1 ▲ Preheat the oven to 325°F. Grease a deep 8-inch cake pan. Line with waxed or parchment paper and grease the paper. Secure a band of brown paper around the outside.

2 ▲ Sift the flours, baking powder and salt into a mixing bowl with the spice and make a well in the center.

Teatime Treats

Here you will find a tempting array of cakes to enjoy with morning coffee or afternoon tea. Featuring popular classics from around the world, from light sponges, chocolate brownies and jelly rolls to delicious meringues, this chapter includes indulgent cakes for all tastes.

Chestnut Cake

An Italian speciality, this is definitely a cake to mark an occasion. Rich, moist and heavy, it can be made up to a week in advance and kept, undecorated, wrapped and stored in an airtight container. Allow the cake to come to room temperature before serving.

INGREDIENTS
Serves 8–10
1¼ cups flour
pinch of salt
1 cup butter, softened
¾ cup sugar
15½ oz can chestnut purée
9 large eggs, separated
7 tbsp dark rum
1¼ cups heavy cream

To Decorate
marrons glacés, chopped
confectioners' sugar, sifted

1 Preheat the oven to 350°F. Grease an 8½ inch springform cake pan, line the base with waxed paper and grease the paper.

2 Sift together the flour and salt, and set aside. Place the butter and three-quarters of the sugar in a bowl and beat until fluffy.

3 ▲ Fold in two-thirds of the chestnut purée, alternating with the egg yolks, and beat. Fold in the flour and salt.

4 ▲ Whisk the egg whites in a clean, dry bowl until stiff. Beat a little of the egg whites into the chestnut mixture, until evenly blended, then fold in the remainder.

5 ▲ Transfer the cake mixture to the prepared pan and smooth the surface. Bake in the center of the oven for about 1¼ hours, or until a skewer inserted into the center of the cake comes out clean.

6 Place the cake, still in the pan, on a wire rack. Using a skewer, pierce holes evenly all over the cake. Sprinkle 4 tbsp of the rum over the top, then allow the cake to cool completely.

7 ▲ Remove the cake from the pan, peel off the lining paper and cut horizontally into two layers. Place the bottom layer on a serving plate. Whisk the cream in a mixing bowl with the remaining rum, sugar and chestnut purée until thick and smooth.

8 To assemble the cake, spread two-thirds of the chestnut cream mixture over the bottom layer and place the other layer on top. Spread some of the remaining chestnut cream over the top and sides of the cake, then fill a waxed paper piping bag, fitted with a star nozzle, with the rest of the chestnut mixture. Pipe big swirls around the outside edge. Decorate with the marrons glacés and sifted confectioners' sugar.

Tip

In order to have the most control over a piping bag, it is important to hold it in a relaxed position. You may find it easier to hold it with one or both hands.

Crunchy-topped Madeira Cake

Traditionally served with a glass of Madeira wine in Victorian England, this light sponge cake still makes a perfect tea-time treat.

INGREDIENTS
Serves 8–10
⁷/₈ cup butter, softened
finely grated zest of 1 lemon
³/₄ cup sugar
3 large eggs
³/₄ cup flour, sifted
1¼ cups self-rising flour, sifted

For the Topping
3 tbsp clear honey
³/₄ cup plus 2 tbsp chopped mixed
citrus peel
¹/₂ cup flaked almonds

1 Preheat the oven to 350°F. Grease a 1 lb loaf pan, line the base and sides with waxed paper and grease the paper.

2 ▲ Place the butter, lemon zest and sugar in a mixing bowl and beat until light and fluffy. Beat in the eggs, one at a time, until evenly blended.

3 ▲ Sift together the flours, then stir into the egg mixture. Transfer the cake mixture to the prepared pan and smooth the surface.

4 ▲ Bake in the center of the oven for 45–50 minutes or until a skewer inserted into the center of the cake comes out clean. Leave the cake in the pan for about 5 minutes. Turn out on to a wire rack, peel off the lining paper and leave to cool completely.

5 ▲ To make the topping, place the honey, chopped mixed peel and almonds in a small saucepan and heat gently until the honey melts. Remove from the heat and stir briefly to coat the peel and almonds, then spread over the top of the cake. Allow to cool completely before serving.

 Banana Coconut Cake

Slightly over-ripe bananas are best for
this perfect coffee morning cake.

INGREDIENTS
Serves 8–10
1½ cups shredded coconut
½ cup butter, softened
½ cup superfine sugar
2 large eggs
1 cup self-rising flour
½ cup flour
1 tsp baking soda
½ cup milk
2 large bananas, peeled and mashed

For the Topping
2 tbsp butter
2 tbsp honey
2 cups shredded coconut

3 Place the butter and sugar in a mixing bowl and beat until they are smooth and creamy. Beat in the eggs, one at a time.

4 Sift together the flours and baking soda, then sift half of this mixture into the butter and egg mixture and stir to mix thoroughly.

5 Mix together the milk and mashed banana in a small bowl, then add half to the egg mixture. Beat well to combine, then add the remaining flour and toasted coconut together with the remaining banana mixture. Stir to mix, then transfer to the prepared cake pan and smooth the surface.

6 Bake in the center of the oven for about 1 hour, or until a skewer inserted into the center of the cake comes out clean. Leave the cake in the pan for about 5 minutes, then turn out on to a wire rack, peel off the lining paper and leave to cool completely.

7 To make the topping, place the butter and honey in a small saucepan and heat gently until melted. Stir in the shredded coconut and cook, stirring constantly, for about 5 minutes or until lightly browned. Remove from the heat and allow to cool slightly.

8 ▲ Spoon the topping over the top of the cake and allow to cool completely before serving.

1 Preheat the oven to 375°F. Grease a deep 7 inch square cake pan, line the base and sides with waxed paper and then grease the paper.

2 ▲ Spread the shredded coconut out on a baking sheet and place under a hot broiler for about 5 minutes, stirring and turning the coconut all the time until evenly toasted.

lmond and Apricot Cake

Although canned apricots can be used in this recipe, nothing quite beats using the fresh fruit in season. Choose sweet-smelling, ripe fruit for this delicious cake.

INGREDIENTS
Serves 6–8
4–5 tbsp fine dry white bread crumbs
1 cup butter, softened
1 cup plus 2 tbsp superfine sugar
4 large eggs
1½ cups self-rising flour
1–2 tbsp milk
1⅓ cups ground almonds
few drops of almond extract
1 lb fresh apricots, pitted and halved
sifted superfine sugar, to decorate

3 ▲ Place the butter and sugar in a mixing bowl and beat with electric beaters until light and fluffy. Beat in the eggs, one at a time, then fold in the flour, milk, ground almonds and almond extract.

4 ▲ Spoon half of the cake mixture into the prepared pan and smooth the surface. Arrange half of the apricots over the top, then spoon over the remaining cake mixture. Finish with the other half of the apricots. Bake the cake in the center of the oven for 30–35 minutes, or until a skewer inserted into the center of the cake comes out clean.

5 Turn the cake out on to a wire rack, peel off the lining paper and sprinkle over the sifted superfine sugar. Serve warm or leave to cool.

1 Preheat the oven to 350°F. Grease a 9 inch round cake pan, line the base with waxed paper and grease the paper.

2 ▲ Sprinkle the bread crumbs into the prepared cake pan and tap them around the pan to coat the base and sides evenly.

Upside-down Pear & Ginger Cake

A light spicy sponge cake topped with glossy baked fruit and ginger. This is also good served warm for dessert.

INGREDIENTS
Serves 6–8
1 x 2 lb can pear halves, drained
8 tbsp finely chopped preserved ginger
8 tbsp ginger syrup from the jar
1½ cups self-rising flour
½ tsp baking powder
1 tsp ground ginger
¾ cup soft light brown sugar
¾ cup butter, softened
3 large eggs, lightly beaten

4 ▲ Carefully spoon the mixture into the tin and smooth the surface.

5 ▲ Bake in the center of the oven for about 50 minutes, or until a skewer inserted in the center of the cake comes out clean. Leave the cake to cool in the pan for about 5 minutes. Turn out on to a wire rack, peel off the lining paper and leave to cool completely. Add the reserved chopped ginger to the pear halves and drizzle over the remaining ginger syrup.

1 Preheat the oven to 350°F. Grease a deep 8 inch round cake pan with butter or vegetable oil, line the base with waxed paper and grease the paper.

2 ▲ Fill the hollow in each pear with half the chopped ginger. Arrange the pear halves, flat sides down, over the base of the cake pan, then spoon half the ginger syrup over the top.

3 Sift the flour, baking powder and ground ginger into a mixing bowl. Stir in the soft brown sugar and butter, then add the eggs and beat together for 1–2 minutes until level and creamy.

One-stage Victoria Sandwich

Originally made in an oblong shape, today's Victoria sandwich is made using a variety of different flavorings and decorations, and is baked and cut into all sorts of shapes and sizes. Use this basic recipe to suit the occasion.

INGREDIENTS
Serves 6–8
1½ cups self-rising flour
pinch of salt
¾ cup butter, softened
¾ cup superfine sugar
3 large eggs

To Finish
4–6 tbsp raspberry jam
superfine or confectioners' sugar

3 ▲ Place one of the cakes on a serving plate and spread with the raspberry jam. Place the other cake on top, then dredge with superfine or confectioners' sugar, to serve.

2 ▲ Cut the cake into individual sized shapes, such as fingers, diamonds, squares or small rounds, using a knife or cookie cutters. Using one quantity of Butter Icing, cover with decorative piping. You can flavor or color the butter icing by substituting orange or lemon juice for the milk and/or adding a few drops of food coloring.

3 For alternative decorations, you could try a selection of the following: glacé cherries, angelica, jellied fruits, grated chocolate, chopped or whole nuts, or choose one of your own ideas.

1 Preheat the oven to 375°F. Grease two deep 7 inch round cake pans, line the bases with waxed paper and grease the paper.

2 ▲ Place all the ingredients in a mixing bowl and whisk together using electric beaters. Divide the mixture between the prepared pans and smooth the surfaces. Bake in the center of the oven for 25–30 minutes, or until a skewer inserted into the center of the cakes comes out clean. Turn out on to a wire rack, peel off the lining paper and leave to cool completely.

Variation
Makes 8–10 iced fancies

1 ▲ Place the cake mixture in a greased and lined 9 x 13 inch jelly roll pan and smooth the surface. Bake in the center of the oven for 25–30 minutes, or until a skewer inserted into the center of the cake comes out clean. Turn out on to a wire rack, peel off the lining paper and leave to cool completely.

Tip

To make the decorative stenciled pattern with confectioners' sugar shown here, cut out star shapes from paper. Lay the paper stars over the top of the cake and then dredge with confectioners' sugar. Remove the paper shapes carefully to reveal the stenciled pattern. You could also use a paper doiley as a stencil.

Carrot and Almond Cake

*Made with grated carrots and ground almonds, this unusual
fat-free sponge cake makes a delicious afternoon treat.*

INGREDIENTS
Serves 8–10
*5 large eggs, separated
finely grated zest of 1 lemon
1¹⁄₃ cups superfine sugar
5–6 medium-size carrots, peeled and
finely grated
1¹⁄₄ cups ground almonds
1 cup self-rising flour, sifted
sifted confectioners' sugar, to
decorate
marzipan carrots, to decorate*

Tip

To make the marzipan carrots, knead a little orange food coloring into 4 oz marzipan until evenly blended. On a work surface lightly dusted with confectioners' sugar, divide the marzipan into even-sized pieces, about the size of small walnuts. Mold into carrot shapes and press horizontal lines along each carrot with a knife blade. Press a tiny stick of angelica into the end of each piece to resemble the carrot top. Position the marzipan carrots on the cake, to decorate.

1 Preheat the oven to 375°F. Grease a deep 8 inch round cake pan, line the base with waxed paper and grease the paper.

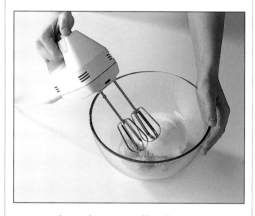

2 ▲ Place the egg yolks, lemon zest and sugar in a bowl. Beat with electric beaters for about 5 minutes, until the mixture is thick and pale.

3 ▲ Mix in the grated carrot, ground almonds and flour and stir until evenly combined.

4 In a clean, dry bowl, whisk the egg whites until stiff. Using a large metal spoon or rubber spatula, mix a little of the whisked egg whites into the carrot mixture, then fold in the rest.

5 ▲ Spoon the mixture into the prepared cake pan and bake in the center of the oven for about 1¹⁄₄ hours, or until a skewer inserted into the center of the cake comes out clean. Leave the cake in the pan for about 5 minutes, then turn out on to a wire rack, peel off the lining paper and leave to cool completely.

6 ▲ Decorate with sifted confectioners' sugar and marzipan carrots.

Flourless Fruit Cake

A really easy recipe which everyone will enjoy. Children can have fun crushing the cornflakes and helping you to beat the ingredients together.

INGREDIENTS

Serves 12–15

1 x 1 lb jar mincemeat
2 cups dried mixed fruit
1 cup no-soak,
ready-to-eat dried apricots, chopped
1 cup no-soak, ready-to-eat dried figs, chopped
½ cup glacé cherries, halved
1 cup walnut pieces
8–10 cups cornflakes, crushed
4 large eggs, lightly beaten
1 x 14½ oz can evaporated milk
1 tsp ground allspice
1 tsp baking powder
mixed glacé fruits, chopped, to decorate

1 Preheat the oven to 300°F. Grease a 10 inch round cake pan, line the base and sides with a double thickness of waxed paper and grease the paper.

2 Put all the ingredients into a large mixing bowl. Beat together well.

3 ▲ Turn into the prepared pan and smooth the surface with the back of a spoon.

4 ▲ Bake in the center of the oven for about 1¾ hours, or until a skewer inserted in the center of the cake comes out clean. Allow the cake to cool in the pan for 10 minutes, then turn out on to a wire rack, peel off the lining paper and leave to cool completely. Decorate with the chopped glacé fruits.

Tip

This cake may be iced and marzipanned to make a Christmas or birthday cake. A useful recipe for anyone who needs to avoid eating wheat flour.

Vegan Chocolate Gâteau

It isn't often that vegans can indulge in a slice of chocolate cake, and this one tastes so delicious, they'll all be back for more!

INGREDIENTS
Serves 8–10
2½ cups self-rising whole wheat flour
⅓ cup cocoa powder
3 tsp baking powder
1¼ cups superfine sugar
few drops of vanilla extract
9 tbsp sunflower oil
1½ cups water
sifted cocoa powder, to decorate
¼ cup chopped nuts, to decorate

For the Chocolate Fudge
¼ cup soy margarine
3 tbsp water
2⅓ cups confectioners' sugar
2 tbsp cocoa powder
1–2 tbsp hot water

1 Preheat the oven to 325°F. Grease a deep 8 inch round cake pan, line the base and sides with waxed paper and grease the paper.

2 Sift the flour, cocoa powder and baking powder into a large mixing bowl. Add the superfine sugar and vanilla extract, then gradually beat in the sunflower oil and water to make a smooth batter.

3 Pour the cake mixture into the prepared pan and smooth the surface with the back of a spoon.

4 ▲ Bake in the center of the oven for about 45 minutes or until a skewer inserted into the center of the cake comes out clean. Leave in the pan for about 5 minutes, then turn out on to a wire rack, peel off the lining paper and leave to cool. Cut the cake in half.

5 ▲ To make the chocolate fudge, place the margarine and water in a pan and heat gently until the margarine has melted. Remove from the heat and add the sifted confectioners' sugar and cocoa powder, beating until smooth and shiny. Allow to cool until firm enough to spread and pipe.

6 ▲ Place the bottom layer of cake on a serving plate and spread over two-thirds of the chocolate fudge mixture. Top with the other layer of cake. Fit a piping bag with a star nozzle, fill with the remaining chocolate fudge and pipe stars over the cake. Sprinkle with cocoa powder and chopped nuts.

Lemon and Apricot Cake

This tasty cake is topped with a crunchy layer of flaked almonds and pistachio nuts, and is soaked in a tangy lemon syrup after baking to keep it really moist.

INGREDIENTS
Serves 10–12
¾ cup butter, softened
1½ cups self-rising flour, sifted
½ tsp baking powder
¾ cup superfine sugar
3 large eggs, lightly beaten
finely grated zest of 1 lemon
1½ cups no-soak, ready-to-eat dried apricots, finely chopped
1 cup ground almonds
⅓ cup unsalted pistachio nuts, chopped
⅓ cup flaked almonds
2 tbsp unsalted whole pistachio nuts

For the Syrup
freshly squeezed juice of 1 lemon
3 tbsp superfine sugar

1 Preheat the oven to 350°F. Grease a 2 lb loaf pan, line the base and sides with waxed paper and grease the paper.

2 Place the butter together with the sifted flour and baking powder into a mixing bowl, then add the sugar, eggs and lemon zest. Beat for 1–2 minutes until smooth and glossy, and then stir in the apricots, ground almonds and the chopped pistachio nuts.

3 ▲ Spoon the mixture into the prepared pan and smooth the surface. Sprinkle with the flaked almonds and the whole pistachio nuts. Bake in the center of the oven for about 1¼ hours, or until a skewer inserted into the center of the cake comes out clean. Check the cake after about 45 minutes and cover with a piece of foil when the top is nicely brown. Leave the cake to cool in the pan.

4 ▲ To make the lemon syrup, put the lemon juice and superfine sugar into a small saucepan and heat gently, stirring until the sugar has dissolved.

5 ▲ Spoon the syrup over the cake. When the cake is completely cooled, turn it carefully out of the pan and peel off the lining paper.

Gooseberry Cake

*This cake is delicious served warm
with fresh whipped cream.*

INGREDIENTS
Serves 6–8
½ cup butter
1⅓ cups self-rising flour
1 tsp baking powder
2 large eggs, beaten
½ cup superfine sugar
1–2 tsp rose water
pinch of freshly grated nutmeg
1 x 4 oz jar gooseberries in syrup,
drained, juice reserved
superfine sugar, to decorate
whipped cream, to serve

4 ▲ Mix in 1–2 tbsp of the reserved
gooseberry juice, then pour half of
the batter mixture into the prepared
pan. Scatter over the gooseberries. Pour
over the remaining batter mixture,
evenly covering the gooseberries.

5 Bake in the center of the oven for
about 45 minutes, or until a skewer
inserted into the center of the cake
comes out clean.

6 ▲ Leave in the cake pan for about
5 minutes, then turn out on to a
wire rack, remove the lining paper and
allow to cool for a further 5 minutes.
Dredge with superfine sugar and serve
immediately with whipped cream, or
leave the cake to cool completely before
decorating and serving.

1 Preheat the oven to 350°F. Grease a
7 inch square cake pan, line the base
and sides with waxed paper and then
grease the paper.

2 Place the butter in a medium
saucepan and melt over a gentle
heat. Remove the pan from the heat,
transfer the melted butter to a mixing
bowl and allow to cool.

3 ▲ Sift together the flour and baking
powder and add to the melted
butter. Beat in the eggs, one at a time,
the sugar, rose water and grated
nutmeg, to make a smooth batter.

Chocolate Mint-Filled Cupcakes

For extra minty flavor, chop 8 thin mint cream-filled after-dinner mints and fold into the cake batter before filling paper liners. Omit the cream filling if you wish.

INGREDIENTS
Makes 12
2 cups all-purpose flour
1 teaspoon baking soda
pinch of salt
½ cup unsweetened cocoa
10 tablespoons (⅔ cup) unsalted butter, softened
1½ cups superfine sugar
3 eggs
1 teaspoon peppermint extract
1 cup milk

For the Mint Cream Filling
1¼ cups heavy or whipping cream
1 teaspoon peppermint extract

For the Chocolate Mint Glaze
6 ounces semisweet chocolate
8 tablespoons (½ cup) unsalted butter
1 teaspoon peppermint extract

1 ▲ Preheat the oven to 350°F. Place paper liners on a baking sheet. Sift together the flour, baking soda, salt and cocoa into a bowl. In a large mixing bowl with an electric mixer, beat the butter and sugar until light and creamy, 3–5 minutes. Add the eggs one at a time, beating well after each addition; beat in the peppermint extract. On low speed, beat in the flour-cocoa mixture alternately with the milk, until just blended. Spoon the batter into the paper liners.

2 Bake for 12–15 minutes, until a cake tester inserted into the center comes out clean; do not overbake. Immediately remove the cupcakes to a wire rack to cool completely. When cool, remove paper liners.

3 Prepare the filling. In a small bowl, whip the cream and peppermint extract with an electric mixer until stiff peaks form. Spoon into a small piping bag fitted with a small plain tip. Push the tip into the bottom of a cupcake and squeeze gently, releasing about 1 tablespoon of cream into the center. Repeat with the remaining cupcakes.

4 ▲ Prepare the glaze. In a saucepan over low heat, melt the chocolate and butter, stirring until smooth. Remove from the heat and stir in the peppermint extract. Cool, then spread on top of each cupcake.

 utumn Cake

*Greengages, plums or pitted semi-dried prunes
are delicious in this recipe.*

INGREDIENTS
Serves 6–8
1/2 cup butter, softened
3/4 cup sugar
3 large eggs, beaten
1 cup ground hazelnuts
1 1/4 cup shelled pecan nuts,
chopped
1/2 cup flour
1 tsp baking powder
1/2 tsp salt
1 1/2 lb pitted plums, greengages or
semi-dried prunes
4 tbsp lime marmalade
1 tbsp lime juice
2 tbsp blanched almonds,
chopped, to decorate

4 ▲ Bake in the center of the oven for 45–50 minutes or until a skewer inserted into the center of the cake comes out clean.

5 ▲ Remove from the oven and carefully arrange the fruit on top. Return to the oven and bake for a further 10–15 minutes until the fruit has softened. Transfer to a wire rack to cool completely, then remove the cake from the pan.

6 Place the marmalade and lime juice in a small saucepan and warm gently. Brush over the fruit, then sprinkle with the almonds. Allow to set, then chill before serving.

1 Preheat the oven to 350°F. Grease a 9 inch round fluted tart pan.

2 ▲ Place the butter and sugar in a mixing bowl and beat with an electric mixer until light and fluffy. Gradually beat in the eggs, alternating with the ground hazelnuts, until they are evenly combined.

3 Stir in the pecan nuts, then sift in the flour, baking powder and salt. Fold in until evenly combined, then transfer the mixture to the prepared pan.

Carrot Cup Cakes

Perfect for a tea party or picnic lunch, this carrot cake mixture can also be made as one big cake to serve for a celebration or as a dessert.

INGREDIENTS
Makes 24
$^3/_4$ cup butter, melted
$^7/_8$ cup soft light brown sugar
1 cup carrots, peeled and finely grated
1 cup dessert apple, peeled and finely grated
pinch of salt
1–2 tsp ground cinnamon
2 large eggs
$1^3/_4$ cups self-rising flour
2 tsp baking powder
1 cup shelled walnuts, finely chopped

For the Topping
$^3/_4$ cup cream cheese
4–5 tbsp light cream
$^1/_2$ cup confectioners' sugar, sifted
$^1/_4$ cup shelled walnuts, halved
2 tsp cocoa powder, sifted

1 Preheat the oven to 350°F. Arrange 24 cup cake paper cases in two cast-iron muffin pans and put to one side.

2 ▲ Place the butter, sugar, carrots, apple, salt, cinnamon and eggs in a mixing bowl and beat well to combine.

3 ▲ Sift together the flour and baking powder into a small bowl, then sift again into the mixing bowl. Add the chopped walnuts and fold in until evenly blended.

4 ▲ Fill the paper cases half-full with the cake mixture, then bake for 20–25 minutes, or until a skewer inserted into the centers of the cup cakes comes out clean.

5 Leave the cup cakes in the pans for about 5 minutes, before transferring them to a wire rack to cool completely.

6 ▲ To make the topping, place the cream cheese in a mixing bowl and beat in the cream and confectioners' sugar until smooth. Put a dollop of the topping on top of each cake, then decorate with the walnuts. Dust with sifted cocoa powder and allow the icing to set before serving.

Tip

To make one big cake, which will serve 6–8, butter an 8 inch fluted bundt cake pan and line the base with waxed paper. Grease the waxed paper. Place all of the cake mixture in the pan and bake for about 1¼ hours, or until a skewer inserted into the center of the cake comes out clean. Leave the cake in the pan for about 5 minutes. Turn out on to a wire rack, peel off the lining paper and leave to cool completely. Decorate with the topping mixture, halved walnuts and sifted cocoa powder.

Almond and Raspberry Jelly Roll

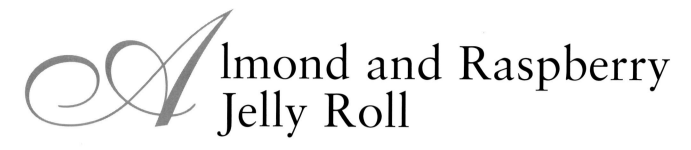

A light and airy whisked sponge cake is rolled up with a delicious fresh cream and raspberry filling, making this a classic jelly roll.

INGREDIENTS
Serves 8
1 quantity Whisked Sponge Cake mixture, replacing 2 tablespoons all-purpose flour with 2 tablespoons ground almonds
a little superfine sugar
1 cup heavy cream
8 ounces fresh raspberries

To Decorate
superfine sugar
reserved raspberries
16 sliced almonds, toasted

1 Preheat the oven to 400°F. Grease a 13 x 90-inch jelly roll pan and line with baking parchment.

2 Make the whisked sponge mixture, spoon into the prepared pan and bake for 10–12 minutes, until risen and springy to the touch.

3 ▲ Lay a sheet of waxed paper on a flat surface and sprinkle superfine sugar over it. Invert the pan onto the sheet, and allow the cake to cool with the pan in place. Remove the pan and peel away the lining paper.

4 ▲ Reserve a little cream for decoration; whip the rest until it holds its shape. Fold in all but eight raspberries and spread the mixture over the cooled cake, leaving a narrow border around the edge.

5 ▲ Carefully roll the cake up from a narrow end to form a jelly roll. Sprinkle liberally with superfine sugar.

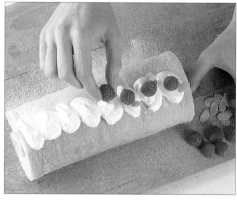

6 ▲ Whip the remaining cream until it just holds its shape and spoon the cream along the center of the cake. Decorate with the reserved raspberries and toasted almonds.

Fudgy Glazed Chocolate Brownies

For a simpler brownie, omit the fudge glaze and dust with confectioners' sugar or cocoa instead.

INGREDIENTS
Serves 18–10
9 ounces bittersweet or semisweet
chocolate, chopped
1 ounce unsweetened
chocolate, chopped
8 tablespoons (½ cup) unsalted
butter, cut into pieces
½ cup packed light brown sugar
¼ cup granulated sugar
2 eggs
1 tablespoon vanilla extract
½ cup all-purpose flour
1 cup pecans or walnuts, toasted
and chopped
5 ounces fine-quality white
chocolate, chopped into
¼-inch pieces
pecan halves to decorate (optional)

For the Fudgy Chocolate Glaze
6 ounces semisweet or bittersweet
chocolate, chopped
4 tablespoons unsalted butter, cut
into pieces
2 tablespoons light corn or
golden syrup
2 teaspoons vanilla extract
1 teaspoon instant coffee powder

1 ▲ Preheat the oven to 350°F. Invert
an 8-inch square baking pan and
mold a piece of foil over the bottom.
Turn the pan over and line with the
molded foil. Lightly grease the foil.

2 ▲ In a medium saucepan over low
heat, melt the chocolate and butter
until smooth, stirring frequently.
Remove the pan from the heat.

3 Stir in the sugars and continue
stirring for 2 more minutes, until
the sugar has dissolved. Beat in the eggs
and vanilla and stir in the flour just
until blended. Stir in the pecans and
white chocolate. Pour the batter into
the prepared pan.

4 ▲ Bake the brownies for 20–25
minutes, until a cake tester inserted
2 inches from the center comes out
with just a few crumbs attached (do not
overbake). Place the pan on a wire rack
to cool for 30 minutes. Using the foil to
lift, remove the brownies from the pan
and cool on the rack for at least
2 hours.

5 ▲ Prepare the glaze. In a medium
saucepan over medium heat, melt
the chocolate, butter, syrup, vanilla and
coffee powder until smooth, stirring
frequently. Remove from the heat.
Refrigerate for 1 hour, or until
thickened and spreadable.

6 ▲ Invert the brownies onto the
wire rack and remove the foil from
the bottom. Turn top side up. Using a
small baking spatula, spread a thick
layer of fudgy glaze over the top of the
brownies just to the edges. Refrigerate
for 1 hour, until set. Cut into squares.
If you like, top each with a pecan half.

Hazelnut Chocolate Meringue Torte with Pears

Do not assemble this torte more than 3–4 hours before serving, as the pears may give off liquid and soften the cream too much.

INGREDIENTS
Serves 8–10
¾ cup granulated sugar
1 vanilla bean, split
scant 2 cups water
4 ripe pears, peeled, halved and cored
2 tablespoons pear- or hazelnut-flavored liqueur
1¼ cups hazelnuts, toasted
6 egg whites
pinch of salt
3 cups confectioners' sugar
1 teaspoon vanilla extract
2 ounces semisweet chocolate, melted

For the Chocolate Cream
10 ounces fine-quality bittersweet or semisweet chocolate, chopped
scant 2 cups whipping cream
¼ cup pear- or hazelnut-flavored liqueur

1 In a saucepan large enough to hold the pears in a single layer, combine the sugar, vanilla bean and water. Over high heat, bring to a boil, stirring until the sugar dissolves. Reduce the heat to medium. Lower the pears into the syrup. Cover the pears and simmer gently for 12–15 minutes, until tender. Remove the pan from the heat and allow the pears to cool in their poaching liquid. Carefully remove the pears from the liquid and drain. Place on a large flat plate lined with layers of paper towel. Sprinkle each pear half with the liqueur. Cover and refrigerate overnight.

2 ▲ Preheat the oven to 350°F. With a pencil, draw a 9-inch circle in the center of each of two sheets of baking parchment or well-greased foil. Turn the sheets of paper over onto two baking sheets (so pencil marks are underneath) or slide foil onto the baking sheets. In a food processor fitted with a metal blade, process the toasted hazelnuts until medium-fine crumbs form.

3 In a large bowl with an electric mixer on medium, beat the egg whites until frothy. Add salt and beat on high speed until soft peaks form. Reduce the mixer speed and gradually add the sugar, beating well after each addition, until all the sugar is added and the egg whites are stiff and glossy; this takes 12–15 minutes.

4 Gently fold in the nuts and vanilla and spoon meringue onto baking sheets, spreading into 9-inch circles and smoothing the top and sides. Bake for 1 hour, until the tops are dry and firm. Turn off the oven and allow to cool in the oven 2–3 hours, or until completely dry. Prepare the chocolate cream. Place the chocolate in a small bowl over a pan of simmering water and turn off the heat. Stir the chocolate until melted and smooth. Cool the chocolate to room temperature.

5 ▲ In a bowl with an electric mixer, beat the cream to soft peaks. Quickly fold the cream into the melted chocolate; fold in the liqueur. Spoon about one-third of the chocolate cream into an icing bag fitted with a star tip. Set aside. To assemble, with a sharp knife, thinly slice each pear half lengthwise. Place one meringue layer on a serving plate. Spread with half the chocolate cream and arrange half the sliced pears evenly over the cream. Pipe a border of rosettes around the edge.

6 ▲ Top with the second meringue layer and spread with the remaining chocolate cream. Arrange the remaining pear slices over the chocolate cream. Pipe a border of rosettes around the edge. Spoon the melted chocolate into a small paper cone and drizzle the chocolate over the pears. Refrigerate for at least 1 hour before serving.

Pear and Cardamom Spice Cake

Fresh pear and cardamom—a classic combination of flavors—are used together in this moist fruit and nut cake to provide a delicious, mouthwatering teatime treat.

INGREDIENTS
Serves 8–12
8 tablespoons (½ cup)
unsalted butter
½ cup superfine sugar
2 eggs, lightly beaten
2 cups all-purpose flour
1 tablespoon baking powder
2 tablespoons milk
crushed seeds from
2 cardamom pods
½ cup walnuts, chopped
1 tablespoon poppy seeds
1¼ pounds dessert pears, peeled,
cored and thinly sliced

To Decorate
*3 walnut halves
reserved pear slices
3 tablespoons honey*

1 Preheat the oven to 350°F. Grease an 8-inch round loose-bottomed cake pan and line the bottom with waxed or parchment paper.

2 Cream the butter and sugar together until pale and light. Gradually beat in the eggs, a little at a time, until incorporated. Sift the flour and baking powder together and fold in with the milk.

3 ▲ Stir in the cardamom, chopped nuts and poppy seeds. Reserve one-third of the pear slices and chop the rest. Fold the chopped pears into the creamed mixture.

4 ▲ Transfer to the prepared pan. Smooth the surface, making a small dip in the center.

5 ▲ Place the three walnut halves in the center of the cake batter, and fan the reserved pear slices around the walnuts, covering the cake batter. Bake for 1¼–1½ hours, or until a skewer inserted in the center of the cake comes out clean.

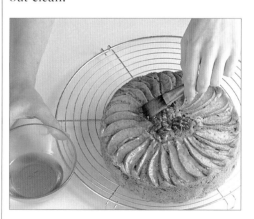

6 ▲ Remove the cake from the oven. Cool in the pan for 20 minutes, then turn out onto a wire rack, brush with the honey and allow to cool completely.

Spiced Honey Nut Cake

A combination of ground pistachio nuts and bread crumbs replaces the flour in this recipe, resulting in a light, moist sponge cake. Soaking the cooled cake is typical of many Middle Eastern cakes, and the combination of pistachio, lemon and cinnamon is mouthwatering.

INGREDIENTS
Serves 8
½ cup superfine sugar
4 eggs, separated
grated zest and juice of 1 lemon
1¼ cups ground pistachio nuts
½ cup dried breadcrumbs
1 lemon
6 tablespoons honey
1 cinnamon stick
1 tablespoon brandy

To Decorate
shredded lemon zest
cinnamon sticks

1 Preheat the oven to 350°F. Grease an 8-inch square cake pan and line the bottom with waxed or parchment paper. Grease the paper.

2 Beat the sugar, egg yolks and lemon zest and juice together until pale and creamy. Fold in 1 cup of the ground pistachio nuts and all the bread crumbs.

3 ▲ Whisk the egg whites until stiff and fold into the creamed mixture. Spoon into the prepared pan and bake for 45 minutes, until risen and springy to the touch. Remove from the oven, cool in the pan for 10 minutes, then turn out onto a wire rack to cool completely.

4 ▲ Meanwhile, to make the syrup, peel the lemon and cut the zest into very thin strips. Squeeze the juice into a small pan and add the honey and cinnamon stick. Bring to a boil, add the shredded zest, and simmer fast for 1 minute. Cool the syrup slightly and stir in the brandy.

5 ▲ Place the cooled cake on a serving plate, prick all over with a skewer and pour the cooled syrup, lemon shreds and cinnamon sticks over.

6 ▲ Sprinkle the reserved ground pistachio nuts in an even layer over the top of the cake.

St. Clement's Marbled Crown

A tangy orange-and-lemon marble cake is transformed into a spectacular centerpiece by the pretty arrangement of fresh flowers in the center of the ring. The icing is decorated with crystallized fruits, dragées and sugared almonds, creating a dramatic jeweled effect.

INGREDIENTS
Serves 8
12 tablespoons (¾ cup)
unsalted butter
½ cup light brown sugar
3 eggs, separated
grated zest and juice of 1 orange
1½ cups self-rising flour
6 tablespoons superfine sugar
grated zest and juice of 1 lemon
2 tablespoons ground almonds

For the Topping
1½ cups heavy cream
1 tablespoon Grand Marnier

To Decorate
16 crystallized orange and
lemon slices
silver dragées
8 gold sugared almonds
fresh flowers

1 Preheat the oven to 350°F. Grease and flour a 3¾-cup ring mold.

2 Cream half the butter and the brown sugar together until pale and light. Gradually beat in the egg yolks and orange zest and juice until incorporated, and fold in ¾ cup of the flour.

3 Cream the remaining butter and sugar together, stir in the lemon zest and juice and fold in the remaining flour and ground almonds. Whisk the egg whites until stiff, and fold in.

4 ▲ Spoon the two batters alternately into the prepared pan.

5 ▲ Using a skewer or small spoon, swirl through the mixture to create a marbled effect. Bake for 45–50 minutes, until risen and a skewer inserted into the cake comes out clean. Cool in the pan for 10 minutes, then turn out onto a wire rack and allow to cool completely.

6 ▲ Whip the cream and Grand Marnier together until lightly thickened. Spread over the cooled cake and swirl a pattern over the cream.

7 ▲ Decorate the ring with the crystallized fruits, dragées and almonds to resemble a jeweled crown. Arrange a few pretty fresh flowers in the center.

Caramel-Frosted Gingerbread

This is an unusual gingerbread, made with all syrup rather than a mixture of syrup and molasses. This gives a lighter batter—and the addition of dried coconut adds a wonderful flavor and texture to the cake. Serve slices of this cake with a warm drink for a light and tasty treat.

INGREDIENTS
Makes 18–20
1½ cups light brown sugar
2 sticks (1 cup) unsalted butter
1¼ cups golden or light corn syrup
6 tablespoons crystallized-ginger syrup
3 cups self-rising flour
2 cups dried coconut
2 tablespoons chopped crystallized ginger
1 teaspoon ground ginger
½ teaspoon baking soda
1¼ cups milk
1 egg, lightly beaten

To Decorate
1 cup dried coconut

1 Preheat the oven to 350°F. Grease a deep 10 x 8-inch rectangular cake pan, line with waxed or parchment paper and grease the paper.

2 ▲ Heat 1 cup of the sugar, 1½ sticks butter, the golden syrup and 4 tablespoons crystallized-ginger syrup together gently until melted. Combine the flour, coconut, crystallized ginger, ground ginger and baking soda in a large bowl. Gradually beat in the melted syrup mixture, milk and egg, and continue beating for 1 minute.

3 Pour into the prepared pan and bake for 1½ hours, or until a skewer inserted in the center comes out clean. Remove from the oven, cool in the pan for 10 minutes then turn out onto a wire rack to cool completely.

4 ▲ Melt the remaining sugar, butter and crystallized ginger syrup together. Increase the heat and boil for 1 minute. Remove from the heat and allow the bubbling to stop. Pour over the cooled cake in one smooth motion, letting a little drizzle over the edges.

5 ▲ Immediately sprinkle the coconut on top, mark into 18–20 slices with a sharp knife and let stand in a cool place until the caramel icing has set. Cut along the marked lines.

Fig, Banana and Brazil Nut Tea Bread

Mashed bananas are a classic ingredient in tea breads. Combined here with dried figs and Brazil nuts, they make an exceptionally moist and flavorful cake, perfect for a midafternoon pick-me-up or with morning coffee.

INGREDIENTS
Serves 8–12
2 cups all-purpose flour
2 teaspoons baking powder
1 teaspoon ground pumpkin pie
spice
8 tablespoons (½ cup) unsalted
butter, diced
½ cup soft light brown sugar
2 eggs, lightly beaten
2 tablespoons milk
2 tablespoons dark rum
2 medium bananas, peeled
and mashed
⅔ cup dried figs, chopped
½ cup Brazil nuts, chopped

To Decorate
8 whole Brazil nuts
4 whole dried figs, halved
2 tablespoons apricot jam
1 teaspoon dark rum

1 Preheat the oven to 350°F. Grease a 9 x 5 x 3-inch loaf pan, line the bottom with waxed or parchment paper and grease the paper.

2 Sift the flour, baking powder and spice into a bowl. Rub in the butter until the mixture resembles fine bread crumbs. Stir in the sugar.

3 ▲ Make a well in the center and work in the eggs, milk and rum until combined. Stir in the remaining ingredients and spoon into the prepared pan.

4 ▲ Press the whole Brazil nuts and halved figs gently into the batter, to form an attractive pattern. Bake for 1¼ hours, or until a skewer inserted in the center comes out clean. Remove from the oven, cool in the pan for 10 minutes, then turn out onto a wire rack.

5 ▲ Heat the jam and rum together in a small pan. Increase the heat and boil for 1 minute. Remove from the heat and pass through a fine sieve. Cool the glaze slightly and brush over the cake while still warm. Allow to cool completely, then store in an airtight container.

Tip

This cake is at its best if stored for 3–4 days in an airtight container before eating.

Chocolate Banana Cake

This chocolate cake is delicious yet low in fat, thanks to the addition of ripe bananas, which result in a moist cake with a good depth of flavor.

INGREDIENTS
Serves 8
2 cups self-rising flour
3 tablespoons cocoa powder
½ cup light brown sugar
2 tablespoons malt extract
2 tablespoons golden or
light corn syrup
2 eggs
4 tablespoons milk
4 tablespoons sunflower oil
2 large, ripe bananas

For the Icing
2 cups confectioners' sugar, sifted
7 teaspoons cocoa powder, sifted
1–2 tablespoons warm water

1 ▲ Preheat the oven to 325°F. Grease a deep 8-inch round cake pan, line the bottom with waxed or parchment paper and grease the paper.

2 ▲ Sift the flour into a mixing bowl with the cocoa powder. Add the sugar and mix together well.

3 ▲ Make a well in the center and add the malt extract, syrup, eggs, milk and oil. Mash the bananas thoroughly and stir them into the mixture until thoroughly combined.

4 ▲ Pour the batter into the prepared pan and bake for 1–1¼ hours, or until the center of the cake springs back when lightly pressed.

5 ▲ Remove the cake from the pan and let sit on a wire rack until completely cool.

6 ▲ Reserve ½ cup confectioners' sugar and 1 teaspoon cocoa powder. Make a darker icing by beating the remaining sugar and cocoa powder with enough of the warm water to make a thick icing. Pour it over the top of the cake and spread evenly to the edges. Make a thinner, lighter icing by mixing the remaining confectioners' sugar and cocoa powder with a few drops of water. Drizzle or pipe this icing across the top of the cake to decorate.

Tip

This cake also makes a delicious dessert when heated in the microwave. The icing melts to a puddle of sauce. Serve a slice topped with a large dollop of fromage frais for a special treat.

Chocolate and Orange Angel Cake

This light-as-air sponge is a variation on the classic angel food cake, made without fat or egg yolks. The dark chocolate cake contrasts dramatically with the sparkling white frosting.

INGREDIENTS
Serves 10
¼ cup all-purpose flour
2 tablespoons cocoa powder
2 tablespoons cornstarch
pinch of salt
5 egg whites
½ teaspoon cream of tartar
½ cup superfine sugar

For the Frosting
scant 1 cup superfine sugar
1 egg white

To Decorate
blanched and shredded zest of
1 orange

1 Preheat the oven to 350°F. Sift the flour, cocoa powder, cornstarch and salt together three times. Beat the egg whites in a large bowl until foamy. Add the cream of tartar, then beat until soft peaks form.

2 ▲ Add the sugar to the egg whites a spoonful at a time, beating after each addition. Sift a third of the flour and cocoa mixture over the meringue and gently fold in. Repeat, sifting and folding in the flour and cocoa mixture two more times.

3 ▲ Spoon the mixture into a non-stick 8-inch ring mold and level the top. Bake for 35 minutes, or until springy when lightly pressed. Invert onto a wire rack and let cool in the pan. Carefully ease out of the pan.

4 ▲ To make the frosting, put the sugar in a pan with 5 tablespoons cold water. Stir over low heat until dissolved. Boil until the syrup reaches a temperature of 240°F on a candy thermometer, or the thread stage. Remove from the heat.

5 ▲ Meanwhile, as soon as the syrup boils, beat the egg white until stiff and dry. Add the syrup in a thin stream, beating all the time. Continue to beat until the mixture is very thick and glossy.

6 ▲ Spread the icing over the top and sides of the cooled cake. Sprinkle the orange zest over the top of the cake to decorate.

Tip

Make sure you do not overbeat the egg whites for the cake mixture. They should not be stiff but should form soft peaks, so that the air bubbles can expand further during cooking and help the cake to rise.

Decorated Cupcakes

These little cakes are perfect for children's parties, with their appealing, colorful decorations.

INGREDIENTS
Makes 16
8 tablespoons (½ cup) unsalted butter,
at room temperature
1 cup granulated sugar
2 eggs, at room temperature
1½ cups all-purpose flour
¼ teaspoon salt
1½ teaspoons baking powder
½ cup plus 1 tablespoon milk
1 teaspoon vanilla extract

For the Icing and Decorations
2 large egg whites
3½ cups sifted confectioners' sugar
1–2 drops glycerin
juice of 1 lemon
food coloring
colored sprinkles, for decorating
candied lemon and orange slices,
for decorating

1 Preheat the oven to 375°F.

2 ▲ Fill 16 muffin cups with fluted paper baking liners, or grease them.

3 With an electric mixer, cream the butter and sugar until light and fluffy. Add the eggs, one at a time, beating well after each addition. Sift together the flour, salt and baking powder. Stir into the butter mixture, alternating with the milk. Stir in the vanilla.

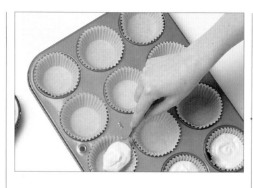

4 ▲ Fill the cups half-full and bake until the tops spring back when touched lightly, about 20 minutes. Let the cupcakes stand in the pan for 5 minutes, then unmold and transfer to a rack to cool completely.

5 For the meringue icing, beat the egg whites until stiff but not dry. Gradually add the sugar, glycerin, and lemon juice and continue beating for 1 minute. The consistency should be spreadable. If necessary, thin with a little water or add some more sifted confectioners' sugar.

6 ▲ Divide the icing among several bowls and tint with food colorings. Spread different colored icings over the cooled cupcakes.

7 ▲ Decorate the cupcakes any way you wish, such as with different colored sprinkles.

8 ▲ Other decorations include candied orange and lemon slices. Cut into small pieces and arrange on top of the cupcakes. Alternatively, use other suitable candies.

9 ▲ To decorate with colored icings, fill paper piping bags with different colored icings. Pipe on faces, or make other designs.

Nectarine Amaretto Cake

Make this delicious cake for afternoon tea or serve it as a dessert with a dollop of fromage frais.

INGREDIENTS
Serves 8
3 eggs, separated
¾ cup superfine sugar
grated zest and juice of 1 lemon
⅓ cup semolina
½ cup ground almonds
¼ cup all-purpose flour

For the Syrup
6 tablespoons superfine sugar
6 tablespoons water
2 tablespoons Amaretto liqueur

To Decorate
2 nectarines or peaches, halved
3 tablespoons apricot jam
1 tablespoon water

1 ▲ Preheat the oven to 350°F. Grease an 8-inch round loose-bottomed cake pan. Whisk the egg yolks, sugar, lemon zest and juice in a bowl until thick, pale and creamy.

2 ▲ Fold in the semolina, almonds and flour until smooth.

3 ▲ Beat the egg whites in a grease-free bowl until fairly stiff. Using a metal spoon, stir a generous spoonful of the whites into the semolina mixture to lighten it, then fold in the remaining egg whites. Spoon the mixture into the prepared cake pan.

4 ▲ Bake for 30–35 minutes, until the center of the cake springs back when lightly pressed. Remove the cake from the oven and carefully loosen around the edge of the cake with a baking spatula. Prick the top with a skewer and let cool slightly in the pan.

5 ▲ Meanwhile, make the syrup. Heat the sugar and water in a small pan, stirring until dissolved, then boil without stirring for 2 minutes. Add the Amaretto liqueur and drizzle slowly over the cake.

6 ▲ Remove the cake from the pan and put it on a serving plate. Slice the nectarines or peaches and arrange them over the top. Heat the jam and water together in a small pan. Remove from the heat and pass through a sieve. Cool the glaze slightly and brush over the cake.

Tip

Use drained canned mandarin orange segments for the topping, if preferred, and use an orange-flavored liqueur instead of the Amaretto.

Cinnamon Apple Cake

A spiced génoise sandwiched with a mouthwatering filling of apples and soft cheese makes a lovely cake for an autumn tea party.

INGREDIENTS
Serves 8
3 eggs
½ cup superfine sugar
¾ cup all-purpose flour
1 teaspoon ground cinnamon

For the Filling and Topping
4 large eating apples
4 tablespoons honey
2 tablespoons water
½ cup golden raisins
½ teaspoon ground cinnamon
1½ cups low-fat soft cheese
4 tablespoons fromage frais
2 teaspoons lemon juice
2 tablespoons apricot jam
mint sprigs, to decorate

1 ▲ Preheat the oven to 375°F. Grease a 9-inch cake pan, line with waxed or parchment paper and grease the paper. Place the eggs and sugar in a bowl and beat with an electric mixer for about 10 minutes, or until thick and pale.

2 Sift the flour and cinnamon over the egg mixture and carefully fold in with a large spoon. Pour into the prepared pan and bake for 25–30 minutes, or until the cake springs back when lightly pressed. Slide a baking spatula between the cake and the pan to loosen the edge, then turn the cake out onto a wire rack to cool.

3 ▲ To make the filling, peel, core and slice three of the apples and put them in a saucepan. Add 2 tablespoons of the honey and 1 tablespoon of the water. Cover and cook over gentle heat for about 10 minutes, until the apples have softened. Add the golden raisins and cinnamon, stir well, replace the lid and let cool.

4 ▲ Put the soft cheese in a bowl with the remaining honey, the fromage frais and half the lemon juice. Beat until the mixture is smooth.

5 ▲ Halve the cake horizontally, place the bottom half on a board and drizzle any liquid from the apples over. Spread with two-thirds of the cheese mixture, then top with the apple filling. Fit the top of the cake in place.

6 ▲ Swirl the remaining cheese mixture over the top of the cake. Core and slice the remaining apple, sprinkle with lemon juice and arrange around the edge. Heat the jam and 1 tablespoon water together in a small pan and pass through a sieve. Cool the glaze slightly, then brush over the apples. Decorate with mint sprigs.

Coffee Almond Flower Gâteau

There are all kinds of reasons for making a cake for someone - sometimes it may be simply to say "thank you."

INGREDIENTS
Serves 8–10
1 quantity Quick-Mix Sponge
Cake mix
¼ cup nuts, such as almonds or
walnuts, finely chopped
1½ x quantity coffee-flavor
Butter Icing
3 x 1oz squares plain chocolate
20 blanched almonds
4 chocolate-coated espresso beans

MATERIALS AND EQUIPMENT
2 x 7 inch round cake pans
serrated scraper
2 waxed paper piping bags
No 2 writing nozzle

1 Preheat the oven to 325°F. Grease the cake pans, line the bases with waxed paper and grease the paper. Fold the nuts into the cake mixture. Divide the mixture evenly between the pans and smooth the surfaces. Bake in the center of the oven for about 20 minutes or until firm to the touch. Turn out on to a wire rack, peel off the lining paper and leave to cool completely.

2 Place one of the cakes on a piece of waxed paper on a turntable. Use the butter icing to sandwich the cakes together and to ice the top and side. Coat the top by spreading the icing smoothly with a palette knife. Coat the side with a serrated scraper. Reserve two spoonfuls of icing for piping.

3 ▲ Melt the chocolate in a heatproof bowl over a pan of hot water. Remove from the heat, then dip half of each almond into the chocolate at a slight angle. Shake off any excess chocolate and leave the almonds to dry on baking parchment. Return the chocolate to the pan of hot water (off the heat) so it does not set. Remove and allow to cool slightly before using for piping.

4 Arrange the almonds on top of the cake to represent flowers.

5 ▲ Place a chocolate-coated espresso bean in the center of each almond flower. Spoon the remaining melted chocolate into a waxed paper piping bag. Cut a small piece off the end in a straight line. Pipe the chocolate in wavy lines over the top of the cake and in small beads around the top edge.

6 Transfer the cake to a cake stand or serving plate. Work quickly so the chocolate in the piping bag does not become too firm to pipe. Place the reserved butter icing in a fresh piping bag fitted with the No 2 writing nozzle. Pipe beads of icing all around the bottom of the cake, then top with small beads of chocolate, allowing the chocolate to drizzle on to the stand.

ummer Strawberry Shortcake

A summer-time treat. Serve with a cool glass of pink sparkling wine for a truly refreshing dessert.

INGREDIENTS
Serves 6–8
2 cups flour
1 tbsp baking powder
½ tsp salt
4 tbsp sugar
4 tbsp butter, softened
⅔ cup milk
1¼ cups heavy cream
1 lb fresh strawberries, halved and hulled

3 ▲ Turn out the dough on to a lightly floured work surface and pat, using your fingers, into a 12 x 6 inch rectangle. Using a template, cut out two 6 inch rounds, indent one of the rounds dividing it into eight equal portions, and place them on the prepared cookie sheet.

4 ▲ Bake in the center of the oven for 10–15 minutes or until slightly risen and golden. Leave the shortcake on the cookie sheet for about 5 minutes, then transfer to a wire rack, peel off the lining paper and leave to cool completely.

5 Place the cream in a mixing bowl and whip with an electric mixer until it holds soft peaks. Place the unmarked shortcake on a serving plate and spread or pipe with half of the cream. Top with two-thirds of the strawberries, then the other shortcake. Use the remaining cream and strawberries to decorate the top layer. Chill the shortcake for at least 30 minutes before serving.

1 Preheat the oven to 425°F. Meanwhile, grease a cookie sheet, line the base with waxed paper and grease the paper.

2 ▲ Sift the flour, baking powder and salt together into a large mixing bowl. Stir in the sugar, cut in the butter and toss into the flour mixture until it resembles coarse breadcrumbs. Stir in just enough milk to make a soft dough.

Spiced Easter Cake

If you can't resist the lure of a slice of iced cake, you'll love this moist, spiced sponge with its delicious creamy topping.

INGREDIENTS
Serves 10
1 medium carrot
1 medium zucchini
3 eggs, separated
½ cup light brown sugar
2 tablespoons ground almonds
finely grated zest of 1 orange
1 cup whole-wheat flour
1½ teaspoons baking powder
½ teaspoon salt
1 teaspoon ground cinnamon

For the Topping
¾ cup low-fat soft cheese
1 teaspoon honey

To Decorate
fondant carrots and zucchini

1 ▲ Preheat the oven to 350°F. Line a 7-inch square pan with baking parchment. Coarsely grate the carrot and zucchini.

2 Put the egg yolks, brown sugar, ground almonds and orange zest into a bowl and beat until very thick and light.

3 ▲ Sift the flour and cinnamon together and fold into the mixture with the grated vegetables. Add any bran left from the flour in the sieve.

4 ▲ Whisk the egg whites until stiff and carefully fold them in, one-half at a time. Spoon into the prepared pan. Bake for 1 hour, covering the top with foil after 40 minutes.

5 ▲ Allow to cool in the pan for about 5 minutes, then turn out onto a wire rack and carefully remove the lining paper.

6 ▲ For the topping, beat together the cheese and honey and spread over the cake. Decorate with fondant carrots and zucchini.

Banana Gingerbread Slices

Bananas make this spicy gingerbread delightfully moist. The flavor develops on keeping, so store the gingerbread for a few days before cutting into slices, if possible.

INGREDIENTS
Makes 20 slices
2½ cups all-purpose flour
1 teaspoon baking soda
4 teaspoons ground ginger
2 teaspoons pumpkin pie spice
½ cup light brown sugar
4 tablespoons sunflower oil
2 tablespoons molasses
2 tablespoons malt extract
2 eggs
4 tablespoons orange juice
3 ripe bananas
⅔ cup raisins or golden raisins

1 ▲ Preheat the oven to 350°F. Lightly grease an 11 x 7-inch shallow baking pan, line with waxed or parchment paper and grease the paper.

2 ▲ Sift the flour, baking soda and spices into a bowl. Sieve in the brown sugar.

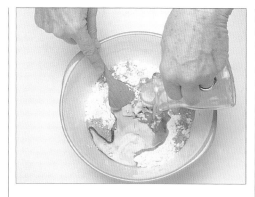

3 ▲ Make a well in the center of the dry ingredients and add the oil, molasses, malt extract, eggs and orange juice. Mix thoroughly.

4 ▲ Mash the bananas on a plate. Add the raisins to the gingerbread mixture, then mix in the mashed bananas.

5 ▲ Pour the mixture into the prepared baking pan. Bake for 35–40 minutes, or until the center of the gingerbread springs back when lightly pressed with your finger.

6 ▲ Let the gingerbread cool in the pan for 5 minutes, then turn out onto a wire rack to cool completely. Transfer to a board and cut into 20 slices to serve.

Tip

If your brown sugar is lumpy, mix it with a little flour and it will be easier to sift.

Banana and Apricot Chelsea Buns

Traditional English favorites are given a new twist with a delectable fruit filling.

INGREDIENTS
Makes 9
6 tablespoons warm milk
1 teaspoon dried yeast
pinch of sugar
2 cups bread flour
2 teaspoons pumpkin pie spice
½ teaspoon salt
2 tablespoons butter
¼ cup superfine sugar
1 egg

For the Filling
1 large ripe banana
1 cup dried apricots
2 tablespoons light brown sugar

For the Glaze
2 tablespoons superfine sugar
2 tablespoons water

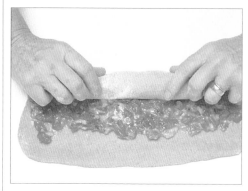

1 ▲ Grease a 7-inch square cake pan. Put the warm milk in a measuring cup. Sprinkle the yeast on top. Add a pinch of sugar to help activate the yeast, mix well and let sit for 30 minutes.

2 ▲ Sift the flour, spice and salt into a mixing bowl. Rub in the butter, then stir in the sugar. Make a well in the center and pour in the yeast mixture and the egg. Gradually mix in the flour to make a soft dough, adding extra milk if the mixture is too dry.

3 ▲ Turn the dough out onto a floured surface and knead for 5 minutes, until smooth and elastic. Return to the clean bowl, cover with a damp dish towel and let stand in a warm place to rise for about 2 hours, until doubled in bulk.

4 ▲ Meanwhile, prepare the filling. Mash the banana in a bowl. Using kitchen scissors, snip the apricots, then stir them into the mashed banana with the sugar.

5 ▲ Knead the risen dough on a floured surface for 2 minutes, then roll out to a 12 x 9-inch rectangle. Spread the banana and apricot filling over the dough and roll up lengthwise like a jelly roll, with the seam underneath.

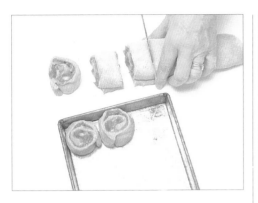

Tip

Do not leave the buns in the pan for too long or the glaze will stick to the sides, making them very difficult to remove.

6 ▲ Cut the roll into nine pieces and place, cut side down, in the prepared pan. Cover and let rise in a warm place for about 30 minutes. Preheat the oven to 400°F.

7 ▲ Bake the buns for 20–25 minutes, until golden brown and cooked in the center. Meanwhile, make the glaze. Mix the sugar and water in a small saucepan. Heat, stirring, until dissolved, then boil for 2 minutes. Brush the glaze over the buns while still hot, then remove the buns from the pan and let them cool on a wire rack.

Chocolate and Banana Brownies

Nuts traditionally give brownies their chewy texture. Here oat bran is used instead, creating a moist, delicious yet healthy alternative.

INGREDIENTS
Makes 9

5 tablespoons cocoa powder
1 tablespoon superfine sugar
5 tablespoons milk
3 large bananas, mashed
1 cup light brown sugar
1 teaspoon vanilla extract
5 egg whites
¾ cup self-rising flour
¼ cup oat bran
1 tablespoon confectioners' sugar,
for dusting

1 ▲ Preheat the oven to 350°F. Line an 8-inch square pan with baking parchment.

2 ▲ Blend the cocoa powder and superfine sugar with the milk. Add the bananas, brown sugar and vanilla.

3 ▲ Lightly beat the egg whites with a fork. Add the chocolate mixture and beat well. Sift the flour over the mixture and fold in with the oat bran. Pour into the prepared pan.

4 ▲ Bake for 40 minutes, or until firm. When completely cool, cut into squares and lightly dust with confectioners' sugar before serving.

White Chocolate Brownies with Milk Chocolate Macadamia Topping

White chocolate makes a light-colored mixture for these brownies, which are dotted with dark chocolate chips and finished with a sensational topping of chunky macadamia nuts.

INGREDIENTS
Serves 12
1¼ cups all-purpose flour
½ teaspoon baking powder
pinch of salt
6 ounces fine-quality white
  chocolate, chopped
scant ½ cup superfine sugar
8 tablespoons (½ cup) unsalted
  butter, cut into pieces
2 eggs, lightly beaten
1 teaspoon vanilla extract
6 ounces semisweet chocolate chips
  or chopped chocolate

For the Topping
7 ounces milk chocolate, chopped
1 cup unsalted macadamia nuts,
  chopped

3 ▲ Bake for 20–25 minutes, until a skewer inserted 2 inches from the side of the pan comes out clean; do not overbake. Remove from the oven to a heatproof surface. Immediately sprinkle the chopped milk chocolate evenly over the surface (avoid touching the side of pan) and return to the oven for 1 minute.

4 ▲ Remove from the oven and gently spread the softened chocolate evenly over the top. Sprinkle with the macadamia nuts and gently press into the chocolate. Cool on a wire rack for 30 minutes, then refrigerate for 1 hour. Run a sharp knife around the pan to loosen, then unclip the springform-pan side and carefully remove. Cut into thin wedges.

1 Preheat the oven to 350°F. Grease a 9-inch springform pan. Sift together the flour, baking powder and salt and set aside.

2 ▲ In a medium saucepan over medium heat, melt the white chocolate, sugar and butter until smooth, stirring frequently. Cool slightly, then beat in the eggs and vanilla. Stir in the flour until well blended. Stir in the chocolate chips or chopped chocolate. Spread evenly in the prepared pan, smoothing the top.

Marbled Chocolate Peanut Butter Cake

This cake cannot be tested with a skewer because the peanut butter remains soft in the center.
Rely on the fingertip method: the cake should spring back when touched after 50–60 minutes.

INGREDIENTS
Serves 12–14
4 ounces unsweetened
chocolate, chopped
2 sticks (1 cup) unsalted butter,
softened
1 cup smooth or crunchy
peanut butter
1 cup granulated sugar
1 cup (packed) light brown sugar
5 eggs
2½ cups all-purpose flour
2 teaspoons baking powder
½ teaspoon salt
½ cup milk
⅓ cup chocolate chips

For the Chocolate Peanut Butter Glaze
2 tablespoons unsalted butter, cut up
2 tablespoons smooth peanut butter
3 tablespoons golden or
light corn syrup
1 teaspoon vanilla extract
6 ounces semisweet chocolate,
broken into pieces
1 tablespoon water

1 ▲ Preheat the oven to 350°F. Generously grease and flour a 10-inch ring mold. In the top of a double boiler over low heat, melt the chocolate.

2 ▲ Place the butter, peanut butter and sugars in a large bowl and beat with an electric mixer until light and creamy, 3–5 minutes, scraping the side of the bowl occasionally. Add the eggs one at a time, beating well after each addition.

3 In a medium bowl, stir together the flour, baking powder and salt. Add to the butter mixture alternately with the milk until just blended.

4 ▲ Pour half the batter into another bowl. Stir the melted chocolate into one half of the batter until well blended. Stir the chocolate chips into the other half of the batter.

5 ▲ Using a large spoon, drop alternate spoonfuls of chocolate batter and peanut butter batter into the prepared pan. Using a knife, pull through the batters to create a swirled, marbled effect; do not let the knife touch the side or bottom of the pan and do not overmix. Bake the cake for 50–60 minutes, until the top springs back when lightly pressed. Cool in the pan on a wire rack for 10 minutes, then turn out onto the rack and allow to cool completely.

6 ▲ To prepare the glaze, combine all the ingredients in a small pan. Melt over low heat, stirring until well blended and smooth. Cool slightly. When slightly thickened, drizzle the glaze over the cake, allowing it to run down the side.

Special Occasions

Special occasions deserve equally special cakes.
For inspired ideas for weddings, christenings, birthdays
and anniversaries, this chapter provides a tempting
selection. Featuring intricate designs that use a variety of
different techniques, these recipes range from chocolate
extravaganzas to iced masterpieces that will ensure that
you have a cake that will truly match the occasion.

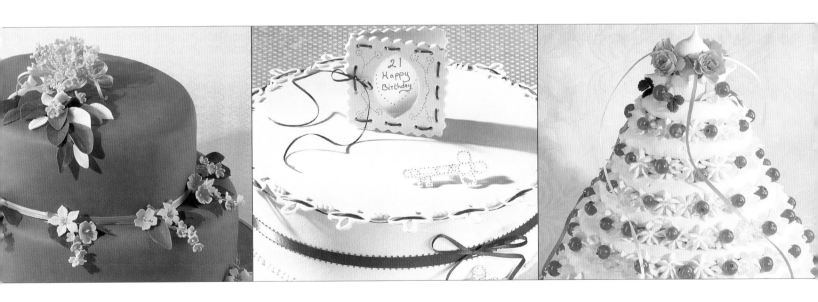

Teddy Bear Christening Cake

To personalize the cake, make a simple plaque for the top and pipe or write the name of the new baby with a food coloring pen.

INGREDIENTS
Serves 30
*8 inch square Light
Fruit Cake
3 tbsp apricot jam, warmed and
sieved
2 lb marzipan
1³/₄ lb/2¹/₃ x quantity Sugarpaste
Icing
peach, yellow, blue and brown
food colorings
¹/₆ quantity Royal Icing*

MATERIALS AND EQUIPMENT
*10 inch square cake board
crimping tool
blossom cutter or plunger
foam pad
3 inch round cutter
frill cutter
wooden toothpick
peach ribbon
small blue ribbon bow*

1 Brush the cake with the apricot jam. Roll out the marzipan on a work surface which is lightly dusted with confectioners' sugar, then use to cover the cake. Leave to dry for 12 hours.

2 Color 1¼ lb of the sugarpaste icing peach. Roll out the icing. Brush the marzipan with a little water and cover the cake with the icing.

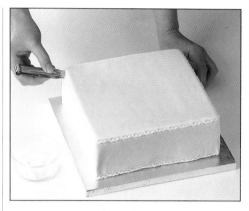

3 ▲ Position the cake on the cake board. Using a crimping tool dipped in cornstarch, crimp the top and bottom edges of the cake.

4 Divide the remaining sugarpaste into three portions. Leave one-third white and color one-third yellow. Cut the remaining third in half and color one portion peach and the other blue.

5 ▲ To make the flowers, roll out the peach and blue sugarpaste thinly on a work surface lightly dusted with confectioners' sugar. Dip the end of the blossom cutter or a plunger in cornstarch and cut out small and larger flowers. Place a small ball of peach icing in the center of the blue flowers; and a small ball of blue icing in the center of the peach flowers. Secure with water, if necessary. Leave the flowers to dry on a foam pad for several hours or overnight. Gather together the blue icing trimmings and set aside, wrapped in plastic wrap.

6 ▲ Make the teddy bear with the yellow icing. Shape the head, body, arms and ears of the bear and press together with a little water to secure. Make the button for the chest out of a little blue icing. Paint on highlights, such as eyes, nose and mouth, with brown food coloring. Leave the bear to dry on a piece of waxed paper for several hours or overnight.

7 To make the blanket, roll out the blue icing and cut out a circle with the 3 inch round cutter. Slice off a small piece, about ½ inch, to give a straight line for the top. Set aside. Roll out the white icing thinly and, using the frill cutter, cut out a ring. Put the end of the wooden toothpick over about ¼ inch of the outer edge of the ring. Roll the stick around the edge firmly back and forth with your finger so the edge becomes thinner and begins to frill. Continue until the ring is completely frilled. Using a sharp knife, cut through the ring once to open it up. Gently ease it open.

8 ▲ Brush the edge of the blue blanket with water and secure the white frill on to the edge.

9 Decorate the cake with the ribbon. Position the bear on top and lay the blanket over it, securing with a little water or royal icing. Secure the flowers with a little royal icing and then the bow to the bear's neck in the same way.

Daisy Christening Cake

A ring of molded daisies sets off this pretty pink christening cake. It can be made in easy stages, giving time for the various icings to dry before adding the next layer.

INGREDIENTS
Serves 20–25
8 inch round Rich Fruit Cake
3 tbsp apricot jam, warmed and sieved
1½ lb marzipan
2 lb/1⅓ x quantity Royal Icing
4 oz/⅓ quantity Sugarpaste Icing
pink and yellow food colorings

MATERIALS AND EQUIPMENT
10 inch round cake board
2 inch fluted cutter
wooden toothpick
2 waxed paper piping bags
No 42 nozzle
pink and white ribbons

1 Brush the cake with the apricot jam. Roll out the marzipan on a work surface lightly dusted with confectioners' sugar and use to cover the cake. Leave to dry for 12 hours.

2 Secure the cake to the cake board with a little of the icing. Color three-quarters of the icing pink. Flat ice the cake with three or four layers of smooth icing, using the white icing for the top and the pink for the sides. Allow each layer to dry overnight before applying the next. Set aside a little of both icings in airtight containers, to decorate the cake.

3 Meanwhile, make the daisies. You will need about 28. For each daisy cut off a small piece of sugarpaste icing. Dust your fingers with a little cornstarch to prevent sticking.

4 ▲ Shape the icing with your fingers to look like a golf tee, with a stem and a thin, flat, round top.

5 ▲ Using scissors, make small cuts all the way around the edge of the daisy. Carefully curl the cut edges slightly in different directions. Place the daisies on a sheet of waxed paper to dry.

6 ▲ When dry, trim the stems and paint the edges with pink and the centers with yellow food coloring.

7 ▲ To make the plaque, roll out the remaining sugarpaste icing on a work surface lightly dusted with confectioners' sugar and cut out a circle with the fluted cutter. Position the end of a wooden toothpick over ¼ inch of the outer edge of the circle. Roll the toothpick firmly back and forth around the edge with your finger until the edge becomes thinner and begins to frill. Continue until the edge of the plaque is completely frilled. Place on a sheet of waxed paper to dry, then paint the name in the center of the plaque and the edges with pink food coloring.

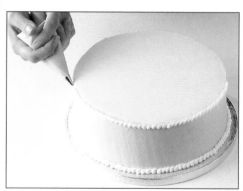

8 ▲ Fit a paper piping bag with the nozzle and pipe a twisted rope around the top and bottom edges of the cake with the remaining white royal icing. Wash the nozzle, fit it in a fresh paper piping bag and pipe a row of stars around the top of the cake with the remaining pink icing.

9 Secure the plaque to the center of the cake with a little royal icing. Arrange the daisies on the cake, also securing with the icing, and decorate with the ribbons.

Frills and Flowers Christening Cake

This pretty cake, decorated with flowers and frills, is perfect for a baby girl's christening, and would be ideal for a little girl's birthday cake, too.

INGREDIENTS
Serves 50
8-inch round Rich Fruit Cake
2 tablespoons apricot jam,
warmed and sieved
1¾ pounds marzipan
2½ pounds/3⅓ x quantity Sugar
paste Icing (Fondant)
pink and red food coloring
⅙ quantity Royal Icing

MATERIALS AND EQUIPMENT
9-inch round silver
cake board
deep pink ribbon, ¾ inch,
½ inch and ¼ inch wide
crimping tool
waxed paper
waxed or parchment paper piping
bag
No. 1 writing nozzle
frill cutter
large and medium plunger
blossom cutters
food coloring pen

1 Brush the cake with apricot jam, place on the cake board and cover the cake with marzipan. Tint the sugar paste pale pink using a few drops of pink food coloring. Using two-thirds of the sugar paste icing, cover the cake. Fit the widest ribbon around the cake board and the narrowest ribbon around the base of the cake. Secure with a bead of icing.

2 Using a crimping tool, crimp the top edge of the cake by pressing the crimper into the icing but not squeezing it together.

3 ▲ Cut a strip of waxed paper to fit around the cake and of the same height. Fold the paper into six equal divisions, position a plate half-way over the template and draw around the shape. Cut out the shape to form the template and reserve the cut-out piece. Fit the template around the cake and mark the shape with a scriber or pin. Remove the paper template.

4 Fill a paper piping bag fitted with a No. 1 writing nozzle with royal icing. Using some of the remaining sugar paste icing, roll and cut out a frill, but cut out a larger center circle to make a thinner frill. Frill the edges. Pipe a line of royal icing following one of the scalloped shapes marked on the cake and attach the frill. Repeat to make a total of six frills.

5 ▲ Using a cut-out piece of the template, mark ten ½-inch lines in a semicircle for the ribbon insertion cuts. Transfer these marks to the side of the cake under each frill and cut the slits. Cut the ½-inch-wide ribbon into pieces to fit the gaps and insert five pieces under each frill.

6 Mark a 4-inch circle on top of the cake and mark 34 ribbon insertion lines. Cut the slits and insert 17 pieces of ½-inch ribbon.

7 Knead all the sugar paste icing trimmings together and tint half dark pink to match the ribbon, using pink and red food coloring. Cut out 22 large and 40 medium light plunger blossom flowers, and 24 medium and 6 large dark plunger blossom flowers. Pipe a bead of icing in the center of each.

10 Secure the medium light pink flowers in between the ribbon inserts on top of the cake, and the small flowers on the side of the cake between the ribbon inserts. Secure the remaining light pink flowers between each frill. Allow the cake to dry.

8 ▲ Roll out a piece of dark pink sugar paste icing thinly and cut out a round using the frill cutter. Frill the edges. Roll out the pale pink sugar paste icing and cut out a 2-inch fluted circle and place on top of the dark pink frill. Allow to dry. Arrange ten plunger blossom flowers at opposite sides of the plaque and secure with royal icing.

9 ▲ Using a food coloring pen, dot in the design and write the child's name across the center. Place the plaque in position on top of the cake. Mark the dark centers on the blossom flowers with the food coloring pen. Attach the medium dark pink flowers to the top edge of the cake and the large ones in the center of each frilled scallop.

Christening Sampler

Instead of embroidering a sampler to welcome a new-born baby, why not make a sampler cake to celebrate?

INGREDIENTS
Serves 30
8 in square Rich Fruit Cake
3 tbsp apricot jam, warmed and strained
1 lb marzipan
1¹/₂ lb/2 x quantity Sugarpaste Icing
brown, blue, pink, yellow, orange, green, cream, and purple food colorings

MATERIALS AND EQUIPMENT
10 in square cake board
paintbrush
small heart-shaped cookie cutter

 Tip

Using the same techniques described here, you can change the overall design by modeling different figures and choosing different colors. You could also make a larger name plaque and pipe the baby's first name on to it.

1 Brush the cake with the apricot jam. On a work surface lightly dusted with confectioner's sugar, roll out the marzipan and use to cover the cake. Allow to dry for 12 hours.

2 Take two-thirds of the sugarpaste icing and cut off one-third of this. Roll out the smaller portion to the size of the top of the cake. Brush the top of the cake with a little water and cover with the icing.

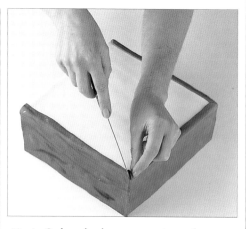

3 ▲ Color the larger portion of sugarpaste icing brown and divide into four equal amounts. Roll out each to the width of the cake side and about ¹/₂ in longer than the height. Brush each cake side with a little water, than press the brown icing into place, folding over the extra at the top to represent a picture frame. Cut off each corner at an angle to make a mitered joint. Reserve any trimmings, wrapped in plastic wrap. Place the cake on the cake board.

4 ▲ Paint the sides with brown food coloring, thinned with a little water, to represent wood grain.

5 ▲ Take the remaining sugarpaste icing and color small amounts yellow, orange, brown, purple, cream, and two shades each of blue, green, and pink. Leave a little white. Use these colors to shape the ducks, teddy bear, bulrushes, water, and apple-blossom branch and leaves. Roll out a small piece of pink icing and cut out a heart with the small heart-shaped cookie cutter. Roll out a small piece of white icing and cut out the baby's initial.

6 For the border, roll out strips of light blue and yellow icing and cut into oblongs and squares. Make small balls and squares from the purple icing. For the apple blossom, gently work together the two pinks and the white sugarpaste to give a marbled effect. Shape the flowers and add a small white ball in the center of each. Stick all the decorations to the cake with a little water as you make them.

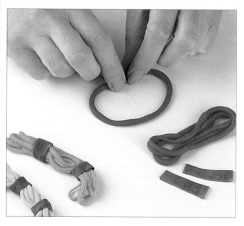

7 ▲ With any leftover colored icing, roll out long strips of icing with your hands to make the embroidery threads. Form these into loops and use small strips of reserved brown icing to hold the threads together. Arrange around the base of the cake.

Bunny and Bib Cake

This delicate cake may be made for a girl or a boy, using any pastel shade of icing. Make the decorations in advance and store in a warm, dry place. The bib may be kept as a keepsake.

INGREDIENTS
Serves 50
10 x 8-inch oval Rich or Light Fruit Cake (make using quantities for a standard 10-inch round cake)
4 tablespoons apricot jam, warmed and sieved
2½ pounds marzipan
2½ pounds/2 x quantity Royal Icing
½ quantity Petal Paste
blue food coloring

MATERIALS AND EQUIPMENT
12 x 9-inch oval silver cake board
card stock for template
small crimping tool
medium-sized heart-shaped plunger cutter
No. 3 and No. 1 writing nozzles
waxed or parchment paper piping bag
bunny-shaped cutter
blue food coloring pen
pale blue ribbon, ¾ inch, ½ inch, ¼ inch and ⅛ inch wide

1 Brush the cake with apricot jam, cover with marzipan and place on the cake board. Let dry for 12 hours. Flat-ice the top and sides of the cake with three layers of smooth icing. Allow the cake to dry, then ice the cake board. Reserve the remaining royal icing for decorating the cake.

2 Tint the petal paste pale blue with a few drops of blue food coloring. Cut out a template of the bib. Roll out a small piece of petal paste very thinly. Place the template on top and cut around the shape using a pointed knife.

3 ▲ Using a small crimping tool, crimp the edge to give a fluted finish. Using the medium-sized heart-shaped plunger cutter, cut out five heart shapes around the edge of the bib. Use the end of a No. 3 writing nozzle to cut out six small rounds between the heart shapes.

4 ▲ Half-fill a paper piping bag fitted with a No. 1 writing nozzle with royal icing. Pipe fine threads of icing following the outlines of the cut-out shapes. Pipe alternate scrolls and three beads of icing as a border design, following the shape of the bib.

5 Pipe the child's name across the center. Allow to dry overnight.

6 ▲ Roll out another piece of blue petal paste thinly and cut out 32 hearts using the plunger cutter. Then roll out some more icing thinly and use a tiny bunny cutter to cut out 16 bunny shapes. Mark their eyes using a blue food coloring pen. Allow all the cut-out shapes to dry overnight.

7 Measure and fit the wide blue ribbon around the cake board and secure with a pin. Measure and fit the ½-inch-wide ribbon around the base and the ¼-inch-wide ribbon around the top edge of the cake and secure each with a bead of royal icing. Secure alternate bunnies and hearts to the side of the cake between the ribbons with beads of royal icing. Secure 20 hearts around the top of the cake with royal icing.

8 Place the bib in the center of the cake and support it with a piece of petal paste; arrange the remaining five bunnies around it. Tie a tiny bow in the fine ribbon, leave the ends long, and pull over the scissors to curl the ends. Place in position at the neck of the bib and the side of the cake.

Birthday Bowl of Strawberries

*All kinds of fun designs can be painted on cakes with edible food colorings.
With this one the strawberry theme is carried on into the molded
decorations too, providing a fresh, summery birthday cake.*

INGREDIENTS
Serves 20
1 quantity Butter Icing
8 inch petal-shaped Madeira Cake
(make using quantities for an 8 inch
round cake)
3 tbsp apricot jam, warmed and
sieved
1½ lb/2 x quantity Sugarpaste Icing
pink, red, yellow, green and
burgundy food colorings
yellow powdered food coloring

MATERIALS AND EQUIPMENT
10 inch petal-shaped cake board
paint palette or small saucers
thin red and green ribbons

1 Color the butter icing pink. Cut the cake into three horizontal layers and sandwich together with the butter icing. Brush the cake with apricot jam. Roll out 1¼ lb of the sugarpaste icing on a work surface lightly dusted with confectioners' sugar and use to cover the cake. Position on the cake board and leave to dry for 12 hours.

2 ▲ To make the strawberries, color three-quarters of the remaining sugarpaste icing red, and equal portions of the rest yellow and green. Dust your fingers with cornstarch to prevent sticking, and mold the red icing into strawberry shapes. Make tiny oval shapes from the yellow icing to represent seeds and lightly press on to the strawberries. Secure with water if necessary. Shape the green icing into small flat circles slightly bigger than the tops of the strawberries. Using scissors, make small cuts all the way round the circles and carefully curl the cut edges slightly. Attach to the tops of the strawberries, securing with a little water. Leave to dry on waxed paper.

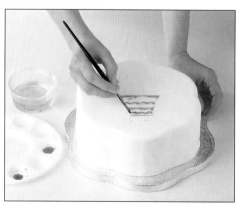

3 ▲ Put the red, green, yellow and burgundy food colorings in a palette and water them down slightly. Draw or paint on an outline of the vase with the burgundy color, then fill in the pattern.

4 ▲ Use a little powdered yellow food coloring to add highlights.

5 ▲ Finish painting the design, filling in the strawberries in the bowl and around the edge of the cake.

6 ▲ Decorate the cake with the ribbons. Secure two strawberries to the top of the cake, and arrange the others around the bottom edge.

Chocolate Fruit Birthday Cake

A moist chocolate Madeira cake is covered in marzipan and chocolate fudge icing. The fruits are molded from colored marzipan and make an eye-catching decoration.

INGREDIENTS
Serves 30
*7-inch square chocolate-flavor
Madeira Cake (see Tip)
3 tablespoons apricot jam,
warmed and sieved
1 pound marzipan
1 pound/1⅓ x quantity
Fudge Frosting
red, yellow, orange, green and
purple food coloring
whole cloves
angelica strips*

MATERIALS AND EQUIPMENT
*8-inch square silver
cake board
wire rack
nylon piping bag
medium-sized star nozzle
yellow ribbon ½ inch wide*

1 Cut a slice off the top of the cake to level if necessary and invert onto the cake board. Brush evenly with apricot jam.

2 ▲ Roll out two-thirds of the marzipan thinly to a 10-inch square. Place over the cake and smooth the top and sides. Trim off the excess marzipan around the base of the cake. Knead the trimmings together and reserve for making the marzipan fruits.

3 ▲ Place the cake on a wire rack over a tray and pour the freshly made fudge frosting over the cake, spreading quickly with a baking spatula. Allow the excess icing to fall on the tray. Let stand for 10 minutes, then place on the cake board.

4 ▲ Place the remaining frosting in a nylon piping bag fitted with a medium-sized star nozzle. Pipe a row of stars around the top edge and base of the cake. Allow to set.

5 ▲ Using the reserved marzipan, food coloring, cloves and angelica strips, model a selection of fruits.

6 Measure and fit the ribbon around the side of the cake and secure with a pin. Decorate the top with marzipan fruits.

Tip

To make a 7-inch chocolate-flavor Madeira Cake, use 1¾ cups all-purpose flour plus 2 tablespoons cocoa powder in place of the full amount of all-purpose flour.

*E*ighteenth Birthday Cake

A really striking cake for a lucky person celebrating his or her eighteenth birthday. Change the shape if you have difficulty finding a diamond-shaped pan.

INGREDIENTS
Serves 80
13½ x 8-inch diamond-shaped Rich or Light Fruit Cake (make using quantities for a standard 9-inch round cake)
3 tablespoons apricot jam, warmed and sieved
2½ pounds marzipan
3½ pounds/4½ x quantity white Sugar paste Icing (Fondant)
black food coloring
2 tablespoons Royal Icing

MATERIALS AND EQUIPMENT
15 x 10-inch diamond-shaped silver cake board
"1" and "8" numeral cutters or templates
small triangular cutter
very small round cutter
waxed or parchment paper piping bag
No. 1 writing nozzle
white ribbon, 1 inch wide
black ribbon, ⅛ inch wide

1 Brush the cake with apricot jam and place on the cake board. Cover with marzipan.

2 Cover the cake using 3⅓ x quantity sugar paste icing. Knead the trimmings into the remaining sugar paste and color using black food coloring.

3 Roll out two-thirds of the black sugar paste icing and cut into four strips the width and length of each section of the cake board. Brush the board with apricot jam and place each strip in position; trim to fit neatly.

4 ▲ Roll out one-quarter of the remaining sugar paste icing and cut out the number 18 using special cutters or by cutting around templates. Let stand on a foam pad to dry.

5 ▲ Roll out some more icing thinly and cut out 40 triangles for the bow ties and 20 for the wineglasses.

6 ▲ Use a tiny round cutter or the end of a plain nozzle to cut out 20 music notes and 10 bases for the glasses, cut in half. Cut out thin strips of icing for the tails of the music notes and the stems of the glasses.

7 Half-fill a paper piping bag fitted with a No. 1 writing nozzle with black royal icing. Join the bow ties together with tiny beads of icing. Attach the music notes to their tails and the glasses to the stems and bases. Allow to dry.

8 ▲ Measure and fit the white ribbon around the cake board and secure with a pin. Arrange the motifs over the top and sides of the cake and attach each with a bead of icing. Make tiny bows using black ribbon; attach to the corners of the cake with beads of icing.

Twenty-first Birthday Cake

This cake looks good in white or any pale color to suit the occasion. Add more color with the ribbons and write your own personal message in the card.

INGREDIENTS
Serves 80
10-inch round Rich Fruit Cake
3 tablespoons apricot jam,
warmed and sieved
2½ pounds marzipan
3 pounds/2 x quantity Royal Icing
blue food coloring
1¼ pounds/1 quantity Petal Paste

MATERIALS AND EQUIPMENT
12-inch round silver cake board
3-inch square fluted cutter
2-inch plain oval cutter
No. 2 and 3 writing nozzles
club-shaped cocktail cutter
tiny petal cutter
royal blue ribbon, ⅛ inch,
¼ inch and ½ inch wide
pale blue ribbon, ¾ inch wide
looped royal blue ribbon,
⅝ inch wide
waxed or parchment paper piping
bag
blue food coloring pen

1 Brush the cake with apricot jam, cover with marzipan and place on the cake board. Allow to dry for 12 hours.

2 Color the royal icing pale blue with a few drops of blue food coloring. Flat-ice the top and sides of the cake with three layers of smooth royal icing. Let the cake dry, then ice the cake board. Reserve the remaining royal icing for decorating.

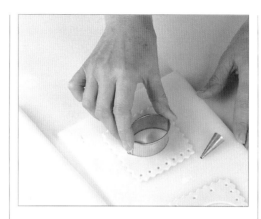

3 ▲ Color the petal paste pale blue with a few drops of blue food coloring. Roll out about one-third of the paste thinly on a surface sprinkled with cornstarch. Cut out two squares using the square fluted cutter. Cut out an oval shape from one square using the plain oval cutter. Make two tiny holes using a No. 2 writing nozzle on the left-hand edge, and match these on the plain square so that the ribbons will meet to tie the card together. Continue to make a cut-out pattern all around the card for the ribbon to thread through. Let stand on a foam pad to dry.

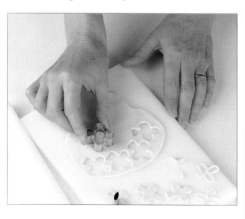

4 ▲ Roll out some more petal paste thinly and, using a club-shaped cocktail cutter, cut out 25 shapes, allowing extras for breakages. Use a tiny petal cutter to cut out three shapes on each piece. Allow to dry.

5 ▲ To make the keys, roll out the paste thinly and cut two end shapes with the club cutter. Then, using a sharp knife, cut out two key shapes. Make a pattern on the keys using tiny cutters. Allow to dry.

6 Fit the pale blue ribbon and the ½-inch royal blue ribbon around the board, securing with a pin. Fit a paper piping bag with a No. 3 writing nozzle and fill with blue icing. Fit the looped ribbon around the side of the cake and secure with a bead of icing.

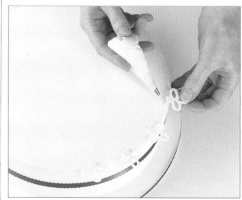

7 ▲ Arrange 18 cut-out sugar pieces around the top edge of the cake and secure each with a bead of icing. Allow to dry. Pipe a shell edging around the base of the cake and beads of icing in between the cut-out pieces around the top edge.

10 Thread the remaining royal blue ribbon (¼ inch) in and out of the cut-out sugar pieces on the top edge of the cake and join the ends together with a bead of icing underneath. Tie a bow and attach it to the side of the cake with a bead of icing. Arrange the card and one key on top of the cake and place the remaining key on the cake board. Secure each with a little icing. Allow the cake to dry.

8 ▲ Using the food coloring pen, write the message on the plain card and decorate the keys.

9 ▲ Thread the ⅛-inch royal blue ribbon through the matching holes to join the card together—do not tie too tightly or the card will not open— and tie a small bow with long ends.

Flower Birthday Cake

A simple birthday cake decorated with piped sugar flowers and ribbons; use any mixture of flowers and ribbons, and pipe a birthday message on the top.

INGREDIENTS
Serves 40
7-inch round Light Fruit Cake
2 tablespoons apricot jam,
warmed and sieved
1½ pounds marzipan
2½ pounds/1⅔ x quantity
Royal Icing
yellow and orange food coloring

MATERIALS AND EQUIPMENT
9-inch round silver cake board
several waxed or parchment
paper piping bags
petal nozzle, No. 1 and 2 writing
nozzles and medium star nozzle
flower nail
white ribbon, ¾ inch wide
coral ribbon, ½ inch and
¼ inch wide

1 Brush the cake with apricot jam and cover with marzipan. Place on the cake board. Allow to dry for 12 hours.

2 Flat-ice the top and side of the cake with three layers of smooth royal icing. Allow the cake to dry, then ice the cake board. Reserve the remaining royal icing for decorating the cake. Store the cake in a box until required.

3 ▲ Snip an inverted V shape off the point of one piping bag. Fit one with a petal nozzle, one with a No. 1 writing nozzle, and another with a medium-sized star nozzle. Color one-third of the icing yellow with yellow food coloring. Color 1 tablespoon of icing orange with orange food coloring. Pipe the narcissi using the petal nozzle for the petals and the plain writing nozzle for the centers: make four white narcissi with yellow centers and nine yellow narcissi with orange centers.

4 ▲ Pipe nine simple white flowers using the snipped bag and add yellow centers with the plain nozzle. Peel the paper off the back of the flowers and arrange them on the top of the cake. Secure each flower with a little icing.

5 ▲ Fill the star nozzle with white icing and pipe a shell edging around the top edge and base of the cake. Using the No. 2 writing nozzle and white icing, pipe the words "Happy Birthday" on the right and left of the flower arrangement. Pipe over the writing using a No. 1 nozzle and some orange icing.

6 ▲ Measure and fit the white ribbon around the cake board and secure with a pin. Fit the coral ribbon around the board and side of the cake, securing with a bead of royal icing. Tie a narrow ribbon bow and attach to the front of the cake with a bead of royal icing. Allow the cake to dry.

Fudge-frosted Starry Roll

*Whether it's a birthday or another occasion you are wanting to celebrate,
this sumptuous looking cake is sure to please.*

INGREDIENTS
Serves 8
1 quantity Jelly Roll mix
½ quantity chocolate-flavor Butter
Icing
2 x 1 oz squares white chocolate
2 x 1 oz squares plain chocolate
1½ x quantity Fudge Frosting

MATERIALS AND EQUIPMENT
9 x 13 inch jelly roll pan
small star cutter
several waxed paper piping bags
No 19 star nozzle

1 Preheat the oven to 350°F. Grease the pan, line the base with waxed paper and grease the paper. Spoon in the cake mixture and gently smooth the surface. Bake for 12–15 minutes, or until springy to the touch.

2 Turn out on to a sheet of waxed paper lightly sprinkled with superfine sugar, peel off the lining paper and roll up the jelly roll, leaving the lining paper inside. When cold, unroll carefully, remove the paper and spread the cake with the butter icing. Re-roll and set aside on a sheet of waxed paper on a wire rack.

3 ▲ To make the chocolate decorations, cover a board with parchment paper and tape it down at each corner. Melt the white chocolate, then pour on to the parchment paper. Spread the chocolate evenly with a spatula and allow to stand until the surface is firm enough to cut, but not so hard that it will break. It should no longer feel sticky when touched with your finger. Press a small star cutter firmly through the chocolate and lift off the paper with a spatula. Set aside.

4 ▲ Melt the plain chocolate and allow to cool slightly. Cover a rolling pin with parchment paper and attach it with tape. Fill a paper piping bag with the chocolate and cut a small piece off the pointed end in a straight line. Pipe lines of chocolate backwards and forwards over the parchment paper, to the size you choose. Make at least nine curls so you have extra in case of breakages. Leave the chocolate lace curls to set in a cool place, then carefully peel off the paper.

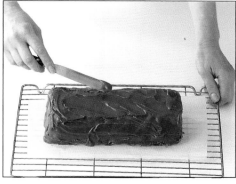

5 ▲ Make the fudge frosting. When cool enough to spread, cover the jelly roll with about two-thirds of it, making swirls with a spatula.

6 ▲ Fit a fresh paper piping bag with the No 19 star nozzle and spoon in the remaining frosting. Pipe diagonal lines, like a twisted rope, on either side of the roll and across both ends.

7 ▲ Position the lace curls in the icing, and arrange the stars. Transfer the cake to a serving plate and decorate with more stars.

The Beautiful Present Cake

For a best friend, mother, grandmother, aunt, or sister, this beautiful cake can mark any special occasion.

INGREDIENTS
Serves 15–20
2 x quantity Quick-Mix Sponge
Cake mix
1 quantity Butter Icing
4 tbsp apricot jam, warmed and
strained
1¼ lb marzipan
2 lb/2⅔ x quantity Sugarpaste Icing
purple and pink food colorings

MATERIALS AND EQUIPMENT
9 in square cake pan
10 in square cake board
heart-shaped cookie cutter
small round fluted cutter
pink food-coloring pen

1 Preheat the oven to 350°F. Grease the pan, line the base and sides with wax paper and grease the paper. Spoon the cake mixture into the prepared pan and smooth the surface. Bake in the center of the oven for 1¼–1½ hours, or until a skewer inserted into the center of the cake comes out clean. Leave the cake in the pan for 5 minutes, then turn out on to a wire rack, peel off the lining paper and leave to cool.

2 Cut the cake in half horizontally and spread with the butter icing. Sandwich the cake together and place in the center of the cake board. Brush the cake with the apricot jam. On a work surface lightly dusted with confectioner's sugar, roll out the marzipan to about a ¼ in thickness and use to cover the cake.

3 Color five-eighths of the sugarpaste icing purple. On a work surface lightly dusted with confectioner's sugar, roll out and use to cover the cake.

4 ▲ Using the heart-shaped cutter, stamp out hearts from the sugarpaste icing to make an even pattern. Remove the hearts with a small, sharp knife, taking care not to damage the surrounding sugarpaste. Knead the hearts together and reserve, wrapped in plastic wrap.

5 ▲ Color the remaining sugarpaste icing pink and roll out to a ¼ in thickness. Using the heart-shaped cutter, cut out as many hearts as you need to fill the spaces left by the purple ones, re-rolling the pink sugarpaste as necessary. Reserve the trimmings, wrapped in plastic wrap. Carefully insert the pink hearts into the spaces.

6 Roll out the reserved pink sugarpaste and cut into three strips about ¾ in wide and 12 in long. Lay one strip across the center of the cake and another at right angles across the center, brushing the strips with a little water to secure. Reserve the trimmings wrapped in plastic wrap.

7 ▲ Divide the remaining strip of pink sugarpaste into quarters and arrange in the center of the cake to make a bow. Secure with a little water and reserve the trimmings.

8 ▲ Roll out the remaining purple and pink sugarpaste and cut out two circles from each color using the small round fluted cutter. With a toothpick, carefully roll out the edges of the circles to make frilled petals. Use a little of the purple sugarpaste to make two tiny balls for the flower centers. Assemble the flowers, securing with a little water and position on the cake. Knead the pink and purple trimmings together, roll out and cut out a name tag. Write a message or a name using the food-coloring pen and position on the cake.

Cloth of Roses Cake

This cake says "congratulations" for whatever reason – passing an exam, getting a new job, getting engaged, or for just achieving a lifelong ambition.

INGREDIENTS
Serves 20–25
8 inch round Light Fruit Cake
3 tbsp apricot jam, warmed and sieved
1½ lb marzipan
2 lb/2⅔ x quantity Sugarpaste Icing
yellow, orange and green food colorings
4oz/⅙ quantity Royal Icing

MATERIALS AND EQUIPMENT
10 inch cake board
2¾ inch plain cutter
petal cutter
thin yellow ribbon

1 Brush the cake with the warmed apricot jam. Roll out the marzipan on a work surface lightly dusted with confectioners' sugar and cover the cake. Leave for 12 hours.

2 Cut off 1½ lb of the sugarpaste icing and divide it in half. Color one-half very pale yellow and the other very pale orange. Wrap separately in plastic wrap and set aside.

3 Cut out a template for the orange icing from waxed paper, as follows. Draw a 10 inch circle using the cake board as a guide. Using the plain cutter, draw half circles 1 inch wide all around the outside of the large circle. Cut out the template.

4 Roll out the yellow sugarpaste icing on a work surface lightly dusted with confectioners' sugar to the same length and height as the side of the cake. Brush the side of the cake with a little water and cover with the sugarpaste icing. Position the cake on the cake board.

5 ▲ Roll out the orange sugarpaste icing to about a 12 inch circle. Place the template on the icing and cut out the scalloped shape.

6 ▲ Brush the top of the cake with water and cover with the orange icing so the scallops fall just over the edge. Bend them slightly to look like a cloth. Leave to dry overnight.

7 Meanwhile make the roses and leaves. Cut off about three-quarters of the remaining sugarpaste icing and divide into four portions. (Wrap the other piece in plastic wrap and reserve for the leaves.) Color the four portions pale yellow, deep yellow, orange, and marbled yellow and orange.

8 ▲ For each rose, dust your fingers with cornstarch, take a small ball of colored icing and form into a cone shape. For each petal, take a small piece of icing and work it with your fingers into a petal shape which is slightly thicker at the base. Wrap the petal around the cone so it sits above the top of it, pressing together to stick. Curl the ends of the petal back. Mold the next petal and attach so it just overlaps the first one. Curl the ends back. Repeat with several more petals, making them slightly larger each time. Cut off the base so the rose will stand on the cake. Make about 18 roses. Leave to dry on waxed paper.

9 ▲ Color the reserved piece of sugarpaste icing green for the leaves. Roll out thinly and cut out leaves with a petal cutter. Make about 24 leaves. Leave to dry on waxed paper.

10 Arrange the leaves and roses, securing with a little royal icing. Decorate the cake with the ribbon.

Double Heart Engagement Cake

For a celebratory engagement party, these sumptuous cakes make the perfect centerpiece.

INGREDIENTS
Serves 20
2 x quantity chocolate-flavor Quick-Mix Sponge Cake mix
12 x 1oz squares plain chocolate
2 x quantity coffee-flavor Butter Icing
confectioners' sugar, for sifting
fresh raspberries, to decorate

MATERIALS AND EQUIPMENT
2 x 8 inch heart-shaped cake pans
2 x 9 inch heart-shaped cake boards

1 Preheat the oven to 325°F. Meanwhile, grease the pans with butter or vegetable oil, line the bases with waxed paper and grease the paper. Divide the cake mixture evenly between the pans and smooth the surfaces. Bake in the center of the oven for 25–30 minutes or until firm to the touch. Turn out on to a wire rack, peel off the lining paper and leave to cool completely.

2 Meanwhile, melt the chocolate in a heatproof bowl over a saucepan of hot water (you may find it easier to work with half the chocolate at a time.) Pour the melted chocolate on to a firm, smooth surface such as a marble or plastic laminate set on a slightly damp cloth to prevent slipping. Spread the chocolate out evenly with a large spatula. Leave the chocolate to cool slightly. It should feel just set, but not hard.

3 ▲ To make the chocolate curls, hold a large sharp knife at a 45° angle to the chocolate and push it along the chocolate in short sawing movements from right to left and left to right. Remove the curls by sliding the point of the knife underneath each one and lifting off. Leave to firm on parchment paper. Repeat with the remaining chocolate.

4 ▲ Cut each of the cakes in half horizontally. Use about one-third of the butter icing to fill both cakes, then sandwich them together.

5 Use the remaining icing to coat the tops and sides of the cakes.

6 ▲ Place the cakes on the cake boards. Generously cover the tops and sides of the cakes with the chocolate curls, pressing them gently into the butter icing.

7 Sift a little confectioners' sugar over each cake and decorate with raspberries. Chill until ready to serve.

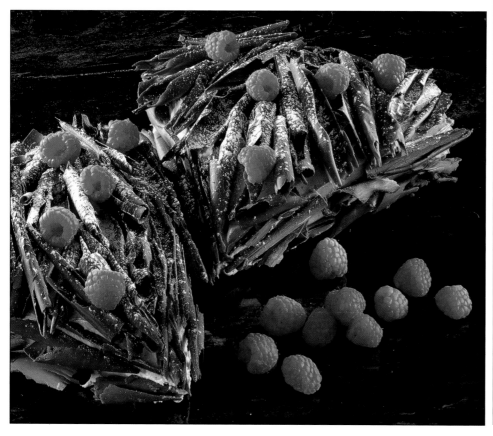

Chocolate-iced Anniversary Cake

This cake is special enough to celebrate any wedding anniversary. Tropical fruits and a glossy chocolate icing make it very appealing for all ages.

4 Cut several chocolate discs into quarters and use to decorate the butter icing.

INGREDIENTS
Serves 12–15
8 inch round Madeira Cake
1½ x quantity chocolate-flavor Butter Icing
1 quantity Satin Chocolate Icing
chocolate discs
selection of fresh fruits, such as kiwi, nectarine or peach, apricot, Cape gooseberries

MATERIALS AND EQUIPMENT
waxed paper piping bag
No 22 star nozzle
thin gold ribbon, about ¼ in wide
florists' wire

3 ▲ Transfer the cake to a serving plate. Fit a paper piping bag with the star nozzle and spoon in the remaining chocolate butter icing. Pipe scrolls around the top edge of the cake.

5 ▲ Prepare the fruit for the top of the cake. Peel and slice the kiwi and cut into quarters, and slice the nectarine or peach, apricot and gooseberries.

6 Arrange the fruit on top of the cake. For each ribbon decoration, make two small loops using the thin gold ribbon. Twist a piece of florists' wire around the ends of the ribbon to secure the loops. Trim the ends of the ribbon. Cut the wire to the length you want and use it to put the loops in position on the cake. Make about seven ribbon decorations. Remove the ribbons and wire before serving.

1 Cut the cake into three horizontal layers and sandwich together with about three-quarters of the chocolate butter icing. Place the cake on a wire rack with a baking sheet underneath.

2 ▲ Make the satin chocolate icing and immediately pour over the cake to coat completely. Working quickly, ease the icing gently over the surface of the cake, using a spatula if necessary. Allow to set.

Rose Blossom Wedding Cake

The traditional white wedding cake, with its classic lines and elegant piping, is still a favorite choice for many brides and grooms.

INGREDIENTS
Serves 80
9 inch square Rich Fruit Cake
6 inch square Rich Fruit Cake
7 tbsp apricot jam, warmed and sieved
3½ lb marzipan
3½ lb/2⅓ x quantity Royal Icing, to coat
1½ lb/1 quantity Royal Icing, to pipe
pink and green food colorings

MATERIALS AND EQUIPMENT
11 inch square cake board
8 inch square cake board
No 1 writing and No 42 nozzles
several waxed paper piping bags
thin pink ribbon
8 pink bows
3–4 cake pillars
about 12 miniature roses
few fern sprigs

1 Brush the cakes with the apricot jam and cover with marzipan, allowing 1 lb marzipan for the 6 inch cake and the remainder for the 9 inch cake. Place the cakes on the cake boards and leave to dry for 12 hours.

2 Make the royal icing for coating the cake. Secure the cakes to the cake boards with a little of the icing. Flat ice the cakes with three or four layers of smooth icing, allowing each layer to dry overnight before applying the next. The royal icing should be very dry before assembling the cake, so it can be made to this stage and stored in cardboard cake boxes for several days.

3 Make the royal icing for piping, and color a small amount pale pink and another small portion pale green. To make the piped sugar pieces, draw the double-triangle design on a piece of waxed paper several times. You will need 40 pieces, but make extra in case of breakages. Tape the paper to a baking sheet or flat board and secure a piece of parchment paper over the top. Tape it down at the corners.

4 ▲ Fit a piping bag with a No 1 writing nozzle. Half-fill with white royal icing and fold over the top to seal. Pipe over each design, carefully following the outlines with a continuous thread of icing. Spoon a little of the pink icing and a little of the green icing into separate paper piping bags fitted with No 1 writing nozzles. Pipe pink dots on the corners of the top triangle in each design and green on the corners of the bottom triangle in each design. Leave to dry for at least two hours.

5 Mark four triangles on the top and side of each cake with a pin. Work from the center of each side, so each triangle is 2½ inches wide at the base and 1½ inches high on the smaller cake, and 3 inches wide at the base and 2 inches high on the larger cake. Fit a paper piping bag with a clean No 1 writing nozzle and half-fill with some of the white icing. Using the pin marks as a guide, pipe double lines to outline the triangles.

6 ▲ Using the same nozzle, pipe cornelli inside all the triangles.

7 ▲ Fit a piping bag with a No 42 nozzle and half-fill with white icing. Pipe shells around the top and bottom edges of each cake, but not within the triangles.

8 Using the piping bags fitted with No 1 writing nozzles and filled with pink and green icing, pipe dots on the corners of each cake.

9 ▲ Remove the piped sugar pieces from the paper by carefully turning it back and lifting off each piece with a spatula. Secure them to the cake and cake board with a little icing.

10 Decorate the cake with the ribbon and bows. Just before serving, assemble the cake with the cake pillars and decorate with the roses and fern sprigs.

*L*ucky Horseshoe

This horseshoe-shaped cake, made to wish "good luck," is made from a round cake and the horseshoe shape is then cut out.

INGREDIENTS
Serves 30–35
10 inch Rich Fruit Cake
4 tbsp apricot jam, warmed and sieved
1¾ lb marzipan
2¼ lb/3 x quantity Sugarpaste Icing
peach and blue food colorings
silver balls
4 oz/⅙ quantity Royal Icing

MATERIALS AND EQUIPMENT
11–12 inch round cake board
crimping tool
large blossom cutter
small blossom cutter
pale blue ribbon, ⅛ in wide

1 Draw a horseshoe shape on a sheet of waxed paper. Cut this shape out of the cake, using the template as a guide. Brush the cake with the apricot jam. Roll out 12 oz of the marzipan to a 10 inch circle on a work surface lightly dusted with confectioners' sugar. Using the template as a guide, cut out the shape and cover the top of the cake with the marzipan. Reserve the trimmings for the inside of the ring.

2 Measure the circumference of the cake as far as the openings of the horseshoe and the height of the side with string. Take the remaining marzipan and roll out for the side, using the string measurement as a guide. Use to cover the side. Using the same method and the reserved trimmings, cover the inside of the horseshoe. Position the cake on the board and leave to dry for 12 hours.

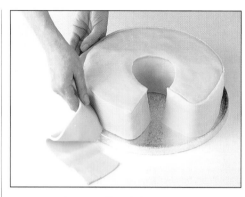

3 ▲ Color 1¾ lb of the sugarpaste icing peach. Brush the marzipan lightly with a little water and cover the cake with the sugarpaste icing in the same way as described for the marzipan, covering first the top, then the side, and finally the inside of the horseshoe shape.

4 Using a crimping tool dipped in cornstarch, carefully crimp the top edge of the cake.

5 Draw and measure the design for the ribbon insertion on the horseshoe template. Cut 13 pieces of pale blue ribbon fractionally longer than the size of each slit.

6 ▲ Place the template on the cake, securing with pins if necessary, and cut through the drawn lines into the icing with a scalpel to make slits for the ribbon. Remove the template.

7 ▲ With the aid of a pointed tool, insert one end of the ribbon into the first slit and the other end into the second slit. Leave a space and repeat, filling all the slits with the pieces of ribbon. Leave to dry for 12 hours.

8 ▲ Draw a small horseshoe shape on a piece of cardboard and cut out. Take the remaining sugarpaste icing and color one-half pale blue and leave the other half white. Roll out the blue icing on a lightly dusted work surface. Using the cardboard template as a guide, cut out nine shapes. Mark small lines around the center of each horseshoe with the knife. Cut out 12 large and 15 small blossoms with the blossom cutters, then press a silver ball into the centers of the larger blossoms. Leave them to dry on waxed paper. Repeat with the white icing.

9 Decorate the cake with the ribbon. Arrange the horseshoes and blossoms on the cake and board, securing with a little royal icing.

*T*ip

Save the discarded section of the round cake to use in the Truffle Mix, if wished. Horseshoe-shaped pans can be purchased or rented from cake decorating specialists.

Golden Wedding Heart Cake

Creamy gold colors, delicate frills and dainty iced blossoms give this cake a special celebratory appeal.

INGREDIENTS
Serves 30
9 inch round Rich Fruit Cake
4 tbsp apricot jam, warmed and sieved
2 lb marzipan
2 lb/2⅔ x quantity Sugarpaste Icing
cream food coloring
4 oz/⅙ quantity Royal Icing

MATERIALS AND EQUIPMENT
11 inch round cake board
crimping tool
small heart-shaped plunger tool
3 inch plain cutter
dual large and small blossom cutter
stamens
frill cutter
foil-wrapped chocolate hearts

1 Brush the cake with apricot jam. Roll out the marzipan on a work surface lightly dusted with confectioners' sugar and use it to cover the cake. Leave to dry for 12 hours.

2 Color 1½ lb of the sugarpaste icing very pale cream. Roll out the icing on a work surface lightly dusted with confectioners' sugar. Brush the marzipan with a little water and cover the cake with the sugarpaste icing. Position the cake on the cake board. Using a crimping tool dipped in cornstarch, carefully crimp the top edge of the cake.

3 ▲ Divide the circumference of the top of the cake into eight equal sections, and stick pins in as markers. Use these as a guide to crimp evenly spaced slanting lines going from the top to the bottom edges of the cake. Using the plunger tool, emboss the bottom edge of the cake. Place the plain cutter lightly in the center of the cake and use as a guide to emboss more hearts in a circle around the cutter. Leave the cake to dry for several hours.

4 ▲ Take the remaining sugarpaste icing and color one-half cream and the other half pale cream. Retain half of each color, and wrap the remainder in plastic wrap. Roll out each color evenly and thinly. Dip the end of the blossom cutter in cornstarch and cut out the flower shapes. Make a pin hole in the center of each larger flower as you make it. Leave to dry on a foam pad. When dry, pipe a little royal icing on to a stamen and thread it through the hole of each larger flower. This will hold it in position. Allow to dry.

5 ▲ To make the frills, roll out the two shades of reserved sugarpaste icing thinly. Using the frill cutter, cut out two rings from each color.

6 ▲ Position the end of a wooden toothpick over ¼ inch of the outer edge of the ring. Roll the toothpick firmly back and forth around the edge with your finger until the edge becomes thinner and begins to frill. Continue until the ring is completely frilled. Repeat with remaining rings. Using a sharp knife, cut each ring in half to make two frills. You should have four frills in each shade.

7 ▲ Using a little water, attach the frills in alternate shades next to the crimped lines running down the side of the cake. Crimp the edges of the deeper colored frills.

8 Arrange the blossom flowers on the top and side of the cake, securing with a little royal icing. Before serving, place the chocolate hearts in the center of the cake.

Trailing Orchid Wedding Cake

A special celebration such as a wedding deserves a very special cake.

INGREDIENTS
Serves 100
12 inch round Madeira
Cake mix
10 inch round Madeira
Cake mix
2 x 1oz squares plain
chocolate
2 x 1oz squares white
chocolate
7½ x quantity Butter Icing
1½ x quantity chocolate-flavor
Butter Icing

MATERIALS AND EQUIPMENT
12 inch oval cake pan
10 inch oval cake pan
about 22 rose leaves
plain scraper
several waxed paper piping bags
No 4 writing and basket-weave
nozzles
14 inch oval thick cake board
10 inch oval thin cake board
orchids

1 Grease the oval cake pans, line with a double thickness of waxed paper and grease the paper. Make the cakes one at a time and bake, following the baking times for the 12 inch and 10 inch round Madeira cakes. Leave to cool slightly in the pan, then turn out on to a wire rack, peel off the lining paper and leave to cool.

2 To make the chocolate leaves, wash and dry the rose leaves well on kitchen paper. Melt the chocolates in two separate heatproof bowls over pans of hot water.

3 ▲ Brush the underside of each leaf, some with plain chocolate and some with the white chocolate. Do not go over to the other side of the leaf. Place the leaves chocolate-side up on baking parchment, and leave to set in a cool place. Peel the leaf from the chocolate. Handle the chocolate as little as possible as the warmth of your hands will melt it. If the chocolate seems too thin then re-coat.

4 Make the butter icings in batches, whisking until smooth. Level off the tops of the cakes if they have domed. Cut each cake in half horizontally, then sandwich each one back together with some of the plain butter icing.

5 Invert each cake on to a board covered with waxed paper. Spread some of the plain butter icing over the sides and smooth with the scraper.

6 ▲ Spread the icing over the top of each cake. To make the surface really smooth, spread the icing with a long metal spatula which has been dipped into hot water.

7 ▲ To pipe the basket-weave design on each cake, spoon some of the chocolate-flavor butter icing into a waxed paper piping bag fitted with a No 4 writing nozzle. (You will need to work in batches with several piping bags). Pipe a vertical line on the side of the cake from the base to the top of the cake. Pipe several more lines.

8 Spoon some of the plain butter icing into a fresh piping bag fitted with a basket-weave nozzle. (You will need to work in batches with several different piping bags). Across the second vertical line of chocolate icing, pipe ¾ inch horizontal lines of basic butter icing, going across the vertical line at ½ inch intervals. You will need about three horizontal lines across each vertical for the smaller cake and three to four for the larger one. Fill in the spaces between the horizontal lines with an alternating row of horizontal lines over the third chocolate vertical. Repeat until the sides of each cake have been completely covered with the design.

9 ▲ Transfer the larger cake to the thick cake board and the smaller cake to the thin one (you should not be able to see the thin board.) Keeping the smaller cake on the thin board, position it on top of the larger cake, to one end. Using a piping bag fitted with a No 4 writing nozzle, pipe beads of chocolate butter icing round the top and bottom edges of each cake. Keep in a cool place overnight. On the day, arrange the chocolate leaves and orchids on the tops of each cake, and keep in a cool place until required.

Chocolate Leaf Wedding Cake

This cake has been designed for lovers of chocolate: a moist chocolate Madeira cake is covered with marzipan and chocolate-flavor sugar paste icing (fondant). The decorations consist of pretty coral-colored sugar flowers and assorted chocolate leaves.

INGREDIENTS
Serves 130

12 x 10-inch oval, deep, chocolate-flavor Madeira Cake (see Tip)
10 x 8-inch oval, deep, chocolate-flavor Madeira Cake
½ cup apricot jam, warmed and sieved
6 pounds marzipan
7 pounds/9 x quantity Sugar paste Icing (Fondant)
4 cups cocoa powder
12 ounces/⅔ quantity Petal Paste
yellow and pink food coloring
1 cup semisweet chocolate chips, melted
¾ cup white chocolate chips, melted
¾ cup milk chocolate chips, melted
4 ounces/⅙ quantity Royal Icing

MATERIALS AND EQUIPMENT

14 x 12-inch oval silver cake board
10 x 8-inch thin oval silver cake board
flower cutter
30 peach pearl stamens
plunger blossom cutter
flower tape and wire
waxed or parchment paper piping bag
No. 1 writing nozzle
peach ribbon, 1 inch and ½ inch wide
coral ribbon, ¼ inch wide
light coral ribbon, ¼ inch wide

To make the cakes

For a 12 x 10-inch and a 10 x 8-inch oval cake, use quantities of cake mix suitable for a 12-inch and a 10-inch round cake. Bake the cakes one at a time and store for up to a week before icing.

1 To level the cakes, cut a slice off the top of each. Invert the cakes onto their cake boards and brush with apricot jam. Cover each cake with marzipan and let dry for 12 hours.

2 Divide the sugar paste icing into three pieces. Knead ½ cup cocoa powder into each piece until the sugar paste icing is evenly colored, then knead all the pieces together. Cover the larger cake using half the sugar paste icing so there is plenty of icing to manipulate, dusting the surface with plenty of cocoa powder and using cocoa powder on your hands to smooth the surface. Repeat to cover the smaller cake and the large cake board. Store the cakes in boxes in a warm, dry place for up to a week.

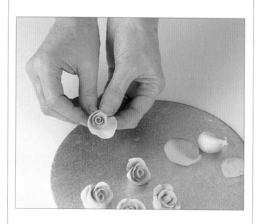

3 ▲ To make the sugar flowers, divide the petal paste into three pieces. Using the yellow and pink food colorings, tint one piece pale, one piece medium and one piece dark coral. Make five roses, starting with dark centers and working out to pale petals.

4 Make 25 cut-out flowers of varying shades of coral paste and add stamens.

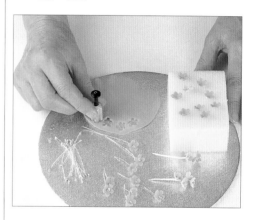

5 ▲ Make 40 plunger blossom flower sprays with the remaining stamens, wire and tape. Allow all the flowers to dry overnight and store in boxes in a warm, dry place. Using a piece of petal paste, press 30 blossom sprays in position to make an arrangement for the top of the cake.

Tip

To make a 12 x 10-inch chocolate-flavor Madeira Cake, use 5½ cups all-purpose flour plus ¼ cup cocoa powder in place of the full amount of all-purpose flour. For a 10 x 8-inch cake, use 4 cups all-purpose flour plus ½ cup cocoa powder.

6 ▲ To make the chocolate leaves, collect a variety of different-shaped leaves (rose, bay, camellia, fruit) and coat 30 with plain chocolate, 15 with white chocolate and 15 with milk chocolate. Store in a cool place until required, then peel off the leaves and keep the chocolate leaves separate on paper towels.

7 The day before the wedding, place the royal icing in a paper piping bag fitted with a No. 1 writing nozzle. Measure and fit the 1-inch-wide peach ribbon around the larger cake board, securing it at the back with a pin. Fit the ½-inch-wide peach ribbon around the base of the larger cake. Fix the coral ribbon over the top, and secure with a bead of royal icing. Arrange the cut-out flowers, roses and assorted chocolate leaves around the base of the cake, securing with royal icing.

8 Measure and fit another length of the ½-inch-wide peach ribbon around the base of the small cake with another coral ribbon over the top, securing with royal icing. Carefully place the cake in position on top of the larger cake so that the backs of the cakes are level.

9 Arrange the sprays of blossom, cut-out flowers and chocolate leaves at intervals around the base of the small cake on the edge of the larger cake. Secure all decorations with royal icing. Carefully remove the top cake. Place the sugar flower arrangement on the top of the cake and arrange the chocolate leaves so they come over the edge. Secure each leaf with royal icing. Using the remaining coral ribbon, the light coral ribbon and fine wire, make some ribbon loops with tails. Press these into the arrangement. Re-box the cakes until the next day, then reassemble just before the reception.

Classic Wedding Cake

The sharp, classical lines of this royal-iced wedding cake give it a very regal appearance. This traditional all-white cake has just a hint of peach in the ribbon decoration.

INGREDIENTS
Serves 100
12-inch square Rich Fruit Cake
5 tablespoons apricot jam,
warmed and sieved
4 pounds marzipan
4½ pounds/3 x quantity
Royal Icing (for covering)
2 pounds/1⅓ x quantity Royal Icing
made with double-strength egg
albumen (for run-outs)

MATERIALS AND EQUIPMENT
14-inch square silver cake board
a sheet of Plexiglas® or glass
baking parchment
waxed or parchment paper piping
bag
white ribbon, 1 inch wide
peach ribbon, ¾ inch and
¼ inch wide
No. 3 plain writing nozzle
medium star nozzle
fresh "paper white" flowers
tiny vase

1 Brush the cake with apricot jam and cover with marzipan. Place the cake on the cake board and allow to dry for 12 hours.

2 Make the royal icing for covering the cake. Flat-ice the top and sides of the cake with three or four smooth layers of royal icing. Allow the cake to dry overnight, then ice the cake board. Place in a cake box and store in a warm, dry place. Reserve the remaining royal icing for decoration.

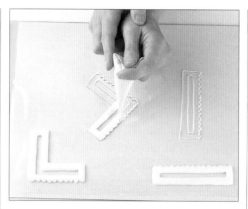

3 ▲ Make the royal icing for the run-outs, unless you have plenty left over from the flat icing, in which case add double-strength egg albumen to dilute it. Draw templates for the side and corner pieces, cover with a piece of plexiglass or glass, and cover with baking parchment. Tape down to secure. As each run-out is piped and filled in, move the Plexiglas® or glass along to reveal the template, and repeat the procedure.

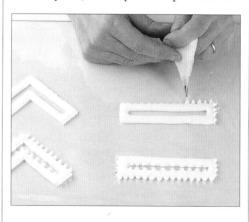

4 ▲ Make six corner pieces and six side pieces, allowing for breakages. Pipe in the details when dry.

5 Measure and fit the white and ¾-inch peach ribbons around the cake board and sides of the cake, securing with beads of royal icing. Make some loops and bows from ¼-inch peach ribbon for the top arrangement.

6 ▲ Carefully release the run-out pieces and half-fill a paper piping bag fitted with a No. 3 writing nozzle with the reserved royal icing. Pipe a line of icing at one corner. Carefully place a corner run-out in position; press very gently to make sure the run-out is secure. Repeat to attach all the corner pieces and the side pieces.

7 ▲ Pipe a bead edging in between the run-outs on the top edge of the cake. Using a medium-sized star nozzle, pipe a star edging around the base of the cake. Make a pretty arrangement of fresh flowers in a tiny vase to go on top of the cake, and decorate with thin peach ribbons and bows.

*M*idsummer Wedding Cake

This lovely meringue wedding cake is fresh and light, and is ideal for a summer wedding when all the soft fruits are in abundance. Picking your own fruits will add an extra personal touch.

INGREDIENTS
Serves 40
8 egg whites
1 teaspoon cream of tartar
2¼ cups superfine sugar
2½ cups heavy cream
1¼ cups whipping cream
2 cups red currants
2 cups white currants
2 cups raspberries
2 cups fraises des bois or
tiny strawberries
2 cups blueberries
2 tablespoons kirsch

MATERIALS AND EQUIPMENT
4 large baking sheets
baking parchment
nylon piping bags
½-inch plain and small star nozzles
looped white ribbon,
¾ inch wide
looped dark pink ribbon,
½ inch wide
12-inch round silver cake board
8 tiny pink rosebuds
plain dark pink ribbon,
¼ inch wide
plain light pink ribbon,
¼ inch wide
small fresh strawberry leaves

1 Preheat the oven to 225°F. Line two large baking sheets with baking parchment. Draw a 10-inch circle on one sheet and 7-inch and 6-inch circles on the remaining sheet of paper. Invert the sheets of paper.

2 To make the meringue, whisk 4 egg whites and ½ teaspoon cream of tartar until stiff. Gradually whisk in 1 generous cup of sugar, whisking well between each addition, until the meringue stands up in stiff peaks. Place the meringue in a large nylon piping bag fitted with a ½-inch plain nozzle.

3 ▲ Pipe a continuous circle of meringue following the marked lines on each circle. Then pipe a coil from the center to the edge to fill in each round. Pipe leftover meringue into 5 small rounds in between the circles. Bake for 2–3 hours, until the meringue is dry and the paper peels away easily.

4 Meanwhile line two more baking sheets with baking parchment and draw a 9-inch, a 4-inch and a 2-inch circle on one sheet of paper and an 8-inch, a 5-inch and a 3-inch circle on the remaining sheet of paper. Invert the two papers.

5 Using the remaining egg whites, cream of tartar and sugar, make the meringue circles following the above instructions. When all the meringues are cool, cut around the paper to separate them. Store them in airtight containers on the paper in a warm, dry place until required.

6 ▲ Measure and fit the white and the wide pink ribbons around the edge of the cake board, securing them with a pin.

7 Place the creams in a bowl and whip until just thick; reserve one-third for piping. Whisk the remaining cream until slightly thicker.

8 ▲ Reserve several stems of red and white currants for decoration and remove the stems and hulls from the remaining fruits. Mix all the fruits together in a large bowl and sprinkle with kirsch. Add the fruit to the cream and fold in until well blended. Place one-third of the reserved cream in a nylon piping bag fitted with a small star nozzle.

9 ▲ Place the largest circle of meringue on the cake board and spread evenly with the cream and fruit mixture to give about a ¾-inch-deep layer. Top with the next size of meringue round and spread with more of the filling. Cover with the next meringue layer and repeat to use all the layers.

10 ▲ Pipe small stars of cream in between the layers to seal in the filling and to decorate the joins. Pipe a swirl of cream on the top and arrange 4 tiny meringue rounds in a circle and one on the top.

11 ▲ Press red currants or other fruits into alternate cream stars and 4 tiny rosebuds around the top. Fit 3 dark and 3 light ribbon lengths from the top of the cake to the board. Decorate the board with reserved currants, leaves and rosebuds. Keep in a cold place for 4 hours.

Basket Weave Wedding Cake

This wonderful wedding cake can be made in any flavor. The butter icing design is really very easy and looks so special.

INGREDIENTS
Serves 150
10-inch, 8-inch and 6-inch square Madeira Cake
6 pounds/8 x quantity Butter Icing

MATERIALS AND EQUIPMENT
12-inch square cake board
8-inch thin cake board
6-inch thin cake board
12 waxed or parchment paper piping bags
basket and No. 4 writing nozzles
lilac ribbon, 1 inch wide
deep lilac ribbon, ¼ inch wide
30 fresh freesias or other flowers

1 Make and bake the cakes one at a time, allow to cool, wrap in foil and store in a tin for up to a week before decorating. If the cake tops have domed, cut off a slice to level them, then invert the cakes onto their appropriate cake boards.

2 Make the icing in three batches. A food processor is worth using to obtain a very light texture and well-mixed icing. Spread each cake evenly with icing, dipping the baking spatula in hot water for easy spreading. Use a side scraper to smooth the sides and the spatula to smooth the top. Allow to set in a cool place for at least one hour.

Tip

It is a good idea to buy two larger thin cake boards to sit the smaller cakes on while they are being decorated, to keep the edges neat. Allow an extra 1–2 inches.

3 Fit a basket-weave nozzle in one piping bag and a No. 4 writing nozzle in a second bag. Fill each with icing and fold down the tops.

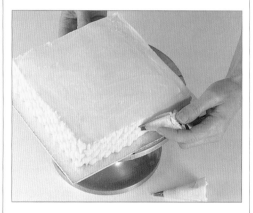

4 ▲ Start piping the basket-weave design by piping a line of icing from the plain nozzle onto the corner of the large cake, from the base of the cake to the top. Using the basket-weave nozzle, pipe three horizontal lines across the vertical line, starting at the top of the cake and equally spacing the lines apart. Pipe another vertical line of icing on the edge of the horizontal lines, then pipe three horizontal lines across this between the spaces formed by the previous horizontal lines to form a basket weave. Pipe all around the side of the cake and neaten the top edge with a shell border, using the basket-weave nozzle. Repeat for the second cake.

5 To decorate the small cake with piping, pipe the top first by starting on the edge with one straight plain line, then pipe across with the basket-weave nozzle, spacing the lines equally apart, about the width of the nozzle. When the top is complete, continue working the design around the sides, making sure the top and side designs meet. Allow all the cakes to set overnight in a cold place before assembling.

6 Measure and fit the wide and narrow lilac ribbons around the large board, securing with a pin. Use more narrow ribbon to tie eight small bows with long tails. Select the flowers and trim off the stems.

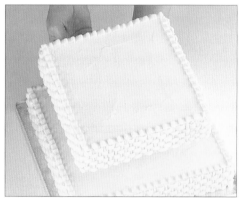

7 ▲ Carefully place the middle cake, still on its board, in position on the base cake. Use a baking spatula at the back of the cake to position it. Place the top cake on its board in position, using the baking spatula at the back.

8 ▲ Position the bows on the top and bottom corners of the cake. Place the flowers on each side of each cake, at the corners of the board and in a tiny arrangement on the top. Keep in a cool place; if the weather is warm, position the flowers at the last minute.

Champagne Wedding Cake

An unusual combination of colors—champagne sugar paste icing (fondant) and coffee-colored ribbons and decorations—gives this cake an elegant, delicate appearance.

INGREDIENTS
Serves 120
10-inch, 8-inch and 6-inch round
Rich Fruit Cake
½ cup apricot jam,
warmed and sieved
5½ pounds marzipan
7 pounds/9½ x quantity
champagne-colored
Sugar paste Icing (Fondant)
1 pound/⅔ quantity Royal Icing
1¼ pounds/1 quantity Petal Paste
old gold and dark brown
food coloring

MATERIALS AND EQUIPMENT
12-inch, 10-inch and 8-inch
round silver cake boards
waxed or parchment paper piping
bags
No. 0 and 1 writing nozzles
champagne ribbon, ¾ inch wide
waxed or parchment paper
coffee ribbon, ½ inch wide
frill cutter
crimping tool
coffee ribbon, ¼ inch wide
champagne ribbon, ¼ inch wide
6 champagne-colored cake pillars
5 acrylic cake skewers
fresh cream or white flowers

1 Place each cake on its cake board and brush with apricot jam. Cover each cake with marzipan.

2 Reserving 2½ x quantity sugar paste icing for the cake boards, use the remainder to cover each cake smoothly, starting with the largest cake. Let stand in boxes overnight to dry in a warm, dry place, without the cake boards. Knead enough sugar paste icing and trimmings together to cover the cake boards. Replace the cakes on their boards and return to their boxes.

3 Make the royal icing and the petal paste. Tint both these icings with old gold food coloring to obtain the same champagne color of the sugar paste icing. Half-fill a paper piping bag fitted with a No. 1 writing nozzle with royal icing. Measure and fit the wide champagne-colored ribbon around each cake board, securing it with a pin.

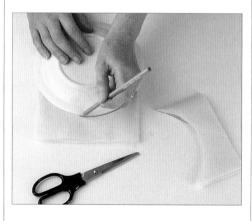

4 ▲ To make the templates, measure and fit a band of waxed or parchment paper the same height around each cake. Fold the largest strip of paper into six equal sections, the next size into five sections and the small band into four sections. Place a plate on the edge of each template so that it comes halfway down the width. Draw around the shape and cut out.

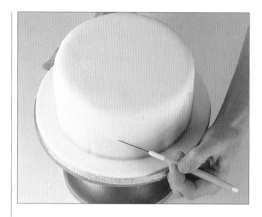

5 ▲ Fit the appropriate template around each cake and mark the scalloped shape with an icing marker or pin. Remove the template. Fit the wide coffee-colored ribbon around the base of each cake and secure with a bead of royal icing.

6 ▲ Knead the remaining sugar paste icing into the petal paste and, using a small piece at a time, make the frills one at a time. On the large cake pipe a line of icing following the design and apply the frill, pressing gently onto the cake. Once the first six frills have been fitted, apply the second layer of frills. Use a crimping tool to neaten the join. Repeat on each cake.

7 ▲ Pipe the bead and scroll design following the top edge of the frills and in between the frills at the base. Color some of the royal icing dark brown and pipe over the design using a No. 0 writing nozzle. Tie 15 coffee-colored bows and 15 champagne-colored bows made from the fine ribbons and attach above and below the frills, where they join. Leave the cakes in their boxes to dry.

8 ▲ Just before the wedding, place the cake pillars in position on the large and middle tier cakes. Press the skewers through the pillars into the cake. Mark the skewers level with the top of the pillars and carefully remove. Cut off the excess skewer above the pillars. Reassemble the cakes with the skewers and pillars, carefully placing each cake on top of the other. Decorate with a fresh flower arrangement on top of the cake and insert flowers between the pillars.

Golden Wedding Cake

For 50 years of marriage, you must have a special cake. With a fine lace edging, embossed horseshoes, bells and flowers, this anniversary cake will be exactly right.

INGREDIENTS
Serves 80
9-inch hexagonal Rich Fruit Cake
(make using quantities for a
standard 9-inch round cake)
3 tablespoons apricot jam,
warmed and sieved
2½ pounds marzipan
3 pounds/4 x quantity champagne-
colored Sugar paste Icing (Fondant)
gold petal dust
13 ounces/⅔ quantity Petal Paste
old gold food coloring
1 pound/⅔ quantity Royal Icing

MATERIALS AND EQUIPMENT
11-inch hexagonal gold cake board
gold ribbon, 1 inch wide
gold ribbon, ¾ inch wide
horseshoe-shaped embossing tool
bell mold
foam pad
plunger blossom cutter
flower stamens
wire and tape
sheet of Plexiglas® or glass
baking parchment
waxed or parchment paper piping
bag
No. 0 writing nozzle
30 gold balls
"50" gold emblem
6 gold paper leaves

1 Brush the cake with apricot jam, place on the cake board and cover with marzipan. Using three-quarters of the sugar paste icing, cover the cake smoothly.

2 Fit the wide ribbon around the base of the cake and secure with a pin. Measure and fit the narrower ribbon around the cake board, securing with a pin.

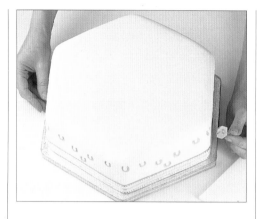

3 ▲ Using a horseshoe-shaped embossing tool and gold petal dust, emboss the sides of the cake with five horseshoes on each side and one on each corner. Place the cake in a box and allow to dry in a warm place.

4 Tint the petal paste to a champagne color using old gold food color. Fill a well-cornstarched bell mold with a small piece of petal paste, pressing into the mold and rubbing the paste against the mold to make the shape. Trim off the paste at the edge and tap to release.

5 Make three bells using two-thirds of the petal paste and let dry on a foam pad. Dust with gold petal dust when dry. Reserve just a little petal paste.

6 Using the remaining paste, blossom plunger and stamens, wire and tape, make up nine sprays of blossoms and allow to dry.

7 ▲ Tint the royal icing a champagne color with old gold food color. Draw the lace design on a sheet of paper and cover with a sheet of Plexiglas® or glass. Cover this with a piece of baking parchment and secure with tape. Half-fill a paper piping bag fitted with a No. 0 writing nozzle with icing. Follow the lace shapes, piping with fine threads of icing. Move the lace designs and repeat to make 40 pieces, allowing for breakages.

8 Attach the lace pieces to the top edge of the cake with a few beads of icing. Secure gold balls in between, using icing to fix on. Press a small piece of petal paste into each bell shape and secure three sprays of blossoms just inside each bell opening. Arrange the bells in the center of the cake, tilting them and supporting them on tiny pieces of petal paste.

9 Arrange lengths of 1-inch gold ribbon in loops and secure in the center of the bells, with the "50" emblem on top. Place the leaves in pairs between the bells and secure with royal icing. Allow to set.

Silver Wedding Cake

This may look difficult, but it is really a simple cake to decorate once all the sugar pieces have been made.

INGREDIENTS
Serves 80
10-inch round Rich or
Light Fruit Cake
4 tablespoons apricot jam,
warmed and sieved
2½ pounds marzipan
3 pounds/2 x quantity Royal Icing
1¼ pounds/1 quantity Petal Paste

MATERIALS AND EQUIPMENT
12-inch round silver cake board
white ribbon, 1 inch wide
silver ribbon, 1 inch wide
club cocktail cutter
tiny round cutter
waxed or parchment paper piping
bag
No. 1 writing nozzle
50 large silver balls (dragées)
silver ribbon, ¼ inch wide
7 silver leaves
"25" silver emblem

1 Brush the cake with apricot jam and cover with marzipan. Place the cake on the cake board and set aside for 12 hours to dry.

2 Flat-ice the top and sides of the cake with three or four smooth layers of royal icing. Allow to dry overnight, then ice the cake board. Place the cake in a box and dry in a warm, dry place. Reserve the remaining royal icing for decorations.

3 Measure and fit the white ribbon around the cake board and the wide silver ribbon around the side of the cake; secure with a bead of icing.

4 ▲ Roll out small pieces of petal paste one at a time very thinly and, using a club cocktail cutter, cut out the sugar pieces. Using a tiny round cutter, cut four holes out of each sugar piece. Make about 65 cut-out sugar pieces, allowing for breakages, and dry flat overnight.

5 ▲ Arrange 25 cut-out pieces around the top of the cake so that they fit evenly. Half-fill a piping bag fitted with a No. 1 plain writing nozzle with royal icing. Pipe small beads of icing onto the top edge of the cake and fit the sugar pieces in position. Repeat at the base of the cake, tilting the pieces upward slightly. Pipe beads of icing between the sugar pieces and press a silver ball in position on each. Let the cake dry in a box overnight.

6 ▲ Measure the narrow silver ribbon to fit around the top edge of the sugar pieces, allowing enough to join. Very carefully thread the ribbon in and out of the sugar pieces, joining the ribbon at the back underneath the sugar pieces.

7 ▲ Arrange a circle of seven sugar pieces in the center of the cake and secure each one with a bead of icing with seven silver balls in between. Thread a length of narrow ribbon through the sugar pieces as before. Place the silver leaves and "25" emblem in position and secure with icing.

Bluebird Bon Voyage Cake

This cake is sure to see someone off on an exciting journey in a very special way.

INGREDIENTS
Serves 12–15
1 lb/²⁄₃ quantity Royal Icing
blue food coloring
1³⁄₄ lb/2¹⁄₃ x quantity Sugarpaste
Icing
8 inch round Madeira Cake
1 quantity Butter Icing
3 tbsp apricot jam, warmed and
sieved
silver balls

MATERIALS AND EQUIPMENT
10 inch round cake board
waxed paper piping bags
No 1 writing nozzle
thin pale blue ribbon

1 Make up the royal icing, keeping about two-thirds softer for filling in, and the rest stiffer for the outlines and further piping. Color the softer icing blue. Cover the icings and leave them overnight. Stir before using.

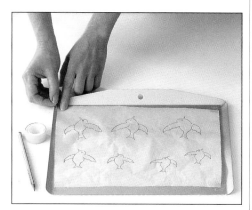

2 ▲ On waxed paper, draw the birds several times in two sizes. Tape the paper to a baking sheet with masking tape, then secure a piece of parchment paper over the top.

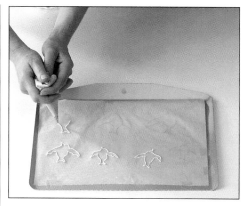

3 ▲ Fit a paper piping bag with a No 1 writing nozzle and spoon in some of the stiffer icing for piping the outlines. Pipe over the outlines of the birds with a continuous thread of icing.

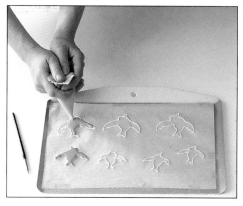

4 ▲ Half-fill a fresh paper piping bag with the blue icing. Cut the pointed end off the bag in a straight line. Do not make the opening too large or the icing will flow too quickly. Pipe the icing into the outlines to fill, working from the outlines into the center. Do not touch the outlines or they may break. To prevent air bubbles, keep the end of the bag in the icing. The icing should look overfilled and rounded, as it will shrink slightly as it dries.

5 Working quickly, brush through the icing to fill in any gaps and to ensure it goes right to the outlines. If any air bubbles appear, smooth them out or burst with a pin. Leave the run-outs on the paper for two days to dry.

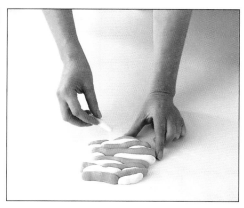

6 ▲ Color two-thirds of the sugar-paste icing blue and leave the rest white. Form the icing into small rolls and place them together on a work surface lightly dusted with confectioners' sugar, alternating the colors. Form into a round and lightly knead together until the icing is marbled. Do not over-knead or you will lose the effect. Cut off about one-quarter of the sugarpaste icing, wrap in plastic wrap and set aside.

7 Cut the cake horizontally into three even layers and sandwich together with the butter icing. Brush with the apricot jam. Roll out the marbled sugarpaste icing and use it to cover the cake. Roll out the reserved sugarpaste icing to a 10 inch circle and use it to cover the cake board.

8 ▲ Position the cake to one edge of the board. Fit a piping bag with the writing nozzle and half-fill with the remaining stiffer royal icing. Pipe a wavy line all around the edge of the cake board. Working quickly before the icing dries, position the silver balls so they are evenly spaced in the icing.

9 Remove the birds from the waxed paper using a spatula and secure them to the cake with a little royal icing. Pipe a bead of white icing on each for the eye and place a silver ball in the center. Drape the ribbon between the birds' beaks, securing it with a little icing.

$\mathcal{P}$ansy Retirement Cake

Sugar-frosted edible flowers make a very effective cake decoration. If pansies are not in season, use other edible flowers such as nasturtiums, roses or tiny daffodils to wish someone a happy retirement. Just co-ordinate the color of the icing, piping and ribbon with the color of the flowers.

INGREDIENTS
Serves 20–25
8 inch round Light Fruit Cake
3 tbsp apricot jam, warmed and sieved
1½ lb marzipan
2½ lb/1²/₃ x quantity Royal Icing
orange food coloring
1 large egg white, lightly beaten
sugar, for frosting
about 7 pansies (orange and purple)

MATERIALS AND EQUIPMENT
10 inch round cake board
2 waxed paper piping bags
No 19 star and No 1 writing nozzles
³/₄ inch wide purple ribbon
¹/₈ inch wide dark purple ribbon

1 Brush the cake with the apricot jam. Roll out the marzipan on a work surface which is lightly dusted with confectioners' sugar and cover the cake. Leave to dry for 12 hours.

2 Secure the cake to the cake board with a little of the royal icing. Color one-quarter of the royal icing pale orange. Flat ice the cake with three or four layers of smooth icing, allowing each layer to dry overnight before applying the next, using the orange icing for the top and the white for the sides. Set aside a little of both icings in airtight containers, to decorate the cake.

3 ▲ To sugar-frost the pansies, have ready a small mixing bowl with the egg white and a small plate with sugar. Dry the pansies on paper towels. If possible, leave some stem attached. Evenly brush the pansies all over on both sides of the petals with the egg white. Holding the flowers by their stems, sprinkle them evenly with the sugar, then shake off any excess. Place the frosted flowers on a flat board or wire rack covered with waxed paper or paper towels and leave to dry in a warm place overnight.

4 ▲ Spoon the reserved white royal icing into a waxed paper piping bag fitted with a No 19 star nozzle. Carefully pipe a row of scrolls around the top of the cake.

5 ▲ Reverse the direction of the scrolls and pipe another row directly underneath the first row.

6 ▲ Pipe another row of scrolls around the bottom of the cake. Spoon the reserved orange icing into a fresh piping bag fitted with a No 1 writing nozzle. Pipe around the outline of the top of each scroll.

7 Using the same piping bag, pipe a row of single dots underneath the top row of reverse scrolls and a double row of dots above the bottom row of scrolls. Arrange the sugar-frosted pansies on top of the cake. Decorate with the ribbons, centering the narrow, darker ribbon on top of the wider one.

$\mathcal{R}$etirement Cake

This easily decorated hexagonal cake bears good wishes for a happy retirement. With its simple lines and stylish appearance, it would be equally suitable for a man or a woman.

INGREDIENTS
Serves 80
10½-inch hexagonal Rich Fruit Cake
(make using quantities for a standard
10-inch round cake)
3 tablespoons apricot jam,
warmed and sieved
2½ pounds marzipan
3 pounds/4 x quantity
Sugar paste Icing (Fondant)
ice-blue food coloring
4 ounces/⅙ quantity Royal Icing

MATERIALS AND EQUIPMENT
12-inch hexagonal silver
cake board
3-inch square fluted cutter
No. 3 writing nozzle
wooden dowel
light green looped ribbon,
¾ inch wide
dark green looped ribbon,
¼ inch wide
light green looped ribbon,
¼ inch wide
light green ribbon, ⅛ inch wide
dark green ribbon, ⅛ inch wide
food-color pen

1 Brush the cake with apricot jam. Cover with marzipan.

2 ▲ Add a few drops of blue food coloring to the sugar paste icing.

3 ▲ Only partially knead in the color to create a marbled effect. Cover the cake with the marbled sugar paste icing and allow to set overnight.

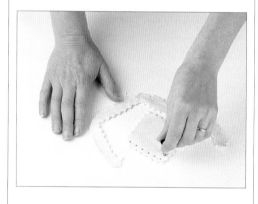

4 ▲ Remove the cake from the board. Press the sugar paste icing trimmings together and use to cover the cake board. Replace the cake carefully on the cake board and allow to dry. Roll out the remaining trimmings and cut out a square using the fluted cutter. Make small holes around the border using a No. 3 writing nozzle.

5 Allow to dry over a small piece of wooden dowel to shape.

6 ▲ Measure and fit the ¾-inch-wide light green looped ribbon around the cake board and secure with a pin. Measure and fit the ¼-inch-wide dark green looped ribbon around the board, base and the top of the cake. Secure with beads of royal icing. Cut six lengths of light and six lengths of dark green ¼-inch looped ribbon the depth of the cake. Fit one strip of each colored ribbon 2 inches in from one corner on each side of the cake. Secure with beads of icing behind the bands of ribbon. Attach fine ribbon bows to the side ribbons.

7 Cut two strips of each ribbon to fit parallel across the top of the cake, leaving a space in the center. Secure with beads of royal icing.

8 Using a food color pen, write the message or name on the plaque and place on the cake. Attach two bows to the sugar plaque. Thread the fine dark green ribbon in and out of the plaque and secure the ends underneath with icing. Attach fine ribbon bows to the top of the cake with beads of icing.

Cakes for Entertaining

For the host eager to create the right impression, this chapter contains cakes that cannot fail to win over even the most demanding of social gatherings. Featuring sumptuous desserts for dinner parties, from cappuccino cakes to luxurious white chocolate cheesecakes, these recipes will guarantee a spectacular finale to any meal.

Chocolate Chestnut Roulade

A traditional version of the classic Bûche de Nöel, the famous and delicious French Christmas gâteau.

INGREDIENTS
Serves 6–8
8 x 1 oz squares plain chocolate
2 x 1 oz squares white chocolate
4 large eggs, separated
½ cup superfine sugar, plus extra for dredging

For the Chestnut Filling
⅔ cup heavy cream
1 x 8 oz can chestnut purée
4–5 tbsp confectioners' sugar, plus extra for dredging
1–2 tbsp brandy

1 Preheat the oven to 350°F. Grease a 9 x 13 inch jelly roll pan, line with waxed paper and grease the paper.

2 Place 2 oz of the plain chocolate and the white chocolate in two bowls and set over saucepans of hot water. Stir until melted.

3 ▲ Pour the plain chocolate on to a plastic chopping board and spread out evenly. When just set, do the same with the white chocolate. Leave to set.

4 To make the chocolate curls, hold a long, sharp knife at a 45° angle to the chocolate and push it along the chocolate, turning the knife in a circular motion. Carefully place the plain and white chocolate curls on a baking sheet lined with waxed paper and set aside until needed.

5 ▲ Place the remaining plain chocolate in another bowl set over a saucepan of hot water and stir until melted. Set aside. Place the egg yolks and superfine sugar in a mixing bowl and beat with electric beaters until thick and pale. Stir in the chocolate.

6 Whisk the egg whites in a clean dry bowl, until they hold stiff peaks. Fold into the chocolate mixture and then turn into the prepared pan. Bake in the center of the oven for 15–20 minutes, or until risen and firm. Place on a wire rack, cover with a just-damp cloth and leave to cool completely.

7 Place a sheet of waxed paper on the work surface and sprinkle with a little superfine sugar. Turn the roulade out on to the waxed paper. Peel away the lining paper and trim the edges of the roulade. Cover again with a just-damp cloth.

8 To make the filling, whip the heavy cream in a mixing bowl, until it holds soft peaks.

9 ▲ Place the chestnut purée and confectioners' sugar in a clean bowl. Add the brandy and beat until smooth and evenly combined, then fold in the whipped cream.

10 ▲ Spread the mixture over the roulade, leaving a little border at the top edge. Roll up the roulade, using the waxed paper to help, and transfer it to a serving plate. Top with the chocolate curls and sprinkle with sifted confectioners' sugar, to serve.

Chocolate Gâteau Terrine

A spectacular finale to a special occasion meal.
You'll find this is well worth the time and effort to make.

INGREDIENTS
Serves 10–12
1/2 cup butter, softened
few drops of vanilla extract
1/2 cup sugar
2 large eggs
1 cup self-rising flour, sifted
1/4 cup milk
1/2 cup shredded coconut, to
decorate
fresh bud roses, or other flowers, to
decorate

For the Light Chocolate Filling
1/2 cup butter, softened
2 tbsp confectioners' sugar, sifted
3 x 1oz squares plain chocolate,
melted
1 cup heavy cream, lightly whipped

For the Dark Chocolate Filling
4 x 1oz squares plain chocolate,
chopped
1/2 cup butter
2 large eggs
2 tbsp sugar
1 cup heavy cream, lightly whipped
1/2 cup cocoa powder
1 tbsp dark rum (optional)
2 tbsp gelatine powder dissolved in
2 tbsp hot water

For the White Chocolate Topping
8 x 1oz squares white chocolate
1/2 cup butter

1 Preheat the oven to 350°F. Meanwhile, grease a 2 lb loaf pan, line the base and sides with waxed paper and grease the paper.

2 To make the cake, place the butter, vanilla extract and sugar in a mixing bowl and beat until light and fluffy. Add the eggs, one at a time, beating well after each addition. Sift the flour again and fold it and the milk into the cake mixture.

3 Transfer the cake mixture to the prepared pan and bake in the center of the oven for 25–30 minutes or until a skewer inserted into the center of the cake comes out clean. Leave the cake in the pan for about 5 minutes, then turn out on to a wire rack, peel off the lining paper and leave to cool completely.

4 ▲ To make the light chocolate filling, place the butter and confectioners' sugar in a mixing bowl and beat until creamy. Add the chocolate and cream until evenly blended. Cover and set aside in the

5 To make the dark chocolate filling, place the chocolate and butter in a small saucepan and heat very gently, stirring frequently, until melted. Set aside to cool. Place the eggs and sugar in a bowl and beat with an electric mixer until thick and frothy. Fold in the cream, cocoa, rum and dissolved gelatine until evenly blended.

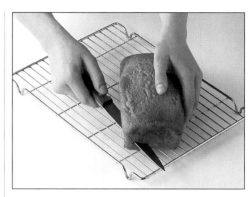

6 ▲ To assemble the terrine, wash and dry the loaf pan, then line with plastic wrap, allowing plenty of wrap to hang over the edges. Using a long serrated knife, cut the cake horizontally into three even layers.

7 ▲ Spread two of the layers with the light chocolate filling, then place one of these layers, filling side up, in the base of the pan.

8 Cover with half of the dark chocolate filling, then chill for about 10 minutes. Place the second light chocolate-topped layer in the terrine, filling side up. Spread over the remaining dark chocolate filling, then chill for another 10 minutes. Top with the remaining layer of cake and chill the terrine again for about 10 minutes.

9 To make the white chocolate topping, place the chocolate and butter in a small saucepan and heat very gently, stirring frequently, until melted and well blended. Allow the topping to cool slightly.

10 To finish the terrine, turn it out on to a wire rack, removing the plastic wrap. Trim the edges with a long, sharp knife, then pour over the white chocolate topping, spreading it evenly over the sides. Sprinkle the coconut over the top and sides. Allow to set before transferring the terrine to a serving plate and decorating with fresh bud roses.

Chocolate and Fresh Cherry Cake

The addition of spices to this attractive cake adds an exotic kick. A compote of fresh cherries fills the hollowed-out center, and the cake is coated with a rich chocolate icing. With the dipped cherries and chocolate-coated leaves, this is a cake for a special occasion.

INGREDIENTS
Serves 8
8 tablespoons (½ cup) unsalted butter
⅔ cup superfine sugar
3 eggs, lightly beaten
1 cup semisweet chocolate chips, melted
4 tablespoons kirsch
1¼ cups self-rising flour
1 teaspoon ground cinnamon
½ teaspoon ground cloves
2 cups fresh cherries, stoned and halved
3 tablespoons Morello cherry jam
1 teaspoon lemon juice

For the Frosting
⅔ cup semisweet chocolate chips
4 tablespoons unsalted butter
4 tablespoons heavy cream

To Decorate
½ cup white chocolate chips
14–18 fresh cherries
a few rose leaves, washed and dried

1 Preheat the oven to 325°F. Grease an 8-inch springform cake pan, line the bottom with waxed or parchment paper and grease the paper. Dust the inside of the pan with flour.

2 Cream the butter and ½ cup sugar together until pale and light. Gradually beat in the eggs until incorporated. Stir in the melted chocolate and 2 tablespoons of the kirsch.

3 Sift the flour and spices together and fold into the creamed mixture. Transfer to the prepared pan, smooth the surface and bake for 55–60 minutes, or until a skewer inserted into the center of the cake comes out clean. Remove from the oven and let cool.

4 ▲ Meanwhile, prepare the filling. Place the halved cherries, remaining kirsch and sugar in a small pan. Heat gently to dissolve the sugar, bring to a boil, cover and simmer for 10 minutes. Remove the lid and simmer for another 10 minutes, until the mixture is thick and syrupy. Let cool.

5 ▲ Cut the cake in half. Using a saucer as a template, cut out a circle about ½ inch deep from the center of the bottom half. Crumble into the cherry syrup mixture, stirring well, to form a thick paste.

6 ▲ Use the mixture to fill the hollowed section of cake, smoothing over the surface. Cover with the top half of the cake.

7 Heat the jam and lemon juice and boil for 1 minute. Strain through a fine sieve and brush all over the cake.

8 To make the frosting, heat the chocolate, butter and cream in a small pan until melted. Cool slightly, until the mixture starts to thicken. In one fluid motion, pour over the glazed cake, completely covering the top and sides. Smooth over the sides with a baking spatula, if necessary. Allow to set in a cool place.

9 ▲ Melt the white chocolate chips in a small bowl over a pan of gently simmering water. Dip each cherry halfway into the white chocolate, so that it is half white and half red, and allow to set on baking parchment. Using a paintbrush, coat the underside of the rose leaves with a thick layer of the remaining chocolate. Allow to set on baking parchment.

10 ▲ When set, carefully peel away the leaves from the chocolate coating. Decorate the top of the cake with an arrangement of cherries and chocolate leaves.

White Chocolate Mousse Strawberry Cake

Layers of rich white chocolate mousse are enhanced by fresh strawberries and strawberry liqueur in this tempting cake.

INGREDIENTS
Serves 10
4 ounces white chocolate, chopped
½ cup heavy cream
½ cup milk
1 tablespoon rum or vanilla extract
8 tablespoons (½ cup) unsalted butter, softened
¾ cup sugar
3 eggs
2 cups all-purpose flour
1 teaspoon baking powder
pinch of salt
1½ pounds fresh strawberries, sliced, plus extra to decorate
3 cups whipping cream
2 tablespoons rum or strawberry-flavored liqueur

For the Mousse Filling
9 ounces white chocolate, chopped
1½ cups whipping or heavy cream
2 tablespoons rum or strawberry-flavored liqueur

1 ▲ Preheat the oven to 350°. Grease two deep 9-inch cake pans. Line the bottoms of the pans with baking parchment. Melt the chocolate and cream in a double boiler over low heat, stirring until smooth. Stir in the milk and rum or vanilla extract; set aside to cool.

2 ▲ In a large mixing bowl, beat the butter and sugar for 3–5 minutes until light and creamy, scraping the sides of the bowl occasionally. Add the eggs one at a time, beating well after each addition. In a small bowl, sift together the flour, baking powder and salt. Alternately add the flour and melted chocolate to the egg mixture until just blended. Divide the mixture between the pans and spread evenly.

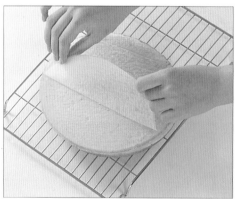

3 ▲ Bake for 20–25 minutes, or until a skewer inserted into the center of one of the cakes comes out clean. Cool in the pans for 10 minutes. Turn the cakes out onto a wire rack, peel off the paper and allow to cool completely.

4 Prepare the filling. Melt the chocolate in the cream over low heat until smooth, stirring frequently. Stir in the rum or liqueur and pour into a bowl. Chill until the mixture is just set. With a wire whisk, whip lightly until the mixture is mousselike.

5 ▲ Slice both cake layers in half, making four layers. Place one layer on a plate and spread with one-third of the mousse. Arrange about one-third of the sliced strawberries over the mousse. Add two more layers in the same way, then cover with the last cake layer.

6 Whip the cream with the rum or liqueur. Spread about half the whipped cream over the top and sides of the cake. Use the remaining cream to pipe scrolls on top of the cake. Fill in the rest of the cake with the remaining strawberries.

Chocolate Cappuccino Cake

If you prefer, this cake can be left whole and rolled roulade-style, or the mixture can be baked in two 9-inch pans and layered to make a round cake.

INGREDIENTS
Serves 8–10
6 ounces semisweet chocolate, chopped
2 teaspoons instant espresso powder (or 1 tablespoon instant coffee powder) dissolved in 3 tablespoons boiling water
6 eggs, separated
²⁄₃ cup sugar
pinch of cream of tartar
cocoa, for sifting

For the Coffee Cream Filling
¼ cup whipping or heavy cream
2 tablespoons sugar
1 cup mascarpone or cream cheese, softened
2 tablespoons coffee-flavor liqueur
1 ounce semisweet chocolate, grated

For the Coffee Buttercream
4 egg yolks, at room temperature
5 tablespoons light corn syrup or golden syrup
¼ cup sugar
2 sticks (1 cup) unsalted butter, cut into small pieces and softened
1 tablespoon instant espresso powder dissolved in 1–2 teaspoons boiling water
1–2 tablespoons coffee-flavored liqueur

To Decorate
chocolate coffee beans

1 Preheat the oven to 350°F. Grease a 16 x 10½-inch baking sheet. Line with baking parchment, leaving a 2-inch overhang at each narrow end. Grease the parchment. In the top of a double boiler over low heat, heat the chocolate and dissolved coffee powder until melted and smooth, stirring frequently. Set aside.

2 ▲ In a bowl with an electric mixer, beat the egg yolks and sugar for 3–5 minutes, until thick and light-colored. Reduce speed to low and beat in the chocolate mixture until blended.

3 ▲ In a large bowl with an electric mixer with cleaned beaters, beat the egg whites and cream of tartar until stiff peaks begin to form. Do not overbeat. Stir a spoonful of whites into the chocolate mixture to lighten it, then fold in the remaining whites.

4 Pour the batter into the prepared pan, spreading into the corners and smoothing the top evenly. Bake for 12–15 minutes, until the cake springs back when touched lightly with a fingertip. Sprinkle a clean dish towel with cocoa to cover and turn the cake out onto to the towel. Peel off the paper and cool.

5 ▲ Prepare the filling. In a medium bowl with an electric mixer, whip the cream and sugar until soft peaks form. In another bowl, beat the mascarpone or cream cheese and liqueur until light and smooth. Stir in the grated chocolate and fold in the whipped cream. Cover and refrigerate until ready for use.

6 ▲ Prepare the buttercream. In a bowl with an electric mixer on high speed, beat the yolks for 5–6 minutes, until thick and pale-colored. In a saucepan over medium heat, cook the syrup and sugar until the mixture boils, stirring constantly.

7 With the mixer on medium-low speed, slowly pour the hot syrup over the beaten yolks in a slow stream. Continue beating until the mixture feels cool, 5–6 minutes. Beat in the butter, a few pieces at a time, until the mixture is smooth. Beat in the dissolved coffee and liqueur. Refrigerate until ready to use, but bring to room temperature before spreading.

Tip

If you don't have instant espresso powder, any instant coffee powder can be used for this cake.

8 ▲ Assemble the cake. With a serrated knife, trim off any crisp edges of cake. Cut the cake crosswise into three equal strips. Place one cake strip on a cake plate and spread with half the coffee cream filling. Cover with a second cake strip and the remaining filling. Top with the last cake strip.

9 ▲ Spoon about one-third of the coffee buttercream into a small piping bag fitted with a small star nozzle. Spread the remaining buttercream on the top and sides of the cake. Pipe a lattice or scroll design on top and around the edges of the cake and decorate with chocolate coffee beans. Refrigerate the cake if you are not serving it immediately, but allow to stand at room temperature for 30 minutes before serving.

Gorgeous Chocolate Cake

This recipe will definitely make you famous.
Make sure you serve it with paper and pens, as everyone will want
to take down the recipe.

INGREDIENTS
Serves 8–10
³/₄ cup butter, softened
¹/₂ cup sugar
9 x 1oz squares plain chocolate,
melted
2¹/₃ cups ground
almonds
4 large eggs, separated
4 x 1oz squares white chocolate,
melted, to decorate

4 ▲ Place the remaining butter and remaining melted plain chocolate in a saucepan. Heat very gently, stirring constantly, until melted. Pour over the cake, allowing the topping to coat the sides of the cake too. Leave to set for at least an hour. To decorate, fill a paper piping bag with the melted white chocolate and snip the end. Drizzle all around the edges. Use any remaining chocolate to make leaves (see Trailing Orchid Wedding cake, steps 2 and 3). Allow to set.

3 ▲ Whisk the egg whites in another clean, dry bowl until stiff. Fold them into the chocolate mixture, then transfer to the prepared pan and smooth the surface. Bake for 50–55 minutes or until a skewer inserted into the center of the cake comes out clean. Leave the cake in the pan for about 5 minutes, then turn out on to a wire rack, peel off the lining paper and leave to cool completely.

Tip

Place a large sheet of waxed paper or a cookie sheet under the wire rack before pouring the chocolate topping over the cake. This will catch all the drips and keep the work surface clean.

1 Preheat the oven to 350°F. Grease a deep 8¹/₂ inch springform cake pan, then line the base with waxed paper and grease the paper thoroughly.

2 ▲ Place ¹/₂ cup of the butter and all the sugar in a mixing bowl and beat until light and fluffy. Add two-thirds of the plain chocolate, the ground almonds and the egg yolks and beat together until evenly blended.

French Chocolate Cake

This very dense chocolate cake can be made up to three days before serving, but decorate it with confectioners' sugar on the day it is to be served.

INGREDIENTS
Serves 10
9 ounces bittersweet chocolate, chopped
2 sticks (1 cup) unsalted butter, cut into pieces
½ cup granulated sugar
2 tablespoons brandy or orange-flavor liqueur
5 eggs
1 tablespoon all-purpose flour
confectioners' sugar for dusting
whipped or sour cream, for serving

1 Preheat the oven to 350°F. Generously grease a 9-inch springform pan. Line the bottom with baking parchment and grease the parchment. Wrap the outside of the pan in foil to prevent water from seeping into the cake. In a saucepan over low heat, melt the chocolate, butter and sugar, stirring frequently until smooth; let cool slightly. Stir in the liqueur. In a large mixing bowl with an electric mixer, beat the eggs lightly. Beat in the flour, then slowly beat in the chocolate mixture until well blended. Pour the batter into the pan.

2 Place the pan in a large roasting pan and pour boiling water into the roasting pan to come ¾ inch up the side of the springform pan. Bake for 25–30 minutes, until the edge of the cake is set but the center is still soft. Remove the pan from the water bath and remove the foil. Let cool completely on a wire rack (the cake will sink in the center and may crack).

3 ▲ Remove the side of the springform pan and turn the cake out onto a wire rack. Remove the springform pan bottom and peel off the lining paper, so the bottom of the cake becomes the top.

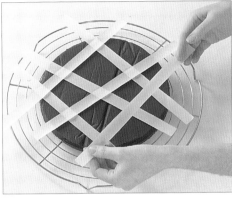

4 ▲ Cut six to eight strips of baking parchment 1 inch wide and place randomly over the cake, or make a lattice-style pattern if you wish. Dust the cake with confectioners' sugar, then carefully remove the paper. Serve with cream.

Death by Chocolate

There are many versions of this irresistible cake; here is a very rich one that is ideal for a large party, and guarantees there won't be a single slice left at the end of the evening.

INGREDIENTS
Serves 18–20
7 ounces semisweet chocolate, chopped
1 stick (½ cup) unsalted butter, diced
⅔ cup water
1⅓ cups granulated sugar
2 teaspoons vanilla extract
2 eggs, separated
¾ cup sour cream
3 cups all-purpose flour
2 teaspoons baking powder
1 teaspoon baking soda

For the Filling and Glaze
1 pound 5 ounces semisweet chocolate, chopped
2 sticks (1 cup) unsalted butter
8 tablespoons brandy
¾ cup seedless raspberry jam
1 cup heavy cream

To Decorate
chocolate curls
raspberries
confectioners' sugar, sifted, for dusting

1 Preheat the oven to 350°F. Grease a 10-inch springform pan and line the bottom with baking parchment. In a saucepan over low heat, melt the chocolate, butter and water, stirring.

2 ▲ Remove from the heat, beat in the sugar and vanilla and let cool. Beat the egg yolks lightly, then beat into the chocolate mixture; gently fold in the sour cream. Sift the flour, baking powder and baking soda over, then fold in. Beat the egg whites until stiff, then fold gently into the chocolate mixture.

3 ▲ Pour the batter into the pan and bake for 50–60 minutes, until the cake begins to shrink away from the side of the pan. Put the pan on a wire rack to cool for 10 minutes (the cake may sink in the center; this is normal). Run a sharp knife around the edge of the cake, then remove the side of the pan. Invert the cake onto the rack, remove the bottom of the pan and allow to cool completely. Wash and dry the pan.

4 ▲ Prepare the filling and glaze. Melt 14 ounces of the chocolate with the butter and 4 tablespoons of the brandy. Cool, then chill until thickened. Cut the cake horizontally into three equal layers. Heat the raspberry jam and 1 tablespoon brandy, stirring until melted and smooth. Spread a thin layer over each cake layer and allow to set.

5 ▲ When the filling is spreadable, place the bottom cake layer back in the pan. Spread with half the filling and top with the second layer of cake, then spread with the remaining filling; top with the final cake layer, jam side down. Gently press the layers together, cover and chill for 4–6 hours or overnight.

6 ▲ Run a knife around the edge of the cake, then remove the side of the pan. Set the cake on a wire rack over a baking sheet. Bring the cream to the boil. Remove from the heat and add the remaining chocolate, stirring until melted. Stir in the remaining brandy and strain into a bowl. Allow to cool.

7 ▲ Beat the chocolate mixture until it begins to hold its shape. Smooth it over the cake and allow to set. Slide the cake onto a serving plate and decorate with chocolate curls and raspberries. Dust with confectioners' sugar. Serve at room temperature.

Tip

It's easy to make your own chocolate curls: bring a thick bar of chocolate to room temperature and pull a vegetable peeler firmly across the edge of the chocolate. Use a skewer or toothpick to transfer the curls to the cake, as fingers will melt them.

Luxury White Chocolate Cheesecake

Despite its pure, creamy white looks, this is a wickedly indulgent cake. No white chocolate lover will be able to refuse a piece.

INGREDIENTS
Serves 16–20
5 ounces graham crackers or
digestive biscuits
½ cup blanched hazelnuts, toasted
4 tablespoons unsalted butter, melted
½ teaspoon ground cinnamon

For the Filling
12 ounces white chocolate, chopped
½ cup heavy cream
3 cups cream cheese, softened
¼ cup granulated sugar
4 eggs
2 tablespoons hazelnut-flavor
liqueur or 1 tablespoon vanilla
extract

For the Topping
1¼ cup sour cream
¼ cup granulated sugar
1 tablespoon hazelnut-flavored
liqueur or 1 teaspoon
vanilla extract

To Decorate
white chocolate curls
cocoa for dusting (optional)

1 Preheat the oven to 350°F. Lightly grease a 9-inch springform pan. In a food processor, process the biscuits and hazelnuts until fine crumbs form. Pour in the butter and cinnamon. Process just until blended; do not overmix.

2 Using the back of a spoon, press the mixture over the bottom and side of the pan to within ½ inch of the top. Bake for 5–7 minutes, until just set. Place on a wire rack to cool. Lower the oven temperature to 300°F.

3 ▲ Prepare the filling. In a small saucepan over low heat, melt the white chocolate and cream until smooth, stirring frequently. Set aside to cool.

4 ▲ In a large bowl, beat the cream cheese and sugar with an electric mixer until smooth. Add the eggs one at a time, beating well after each addition and scraping the bowl occasionally. Slowly beat in the white chocolate mixture and liqueur or vanilla extract.

5 Pour into the baked crust. Place the pan on a baking sheet. Bake for 45–55 minutes, or until the edge of the cake is firm but the center is still slightly soft; do not allow to brown. Let stand on a wire rack while preparing the topping. Increase the oven temperature to 400°F.

6 ▲ Prepare the topping. In a small bowl whisk the sour cream, sugar and liqueur or vanilla. Pour over the cheesecake, spreading evenly, and return to the oven. Bake for another 5–7 minutes. Turn off the oven, but do not open the door for 1 hour.

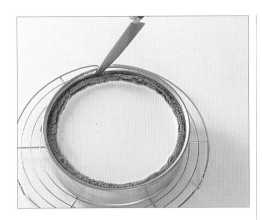

7 ▲ Place the cake, in the pan, on a wire rack to cool to room temperature. Run a sharp knife around the edge of the cake to separate it from the pan; this helps prevent cracking. Cool completely, then refrigerate, loosely covered, overnight.

8 ▲ Decorate the top of the cake with chocolate curls and dust lightly with cocoa.

9 If you like, slide a sharp knife under the crust to separate the cake from the bottom. Alternatively, leave the bottom of the tin in place to avoid breaking the crust and serve the cake from it.

Tip

To ensure an even crust, use a metal spoon to press the crumbs to the bottom and side of the pan.

Exotic Celebration Gâteau

Use any tropical fruits you can find to make a spectacular display of colors and tastes.

INGREDIENTS
Serves 8–10
3/4 cup butter, softened
3/4 cup superfine sugar
3 large eggs, beaten
2 1/4 cups self-rising flour
2–3 tbsp milk
6–8 tbsp light rum
scant 2 cups heavy or whipping cream
1/4 cup confectioners' sugar, sifted

To Decorate
1 lb mixed fresh exotic and soft fruits, such as figs, red currants, star fruit, kiwi fruit, etc.
6 tbsp apricot jam, warmed and sieved
2 tbsp warm water
sifted confectioners' sugar

3 Spoon the cake mixture into the prepared pan and smooth the surface. Bake in the center of the oven for about 45 minutes, or until a skewer inserted into the center of the cake comes out clean. Turn out on to a wire rack and leave to cool completely.

4 ▲ Place the cake on a serving plate, then use a thin skewer to make holes randomly over the cake. Drizzle over the rum and allow to soak in.

5 ▲ Place the cream and confectioners' sugar in a mixing bowl and beat with electric beaters until the mixture holds soft peaks. Spread all over the top and sides of the cake.

6 Arrange the fruits attractively in the hollow center of the cake, allowing the fruits to overhang the edges a little. Mix together the apricot jam and water, then use to brush evenly over the fruit. Sift over a little confectioners' sugar.

1 Preheat the oven to 375°F. Lightly grease and flour a deep 8 inch ring mold.

2 ▲ Place the butter and sugar in a mixing bowl and beat until light and fluffy. Gradually beat in the eggs, then fold in the flour with the milk.

Chocolate Pecan Torte

This torte uses finely ground nuts instead of flour. Toast and then cool the nuts before grinding finely in a food processor. Do not overgrind the nuts, as the oils will form a paste.

INGREDIENTS
Serves 16
7 ounces bittersweet or semisweet
chocolate, chopped
10 tablespoons (⅔ cup) unsalted
butter, cut into pieces
4 eggs
scant ½ cup superfine sugar
2 teaspoons vanilla extract
1 cup ground pecans, toasted
2 teaspoons ground cinnamon

For the Chocolate Honey Glaze
4 ounces bittersweet or semisweet
chocolate, chopped
4 tablespoons butter, cut
into pieces
2 tablespoons honey
pinch of ground cinnamon

To Decorate
24 toasted pecan halves

3 ▲ Prepare the glaze. In a small saucepan over low heat, melt the chocolate, butter, honey and cinnamon, stirring until smooth; remove from the heat. Carefully dip the toasted pecan halves halfway into the glaze and place on a baking parchment-lined baking sheet until set. The glaze will have thickened slightly.

4 ▲ Remove the side from the springform pan and invert the cake onto a wire rack. Remove the pan bottom and lining paper. Pour the thickened glaze over the cake, tilting the rack slightly to spread the glaze. Use a baking spatula to smooth the sides. Arrange the nuts around the outside edge of the torte and allow the glaze to set.

1 Preheat the oven to 350°F. Grease an 8-inch springform pan; line the bottom with baking parchment, then grease the parchment. Wrap the outside of the pan with foil to prevent water from seeping in. In a saucepan over low heat, melt the chocolate and butter, stirring until smooth. Remove from the heat. In a mixing bowl, beat the eggs, sugar and vanilla with an electric mixer until frothy. Stir in the melted chocolate, toasted ground nuts and cinnamon. Pour into the prepared pan.

2 Place the foil-wrapped pan in a large roasting pan and pour boiling water into the roasting pan to come ¼ inch up the side of the springform pan. Bake for 25–30 minutes, until the edge of the cake is set but the center is soft. Remove from the water bath and remove the foil. Cool on a wire rack.

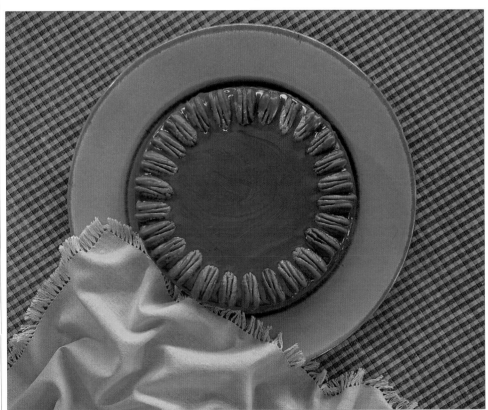

Jewel Cake

This pretty tea-time cake is excellent
served as an afternoon snack with tea or coffee.

INGREDIENTS
Serves 10–15
½ cup mixed colored glacé cherries,
halved, washed and dried
¼ cup preserved ginger in syrup,
chopped, washed and dried
⅓ cup chopped mixed citrus peel
1 cup self-rising flour
¾ cup flour
3 tbsp cornstarch
¼ cup butter
¾ cup superfine sugar
3 large eggs
finely grated zest of 1 orange

To Decorate
1½ cups confectioners' sugar,
sifted
2–3 tbsp freshly squeezed orange
juice
¼ cup mixed colored glacé cherries,
chopped
2½ tbsp mixed citrus peel,
chopped

Tip

For variation, bake the cake in a 7 inch round cake pan, if wished. Use the same quantities of ingredients and follow the method as described here. Decorate with crystallized fruits instead of the glacé cherries and mixed citrus peel.

1 Preheat the oven to 350°F. Grease a 2 lb loaf pan, line the base and sides with waxed paper and then grease the paper.

2 ▲ Place the cherries, preserved ginger and mixed citrus peel in a plastic bag with 1 tbsp of the self-rising flour and shake to coat evenly. Sift the remaining flours and cornstarch into a small bowl.

3 ▲ Place the butter and sugar in a mixing bowl and beat until light and fluffy. Beat in the eggs, one at a time, until evenly blended. Fold in the sifted flours with the orange zest, then stir in the dried fruit.

4 ▲ Transfer the cake mixture to the prepared pan and bake in the center of the oven for about 1¼ hours, or until a skewer inserted into the center of the cake comes out clean. Leave the cake in the pan for about 5 minutes, then turn out on to a wire rack, peel off the lining paper and leave to cool completely.

5 ▲ To decorate the cake, place the confectioners' sugar in a mixing bowl. Stir in the orange juice and mix until smooth. Drizzle the icing over the cake. Mix together the chopped glacé cherries and mixed citrus peel in a small bowl, then use to decorate the cake. Allow the icing to set before serving.

Fresh Fruit Genoese

This Italian classic, "Genovese con Panne e Frutta,"
can be made with any type of ripe fresh fruit.

INGREDIENTS
Serves 8–10
For the Sponge Cake
1½ cups flour, sifted
pinch of salt
4 large eggs
½ cup sugar
6 tbsp orange-flavored liqueur

For the Filling and Topping
2½ cups heavy cream
4 tbsp vanilla sugar
1 lb fresh soft fruit, such as
raspberries, blueberries, cherries,
peaches, etc.
1¼ cups shelled pistachio nuts,
finely chopped
4 tbsp apricot jam, warmed and
sieved, to glaze

Tip

To save time and money, use shop-bought chopped mixed nuts to coat the sides of the cake instead of pistachios.

1 Preheat the oven to 350°F. Meanwhile, grease an 8½ inch round springform cake pan with butter or vegetable oil, line the base with waxed paper and grease the paper.

2 ▲ Sift the flour and salt together three times, then set aside.

3 Place the eggs and sugar in a mixing bowl and beat with an electric mixer for about 10 minutes or until thick and pale.

4 ▲ Sift the reserved flour mixture into the mixing bowl, then fold in very gently. Transfer the cake mixture to the prepared pan. Bake in the center of the oven for 30–35 minutes or until a skewer inserted into the center of the cake comes out clean. Leave the cake in the pan for about 5 minutes, then turn out on to a wire rack, peel off the lining paper and leave to cool completely.

5 Cut the cake horizontally into two layers, and place the bottom layer on a serving plate. Sprinkle the orange-flavored liqueur over both layers.

6 ▲ Place the heavy cream and vanilla sugar in a mixing bowl and beat with an electric mixer until it holds peaks.

7 ▲ Spread two-thirds of the cream mixture over the bottom layer of cake and top with half the fruit. Place the second layer of the cake on top and spread the remaining cream over the top and sides.

8 Using a knife, lightly press the chopped nuts evenly around the sides. Arrange the remaining fresh fruit on top and brush over a light glaze using the apricot jam.

Hazelnut Praline and Apricot Génoise

Génoise is the name associated with the most classic of all whisked sponge cakes. Here it is layered with an apricot- and maple-flavored buttercream and topped with apricots and whole praline-coated hazelnuts. Delicious and elegant, this is an ideal cake for any occasion.

INGREDIENTS
Serves 12
1¼ cups all-purpose flour
pinch of salt
4 eggs
½ cup superfine sugar
2 tablespoons toasted
ground hazelnuts

For the Praline
6 tablespoons granulated sugar
¾ cup unblanched hazelnuts

For the Icing
6 egg yolks
¾ cup superfine sugar
⅔ cup milk
1½ cups unsalted butter, diced
2 tablespoons maple or golden syrup
1 tablespoons apricot brandy or apricot
juice from canned apricots

For the Topping
14-ounce can apricot halves in natural
juice, drained
12 praline-coated hazelnuts

1 Preheat the oven to 350°F. Grease a 9-inch round springform cake pan, line the bottom with waxed or parchment paper and grease the paper. Dust with flour. Oil a baking sheet.

2 Sift the flour and salt together three times. Beat the eggs and sugar with an electric mixer for about 10 minutes, or until thick and pale. Sift the flour into the bowl, add the ground hazelnuts and fold gently. Transfer the mixture to the pan. Bake in the center of the oven for 30–35 minutes, or until a skewer inserted into the center of the cake comes out clean. Let the cake stand in the pan for 5 minutes, then turn out onto a wire rack, peel off the lining paper and let cool completely.

3 To make the praline, heat the granulated sugar and nuts together in a small heavy-bottomed pan until the sugar melts. Increase the heat and stir with a wooden spoon until the sugar turns golden. Be careful not to allow the sugar to burn. Remove from the heat immediately.

4 ▲ Carefully scoop out 12 coated nuts with a metal spoon and place separately on the oiled baking sheet. Pour the remaining mixture onto the sheet and set aside until completely cool and set hard. Break into pieces and grind in a blender or food processor to form a rough paste. Cover and set aside.

5 To make the icing, beat the egg yolks and superfine sugar together until pale and thick. Heat the milk until it just boils and pour over the creamed mixture, still beating. Return to the pan and stir over low heat until the mixture coats the back of the spoon. Do not let the mixture become too hot or it will curdle. Remove from the heat and strain through a fine sieve into a large bowl.

6 Beat the mixture for 1–2 minutes, until tepid. Gradually beat in the butter, a little at a time, until the mixture thickens and becomes glossy. Beat in the maple syrup and apricot brandy or fruit juice. (Just before the mixture thickens it will appear to be curdling. Continue beating and the correct consistency will be achieved.)

7 ▲ Cut the cake into three equal layers. Reserve four apricot halves and chop the rest. Dry well and fold the chopped fruit into one-third of the icing along with 3 tablespoons of praline.

8 ▲ Place one layer of sponge cake on a turntable, spread with half the filling, top with the next layer of sponge cake and repeat.

11 Fan the remaining apricot slices in the center of the cake and top with a single praline-coated hazelnut.

9 ▲ Reserve a little of the remaining icing for decoration. Use the rest to cover the top and sides of the cake. Coat the sides with 3 more tablespoons of praline and swirl a pattern over the top with a baking spatula.

10 ▲ Transfer the remaining icing to a piping bag fitted with a medium star nozzle and pipe 24 rosettes around the top of the cake. Decorate alternate rosettes with the reserved apricots, thinly sliced, and whole praline-coated nuts.

Iced Paradise Cake

A whisked sponge cake mixture is piped into fingers. These are then used to line a loaf pan to make a luxurious frozen cake, finished off with a coating of melted chocolate, butter and cream.

INGREDIENTS
Serves 12
For the Sponge Fingers
1 quantity Whisked Sponge Cake, substituting 2 tablespoons all-purpose flour with 2 tablespoons cornstarch
6 tablespoons dark rum

For the Filling and Icing
1½ cups semisweet chocolate chips
2 tablespoons golden or light corn syrup
2 tablespoons water
1⅔ cups heavy cream
2 cups dried coconut, toasted
2 tablespoons unsalted butter
2 tablespoons light cream

To Decorate
⅓ cup white chocolate chips
dried coconut or coconut curls
cocoa powder, for dusting

1 Preheat the oven to 400°F. Grease and flour two baking sheets. Line a 9 x 5 x 3-inch loaf pan with a layer of plastic wrap.

2 ▲ Make the whisked sponge cake mixture and transfer to a piping bag fitted with a ½-inch plain nozzle. Pipe 28–30 3-inch fingers onto the prepared baking sheets and bake for 8–10 minutes, until risen and springy to the touch. Remove from the oven, cool slightly and transfer to a wire rack to cool completely.

3 ▲ Line the bottom and sides of the prepared loaf pan with sponge fingers, trimming them as necessary to fit the pan. Brush with a little rum.

4 Melt ½ cup of the chocolate chips, the syrup, water and 2 tablespoons rum in a bowl over a pan of gently simmering water. Allow to cool slightly.

5 ▲ Whip the cream until it holds its shape and stir in the chocolate mixture and toasted coconut. Pour into the pan, tap the bottom gently to clear any air bubbles, and place the remaining sponge fingers over the top. Brush with the remaining rum. Cover with plastic wrap and freeze for several hours, until firm.

6 Melt the remaining chocolate, butter and cream in a bowl over a pan of gently simmering water. Remove from the heat and let cool slightly.

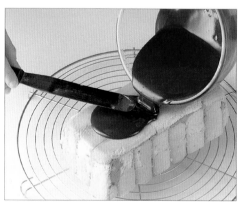

7 ▲ Remove the cake from the freezer and unmold onto a wire rack. Pour the icing over in one smooth motion to coat the top and sides of the cake. Use a baking spatula to smooth the sides, if necessary.

8 Refrigerate for 10–15 minutes, until the chocolate icing is set. (Alternatively, the cake can be returned to the freezer at this time and stored for up to 3 months.)

Tip

To make coconut curls, draw a swivel-bladed peeler along the curved edge of a piece of fresh coconut. This will make thin, wide curls with a brown edge. Use these to decorate the top of the cake.

9 ▲ To make the decorations, melt the white chocolate chips and transfer to a paper piping bag. Snip the end off the bag and drizzle a pattern over the chocolate icing. Allow the cake to soften in the refrigerator for 20–30 minutes, or until a knife will cut through easily.

10 ▲ Just before serving, decorate the top with a little dried coconut or coconut curls, and dust lightly with cocoa powder.

Mocha Brazil Layer Torte

This wonderfully rich dessert is a layer torte, consisting of both sponge cake and meringue disks. The combination of mocha and Brazil nuts is particularly successful, and the simple decorations give an elegant finish to this classic European cake.

INGREDIENTS
Serves 12
3 egg whites
½ cup superfine sugar
3 tablespoons coffee extract
¾ cup Brazil nuts, toasted and finely ground
⅔ cup semisweet chocolate chips
4 eggs
½ cup superfine sugar
1 cup all-purpose flour
1 teaspoon baking powder

For the Icing
1 cup semisweet chocolate chips
2 tablespoons coffee extract
2 tablespoons water
2½ cups heavy cream

To Decorate
⅓ cup semisweet chocolate chips
12 chocolate-coated coffee beans

1 Preheat the oven to 300°F. Draw 8-inch circles on a large sheet of baking parchment. Place on a baking sheet. Grease an 8-inch round springform pan and line the bottom with waxed or parchment paper. Grease the paper and flour the pan.

2 ▲ To make the meringue, beat the egg whites until stiff and gradually beat in the sugar, 1 tablespoon at a time, until thick and glossy. Fold in the coffee extract and nuts until evenly incorporated and transfer to a piping bag fitted with a ½-inch plain nozzle. Starting in the center, pipe circles of the meringue mixture onto the prepared paper.

3 ▲ Bake for 1¾–2 hours, until crisp and golden. Remove from the oven and transfer to a wire rack to cool completely. Peel away the baking parchment. Increase the oven temperature to 350°F.

4 ▲ To prepare the chocolate decorations, melt the chocolate chips and pour over a piece of baking parchment, spreading out to a very thin layer with a baking spatula, and allow to set.

5 To make the sponge, melt the chocolate chips and cool slightly. Beat the eggs and sugar together in a bowl over a pan of gently simmering water until very pale and thick and the whisk leaves a trail through the mixture. Remove from the heat, continue beating until cool and carefully stir in the melted chocolate. Sift the flour and baking powder together and fold into the whisked mixture until incorporated. Transfer to the prepared pan and bake for 40–45 minutes, or until the mixture has risen and is springy to the touch.

6 Remove from the oven, cool in the pan for 10 minutes and transfer to a wire rack to cool completely.

7 To make the icing, melt the chocolate chips, coffee extract and water together in a bowl over a pan of gently simmering water, then remove from the heat. Whip the cream until it holds its shape and stir into the mocha mixture until combined.

8 ▲ Place the cooled cake on a turntable and cut into three equal layers. Trim the meringue disks to the same size and assemble the gateau with a layer of sponge, a little of the icing and a meringue disk, finishing with a layer of sponge.

9 Reserve a little of the remaining icing for decoration; use the rest to completely coat the cake, forming a swirling pattern over the top.

10 ▲ Carefully peel away the paper from the set chocolate and cut out 12 triangles, 4 inches long and 1 inch wide at the top.

11 ▲ Transfer the reserved icing to a piping bag fitted with a large star nozzle, and pipe 24 small rosettes around the top edge of the cake. Top alternately with the coffee beans and chocolate triangles.

Coffee, Peach and Almond Daquoise

This is a traditional meringue cake. The meringue mixture is piped into rounds, baked, and layered with a classic buttercream and peach filling. The French name for this classic style of cake, "succès," is then piped over the top of the finished cake.

INGREDIENTS
Serves 12
5 eggs, separated
scant 2 cups superfine sugar
2 tablespoons cornstarch
2 cups ground almonds, toasted
½ cup milk
2½ sticks (1¼ cups) unsalted butter, diced (at room temperature)
3–4 tablespoons coffee extract
2 x 14-ounce cans peach halves in juice, drained

To Decorate
¾ cup sliced almonds, toasted
confectioners' sugar
3 reserved peach halves
a few mint leaves (optional)

1 Preheat the oven to 300°F. Draw 3 x 9-inch circles on three sheets of baking parchment. Place the sheets on separate baking sheets.

2 Whisk the egg whites until stiff. Gradually whisk in 1¼ cups of the sugar, a little at a time, until thick and glossy. Fold in the cornstarch and almonds until evenly incorporated. Transfer the mixture to a piping bag fitted with a ½-inch plain nozzle.

3 Starting in the center of the prepared circles, pipe the mixture in a continuous tight coil, finishing just within the lines. Bake for 1¾–2 hours, until lightly golden and dried out. Remove from the oven and transfer to a wire rack to cool completely. Peel away the baking parchment.

4 Using the 5 egg yolks, the remaining ¾ cup superfine sugar, the milk and the diced butter, make the icing. See Hazelnut Praline and Apricot Génoise steps 5 and 6 for the method. Substitute the coffee extract for the syrup and brandy in that recipe.

5 ▲ Trim the meringue disks to 9-inch circles, and crush the trimmings. Reserve three peach halves. Chop the rest and fold into half the icing with the crushed meringue. Use this to sandwich together the three meringue disks.

6 ▲ Reserve a little icing for decoration. Coat the top and sides of the cake, and smooth over the sides with a baking spatula.

7 ▲ Cover the top of the cake with toasted sliced almonds and dust liberally with confectioners' sugar.

8 ▲ Cut the reserved peaches into thin slices and use to decorate the outer edges of the cake. Garnish with mint leaves. Place the reserved icing in a piping bag fitted with a small star nozzle and use to pipe the word "succès" in the center of the cake.

Lemon Chiffon Cake

*Lemon mousse provides a tangy filling for this light lemon sponge.
The curly lemon decorations add an extra bite to every piece.*

INGREDIENTS
Serves 8
2 eggs
6 tablespoons superfine sugar
grated zest of 1 lemon
½ cup all-purpose flour, sifted

For the Filling
2 eggs, separated
6 tablespoons superfine sugar
grated zest and juice of 1 lemon
2 tablespoons water
1 tablespoon powdered gelatin
½ cup fromage frais

For the Icing
1 cup confectioners' sugar, sifted
1 tablespoon lemon juice

To Decorate
blanched and shredded zest
of 1 lemon

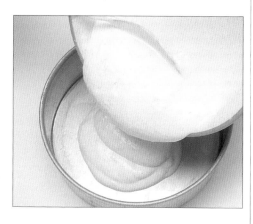

1 ▲ Preheat the oven to 350°F. Grease and line an 8-inch round loose-bottomed cake pan. Beat the eggs, sugar and lemon zest together with an electric mixer until thick and mousselike. Gently fold in the flour, then turn the mixture into the prepared pan.

2 ▲ Bake for 20–25 minutes, until the cake springs back when lightly pressed in the center. Turn onto a wire rack to cool. Once cool, split the cake in half horizontally and return the lower half to the clean cake pan. Set the pan aside.

3 ▲ Make the filling. Place the egg yolks, sugar, lemon zest and juice in a bowl. Beat with an electric mixer until thick, pale and creamy.

4 ▲ Pour the water into a small heatproof bowl and sprinkle the gelatin on top. Let stand until spongy, then place over simmering water and stir until dissolved. Cool slightly, then whisk into the yolk mixture. Fold in the fromage frais. When the mixture begins to set, quickly beat the egg whites to soft peaks. Fold a spoonful into the mousse mixture to lighten it, then fold in the rest.

5 ▲ Pour the lemon mousse over the sponge in the cake pan, spreading it to the edges. Set the second layer of sponge on top and chill until set.

6 ◀Slide a baking spatula dipped in hot water between the pan and the cake to loosen it, then carefully transfer the cake to a serving plate. Make the icing by adding enough lemon juice to the confectioners' sugar to make a mixture thick enough to coat the back of a wooden spoon. Pour over the cake and spread evenly to the edges. Decorate with lemon shreds.

Tip

The mousse mixture should be just on the point of setting when the egg whites are added. This setting process can be speeded up by placing the bowl of mousse in a bowl of iced water.

Tia Maria Cake

This cake is a featherlight coffee sponge with a creamy liqueur-flavored filling, perfect for a sophisticated dessert at the end of a dinner party.

INGREDIENTS
Serves 8
¾ cup all-purpose flour
2 tablespoons instant coffee powder
3 eggs
½ cup superfine sugar

For the Filling
¾ cup low-fat soft cheese
1 tablespoon honey
1 tablespoon Tia Maria
¼ cup crystallized ginger,
roughly chopped

For the Icing
2 cups confectioners' sugar, sifted
2 teaspoons coffee extract
1 tablespoon water
1 teaspoon cocoa powder

To Decorate
coffee beans

1 ▲ Preheat the oven to 375°F. Grease and line a deep 8-inch round cake pan. Sift the flour and coffee powder together onto a sheet of waxed paper.

2 ▲ Beat the eggs and sugar in a bowl with an electric mixer for about 2 minutes, until the mixture is pale and leaves a thick trail when the beaters are lifted.

3 ▲ Gently fold in the flour mixture with a metal spoon, being careful not to knock out any air. Turn the mixture into the prepared pan. Bake the sponge for 30–35 minutes, or until it springs back when lightly pressed. Turn onto a wire rack and let cool completely.

4 ▲ Make the filling. Mix the soft cheese with the honey in a bowl. Beat until smooth, then stir in the Tia Maria and chopped ginger.

5 ▲ Split the cake in half horizontally and sandwich the two halves together with the Tia Maria filling.

6 ◀ Make the icing. In a bowl, mix the confectioners' sugar and coffee extract with enough of the water to make an icing that will coat the back of a wooden spoon. Pour three-quarters of the icing over the cake, spreading it evenly to the edges. Stir the cocoa into the remaining icing until smooth. Spoon into a piping bag fitted with a writing nozzle and pipe the mocha icing over the coffee icing. Decorate with coffee beans, if you like.

Tip

To make a Mocha Cake, replace the coffee powder with 2 tablespoons cocoa powder, sifting it with the flour. Omit the chopped ginger in the filling.

ℳpricot Brandy-snap Roulade

*A magnificent combination of soft
and crisp textures, this cake
looks impressive and is easy to prepare.*

INGREDIENTS
Serves 6–8
4 large eggs, separated
½ tbsp fresh orange juice
½ cup sugar
2 cups ground almonds
4 brandy-snap cookies, crushed,
to decorate

For the Filling
5 oz canned apricots, drained
1¼ cups heavy cream
4 tbsp confectioners' sugar

3 ▲ Whisk the egg whites until they hold stiff peaks. Fold the egg whites into the almond mixture, then transfer to the prepared pan and smooth the surface. Bake in the center of the oven for about 20 minutes or until a skewer inserted into the center comes out clean. Leave to cool in the pan, covered with a clean, just-damp cloth.

4 ▲ To make the filling, place the apricots in a blender or food processor and purée until smooth. Place the cream and confectioners' sugar in a bowl and whip until the cream holds soft peaks. Fold in the apricot purée.

5 Spread out the crushed brandy-snaps on a sheet of waxed paper. Spread about one-third of the cream mixture over the cake, then invert it on to the crushed brandy-snaps. Peel away the lining paper.

6 Use the remaining cream mixture to cover the cake, then, using the waxed paper as a guide, tightly and neatly roll up the roulade from a short end. Transfer to a serving dish, sticking on any additional pieces of crushed brandy-snaps.

1 ▲ Preheat the oven to 375°F. Grease a 13 x 9 inch jelly roll pan, line the base with waxed paper and grease the paper.

2 Place the egg yolks, orange juice and sugar in a mixing bowl and beat with an electric mixer for about 10 minutes until thick and pale. Fold in the ground almonds.

Strawberry Cream Gâteau

Fresh raspberries also work well for this recipe.

INGREDIENTS

Serves 8–10
2 egg yolks
4 large eggs
finely grated zest of 1 lemon
½ cup superfine sugar
1 cup flour, sifted
½ cup butter, melted

For the Strawberry Cream
1½ cups fresh strawberries,
washed, dried and hulled
1¼ cups heavy cream
½ cup confectioners' sugar
1 tbsp strawberry liqueur or Kirsch

1 Preheat the oven to 300°F. Grease an 8 inch round cake pan, line the base with waxed paper and then grease the paper.

2 Place the eggs yolks, egg, lemon zest and sugar in a mixing bowl and beat with electric beaters for about 10 minutes or until thick and pale. Add the flour and melted butter. Beat for a further minute, then transfer to the prepared cake pan.

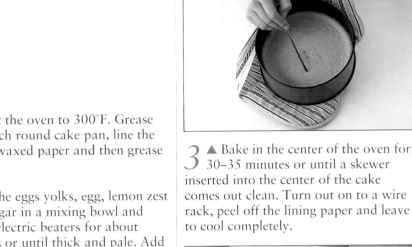

3 ▲ Bake in the center of the oven for 30–35 minutes or until a skewer inserted into the center of the cake comes out clean. Turn out on to a wire rack, peel off the lining paper and leave to cool completely.

4 ▲ To make the strawberry cream, place all but one of the strawberries in a food processor and purée until smooth. Place the heavy cream in a bowl and whip until it holds peaks. Fold the purée into the cream with the confectioners' sugar and liqueur.

5 ▲ Place the cooled cake on a plate and spread the strawberry cream evenly over the top and sides, making swirls for an attractive finish. Decorate with the sliced reserved strawberry.

Seasonal Celebrations

What better way to welcome in the New Year or
celebrate Christmas or Easter than with a really special
cake? With the family gathered around, you really do
have the perfect excuse to bake something special. Make
a blackberry ring to usher in harvest time, celebrate
Christmas French-style with a Bûche de Noël, or
concoct a treat in the shape of a pumpkin to spook
any Halloween gathering.

*S*tarry New Year Cake

Although it is not so traditional to welcome in the New Year with a cake as it is at Christmas, why not start a new tradition?

INGREDIENTS
Serves 15–20
9 inch round Madeira Cake
2 x quantity Butter Icing
1³/₄ lb/2¹/₃ x quantity Sugarpaste Icing
grape violet and mulberry food colorings
gold, lilac shimmer and primrose sparkle powdered food colorings

MATERIALS AND EQUIPMENT
star-shaped cutter
florists' wire
11 inch round cake board purple ribbon with gold stars

1 Cut the cake horizontally into three layers. Sandwich the layers together with three-quarters of the butter icing. Spread the remaining butter icing in a thin layer over the top and sides.

2 Color 1¼ lb of the sugarpaste icing purple with the grape violet and a touch of the mulberry food colorings. Roll out on a work surface lightly dusted with confectioners' sugar and cover the cake. Leave to dry overnight.

3 ▲ Place the cake on a sheet of waxed paper to protect the work surface. Water down a little of the gold and lilac shimmer powdered food colorings, then load up the end of a paintbrush with one of the colors. Position the brush over the area you want to color, then flick your wrist in the direction of the cake, so the color falls on to it in small beads. Repeat with the other color until the whole cake is covered. Leave to dry.

4 To make the stars, divide the remaining sugarpaste icing into three portions. Color one portion purple, the same as the coated cake, one portion with the lilac shimmer and one portion with the primrose sparkle. Roll out each color separately to about ¹/₈ inch thick on a work surface lightly dusted with sugar. Cut out stars with the star-shaped cutter and place on a piece of waxed paper. You will need 30 stars in total. Highlight the stars with the dry powdered colors, brushing gold on the purple stars, primrose on the yellow and lilac on the lilac stars. Using the watered-down gold and lilac colors, flick them on to each star as before.

5 ▲ While the icing is still soft, cut short lengths of florists' wire and carefully push them through the middle of 15 of the stars, but not all the way through. Leave to dry overnight.

6 ▲ Position the cake on the cake board or plate. Arrange three unwired stars in each color in a diagonal line on the top edge of the cake, securing with a little water. Repeat to make four more groupings of the stars. Stick the wired stars at angles all over the top of the cake as you arrange the flat ones.

7 Decorate the base of the cake with the ribbon.

*G*reek New Year Cake

A gold coin wrapped in foil is baked into this cake and tradition holds that good luck will come to the person who finds it.

INGREDIENTS
Serves 8–10
2¹/₂ cups flour
2 tsp baking powder
²/₃ cup ground almonds
1 cup butter, softened
³/₄ cup plus 2 tbsp sugar, plus a little extra
4 large eggs
²/₃ cup fresh orange juice
¹/₂ cup blanched almonds
1 tbsp sesame seeds

1 ▲ Preheat the oven to 350°F. Meanwhile, grease a 9 inch square cake pan with butter or vegetable oil, line the base and sides with waxed paper and grease the paper.

2 ▲ Sift the flour and baking powder into a mixing bowl and stir in the ground almonds.

3 ▲ In another mixing bowl, cream together the butter and sugar until light and fluffy. Beat in the eggs, one at a time, using an electric mixer. Fold in the flour mixture, alternating with the orange juice, until evenly combined.

4 ▲ Add a coin wrapped in foil if you wish to make the cake in the traditional manner, then spoon the cake mixture into the prepared pan and smooth the surface. Arrange the almonds on top, then sprinkle over the sesame seeds. Bake in the center of the oven for 50–55 minutes or until a skewer inserted into the center of the cake comes out clean. Leave to cool in the pan for about 5 minutes, then turn out on to a wire rack, peel off the lining paper and leave to cool completely. Serve cut into diamond shapes.

Valentine's Heart Cake

Cakes decorated with hearts can be very adaptable. Although this one was designed with Valentine's Day in mind, it could also be used to celebrate a birthday for someone special, an anniversary, or be made as two tiers for a wedding cake.

INGREDIENTS
Serves 30
8 inch square Light Fruit Cake
3 tbsp apricot jam, warmed and sieved
2 lb marzipan
3 lb/2 x quantity Royal Icing
4 oz/¹/₃ quantity Sugarpaste Icing
red food coloring

MATERIALS AND EQUIPMENT
1 x 10 inch square cake board
2 inch heart-shaped cutter
1 inch heart-shaped cutter
4 waxed paper piping bags
No 1 and No 2 writing and No 42 star nozzles
heart-patterned ribbon

1 Brush the cake with the apricot jam. Roll out the marzipan on a surface lightly dusted with confectioners' sugar and cover the cake. Leave to dry for at least 12 hours.

2 Secure the cake to the cake board with a little of the royal icing. Flat ice the cake with three or four layers of smooth icing, allowing each layer to dry overnight before applying the next. Set aside a little of the royal icing in an airtight container for piping.

3 ▲ To make the heart decorations, color the sugarpaste icing red. Roll out the red icing on a work surface lightly dusted with confectioners' sugar and cut out 12 hearts with the 2 inch heart-shaped cutter. Place the 1 inch heart-shaped cutter in the center of each larger heart and cut out a smaller heart, so you have 12 small hearts and 12 larger hollow hearts. Cut out four more smaller hearts from the remaining red icing so that you have 16 hearts in total. Place the hearts on a board covered with waxed paper.

4 ▲ Spoon a little of the reserved royal icing into a waxed paper piping bag fitted with a No 1 writing nozzle. Pipe wavy lines around the edges of four of the small hearts. Leave all the hearts to dry for several hours or overnight.

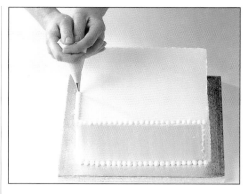

5 ▲ Spoon some more royal icing into a fresh piping bag fitted with a No 42 nozzle. Pipe swirls around the top and bottom edges of the cake with some of the royal icing.

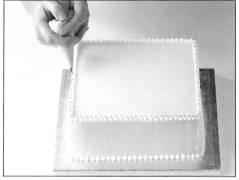

6 ▲ Color a heaped tablespoon of the remaining royal icing red and spoon into a fresh piping bag fitted with a clean No 1 writing nozzle. Pipe red dots on top of each white swirl of icing.

7 ▲ Arrange four of the large hearts on top of the cake, securing with a little royal icing.

8 Decorate with the ribbon. Spoon the remaining white royal icing into a fresh piping bag fitted with a No 2 writing nozzle. Pipe beads of icing down each side of the cake, above and below the ribbon. Allow all the piping to dry for several hours.

9 Arrange the remaining large hearts on top of the cake, securing with a little royal icing. Arrange the remaining small hearts on the sides.

Valentine's Box of Chocolates

This special cake would also make a wonderful gift for Mother's Day. Choose your favorite chocolates to go inside.

INGREDIENTS
Serves 10–12
1½ x quantity chocolate-flavor Quick-Mix Sponge Cake mix
10 oz yellow marzipan
8 tbsp apricot jam, warmed and sieved
2 lb/2⅔ x quantity Sugarpaste Icing
red food coloring
8 oz/about 16–20 hand-made chocolates

MATERIALS AND EQUIPMENT
heart-shaped cake pan
9 inch square piece of stiff cardboard
9 inch square cake board
piece of string
small heart-shaped cutter
length of ribbon and a pin
paper petits fours cases

1 Preheat the oven to 350°F. Grease the pan, line the base with waxed paper and grease the paper. Spoon the cake mixture into the pan and smooth the surface. Bake in the center of the oven for 45–50 minutes, or until a skewer inserted into the center of the cake comes out clean. Leave the cake in the pan for about 5 minutes, then turn out on to a wire rack, peel off the lining paper and leave to cool completely.

2 ▲ Place the cake on the piece of cardboard and draw around it with a pencil. Cut the heart shape out of the cardboard and set aside. This will be used as the support for the box lid.

3 ▲ Using a large, sharp knife, cut through the cake horizontally just below where the cake starts to dome. Carefully lift the top section on to the heart-shaped cardboard and place the bottom section on the cake board.

4 Use the piece of string to measure around the outside of the bottom section of cake.

5 ▲ On a work surface lightly dusted with confectioners' sugar, roll out the marzipan into a long sausage shape to the same length as the string. Place the marzipan sausage on the cake around the outside edge. Brush the bottom and lid sections evenly with apricot jam.

6 Color the sugarpaste icing red and cut off about one-third. Cut another portion from the larger piece, about 2 oz in weight. Wrap these two portions separately in plastic wrap and set aside. On a work surface lightly dusted with confectioners' sugar, roll out the icing to a 14 inch square and use it to cover the bottom section of cake.

7 ▲ Stand the lid on a raised surface, such as a glass or bowl. Roll out the reserved one-third of sugarpaste icing to a 12 inch square and cover the lid section of the cake. Roll out the remaining piece of icing and stamp out small hearts with the cutter. Stick them around the edge of the lid with a little water. Tie the ribbon in a bow and secure on top of the lid with the pin. Carefully lift the top section on to the heart-shaped cardboard and place the bottom section on the cake board.

8 Place the chocolates in the *petits fours* cases and arrange in the bottom section of the cake. Position the lid, placing it slightly off center, to reveal the chocolates inside. Remove the ribbon and pin before serving.

Sweetheart Cake

This romantic cake would be ideal for Valentine's Day, or to celebrate an engagement or anniversary. Change the icing colors to suit the particular occasion.

INGREDIENTS
Serves 70
8-inch heart-shaped Light Fruit Cake (make using quantities for standard 9-inch round cake)
2 tablespoons apricot jam, warmed and sieved
2 pounds marzipan
2 pounds/2⅔ x quantity Sugar paste Icing (Fondant)
red food coloring
8 ounces/⅓ quantity Royal Icing

MATERIALS AND EQUIPMENT
10-inch silver heart-shaped cake board
large and medium-sized heart-shaped plunger cutters
red ribbon, 1 inch and ¼ inch wide
looped red ribbon, ½ inch wide
waxed or parchment paper piping bag
medium star nozzle
fresh red rosebuds

1 ▲ Brush the cake with apricot jam, place on the cake board and cover with marzipan. Using about three-quarters of the sugar paste icing, cover the cake smoothly.

2 ▲ Trim away the excess sugar paste icing. Knead the trimmings together with the remaining sugar paste icing and use to cover the cake board. Return the cake to the cake board and let dry overnight in a cake box.

3 ▲ Color the remaining sugar paste icing bright red with red food coloring. Roll out thinly and cut out 18 large and 21 medium-sized hearts. Allow to dry flat.

4 Measure and fit the wide ribbon around the cake board and secure with a pin. Fit a band of the looped ribbon around the side of the cake, securing with a bead of icing. Tie a bow with long tails in the narrow ribbon and attach to the side of the cake with a bead of icing.

5 ▲ Fill a paper piping bag fitted with a medium-sized star nozzle with royal icing. Pipe a row of stars around the base of the cake and attach a medium-sized heart to alternate stars. Arrange the large red hearts around the top of the cake, and pipe a star to secure each one.

6 ▲ Choose several tiny rosebuds or one large rose and tie a bow with narrow ribbon. Place on top of the cake just before serving.

Heart Cake

This is a delightful variation of the Sweetheart Cake—a fun way to show someone special how you feel.

INGREDIENTS
Serves 8–10
2 sticks (1 cup) unsalted butter or margarine, at room temperature
1 cup sugar
4 eggs, at room temperature
1½ cups flour
1 teaspoon baking powder
½ teaspoon baking soda
2 tablespoons milk
1 teaspoon vanilla extract

To Decorate
3 egg whites
1¼ cups granulated sugar
2 tablespoons cold water
2 tablespoons fresh lemon juice
¼ teaspoon cream of tartar
pink food coloring
1½–2 cups confectioners' sugar

1 Preheat the oven to 350°F. Line an 8-inch heart-shaped pan with waxed or parchment paper and grease.

2 ▲ With an electric mixer, cream the butter or margarine and sugar until light and fluffy. Add the eggs, one at a time, beating thoroughly after each addition.

3 Sift the flour, baking powder, and baking soda together. Fold the dry ingredients into the butter mixture in three batches, alternating with the milk. Stir in the vanilla.

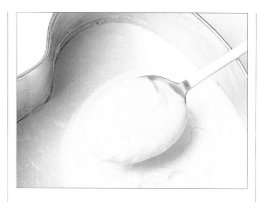

4 ▲ Spoon the batter into the prepared pan and bake for 35–40 minutes. Let the cake stand for 5 minutes, then unmold and transfer to a rack to cool completely.

5 For the frosting, combine 2 of the egg whites, the granulated sugar, water, lemon juice and cream of tartar in the top of a double boiler or in a bowl set over simmering water. With an electric mixer, beat until the mixture is thick and holds soft peaks, about 7 minutes. Remove from the heat and continue beating until the mixture is thick enough to spread. Tint the frosting with the pink food coloring.

6 ▲ Put the cake on a board about 12 inches square, covered in foil or in paper suitable for contact with food. Spread the frosting evenly on the cake. Smooth the top and sides. Allow to set 3–4 hours, or overnight.

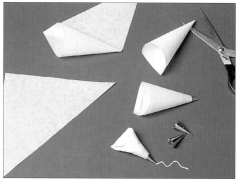

7 ▲ For the paper piping bags, fold an 11 x 8-inch sheet of baking parchment or waxed paper in half diagonally, then cut into two pieces along the fold mark. Roll over the short side, so that it meets the right-angled corner and forms a cone. To form the piping bag, hold the cone in place with one hand, wrap the point of the long side of the triangle around the cone, and tuck inside, folding over twice to secure. Snip a hole in the pointed end and slip in a small metal piping tip to extend about ¼ inch.

8 For the piped decorations, place 1 tablespoon of the remaining egg white in a bowl and whisk until frothy. Gradually beat in enough confectioners' sugar to make a stiff mixture suitable for piping.

9 ▲ Spoon into a paper piping bag to half-fill. Fold over the top and squeeze to pipe decorations on the cake.

Simnel Cake

A traditional cake for Easter.

INGREDIENTS
Serves 10–12
1 cup butter, softened
1 cup superfine sugar
4 large eggs, beaten
3 cups mixed dried fruit
such as apricots or prunes
½ cup glacé cherries
3 tbsp sherry (optional)
2½ cups flour, sifted
3 tsp ground allspice
1 tsp baking powder
1½ lb yellow marzipan
1 egg yolk, beaten
ribbons and sugared eggs, to
decorate

1 Preheat the oven to 325°F. Lightly grease a deep 8 in round cake pan, line with a double thickness of waxed paper and grease the paper.

2 Place the butter and sugar in a large mixing bowl and beat until light and fluffy. Gradually beat in the eggs. Stir in the dried fruit, glacé cherries and sherry, if using.

3 ▲ Sift together the flour, allspice and baking powder, then fold into the cake mixture. Set aside.

4 ▲ Cut off half of the marzipan and roll out on a work surface dusted with confectioners' sugar to an 8 inch round. Spoon half of the cake mixture into the prepared pan and smooth the surface with the back of a spoon. Place the marzipan round on top, then add the other half of the cake mixture and smooth the surface.

5 Bake in the center of the oven for about 2½ hours or until golden and springy to the touch. Leave the cake in the pan for about 15 minutes, then turn out on to a wire rack, peel off the lining paper and leave to cool completely.

6 ▲ Roll out the other half of the marzipan to a round to fit on top of the cooled cake. Brush the top of the cake with a little of the egg yolk and position the marzipan round on top. Flute the edges of the marzipan and, if liked, make a decorative pattern on top with a fork. Brush with more egg yolk.

7 Put the cake on a baking sheet and place under a broiler for 5 minutes or until the top is lightly browned. Leave to cool before decorating with ribbons and sugared eggs.

Easter Egg Nest Cake

Celebrate Easter with a fresh-tasting lemon sponge cake, colorfully adorned with marzipan nests and chocolate eggs.

INGREDIENTS
Serves 10
1 quantity lemon-flavor Quick-Mix Sponge Cake mix
1 quantity lemon-flavor Butter Icing
8 oz marzipan
pink, green and purple food colorings
foil-wrapped chocolate eggs

MATERIALS AND EQUIPMENT
8 inch ring mold
10 inch cake board

1 Preheat the oven to 325°F. Grease and flour the ring mold. Spoon the cake mixture into the mold and smooth the surface. Bake in the center of the oven for about 25 minutes, or until golden in color and firm to the touch. Turn out on to a wire rack and leave to cool completely.

2 ▲ Cut the cake in half horizontally and sandwich together with about one-third of the butter icing. Position the cake on the cake board. Spread the remaining icing over the outside of the cake to cover completely.

3 Smooth the top of the cake with a spatula and swirl the icing around the side of the cake.

4 ▲ To make the marzipan braids, divide the marzipan into three portions and color it pink, green and purple. Cut each portion in half. Using one-half of each of the colors, roll each one out with your fingers on a work surface lightly dusted with confectioners' sugar to make a thin sausage shape long enough to go around the bottom edge of the cake. Pinch the ends together at the top, then twist the individual strands into a rope. Pinch the other ends to seal neatly.

5 ▲ Place the rope on the cake board around the bottom edge of the cake.

6 To make the nests, take the remaining portions of colored marzipan and divide each color into five. Roll each piece into a rope about 6 ½ inches long. Take a rope of each color, pinch the ends together, twist to form a multi-colored rope and pinch the other ends. Form the rope into a circle and then repeat the process to make the remaining four nests.

7 ▲ Arrange the nests so they are evenly spaced on the top of the cake and place several chocolate eggs in the middle of each.

Easter Sponge Cake

For a special Easter celebration, serve your family this light lemon quick-mix sponge cake, decorated with lemon butter icing and cut-out marzipan flowers.

INGREDIENTS
Serves 10–12
1½ x quantity lemon-flavor
Quick-mix Sponge Cake mix
2 x quantity lemon-flavor
Butter Icing
½ cup sliced almonds, toasted
2 ounces marzipan
green, orange and yellow
food coloring

MATERIALS AND EQUIPMENT
8-inch round cake pans
nylon piping bag
medium-sized star nozzle
flower cutters

1 Preheat the oven to 325°F. Grease the pans, line the bottoms with waxed or parchment paper and grease the paper. Divide the mixture between the pans and bake the cakes for 35–40 minutes, until the cakes spring back when lightly pressed in the center and are golden brown. Loosen the edges of the cakes with a baking spatula, turn out, remove the lining paper and cool on a wire rack.

2 ▲ Sandwich the cakes together with one-quarter of the butter icing. Spread the side of the cake evenly with another one-quarter of icing.

3 ▲ Press the almonds onto the sides to cover evenly. Spread the top of the cake evenly with another one-quarter of icing and finish with a baking spatula dipped in hot water, spreading backward and forward to give an even lined effect.

4 ▲ Place the remaining icing in a nylon piping bag fitted with a medium-sized star nozzle and pipe a scroll edging.

5 ▲ Using the marzipan and food coloring, make ten green and eight orange marzipan flowers and six marzipan daffodils.

6 ▲ Arrange the marzipan flowers on the cake and allow the icing to set.

Easter Cake

This delicious, spicy Easter fruit cake is decorated with ribbons and miniature eggs made from chocolate modeling paste.

INGREDIENTS
Serves 16
1/2 cup soft margarine
1/2 cup brown sugar
3 eggs
1 1/2 cups flour
2 tsp apple pie spice
3 1/2 cups mixed dried fruit
1/4 cup candied cherries, chopped
1/4 cup hazelnuts
3 tbsp apricot jam, warmed and strained
1 lb marzipan
brown food coloring

For the Chocolate Molding Icing
4 oz dark or milk chocolate
2 tbsp liquid glucose
1 egg white
3 1/2 cups confectioner's sugar
cornstarch, for dusting

For the Chocolate Modeling Paste
2 oz dark chocolate
2 oz white chocolate
2 tbsp liquid glucose
pink food coloring

MATERIALS AND EQUIPMENT
6 1/4 cup pudding mold
10 in round, gold cake board
clean piece of sponge
several 2 1/2 in squares of gold foil
Paintbrush

1 Preheat the oven to 300°F. Grease the mold, line the base with wax paper and grease the paper. Cream together the margarine and brown sugar. Gradually add the eggs with a little of the flour to prevent curdling. Sift the remaining flour and the spice into the bowl and stir in the fruit and nuts.

2 Spoon the cake mixture into the prepared mold and smooth the surface. Bake in the center of the oven for 1 1/2 hours, or until a skewer inserted into the center of the cake comes out clean. Turn the cake out on to a wire rack, peel off the lining paper and then allow to cool.

3 To make the chocolate molding icing, break up the chocolate and place in a bowl with the glucose over a pan of hot water. Leave until melted, cool slightly then add the egg white. Gradually add the confectioner's sugar, beating well each time, until too stiff to stir. Turn out on to a work surface, lightly dusted with confectioner's sugar and knead in the remaining sugar.

4 To make the modeling paste, melt the dark and white chocolate in separate bowls. Add half the glucose to the dark chocolate and mix to a stiff paste. Add some pink food coloring and the remaining glucose to the white chocolate and mix to a stiff paste. Wrap the pastes separately in plastic wrap and chill until firm.

5 ▲ Cut a wedge out of the cake. Place the cake on the board and brush with the apricot jam. On a work surface lightly dusted with confectioner's sugar, roll out the marzipan and use to cover the cake, tucking the marzipan into the cut section. Reserve the trimmings, wrapped in plastic wrap.

6 On a work surface lightly dusted with cornstarch, roll out the chocolate molding icing and use to cover the cake. Cut two thin strips from the marzipan trimmings and stick on the inside edges of the cut-out wedge with a little water.

7 ▲ Thin the brown food coloring with water. Dip the sponge in the color and pat over the surface of the icing. Allow to dry.

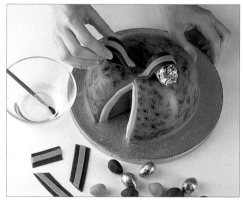

8 ▲ Lightly knead two-thirds of each of the modeling pastes and shape into 18 small eggs. Cover some of the eggs with gold foil and position them all inside the cut-out wedge. To make the bow, roll out the remaining modeling paste and cut two strips 3/4 in wide and 10 in long from the dark paste and two strips 1/4 in wide and 8 in long from the pink paste. Stick the pink strips to the dark ones with a little water. From these strips, cut two 5 in lengths, press the ends together to form loops and secure to the cake. Secure two 3 in lengths for ribbons ends and cover the center of the bow with another small strip. Place a piece of crumpled foil under each strip until hardened.

Mother's Day Basket

Every mother would love to receive a cake like this on Mother's Day. Choose fresh flowers to decorate the top and add ribbons to the basket handle for a pretty finish.

INGREDIENTS
Serves 12
*1½ x quantity orange-flavor
Quick-mix Sponge Cake, made
without baking powder
2 pounds/2⅔ x quantity
orange-flavor Butter Icing*

MATERIALS AND EQUIPMENT
*2-pint fluted ovenproof glass dish
or brioche mold
6-inch round thin silver
cake board
waxed or parchment paper piping
bags
basket-weave nozzle
12 x 3-inch strip kitchen foil
mauve ribbon, ½ inch wide
dotted mauve ribbon,
⅛ inch wide
fresh flowers*

1 Lightly grease the dish. Line the bottom with waxed or parchment paper and grease the paper. Make the cake without any baking powder and bake for 75–85 minutes, until well risen, golden brown and firm to the touch.

2 ▲ Spread the side of the cake with one-third of the orange-flavor butter icing and place upside down on a cake board.

3 ▲ Make plenty of paper piping bags and fit one with a basket-weave nozzle. Half-fill with butter icing and pipe the sides with a basket-weave pattern (see Basket-Weave Wedding Cake).

4 ▲ Invert the cake onto the cake board and spread the top with butter icing. Pipe a shell edging, using the basket-weave nozzle, to neaten the top edge. Continue to pipe the basket-weave icing across the top of the cake, starting at the edge. Set the cake in a cool place.

5 ▲ Fold the strip of foil in half, then in half again; continue to fold until you have a strip several layers thick.

6 ▲ Using the plain ribbon, bind the strip to cover the foil; bend up the end to secure the ribbon. Bend the foil to make a handle; press into the icing.

7 ▲ Make a neat arrangement of fresh flowers tied with narrow ribbon and arrange on top of the cake just before serving. Tie a bow and pin it to the side of the cake.

Terracotta Flowerpot

Ideal for celebrating a gardener's birthday or Mother's Day, this cake is baked in a pudding mold for the flowerpot shape and filled with a colorful arrangement of icing flowers and foliage.

INGREDIENTS
Serves 15
3-egg quantity Madeira Cake mix
6 oz jam
½ quantity Butter Icing
2 tbsp apricot jam, warmed and strained
1¼ lb/1²/₃ x quantity Sugarpaste Icing
4 oz/¹/₆ quantity Royal Icing
dark orange, black, red, silver, green, purple, and yellow food colorings
3 oz chocolate, coarsely grated

MATERIALS AND EQUIPMENT
5 cup pudding mold
string
paintbrush
thin green wire
9 in round cake board

1 Preheat the oven to 325°F. Grease the mold, line the base with wax paper and grease the paper. Spoon the cake mixture into the prepared mold and smooth the surface. Bake in the center of the oven for 1¼ hours, or until a skewer inserted into the center of the cake comes out clean. Cover with foil for the last 10 minutes if the top begir ˙ to brown. Turn the cake out on to a wire rack, peel off the lining paper and allow to cool.

2 Trim the top of the cake flat if it has domed. Cut the cake horizontally into three and fill with the jam and butter icing.

3 Cut out a shallow circle from the top of the cake, leaving a ½ in rim around the edge.

4 ▲ Brush the outside of the cake and the rim with the apricot jam. Color two-thirds of the sugarpaste icing dark orange. Measure the circumference of the cake at its widest part and the height, including a turnover for the rim, with string. On a work surface lightly dusted with confectioner's sugar, roll out the icing to these measurements and use to cover the cake. Reserve any trimmings, wrapped in plastic wrap. Allow the cake to dry for 12 hours.

5 ▲ Using the reserved trimmings, shape the decorations and handles for the flowerpot. Leave to dry on wax paper. Sprinkle the grated chocolate into the top of the flowerpot for soil.

6 Color a small piece of the remaining sugarpaste icing a very pale orange, roll out into an oblong and fold over to make a seed package. Color a little of the icing black and make the seeds. Color two more small pieces of icing red and silver and shape the trowel. Leave to dry on wax paper.

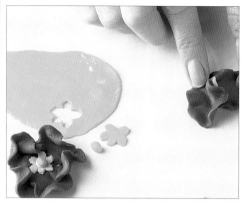

7 ▲ Color the remaining sugarpaste icing green, purple and a very small amount yellow. Mold individual flower petals with the purple icing. Stick them together in flower shapes with royal icing. Roll out the yellow icing and cut out the flower centers with a small knife. Position in the center of each flower with a small ball of yellow icing. Secure with royal icing. Allow to dry on wax paper.

8 ▲ Shape the leaves from the green icing using your fingers and mark the veins with a knife. Insert short pieces of wire up some of the stems so you can arrange them in the flowerpot. Allow to dry over the handle of a wooden spoon. Roll out any remaining green icing and snip to represent grass. Paint a design on the seed package with food colorings.

9 Attach the dark-orange decorations to the flowerpot with royal icing. Arrange the leaves and flowers in the pot. Place the cake on the cake board and position the trowel, seed package, and grass around the outside. Remove the wire from the leaves before serving.

Mother's Day Bouquet

A piped bouquet of flowers can bring as much pleasure as a fresh one for a Mother's Day treat.

INGREDIENTS
Serves 8–10
1 quantity Quick-Mix Sponge Cake mix
2 x quantity Butter Icing green, blue, yellow and pink food colorings

MATERIALS AND EQUIPMENT
2 x 7 inch round cake pans
serrated scraper
5 waxed paper piping bags
No 3 writing and petal nozzles

1 Preheat the oven to 325°F. Grease the cake pans, line the bases with waxed paper and grease the paper. Divide the cake mixture evenly between the pans and smooth the surfaces. Bake in the center of the oven for about 20 minutes or until firm to the touch. Turn out on to a wire rack, peel off the lining paper and leave to cool.

2 ▲ Place one of the cakes on paper on a turntable. Use half to two-thirds of the butter icing to sandwich the cakes together and to coat the top and sides. Coat the top using a spatula and the sides using the scraper.

3 Transfer the cake to a serving plate, then divide the remaining butter icing into four bowls and color one portion green, one portion blue, one portion yellow and one portion pink. Spoon the blue icing into a waxed paper piping bag fitted with the No 3 writing nozzle. Pipe the vase on top of the cake in lines and beads.

4 ▲ Spoon the green icing into a fresh piping bag fitted with a clean No 3 writing nozzle. Pipe the flower stems coming out of the vase.

5 Spoon the pink icing into a fresh piping bag fitted with the petal nozzle. Pipe pink petals on the ends of some of the stems. Pipe beads of blue icing in the centers.

6 Spoon most of the yellow icing into a fresh piping bag fitted with a clean petal nozzle and pipe yellow flowers on the remaining stems. Pipe beads of blue icing in the centers.

7 ▲ Decorate the side of the cake. Pipe stems with leaves evenly spaced all around the side with the green icing, and pipe beads of the blue icing to make flowers at the end of each stem. Spoon the reserved yellow icing into a fresh piping bag fitted with a clean No 3 writing nozzle and pipe small beads in the center of the blue flowers.

8 Pipe beads of green icing round the top and bottom edges of the cake.

*J*azzy Chocolate Gâteau

This cake is made with Father's Day in mind, though really it can be made for anyone who loves chocolate.

INGREDIENTS
Serves 12–15
2 x quantity chocolate-flavor
Quick-Mix Sponge Cake mix
3 x 1 oz squares plain chocolate
3 x 1 oz squares white chocolate
½ quantity Fudge Frosting
½ quantity Glacé Icing
1 tsp weak coffee
8 tbsp chocolate hazelnut spread

MATERIALS AND EQUIPMENT
2 x 8 inch round cake pans
waxed paper piping bag
No 1 writing nozzle

1 Preheat the oven to 325°F. Grease the cake pans, line the bases with waxed paper and grease the paper. Divide the cake mixture evenly between the pans and smooth the surfaces. Bake in the center of the oven for 20–30 minutes, or until firm to the touch. Turn out on to a wire rack, peel off the lining paper and leave to cool completely.

2 Meanwhile, cover a large baking sheet or board (or two smaller ones) with baking parchment and tape it down at each corner. Melt each chocolate in separate bowls over pans of hot water, stirring until smooth, then pour on to the baking parchment. Spread out the chocolates evenly with a spatula. Allow to cool until the surfaces are firm enough to cut, but not so hard that they will break. The chocolate should no longer feel sticky when touched with your finger.

3 ▲ Cut out haphazard shapes of chocolate and set aside.

4 ▲ Make the fudge frosting and, when cool enough to spread, use to sandwich the two cakes together. Place the cake on a stand or plate.

5 Make the glacé icing, using 1 tsp weak coffee (to color it very slightly) along with enough water to form a spreading consistency, and spread on top of the cake almost to the edges. Spread the side of the cake with enough chocolate hazelnut spread to

6 ▲ Arrange the chocolate pieces around the side of the cake, pressing into the hazelnut spread to secure.

7 To decorate, spoon about 3 tbsp of the chocolate hazelnut spread into a piping bag fitted with a No 1 nozzle and pipe 'jazzy' lines over the glacé icing.

Father's Day Cake

Celebrate Father's Day with this coffee-flavored cake smothered in a rich coffee butterscotch frosting and decorated with piped chocolate and cut-out decorations.

INGREDIENTS
Serves 12
1½ x quantity coffee-flavor
Quick- mix Sponge Cake (see Tip)
1½ pound/1½ x quantity
coffee-flavor Butterscotch Frosting
⅔ cup plain chocolate chips
2 tablespoons chocolate and
hazelnut spread

MATERIALS AND EQUIPMENT
deep 7-inch square cake pan
8-inch square silver cake board
baking sheet
waxed or parchment paper piping
bags
star and No. 2 writing nozzles

1 Grease the cake pan. Line with waxed or parchment paper and grease the paper. Make the cake and bake for 45–50 minutes, until well risen, golden brown and firm to the

2 ▲ Place the cake on a rack over a baking sheet and pour the freshly made frosting over to cover the cake completely, allowing the excess frosting to fall into the tray. Allow to set. Place on the cake board.

3 ▲ Melt the chocolate, pour onto a sheet of baking parchment and spread evenly. As the chocolate begins to set, place another sheet of baking parchment on top and turn the chocolate "sandwich" over. Peel off the baking parchment and turn the chocolate sheet over.

4 ▲ Cut out seven 1-inch squares of chocolate with a sharp knife and cut into 14 triangles.

5 ▲ Half-fill a paper piping bag fitted with a star nozzle with chocolate and hazelnut spread. Pipe a shell border around the base and along the top edge of the cake.

6 ▲ Decorate the sides and top of the cake with the chocolate cut-outs. Using a No. 2 writing nozzle, pipe "Happy Father's Day" on the top.

Tip

To make a coffee-flavored Sponge Cake, add 2 teaspoons coffee granules blended with 1 teaspoon boiling water to the cake mixture.

Harvest Blackberry Ring

Gracious blackberry branches twisting their way over the cake, and leaves tinged with reddish-brown, create an autumnal theme.

INGREDIENTS
Serves 20
1 quantity 7 inch round Light Fruit Cake mix
3 tbsp apricot jam, warmed and sieved
1 lb marzipan
2 lb/2²/₃ x quantity Sugarpaste Icing tangerine, purple, green and paprika food colorings

MATERIALS AND EQUIPMENT
8 inch ring mold
10 inch round cake board

1 Preheat the oven to 300°F. Grease the cake pan, line with waxed paper and grease the paper. Spoon in the cake mixture and smooth the surface with the back of a wet metal spoon. Bake in the center of the oven for 1½–2 hours or until a skewer inserted in the center of the cake comes out clean. Leave the cake to cool in the mold on a wire rack. When completely cool, turn out.

2 Brush the cake with the apricot jam. Measure half the circumference of the cake with a piece of string. Measure the height to include the top as well as the sides of the cake (see step 4 for guidance). Take three-quarters of the marzipan and cut in half. Cover the cake in two halves as follows. Roll out each piece of marzipan on a work surface lightly dusted with confectioners' sugar and trim each using the string measurements as a guide. Trim and press the joins together to secure.

3 Measure the height and circumference of the inside of the ring with string. Cover the inside by rolling out the remaining one-quarter of marzipan. Trim to fit and press the joins together to secure. Position the cake on the cake board. Leave to dry

4 ▲ Measure half the circumference of the cake with a piece of string. Measure the height to include the top as well as the sides of the cake.

5 ▲ Colour 1½ lb of the sugarpaste icing pale tangerine. Cut off three-quarters of this and cut in half. Keep the remaining icing well wrapped. Brush the marzipan lightly with water. Cover the top and sides of the cake in two pieces by rolling out each piece of icing. Trim and press the joins together.

6 Measure the height and circumference of the inside of the ring with string. Cover the inside of the ring by rolling out the remaining one-quarter of sugarpaste icing, using the string measurement as a guide. Trim to fit and press the joins together to secure.

7 ▲ Color one-quarter of the white sugarpaste icing purple. To mold the blackberries, take a little of the purple icing and form into balls of different sizes for the bases. Make a number of smaller balls and stick them on the outside of the larger ones, securing with water. Place on a piece of waxed paper and leave to dry while making the leaves and branches.

8 ▲ Color two-thirds of the remaining white sugarpaste icing green and the rest paprika. Reserve half of the green icing for the stems, and knead the remaining green and the paprika icing lightly together until marbled. Roll out and cut out leaf shapes. Make the branches by rolling the green icing into long thin strands.

9 To assemble, arrange the branches on the cake, securing them with a little water and twisting them as necessary, covering any joins in the icing where possible. Attach the leaves, bending them into shape, then arrange the blackberries on the cake, attaching all with a little water.

Halloween Pumpkin Patch

Pumpkins have sprung up all over this orange and chocolate cake, making it the ideal design to celebrate Halloween.

INGREDIENTS
Serves 12–15
2 x quantity chocolate-flavor
Quick-Mix Sponge Cake mix
6 oz/2 x quantity Sugarpaste Icing
orange and brown food colorings
2 x quantity orange-flavor Butter
Icing
chocolate chips
angelica

MATERIALS AND EQUIPMENT
2 x 8 inch round cake pans
9 inch round cake board
serrated scraper
waxed paper piping bag
No 7 writing nozzle

1 Preheat the oven to 325°F. Lightly grease the cake pans, line the bases with waxed paper and then grease the paper.

2 Divide the mixture between the pans and smooth the surfaces. Bake for 20–30 minutes or until firm to the touch. Turn out on to a wire rack, peel off the lining paper and leave to cool.

3 ▲ To make the pumpkins, color a very small piece of the sugarpaste icing brown, and the rest orange. Dust your fingers with a little cornstarch. Shape small balls of the orange icing the size of walnuts and some a bit smaller. Make the ridges with a wooden toothpick. Make the stems from the brown icing and press into the top of each pumpkin, securing with a little water. Paint highlights on each pumpkin with orange food coloring. Leave to dry on waxed paper.

4 Cut each cake in half horizontally. Use one-quarter of the butter icing to sandwich the cakes together. Place the cake on the cake board. Use about two-thirds of the remaining icing to coat the top and sides of the cake.

5 Texture the cake sides with a serrated scraper. Decorate the top with the same scraper, moving the scraper sideways to make undulations and a ridged spiral pattern in a slight fan shape. The texturing should resemble a ploughed field.

6 ▲ Fit a paper piping bag with the writing nozzle and spoon in the remaining butter icing. Pipe a twisted rope pattern around the top and bottom edges of the cake.

7 Decorate the piped pattern with chocolate chips.

8 ▲ Cut the angelica into diamond shapes and arrange on the cake with the pumpkins.

Halloween Coffin

A simple, spooky cake for the centerpiece of a Halloween party.

INGREDIENTS
Serves 4–6
1 quantity Quick-Mix Sponge Cake
mix
5 tbsp apricot jam, warmed and
sieved
12 oz/1 quantity Sugarpaste
Icing
black food coloring
3 oz yellow marzipan
¼ quantity Butter Icing
golden superfine sugar, for dusting

MATERIALS AND EQUIPMENT
2 lb loaf pan
9 inch square piece of thick
cardboard
small fluted oval cutter
small plastic skeleton and other
Halloween toys
piping bag fitted with a small star
nozzle

3 ▲ To make the lid of the coffin, slice about ½ inch off the top of the cake. To make a base to reinforce the coffin and lid, place both pieces of cake on the cardboard and draw around them with a pencil. Remove the cakes and cut out the shapes on the cardboard. Brush the cakes with apricot jam.

4 Use a small, sharp knife to hollow out the base of the coffin, leaving about a ½ inch border. Place the coffin and lid on the cards. Brush the cakes with apricot jam.

5 Color the sugarpaste icing black, then cut off about one-third and set aside, wrapped in plastic wrap. Roll out the larger portion of sugarpaste icing on a work surface lightly dusted with confectioners' sugar and use to cover the base of the coffin, easing it into the hollow and down the sides. Trim the edges. Roll out the remaining black icing and cover the lid. Trim the edges.

6 ▲ To make the coffin handles, pull off six small pieces of the marzipan and shape into sausages with rounded ends. To make the plaque on the lid, roll out the kneaded trimmings of marzipan thinly and stamp out a fluted oval with the cutter. Stick the handles and plaque in position with a little butter icing.

7 Lay the skeleton in the coffin. Color the remaining butter icing black and use to pipe a small star border around the coffin and down the sides. Sprinkle with sifted superfine sugar and decorate with the Halloween toys.

1 Preheat the oven to 350°F. Grease the pan, line the base and sides with waxed paper and grease the paper. Spoon the mixture into the pan and smooth the surface. Bake in the center of the oven for 35–40 minutes, or until a skewer inserted into the cake comes out clean. Leave the cake in the pan for 5 minutes, then turn out on to a wire rack, peel off the lining paper and leave to cool.

2 To shape the cake, use a large, sharp knife to slice off the risen surface to make it completely flat. Turn the cake upside-down and score the shape of the coffin in the cake. Cut off the two top corners at an angle, then cut diagonally down from the corners to the base of the coffin.

*H*alloween Pumpkin

Halloween is a time for spooky cakes—witches may even burst out of them. This one is made in two pudding basins, making it easy to create a pumpkin effect. Make the cake and icing with your favorite flavor and—you are all set for a party full of eerie surprises.

INGREDIENTS
Serves 15
3-egg quantity Madeira Cake mix
9 ounces/³⁄₄ quantity orange-flavor
Butter Icing
1 pound/1¹⁄₃ x quantity
Sugar paste Icing (Fondant)
4 ounces/¹⁄₆ quantity Royal Icing
orange, black and yellow food
coloring

MATERIALS AND EQUIPMENT
2 x 1-quart pudding basins
thin wooden skewer
thin paintbrush
10-inch round cake board

1 Preheat the oven to 325°F. Grease the pudding basins, line the bottoms with waxed or parchment paper and grease the paper. Divide the cake mixture equally between them and bake for 1¼ hours. Turn out and cool on a wire rack.

2 Trim the widest ends of the cakes so they will fit flat against one another to make a round shape. Split each cake in half horizontally and fill with some of the butter icing, then stick the two cakes together with butter icing to form a pumpkin. Trim one of the narrow ends slightly, to make the bottom of the pumpkin. Cover the outside of the cake with the remaining butter icing.

3 Take three-quarters (12 ounces) of the sugar paste icing and color it orange. Roll out to cover the cake, trimming to fit where necessary. Mold it gently with your hands to create a smooth surface. Reserve the trimmings.

4 ▲ With a thin wooden skewer, mark the segments onto the pumpkin. With a fine paintbrush and watered-down orange food coloring, paint on the markings for the pumpkin skin. Use orange sugar paste icing trimmings to make the top of the cake where the witch bursts out, by cutting and tearing rolled-out pieces to create jagged edges. Attach to the top of the cake with a little water.

5 ▲ Take the remaining sugar paste icing and color three-quarters black. Of the remainder, color a little yellow and leave the rest white. Use some of the black and white to make the witch, molding the head, arms and body separately and securing with royal icing. When set, roll out some black icing and cut jagged edges to form a cape.

6 Drape the shapes over the arms and body, securing with a little water. Make the hat in two pieces—a circle and a cone—and secure with royal icing. Let dry on waxed paper. Shape the cauldron, broomstick and cat's head out of more of the black, white and yellow icing, securing the handle of the cauldron with royal icing when dry. Allow all to dry completely on waxed paper.

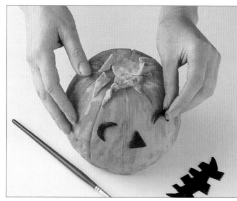

7 ▲ Use the remaining black icing for the pumpkin features. Roll out and cut out the eyes, nose and mouth with a sharp knife. Attach to the pumpkin with a little water. Place the cake on the cake board, secure the witch on top of the cake with royal icing and arrange the cat, cauldron and broomstick around the base.

*S*piders' Web Cake

A spooky cake for any occasion, fancy dress or otherwise. Put as many spiders as you like on the cake, but any leftover ones can be put on the children's plates or arranged to look like they're crawling all over the table.

INGREDIENTS
Serves 6–8
1 quantity lemon-flavor Quick-Mix
Sponge Cake mix
1 quantity lemon-flavor Glacé Icing
yellow and black food colorings

For the Spiders
4 x 1 oz squares plain chocolate,
broken into pieces
²/₃ cup heavy cream
3 tbsp ground almonds
cocoa powder, for dusting
chocolate sprinkles
8 strands black liquorice, cut in half
lengthwise
½ oz Sugarpaste Icing

MATERIALS AND EQUIPMENT
2 lb fluted dome-shaped pan or
Pyrex bowl
8 inch cake board
small waxed paper piping bag
wooden skewer

1 Preheat the oven to 350°F. Grease and flour the fluted dome-shaped pan or Pyrex bowl. Spoon in the cake mixture and smooth the surface. Bake in the center of the oven for 35–40 minutes or until a skewer inserted into the center of the cake comes out clean.

2 ▲ Leave the cake in the pan for about 5 minutes, then turn out on to a wire rack and leave to cool completely.

3 Place about 3 tbsp of the glacé icing in a small bowl. Stir a few drops of yellow food coloring into the larger quantity of icing and color the small quantity black. Place the cake on the cake board, dome side up, and pour over the yellow icing, allowing it to run, unevenly, down the sides. Fill the piping bag with the black icing. Seal the bag and snip the end, making a small hole for the nozzle.

4 ▲ Starting on the top of the cake, in the center, drizzle the black icing round the cake in a spiral, keeping the line as continuous and as evenly spaced as possible. Use the wooden skewer to draw through the icing, downwards from the center at the top of the cake, to make a web effect. Wipe away the excess icing with a damp cloth, then allow the icing to set at room temperature.

5 To make the spiders, place the chocolate and cream in a small, heavy-based saucepan and heat gently, stirring frequently, until the chocolate melts. Transfer the mixture to a small mixing bowl and allow to cool.

6 ▲ When cool, beat the mixture for about 10 minutes or until thick and pale. Stir in the ground almonds, then chill until firm enough to handle. Dust your hands with a little cocoa, then make a ball the size of a large walnut out of the chocolate mixture. Roll each ball in chocolate vermicelli until evenly coated. Repeat this process until all the mixture is used.

7 ▲ To make the spiders' legs, cut the liquorice into 1½ inch lengths. Make small cuts into the sides of each spider, then insert the legs. To make the spiders' eyes, pull off a piece of sugarpaste icing about the size of a hazelnut and color it with black food coloring. Use the white icing to make tiny balls and the black icing to make even smaller ones. Use a little water to stick the eyes in place. Arrange the spiders on and around the cake.

Ghostly Specter

*This fun Hallowe'en cake is really simple to make, yet very effective.
Use a 7 in square cake of your choice, such as a citrus or chocolate-
flavored Madeira or a light fruit cake.*

INGREDIENTS
Serves 14
2 x quantity orange-flavored Quick-
Mix Sponge Cake mix
2 lb/2²/₃ x quantity Sugarpaste Icing
black food coloring
1 quantity Butter Icing

MATERIALS AND EQUIPMENT
7 in square cake pan
1¹/₄ cup pudding mold
9 in round cake board
paintbrush

1 Preheat the oven to 300°F. Grease
the pan and the pudding mold, line
the bases with wax paper and grease the
paper. Half-fill the mold with the cake
mixture and turn the remainder into the
pan. Smooth the surfaces and bake in
the center of the oven for 25 minutes for
the mold and 1¹/₂ hours for the pan, or
until a skewer inserted into the center of
the cakes comes out clean. Leave to cool
for 5 minutes, then turn out on to a
wire rack, peel off the lining paper and
allow to cool.

2 Knead a little black food coloring
into about one-eighth of the
sugarpaste icing. On a work surface
lightly dusted with confectioner's sugar,
roll out and use to cover the cake board.

3 ▲ Cut two small corners off the
large cake and two larger wedges off
the other two corners. Stand the large
cake on the cake board and secure with
a little butter icing. Halve the large cake
trimmings and wedge around the base
of the cake.

4 ▲ Secure the small cake to the top
of the large cake with a little of the
butter icing for the head. Secure the
small cake trimmings on either side
of the head with butter icing for the
shoulders. Use the remaining butter
icing to cover the cake completely.

5 ▲ On a work surface lightly dusted
with confectioner's sugar, roll out
the remaining sugarpaste icing to an
oval shape about 20 in long and 12 in
wide. Position over the cake, letting the
icing fall into folds around the sides.
Gently smooth the icing over the top
half of the cake.

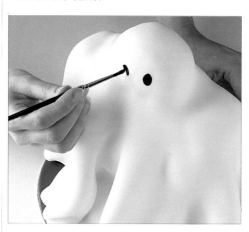

6 ▲ Using black food coloring, paint
two oval eyes on to the head.

Glittering Star

With a quick flick of a paintbrush you can give a sparkling effect to this glittering cake. Add some shimmering stars and moons and you have a cake ready to celebrate a birthday, Christmas, Halloween or silver wedding anniversary—for all the stars in your life.

INGREDIENTS
Serves 20–25
8-inch round Rich Fruit Cake
2½ tablespoons apricot jam, warmed and sieved
1½ pounds marzipan
1 pound/1⅓ x quantity Sugar paste Icing (Fondant)
silver, gold, lilac shimmer, red sparkle, glitter green and primrose sparkle powdered food coloring
4 ounces/¼ quantity Royal Icing

MATERIALS AND EQUIPMENT
paintbrush
stiff paper for templates
10-inch round cake board or plate

1 Brush the cake with the apricot jam. Roll out two-thirds of the marzipan and cover the cake. Allow to dry for at least 12 hours.

2 Roll out the sugar paste icing. Brush the marzipanned cake with a little water to dampen slightly and cover the cake with the sugar paste icing. Allow to dry for several hours.

3 ▲ Place the cake on a large sheet of waxed paper. Water down a little powdered silver food coloring and, using a paintbrush loaded with the color, flick this all over the cake to give a spattered effect. Allow to dry.

4 ▲ Make templates out of stiff paper in two or three different-sized moon shapes and three or four irregular star shapes. Take the remaining marzipan, divide into six pieces and color silver, gold, lilac, pink, green and yellow. Roll out each color and cut into stars and moons using the templates as a guide, cutting some of the stars in half.

5 ▲ Place the cut-out shapes on the waxed paper and brush each with its own color in powdered form to add more glitter. Allow to dry for several hours.

6 ▲ Position the cake on the cake board, securing underneath with a dab of royal icing, or place on a plate. Arrange the stars and moons at different angles all over the cake, attaching with royal icing, and position the halved stars upright as though coming out of the cake. Allow to set.

Glazed Christmas Ring

A good, rich fruit cake is a must at Christmas. This one is particularly festive with its vibrant glazed fruit and nut topping. Made here in a tube pan, it gives the cake an unusual shape, but it is equally successfully made in a 10-inch round cake pan. If using the latter, cook for an extra 15–30 minutes, checking the center with a skewer.

INGREDIENTS
Serves 16–20
1⅓ cups golden raisins
1 cup raisins
1 cup currants
1 cup dried figs, chopped
6 tablespoons whiskey
3 tablespoons orange juice
2 sticks (1 cup) unsalted butter
1 cup dark brown sugar
5 eggs
2 cups all-purpose flour
1 tablespoon baking powder
1 tablespoon pumpkin pie spice
½ cup candied cherries, chopped
1 cup Brazil nuts, chopped
scant ½ cup cut peel
⅔ cup ground almonds
grated zest and juice of 1 orange
2 tablespoons orange marmalade

To Decorate
½ cup orange marmalade
1 tablespoon orange juice
¾ cup candied cherries
¾ cup whole Brazil nuts
⅔ cup dried figs, halved

1 Place the raisins, currants and figs in a large bowl. Pour 4 tablespoons of the whiskey and the orange juice over and marinate overnight.

2 Preheat the oven to 325°F. Grease a 10-inch tube pan and line with a double layer of waxed or parchment paper; grease the paper.

3 Cream the butter and sugar together until pale and light. Beat in the eggs one at a time, beating well after each addition, until incorporated. Add some flour if the mixture starts to curdle.

4 ▲ Sift the remaining flour, baking powder and spice together. Fold into the creamed mixture, alternating with the remaining ingredients, except for the whiskey. Transfer the mixture to the prepared pan and smooth the surface, making a small dip in the center. Bake for 1 hour, reduce the oven temperature to 300°F and bake for another 1¼–2 hours. Test with a skewer to make sure the cake is cooked.

5 ▲ Remove from the oven, prick the cake all over with a skewer and pour the reserved whiskey over. Allow to cool in the pan for 30 minutes and then transfer to a wire rack to cool completely.

6 ▲ To decorate, heat the marmalade and orange juice together and boil gently for 3 minutes. Stir in the cherries, nuts and figs. Remove from the heat and cool slightly.

7 ▲ Spoon the glazed fruits and nuts over the cake in an attractive pattern and allow to set.

*B*ûche de Noël

This is the traditional French Christmas cake, filled with a purée of chestnuts, flavored with honey and brandy, and coated with a classic chocolate ganache. The meringue mushrooms add a whimsical touch to the decoration of this festive cake.

INGREDIENTS
Serves 8
1 egg white
¼ cup superfine sugar,
plus extra for sprinkling
¼ quantity Whisked Sponge Cake
mixture substituting
2 tablespoons all-purpose flour
with 2 tablespoons cocoa powder

For the Filling and Icing
8 ounces unsweetened
chestnut purée
2 tablespoons honey
2 tablespoons brandy
1¼ cups heavy cream
scant 1 cup semisweet
chocolate chips

To Decorate
4 chocolate twigs, crumbled
confectioners' sugar
holly leaves

1 Preheat the oven to 225°F. Grease a baking sheet, line with waxed or parchmentf paper and grease the paper. Grease a 13 x 9-inch jelly roll pan, line with waxed or parchment paper and grease the paper.

2 To make the meringue mushrooms, whisk the egg white until stiff and gradually beat in the sugar, a little at a time, until thick and glossy. Transfer to a piping bag. Pipe eight tall "stalks" and eight shorter "caps" onto the prepared baking sheet. Bake for 2½–3 hours, until crisp and dried out. Remove from the oven and let cool completely. Increase the temperature to 400°F.

3 Make the whisked sponge cake mixture and transfer to the prepared jelly roll pan. Bake for 10–12 minutes, until risen and springy to the touch.

4 Lay a sheet of baking parchment on a lightly dampened dish towel and sprinkle liberally with superfine sugar. Turn the cake over onto the paper and allow to cool completely with the pan in place.

5 To make the filling, blend the chestnut purée with the honey and brandy in a food processor until smooth, and gradually blend in half the cream until thick. Chill until required.

6 To make the icing, heat the chocolate and remaining cream in a small pan over low heat until melted. Transfer to a bowl, cool and chill for 1 hour. Remove from the refrigerator and beat until thick.

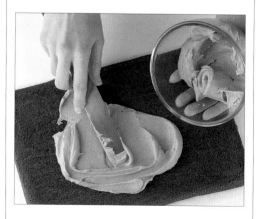

7 ▲ Remove the jelly roll pan and peel away the lining paper from the sponge. Spread with all but 2 tablespoons of the chestnut filling, leaving a border around the edges. Roll up from one narrow end to form a roll. Transfer to a cake board.

8 Coat the top and sides of the roll with the icing, leaving the ends plain. Swirl a pattern over the icing with a baking spatula, to resemble tree bark. Sprinkle the crumbled flakes over the rest of the board.

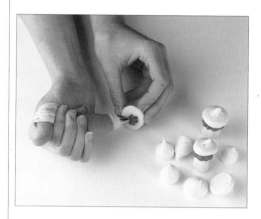

9 ▲ Remove the meringue stalks and caps from the baking sheet. Transfer the reserved chestnut filling to the piping bag fitted with the star nozzle. Pipe a swirl onto the underside of each mushroom cap. Press gently onto the stalks to form the mushroom decorations.

10 Place a small cluster of mushrooms on top of the chocolate log, arranging the rest around the board. Sprinkle a little confectioners' sugar over and add a few festive holly leaves, if you like.

*M*arbled Party Cracker Cake

Here is a Christmas cake decorated in an untraditional way.
The cake can be made well ahead of Christmas and then decorated nearer the time.

INGREDIENTS
Serves 20–25
8 inch round Rich Fruit Cake
3 tbsp apricot jam, warmed and sieved
1½ lb marzipan
1¾ lb/2⅓ x quantity Sugarpaste Icing
red and green food colorings
edible gold balls

MATERIALS AND EQUIPMENT
wooden toothpicks
10 inch round cake board
red, green and gold thin gift wrapping ribbon
3 red and 3 green ribbon bows

1 Brush the cake with jam. Roll out the marzipan on a work surface lightly dusted with confectioners' sugar. Cover the cake. Leave to dry for 12 hours.

2 ▲ Take 1¼ lb of the sugarpaste icing and form a smooth roll. Put some red food coloring on the end of a toothpick and dab a few drops on to the icing. Repeat with the green. Knead just a few times. Roll out the sugarpaste, on a work surface lightly dusted with confectioners' sugar, until marbled.

3 Brush the marzipan with a little water and cover with the icing. Position the cake on the cake board.

4 ▲ Color half of the remaining sugarpaste icing red and the rest green. On a work surface lightly dusted with confectioners' sugar, roll about half of the red icing into five 2 x ½ inch rectangles for the crackers. Roll half of the green icing into a 5 x ½ inch roll and cut off ten ½ inch lengths. These are the ends of the crackers. Attach two green ends to each red cracker with a little water. Gather together any icing trimmings. Roll out a small piece of green icing thinly and cut into two 5 x ½ inch strips. Cut each strip into five diamonds. Attach two green diamonds to each cracker, then press a gold ball in the center. Leave to dry on waxed paper for several hours or overnight.

5 ▲ Meanwhile, roll out the remaining red and green icings, including any trimmings, into ½ inch wide strips. Cut each of the strip's into diamonds – you will need about 24 diamonds in each color.

6 ▲ Attach alternate red and green diamonds around the top and base of the cake, securing with water.

7 ▲ Cut the ribbons into about 4 inch lengths. Run the blade of a pair of scissors or a sharp knife down the length of them to curl.

8 Arrange the crackers in a pile on top of the cake and decorate with the curled ribbons. Attach the bows in alternate colors with a little softened sugarpaste icing, evenly spaced between the diamonds around the top edge of the cake.

*T*ip

Add the color to the icing sparingly at first because the color becomes more intense as the icing stands. It is advisable to leave the icing for about 10 minutes to see if it is the shade you need.

Christmas Tree Cake

*No piping is involved in this bright and colorful Christmas tree cake,
making it a good choice for all the family to help decorate.*

INGREDIENTS
Serves 20–25
8 inch round Rich Fruit Cake
*3 tbsp apricot jam, warmed and
sieved*
2 lb marzipan
*green, red, yellow and purple food
colorings*
*8 oz/¹/₃ quantity Royal Icing
silver balls*

MATERIALS AND EQUIPMENT
10 inch round cake board

1 Brush the cake with the apricot
jam. Color 1½ lb of the marzipan
green. Roll out the green marzipan
on a work surface lightly dusted with
confectioners' sugar and use it to cover
the cake. Leave to dry for 12 hours.

2 ▲ Make the royal icing. Secure the
cake to the cake board with a little
of the icing. Spread the icing evenly on
the side of the cake to cover just half
way up. Starting at the bottom of the
cake, press the flat side of a spatula into
the icing, then pull away sharply to
form a peak. Repeat until the iced area
is covered with peaks.

3 ▲ Draw three Christmas tree shapes
in different sizes on to a piece of
cardboard and cut out. Take half of the
remaining marzipan and color it a
slightly deeper shade of green than the
top. Using the cardboard templates as
a guide, cut out three Christmas tree
shapes. Arrange the trees on top of
the cake.

4 ▲ Divide the remaining marzipan
into three portions and color it red,
yellow and purple. Use a little of the
marzipan to make five 3 inch rolls from
each color. Loop the colored lengths
alternately around the top edge of the
cake, pressing on to the top to secure
them firmly.

5 ▲ Make small balls from red
marzipan and press on to the end
of each loop.

6 ▲ Use the remaining marzipan to
make the tree decorations. Roll the
red marzipan into a thin rope and cut
into eight 1 inch lengths for the candles.
Shape eight flames from the yellow
icing and stick on the end of each
candle. Mold 11 small balls from the
purple icing and press a silver ball into
the center of each.

7 Arrange the candles and balls on
the trees, securing them with a little
water if necessary.

Noël Christmas Cake

For those who prefer a traditional royal-iced cake, this is a simple design using only one icing and easy-to-pipe decorations.

INGREDIENTS
Serves 50
8-inch round Rich Fruit Cake
2 tablespoons apricot jam,
warmed and sieved
1¾ pounds marzipan
2 pounds/1⅓ x quantity
Royal Icing
red and green food coloring

MATERIALS AND EQUIPMENT
9-inch round silver cake board
waxed or parchment paper piping
bag
No. 0 and No. 1 writing nozzles
44 large gold balls (dragées)
gold ribbon, ¾ inch wide
red ribbon, ¼ inch wide

1 Brush the cake with apricot jam, cover with marzipan and place on the cake board. Allow to dry for at least 12 hours.

2 ▲ Flat-ice the top of the cake with two layers of royal icing and let stand until dry. Ice the sides of the cake and, using a baking spatula, peak the royal icing, leaving a space around the center of the side to fit the ribbon. Reserve the remaining royal icing for decorating.

3 ▲ Half-fill a paper piping bag fitted with a No. 1 writing nozzle with royal icing. Pipe beads of icing around the top edge of the cake and attach a gold ball on every other bead of icing.

4 Write "NOEL" across the cake and then pipe holly leaves, stems and berries around the cake.

5 ▲ Measure and fit the gold ribbon around the side of the cake, taking care not to break the peaks. Press into the icing. Measure and fit the red ribbon over the top of the gold, and secure with a bead of icing. Tie a neat red bow and attach it to the front of the cake. Use more ribbon to fit around the cake board, securing with a pin. Allow to dry overnight.

6 ▲ Color 2 tablespoons of the royal icing bright green and 1 tablespoon bright red with food coloring. Use a paper piping bag and a No. 0 writing nozzle to pipe over "NOEL" in red.

7 ▲ Pipe the holly berries and alternate dots around the edge of the cake in red and pipe over the holly in green. Allow to dry.

Christmas Stocking Cake

A bright and happy cake to make for Christmas. You can make the stocking and parcel decorations in advance, and assemble the cake nearer the time.

INGREDIENTS
Serves 50
8-inch square Rich Fruit Cake
3 tablespoons apricot jam,
warmed and sieved
2 pounds marzipan
2½ pounds/3 x quantity
Sugar paste Icing (Fondant)
4 ounces/⅙ quantity Royal Icing
red and green food coloring

MATERIALS AND EQUIPMENT
10-inch square silver cake board
red ribbon, ¾ inch wide
green ribbon, ¾ inch wide
card stock for template

1 Brush the cake with apricot jam and place on the cake board. Cover the cake with marzipan. Reserve one-fifth (8 ounces) sugar paste icing for decorations, and use the remainder to cover the cake smoothly. Place the cake in a box and allow to dry in a warm place. Measure and fit the red ribbon around the board, securing with a pin, and the green ribbon around the cake, securing with royal icing.

2 ▲ Knead the sugar paste icing trimmings together. Reserve 4 ounces and cut the remainder in half; color one half red and the other green with food coloring. Draw a template for the stocking on card stock and cut out. Roll out a piece of white sugar paste icing and cut out around the template.

3 ▲ Roll out the red and green sugar paste icing to ¼ inch thick and cut each into seven ½-inch strips. Remove alternate green strips and replace with red strips. Gently roll the striped sugar paste icing together.

4 ▲ Use the template to cut out a striped stocking shape, allowing an extra ¼ inch all around.

5 Brush the white stocking with apricot jam and, using a baking spatula, lift the striped stocking and place over the white one. Press lightly together and allow to dry.

6 Shape the remaining white sugar paste icing into four parcel shapes and trim each with thin strips of red and green sugar paste icing ribbons.

7 ▲ Knead the remaining green and red sugar paste icing, keeping the colors separate. Roll out each into a 8-inch strip, ½ inch wide. Cut each into two ¼-inch strips. Pipe a bead of royal icing onto each corner of the cake, press alternate green and red strips in position and trim to size. Shape four red and four green balls and press in position where the sugar paste icing strips join, securing with a little royal icing.

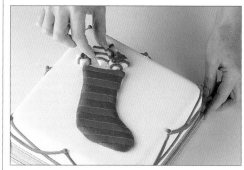

8 ▲ Arrange the stocking and parcels in position on the top of the cake. Set aside to dry.

Mini Christmas Cakes

These little cakes make a welcome gift, especially for friends or relatives on their own. Gift-wrap them in pretty boxes tied with ribbon.

INGREDIENTS
Makes 9
8-inch square Rich Fruit Cake
3 tablespoons apricot jam,
warmed and sieved
1½ pounds marzipan
1 pound/1⅓ x quantity
Sugar paste Icing (Fondant)
1½ pounds/1 quantity Royal Icing
red, green and yellow
food coloring

MATERIALS AND EQUIPMENT
3 silver, 3 red and 3 gold
4-inch thin cake boards
small crimping tool
holly leaf cutter
red ribbon, ¾ inch and
¼ inch wide
green ribbon, ¾ inch and
¼ inch wide
18 gold leaves
3 gold candles
gold ribbon, ¾ inch wide

1 Cut the cake into three strips each way to make nine square cakes. Brush each with apricot jam and place on a cake board.

2 Cut the marzipan into nine pieces. Cut two-thirds off one piece and roll out a strip long enough and wide enough to cover the sides of one cake. Trim to size and wrap around the cake, keeping a good square shape. Roll out the remaining one-third of the marzipan large enough to fit the top. Invert the cake onto the square, trim to shape and replace on the cake board. Repeat to cover all the cakes with marzipan. Knead all the trimmings together and reserve for decorations.

3 ▲ Cut the sugar paste icing into three pieces. On a lightly sugared surface, roll out one piece at a time large enough to cover the top and sides of a cake. Cover the three cakes on the red cake boards. Carefully crimp the top edges of each cake using a small crimping tool.

4 ▲ Cover the three cakes on the gold boards with royal icing and peak the surfaces to finish, working on one cake at a time. Leave a plain strip around the sides to fit the ribbons.

5 Cut the marzipan trimmings into three portions. Color one piece red, one green and the other yellow. Roll out the green marzipan thinly and cut out 27 leaves, using a holly leaf cutter. Mark the veins with a knife and bend the leaves into shape. Make lots of tiny red berries, and form the remaining red marzipan into nine candle shapes—three small, three medium and three large. Shape nine flames from the yellow marzipan.

6 ▲ Arrange the candles, flames, holly leaves and berries on the sugar paste cakes and tie each with a wide red ribbon and a bow. Secure all the decorations with a little royal icing.

7 Arrange a holly garland with a few berries on each of the plain marzipan cakes. Tie each marzipan cake with wide green and fine red and green ribbon and a double bow.

8 Arrange six gold leaves on each peaked royal-icing cake. Position a gold candle in the center and the gold ribbon around each cake with a bow. Allow all the cakes to set overnight before gift-wrapping them.

Hand-painted Christmas Cake

An unusual Christmas cake that is thoroughly enjoyable to make, provided that you like painting and have a reasonably steady hand.

INGREDIENTS
Serves 35
10-inch round Rich Fruit Cake,
covered with
2½ pounds marzipan
3 pounds/4 x quantity
Sugar paste Icing (Fondant)
red, yellow, green and mauve
food coloring

MATERIALS AND EQUIPMENT
13-inch round gold cake board
baking parchment
dressmakers' pins
fine paintbrush
red ribbon, 1 inch wide
red candle

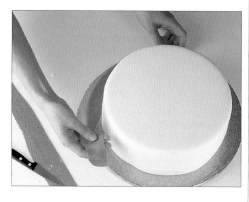

1 ▲ Place the cake on the cake board. Reserve one-twelfth (4 ounces) of the sugar paste icing and use the remainder to cover the cake. Color the reserved sugar paste icing red and roll out thinly on a surface dusted with confectioners' sugar. Dampen the surface of the cake board and cover with strips of icing. Smooth down gently and trim off the excess around the edge of the board. Let stand for at least 24 hours to harden.

2 ▲ Draw a template for one-quarter of the design on baking parchment, using the photograph as a guide. Make a pin mark in the exact center of the cake. Lay the template on top of the cake so that the apex of the template meets the pin mark. Using a pin, press the template lines onto the surface of the cake so that a faint marking can be seen on the cake. Move the template around and repeat on the remaining three-quarters of the cake.

3 Cut another piece of baking parchment long enough to fit around the circumference of the cake and 2½ inches wide. Lay around the side of the cake so that the base of the template rests on the cake board, securing the ends with pins. Using a pin, mark a line on the icing around the top edge of the template. Cut the template in half lengthwise and reposition around the cake as before. Mark another line around the top edge of the template, halfway down the sides of the cake. Remove the template.

4 ▲ Place a little of each food coloring on a large flat plate and thin each with a little water. Paint a red triangle on the cake next to the central circle to within ¹⁄₁₆ inch of the template markings. Paint another triangle opposite the first. Fill in the centers with yellow. Use the green and mauve colors to fill the remaining triangles around the central circle.

5 Using a clean paintbrush dampened with water, lightly smudge the red and yellow colors together. Repeat on the green and mauve triangles.

6 ▲ Using this technique, build up a design over the top and sides of the cake. Leave the area between the two marked lines around the cake blank and attach the ribbon. Place a candle in the center, using a little confectioners' sugar mixed to a paste with water as glue.

Christmas Cracker

A festive cake that is fun to make and fun to eat. To make sure it is really fresh for your Christmas party, the cake can be made and decorated a day or two ahead of time, then cut in half on the day and arranged on the cake board with the colorful decorations to serve.

INGREDIENTS
Serves 8
1 quantity Whisked Sponge Cake
1 cup jam, for filling
2 tablespoons apricot jam,
warmed and sieved
1¹/₂ pounds/2 x quantity
Sugar paste Icing (Fondamt)
Christmas red, mint green, yellow,
black and blue food coloring

To Decorate
red, gold, green and pink foil-wrapped
chocolate eggs, coins and bars

MATERIALS AND EQUIPMENT
13 x 9-inch jelly roll pan
small round cutter
2 small red candles
13–14-inch cake board

1 Preheat the oven to 350°F. Grease the jelly roll pan, line with waxed or parchment paper and grease the paper. Spoon the cake mixture into the prepared pan and bake in the preheated oven for 20–25 minutes. Allow to cool, spread with the jam and make into a roll. Cut 1 inch off each end of the jelly roll. Cut each piece in half. Set aside. Brush the outside of the roll with the apricot jam.

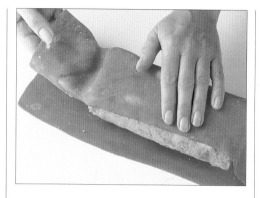

2 ▲ Take two-thirds (1 pound) sugar paste icing and color it red. Roll it out so it is 6 inches longer than the length of the trimmed cake and wide enough to wrap around it. Position the cake in the center of the red sugar paste icing and wrap around to cover, keeping the seam underneath. Secure with water and trim where necessary.

3 ▲ Pinch the icing slightly where it meets the ends of the cake to resemble a cracker, and place the reserved pieces of cake inside each end of the icing to support them. Using any red icing trimmings, cut out two circles the same diameter as the ends of the cracker. Dampen the edges and position one at each end of the cracker, pressing together to seal.

4 Use the remaining icing as follows: color most of it green and yellow for the decorations, leave a little white for the snowman, and color a very small amount black and blue. Roll out the green and yellow icing. Cut strips with a knife and small circles with a small cutter or the end of a large piping nozzle to decorate the cracker. Arrange the decorations on the cracker, securing with a little water.

5 ▲ Make the snowman with the white icing. Shape the body, head, arms and legs separately, then assemble securing the pieces with a little water. Shape the hat, eyes and mouth from the black icing, the bow tie from the green, buttons from the red and a nose from the blue. Position these on the snowman, securing with a little water. Press two small red candles into his arms to hold. Allow to set.

6 When ready to serve, cut the cake in half, making jagged edges, and position on the cake board. Sit the snowman on top of one half and arrange the wrapped sweets around the board.

Marzipan Bell Cake

An unusual Christmas cake, this is decorated purely with marzipan, which gives a holiday feel without the sweetness of icing.

INGREDIENTS
Serves 40
*7-inch round Rich or
Light Fruit Cake
2 tablespoons apricot jam,
warmed and sieved
2 pounds marzipan
green, yellow and red
food coloring*

MATERIALS AND EQUIPMENT
*8-inch round silver cake board
crimping tool
bell cutter
holly leaf cutter
red ribbon, ¾ inch and
¼ inch wide
green ribbon, ¼ inch wide*

1 Brush the cake with apricot glaze and place on the cake board.

2 Color two-thirds of the marzipan pale green with a few drops of green food coloring. Knead until evenly colored.

3 Roll out the marzipan to a 9-inch circle and place over the cake, smoothing across the top and down the side. Trim the excess away from the base of the cake.

4 ▲Use a crimping tool to make a scalloped pattern on the top edge.

5 Color a small piece of marzipan bright yellow, a small piece bright red and the remaining marzipan bright green. Roll out the yellow marzipan and, using a bell cutter, cut out two bells and mold two clappers.

6 ▲ Using some green marzipan, cut two pencil-thin lengths and form into bell ropes, bending them into shape. Roll out the remaining green marzipan and, using a holly cutter, cut out 11 holly leaves. Mark the veins with a knife and bend them to shape. Using the red marzipan, shape some tiny red berries and also two thin strips to wind around the ends of the bell ropes. Allow the decorations to dry.

7 Measure and fit the wide red and fine green ribbon around the side of the cake, securing each with a pin. Tie a neat double bow from fine red and green ribbon and attach to the side with a bead of icing.

8 ▲ Arrange the bells, clappers, bell ropes, holly leaves and berries on top of the cake and secure each with a little icing.

Animal Cakes

*This chapter contains a wide range of ideas to amuse
children of all ages. From tropical parrots to dinosaurs,
from adorable puppies to crazy caterpillars, this section
will encourage you to bring a little bit of fun into baking
that will brighten up any occasion.*

Ladybug Cake

*Create a little animal magic and make this cake
for a nature lover or gardener.*

INGREDIENTS
Serves 10–12
1½ x quantity lemon-flavored
Quick-Mix Sponge Cake mix
½ quantity lemon-flavored Butter
Icing
2 tbsp apricot jam, warmed and
strained
4 tbsp lemon curd, warmed
2¼ lb/3 x quantity Sugarpaste Icing
red, black, and green food colorings
5 marshmallows
2 oz yellow marzipan
edible ladybug icing decorations
(optional)

MATERIALS AND EQUIPMENT
5 cup ovenproof mixing bowl
11 in round cake board
1½ in and 2 in plain round cookie
cutters
garlic press
2 pipe cleaners

1 Preheat the oven to 350°F. Grease the bowl, line the base with wax paper and grease the paper. Spoon the cake mixture into the prepared bowl and smooth the surface. Bake in the center of the oven for 55–60 minutes, or until a skewer inserted into the center of the cake comes out clean. Leave the cake in the bowl for 5 minutes, then turn out on to a wire rack, peel off the lining paper, and allow to cool.

2 ▲ Cut the cake in half horizontally and sandwich together with the butter icing. Cut off about one-third of the cake and brush both pieces of cake with the lemon curd.

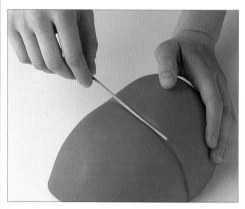

3 ▲ Color a little less than half of the sugarpaste icing red. On a work surface lightly dusted with confectioner's sugar, roll out to about a ¼ in thickness and use to cover the large piece of cake. Using a wooden skewer or the back of a knife, make an indentation down the center of the cake for the wing casings.

4 Color just over half of the remaining sugarpaste icing black. Roll out three-quarters of the icing and use to cover the small piece of cake. Place the cakes on the cake board and assemble the ladybug's head and body, gently pressing them together to secure.

5 Roll out a little of the white sugarpaste icing and cut out two circles for the eyes, using the 2 in round cookie cutter. Stick in position with a little water.

6 ▲ Roll out the reserved black sugarpaste icing and cut out eight circles, using the 1½ in round cookie cutter. Stick one on each eye and stick the rest on to the body with a little water. Reserve the trimmings.

7 Color the remaining sugarpaste icing green. To make the grass, break off small pieces and squeeze through the garlic press. Trim off with a knife. Brush the cake board with a little water and position the grass.

8 ▲ To make the marshmallow flowers, roll the marzipan into a ¾ in long sausage shape and cut into slices. Set aside. On a work surface lightly dusted with confectioner's sugar, flatten each marshmallow with a rolling pin. Snip around the marshmallows to make petals. Press a marzipan circle into the center of each flower.

9 To make the antennae, paint the pipe cleaners with black food coloring and press a small ball of the reserved black sugarpaste icing on to the end of each one. Bend each pipe cleaner slightly and insert into the cake between the head and the body. Arrange the ladybug decorations around the cake, if using.

Rainbow Snake Cake

This wild cake doesn't need any cooking and its heavy texture and sweet flavor make it an excellent party cake. For a large party, double the ingredients to make an extra big snake.

INGREDIENTS
Serves 10–15
1½ lb white marzipan
red, yellow, orange, purple, and green food coloring
1 quantity Truffle Cake mix
2 round red candies
2 cups shredded coconut
jelly snake candies (optional)

MATERIALS AND EQUIPMENT
5 toothpicks
10 in round cake board
small piece of thin red cardboard, cut into a tongue shape
small star-shaped cookie cutter

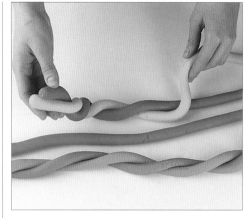

2 ▲ On a work surface lightly dusted with confectioner's sugar, roll out each piece of marzipan into a sausage shape with your hands. They should be about ½ in in diameter. Line up the sausage shapes next to one another and twist together the two outside sausages on either side. Firmly push the twists up against the middle sausage.

4 ▲ Spoon the truffle mix evenly down the center of the marzipan and mold into a sausage shape. Starting at one end, gather up the sides of the marzipan around the cake mixture and pinch the sides together firmly to seal. Shape the head and the tail.

1 ▲ Divide the marzipan into five equal portions and color one portion red, one portion yellow, one orange, one purple and one green. Remove a tiny ball from the green portion and reserve, wrapped in plastic wrap.

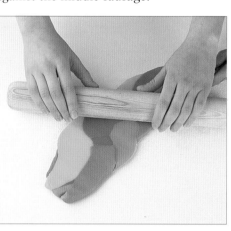

3 ▲ Roll out the marzipan, making short, sharp downward movements with the rolling pin. Starting at one end, roll out the marzipan a little at a time until about 6 in wide. Keep the width even all along the snake. Carefully slide a heavy, sharp knife underneath the marzipan and flip the marzipan over, taking care not to tear it.

5 ▲ Carefully coil the snake on to the cake board. Make a small incision for the mouth and insert the red cardboard tongue. Roll out the reserved green marzipan and cut out two eyes using the small star cookie cutter. Stick the eyes to the head with a little water and press the red candies on top.

6 Place the shredded coconut in a bowl and add a few drops of green food coloring and a little water. Stir until the coconut is flecked with green. Sprinkle around the snake on the cake board for grass.

Elephant Cake

Any medium-sized roasting pan will work for this cake, but one with rounded edges is preferable as this improves the finished result.

INGREDIENTS
Serves 10–12
1½ x quantity lemon-flavor Quick-Mix Sponge Cake mix
1 quantity lemon-flavor Butter Icing (optional)
8 tbsp apricot jam, warmed and sieved
2 lb/2²/₃ x quantity Sugarpaste Icing
pink, blue and grey food colorings

MATERIALS AND EQUIPMENT
12 x 9 inch roasting pan
7 inch round cake pan, or card, to use as a template
16 inch round cake board, with a support for the trunk, or 16 x 10 inch cake board (optional)
wooden toothpick
medium-size round cutter (optional)
bow made from pretty ribbon
pin

1 Preheat the oven to 350°F. Grease the roasting pan, line the base and sides with waxed paper and grease the paper. Spoon in the cake mixture and smooth the surface. Bake in the center of the oven for 45–50 minutes or until a skewer inserted into the center of the cake comes out clean. Leave in the pan for about 5 minutes, then turn out on to a wire rack, peel off the lining paper and leave to cool completely.

2 ▲ Place the cake, dome side down, on the work surface and position the template in the center on the flat surface. Use a sharp knife to cut around the template, holding it steady and firm as you cut. Lift out the cut-out circle, keeping the outside piece intact.

3 ▲ Use the template to cut out the elephant's trunk. Place the template close to one edge of the short side of the remaining cake and cut out a crescent shape. Cut off one end of the crescent to make the elephant's mouth. Cut off the other end of the cake, just past the rounded corners, to make the ear. Discard the two small, middle sections of cake. Cut horizontally through the face, ear, trunk and mouth sections of the cake, then sandwich them back together with lemon butter icing, if you are using it.

4 ▲ Assemble the cake on a board or directly on the table. Place the ear piece on one side of the round face, then place the flat edge of the trunk section up against the face, opposite the ear. Place the mouth section in the space between the trunk and the face. Brush the whole surface with jam.

5 Cut off about 2 oz of sugarpaste icing and set aside, wrapped in plastic wrap. Cut off another 6 oz of sugarpaste icing and color it pink, and ½ oz and color it blue. Set aside, wrapped in plastic wrap. Color the remaining icing grey, cut off about 3 oz and set aside. Dust the work surface with confectioners' sugar then roll out the larger portion of grey icing into a 20 x 10 inch rectangle. Use this to cover the entire cake. Smooth down the sides and edges, snipping with scissors or cutting the icing in the places where it overlaps. Trim the edges.

6 To make the ear piece, roll out the reserved portion of grey icing into a 8 x 4 inch rectangle, then roll it in small sections with the toothpick, to give a ruffled effect (see Teddy Bear Christening Cake, step 7). Lay this section on top of the ear, slightly off center. Cut off about 5 oz of the pink icing and roll it out to a slightly smaller rectangle, then repeat the ruffling process with the toothpick. Lay this piece on top of the grey ruffle.

7 Roll out the reserved blue and white icings and cut out the eye parts, using the round cutter, if preferred. Stick in place with a little water, placing a small round ball of the remaining pink icing in the center. Roll out the remaining pink icing and cut out a triangular piece for the mouth. Shape the remaining white icing into a tusk and then stick them both in place with a little water. Finally, position the bow, securing in place with the pin, which must be removed before serving the cake.

Indian Elephant

Make this cake to celebrate a birthday, to wish someone "Bon Voyage," or for a festive occasion. Be as colorful as you like with the decorations.

INGREDIENTS
Serves 30
12 in square Madeira Cake
2 x quantity Butter Icing
8 oz marzipan
black, green, yellow, and pink food colorings
chocolate coins, silver balls, colored and white chocolate buttons and two candies
2 cups shredded coconut
2 tbsp apricot jam, warmed and strained

MATERIALS AND EQUIPMENT
stiff paper for template
14 in square cake board
toothpick

1 ▲ Make a template from stiff paper in the shape of an elephant. Trace off the design from the photograph of the finished cake and enlarge by 150%, if wished. Place the template on top of the cake and cut out the shape with a sharp knife. Secure the cake to the cake board with a little butter icing.

2 ▲ Color the butter icing pale gray using the black food coloring. Cover the top and sides of the cake with the icing and swirl with a palette knife.

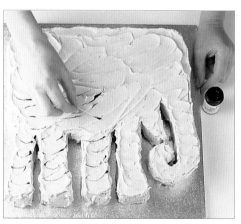

3 ▲ Using a toothpick and black food coloring, swirl black highlights into the surface of the butter icing.

4 ▲ On a work surface lightly dusted with confectioner's sugar, roll out half of the marzipan and cut out shapes for the elephant's tusk, headpiece and blanket. Place them in position on the cake. Color the remaining marzipan green, yellow, and pink. Roll out thinly and cut out patterns for the blanket, headpiece, trunk, and tail. Roll small balls of yellow and pink marzipan to make the ankle bracelets.

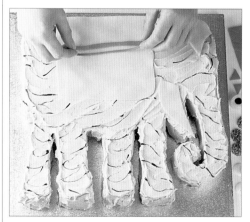

5 ▲ Place all the decorations, including the silver balls, chocolate coins and colored chocolate buttons, in position. Cut the white chocolate buttons in half and use for the toenails and the candies for the eye.

6 Mix a little green food coloring into the coconut. Brush the cake board with a little apricot jam and sprinkle with the coconut for grass.

Fish Cake

A very easy but colorful cake, perfect for a small child's birthday party. Candles can be pressed into the icing covering the board.

INGREDIENTS
Serves 8
*1 quantity Quick-mix
Sponge Cake mix
1 pound/1⅓ x quantity
Sugar paste Icing (Fondant)
blue, orange, red, mauve and green
food coloring
12 ounces/1 quantity Butter Icing
1 blue candy*

MATERIALS AND EQUIPMENT
*large ovenproof mixing bowl
large oval cake board
baking spatula
1-inch plain cookie cutter
waxed or parchment paper piping
bag*

1 Preheat the oven to 325°F. Grease the mixing bowl and line the base with waxed or parchment paper. Spoon the cake mixture into the prepared bowl, level the surface and bake for 40–50 minutes, until just firm. Turn out and let cool.

2 Color two-thirds of the sugar paste icing blue and roll out very thinly on a surface dusted with sugar. Lightly dampen the cake board and cover with the sugar paste icing. Trim off the excess.

3 ▲ Invert the cake and trim to create a fish shape. Trim the edges to give sloping sides. Place on the board.

4 ▲ Color all but 1 tablespoon of the butter icing orange. Cover the cake completely with the orange butter icing and smooth down with a baking spatula. Score curved lines for scales with the baking spatula, starting from the tail end and working up toward the head.

5 ▲ Color half the remaining sugar paste icing red. Shape and position two lips. Thinly roll the remainder and cut out the tail and fins. Mark with lines using a knife and position on the fish.

6 Roll a small ball of white sugar paste icing, flatten slightly and position for the eye. Press the blue candy into the center.

7 Color a small ball of sugar paste icing mauve, cut out crescent-shaped scales using a cookie cutter and place on the fish. Color the remaining sugar paste icing green, roll out and cut long strips. Twist each strip and arrange them around the board.

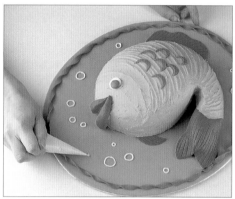

8 ▲ Place the reserved butter icing in a piping bag and snip off the end. Pipe small circles on the cake board around the fish to look like bubbles.

Tip

For a sea-themed birthday party you could decorate small cupcakes with fish designs and other watery motifs, to be given as a gift to take home at the end of the afternoon.

Porcupine Cake

Melt-in-the-mouth strips of chocolate twigs give this porcupine its spiky coat, and a quick-mix moist chocolate cake makes the base. It's a fun cake for a children's or an adult's party.

INGREDIENTS
Serves 15
1½ x quantity chocolate-flavor Quick-mix Sponge Cake
1¼ pound/1⅔ x quantity chocolate-flavor Butter Icing
5–6 chocolate twigs
2 ounces marzipan
black, green, cream, brown and red food coloring

MATERIALS AND EQUIPMENT
waxed or parchment paper
1-quart pudding basin
2½-cup pudding basin
14-inch-long rectangular cake board
toothpick
fine paintbrush

1 Preheat the oven to 325°F. Grease the pudding basins and line the bottoms with waxed or parchment paper. Grease the paper. Spoon the cake mixture into both basins to two-thirds full. Bake, allowing 55 minutes—1 hour for the larger basin and 35–40 minutes for the smaller basin. Turn out and allow to cool on a wire rack.

2 ▲ Place both cakes on a surface so the widest ends are underneath. Slice pieces from the smaller cake to create a pointed nose at one end.

3 ▲ Place the larger cake on the cake board behind the smaller one. Cut one of the cut-off slices in half and position on either side between the larger and small cake to fill in the side gaps. Place the other cut-off piece on top to fill in the top gap, securing all with a little butter icing.

4 ▲ Spread the remaining butter icing all over the cake. On the pointed face part, make markings with a cocktail stick.

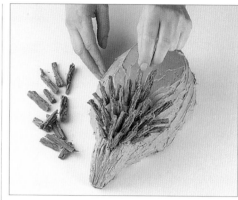

5 ▲ Break or cut the chocolate twigs into thin strips and stick into the butter icing over the body of the porcupine to represent spikes.

6 Reserve a small portion of marzipan. Divide the remainder into three portions and color one portion black, one green and one cream. Color a tiny portion of the reserved white marzipan brown for the apple stems. With the cream marzipan shape the ears and feet, using black and white make the eyes, and with the rest of the black shape the nose and the claws for the feet. With the green marzipan make the apples, painting on red markings with a fine paintbrush. Position the stems. Set everything except the apples in place on the porcupine cake. Finally, place the apples on the board by the front of the porcupine.

Tropical Parrot

Add a tropical feel to your celebration with this colorful, exotic cake, whether for a bon voyage to faraway places or a simple birthday celebration. The cake is made from one round Madeira cake, cut into three easy shapes to give the parrot's body and tail and the branch it sits on. You can then be as decorative as you like with the markings and foliage.

INGREDIENTS
Serves 15
8-inch round Madeira Cake
1 pound/1⅓ quantity
Sugar paste Icing (Fondant)
red, brown, yellow, pink, orange, blue, purple, black and green food coloring
1¼ pounds/1½ x quantity Butter Icing

MATERIALS AND EQUIPMENT
card stock for templates
14-inch square cake board

1 ▲ Make templates out of a circle of stiff paper, using the photograph as a guide, for the parrot's body, tail and branch. Place the templates on top of the cake and cut out the shapes with a sharp knife.

2 Take the sugar paste icing and color about one-third red. Color a quarter of the remaining piece brown and the rest yellow, pink, orange, blue, purple, black, green and light green. Leave a small amount white.

3 ▲ Slice each piece of cake (body, tail and branch) in half horizontally and fill with some of the butter icing. Use the remaining butter icing to coat the outsides of the cake. Measure the length and depth of the cake that forms the branch. Roll out the brown icing in one piece large enough to cover it. Position over the cake branch and trim to fit.

4 Measure the length and depth of the sides of the parrot's body. Roll out some of the red icing and cut strips to match the measurements. Press onto the butter icing to fix in position. Roll out a piece of red icing for the top of the parrot's body, using the template as a guide. Leave out the face, beak and blue body parts.

5 Position the red sugar paste icing on the butter icing, reserving the trimmings. Roll out a piece of white and some black icing for the face and beak, cut to fit and ease into position with your fingers. Do the same with a piece of blue icing to finish off the body, and cover the tailpiece using the rest of the reserved red icing.

6 ▲ Roll out the other colored pieces of icing. Cut out pieces in the shape of feathers, some with jagged edges. Press these into position on the body and tail, easing to fit with your fingers. Secure with a little water, bending and twisting some of the feathers to create different angles and heights. Cut out leaf and flower shapes for the branch out of the green and pink icings.

7 ▲ Place the iced parrot pieces in position on the cake board. Make the eye for the parrot. Secure the eye to the head with water, and use water to fix the leaves and flowers on the branch. If wished, color an additional 4 ounces sugar paste icing green. Roll and cut out more leaves to decorate the cake board.

Daisy Cow

A really fun cake to make for a child who loves animals or the countryside.

INGREDIENTS
Serves 10–12
1½ x quantity Quick-Mix Sponge Cake mix
9 tbsp apricot jam, warmed and sieved
3 lb 12 oz/5 x quantity Sugarpaste Icing
black, brown, blue, yellow and red food colorings

MATERIALS AND EQUIPMENT
2 x deep 7 inch round cake pans
10 x 13 inch cake board
1½ inch and 1 inch plain round pastry cutters
2½ inch fluted round pastry cutter
wooden toothpick
10 inch florists' wire covered in florists' tape

1 Preheat the oven to 350°F. Grease the pans, line the bases with waxed paper and grease the paper. Divide the cake mixture equally between the two pans and smooth the surfaces. Bake in the center of the oven for 30–35 minutes or until a skewer inserted into the center of each cake comes out clean. Turn out on to wire racks, peel off the lining paper and leave to cool completely.

2 ▲ Using a sharp, pointed knife, cut a crescent-shaped piece from the side of one cake, then cut it in half to make the cow's ears.

3 ▲ This is how the cake should be assembled. On the work surface, brush the cake with apricot jam and push the two rounds together to make the face.

4 Color 2 lb 2 oz of the sugarpaste icing with black food coloring. Cut off 1 lb 2 oz and set aside, wrapped in plastic wrap. Roll out the remainder on a work surface dusted with confectioners' sugar into a rectangle about ¼ inch thick. Roll out two-thirds of the white icing, then cut into rounds using plain round cutters. Place some of the rounds of white icing in a random pattern on the rolled-out black icing and roll again lightly with the rolling pin to flatten them into the surface. Cover the cow's face with the black and white icing, trimming it neatly around the bottom edge. Brush the cake board evenly with apricot jam. Roll out 10 oz of the reserved black icing into an oblong large enough to cover the cake board.

5 Arrange the circles of white icing on top of the black icing and roll lightly into the surface. Lay over the cake board and trim the edges. Set aside 2 oz of the black icing, break off two marble-size pieces and set aside from the rest for the cow's eyes. Roll out the icing that is left and use to cover the ear shapes.

6 Carefully lift the cow's head on to the cake board, set aside 3½ oz of the white icing then roll out the rest thinly. Cut out a pear shape for the cow's nose. Brush the back with a little water and stick on to the cake. Roll two small pieces of white icing into walnut-size balls, then flatten with a rolling pin and reserve for the eyes.

7 To make the cow's eyes, color 1½ oz sugarpaste icing brown, then cut out two rounds with the 1½ inch round pastry cutter. Color 1 oz icing blue, then cut out two rounds with the 1 inch round cutter. Following the design, assemble the cow's eyes from the brown and blue rounds and the reserved white and black icings. Stick them in place with a little water.

8 Divide the reserved 2 oz of the black sugarpaste icing in half, hand roll out one half thinly into a rectangle of about 6 x 4 inches. Cut along the icing at intervals, leaving a ½ inch border along the top, to create the fringe. Position between the ears. Divide the remaining sugarpaste icing in half and use for the nose.

9 ▲ Color 1 oz of the remaining icing bright yellow and the rest red. Roll two-thirds of the red icing into a sausage shape, to make a mouth. To make the flower, roll out the remaining red icing and cut out a 2½ inch round, using the fluted cutter.

10 Roll the edge of the red icing using a toothpick to make it frilly (see Teddy Bear Christening Cake, step 7). Roll the yellow icing into a ball to finish off the flower. Push the florists' wire through the cake. Remove before serving.

Dinosaur Cake

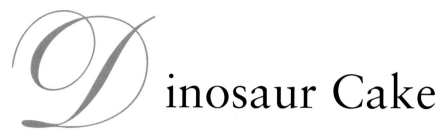

*For a dino-crazy kid, this cake is just the ticket.
Put it on a cake board or build a little scene using bits
and pieces from around the house and garden.*

INGREDIENTS
Serves 8–10
*1 quantity Quick-Mix Sponge
Cake mix*
½ quantity Butter Icing
1 quantity Truffle Cake mix
2 lb/2²⁄₃ x quantity Sugarpaste Icing
*pink, yellow, green and black food
colorings*
*4 tbsp apricot jam, warmed and
sieved*

MATERIALS AND EQUIPMENT
2 qt heart-shaped pan
2 x 10 inch piece of card
*small block of wood, for raising
the cake*

1 Preheat the oven to 350°F. Grease the heart-shaped pan, line the base with waxed paper and grease the paper. Spoon in the cake mixture and smooth the surface. Bake in the center of the oven for 35–40 minutes or until a skewer inserted into the center of the cake comes out clean. Turn out on to a wire rack, peel off the lining paper and leave to cool completely.

2 ▲ Cut the heart-shaped cake in half vertically, then sandwich the halves together with the butter icing so they form a half heart shape. Place the cake in the center of the strip of card, positioned on the long, straight side. Stand the cake on the small block of wood to raise it up slightly.

3 ▲ Divide the truffle mixture in half. Shape one portion into the tail, making it thicker and flattened at one end and more pointed at the other. This will fit on the pointed end of the cake. Mold the other half of the truffle cake mix into the head shape, starting with a ball and then flattening one side, so the diameter matches the width of the head end of the cake. Mold the other end of the head into a pointed shape for the nose.

4 Place the head and tail in position at either end of the cake, molding the truffle cake mix on to the cake a little. Cut off about 1¼ lb of the sugarpaste icing and color it pink. Lightly dust the work surface with confectioners' sugar and roll out the icing to a long, thin, rectangular shape. Brush the cake evenly with jam and cover the dinosaur with the icing in one piece from head to toe. Smooth down the sides and edges with your hands, then trim.

5 ▲ To make the dinosaur's legs, cut off about 4 oz of the remaining sugarpaste icing and color it yellow. Remove about 1 oz and set aside, wrapped in plastic wrap. Use the remainder to roll out 10 evenly sized balls, each about the size of a small walnut. Squeeze together two balls for each of the back legs and three for each of the front ones. Indent the toes with a fork, then using a little water stick the legs on the dinosaur.

6 ▲ Use the reserved yellow sugarpaste icing to make one small and three large horns, then stick these in place with a little water. Cut off about 3 oz of the remaining icing and color it green. Divide it into about 11 evenly sized pieces and shape each into a cone. Stick these on to the dinosaur with a little water. Divide the remaining icing in half and color one portion black. Use the white and black icings to make the mouth, eyes and eyebrows for the dinosaur. Stick on with a little water.

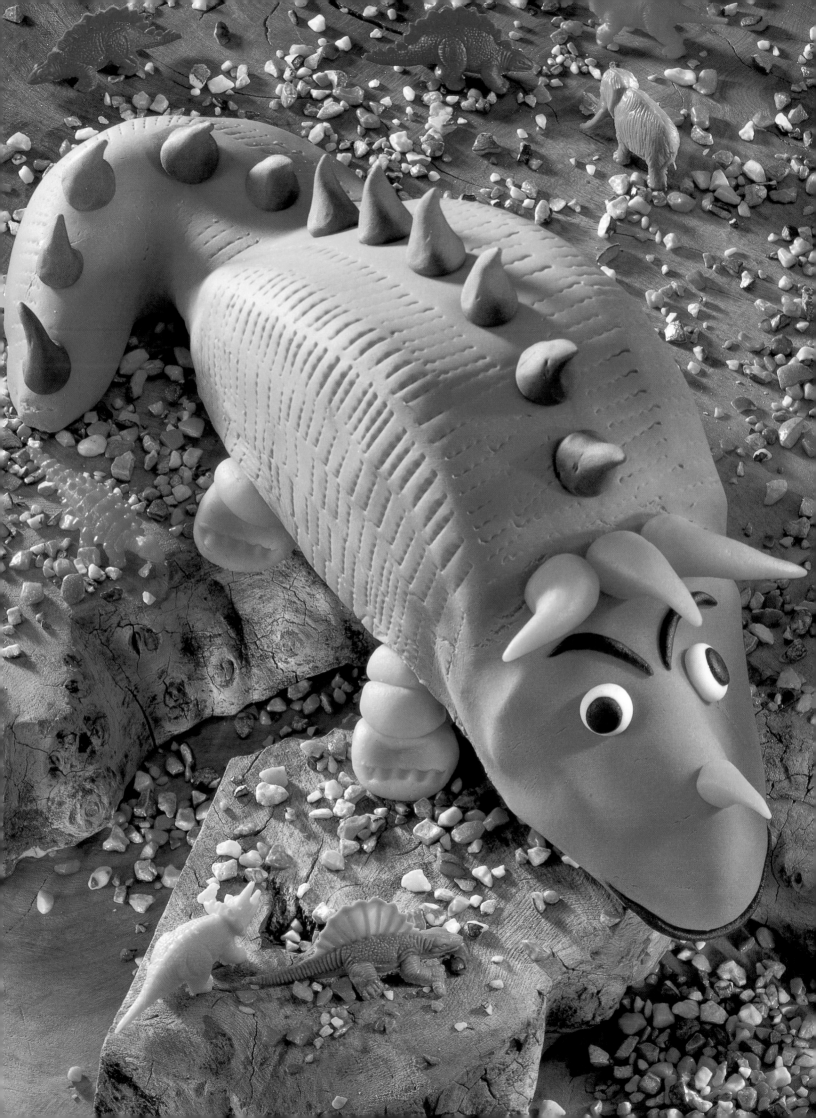

ucks on a Pond

A real treat at a children's party. A scrumptious combination of coconut cake, jelly and cream.

INGREDIENTS
Serves 8–10
1 quantity Quick-Mix Sponge Cake
mix
2¹/₂ cups heavy cream
green, yellow and red food colorings
4 cups shredded coconut
1 x 4¹/₂ oz packet of green jelly,
made up to the manufacturer's
instructions
7 oz/¹/₂ quantity Sugarpaste Icing
a few tiny candies
3 oz marzipan
5 pink marshmallows

MATERIALS AND EQUIPMENT
7 inch pie pan
9 inch round cake board
duck-shaped cutter
toothpicks
garlic press

1 Preheat the oven to 350°F. Grease the pie pan, line the base with waxed paper and grease the paper. Spoon the cake mixture into the prepared pan and smooth the surface. Bake in the center of the oven for 35–40 minutes or until firm to the touch. Leave the cake in the pan for about 3 minutes, then turn out on to a wire rack, peel off the lining paper and leave to cool completely.

2 ▲ Add a few drops of green food coloring to the heavy cream, and beat until it holds soft peaks. Place the cake on the cake board and spread the cream evenly over the cake.

3 ▲ To make the grassy bank, place the coconut in a bowl and add a few drops of green food coloring diluted with a dash of water. Stir until the coconut is speckled green and white.

4 ▲ Cut up the set jelly into ¹/₂ inch pieces. Carefully place the jelly pieces in the center of the cake.

5 To make the ducks, take 3 oz of the sugarpaste icing and color it yellow. Roll out on a work surface lightly dusted with confectioners' sugar until about ¹/₄ inch thick.

6 ▲ Using a duck-shaped cutter, stamp out the ducks, then skewer the bottom of each one with a toothpick. Lay the ducks on a baking sheet and leave them in a warm, dry place to harden.

7 Use the tiny candies, or sugarpaste icing, for the ducks' eyes, securing with a drop of water. Take off a small piece of marzipan, about the size of a hazelnut, then color the remainder green and shape into a frog, using a small, sharp knife to open the mouth and make the feet. Color the reserved piece of marzipan red, shape into the frog's tongue and secure in position with a little water. Use candies or blue and white sugarpaste icing for the eyes. Place the frog on the cake board.

8 To make the grass, color the remaining sugarpaste icing green and push through a garlic press, cutting it off with a small, sharp knife. Place the grass around the pond. To make the flowers, flatten the marshmallows with a rolling pin, then snip the edges with scissors to make the petals. Place the flowers around the pond and put a colored candy in the center of each. The wooden toothpicks must be removed from the ducks before serving.

Puppies in Love

Out of one jelly roll come two gorgeous puppy dogs. This cake looks extremely impressive, without being too difficult to prepare.

INGREDIENTS
Serves 8–10
1 quantity chocolate-flavor Jelly Roll mix
1/4 quantity chocolate-flavor Butter Icing
4 oz yellow marzipan
green, brown, pink and red food colorings
1 1/2 cups unsweetened shredded coconut
1 lb/1 1/3 x quantity Sugarpaste Icing
4 tbsp apricot jam, warmed and sieved

MATERIALS AND EQUIPMENT
13 x 9 inch jelly roll pan
10 inch square cake board
small round cutter
4 inch piece of thin ribbon

STORING
The finished cake can be kept in a cool, dry place for up to two days.

1 Preheat the oven to 350°F. Grease the jelly roll pan with butter or vegetable oil, line with waxed paper and grease the paper. Spoon in the cake mixture and smooth the surface. Bake in the center of the oven for about 12 minutes or until springy when touched in the center. Leave to cool in the pan, on a wire rack, covered with a clean, just-damp cloth. Then invert the cake on to a sheet of waxed paper, dredged with confectioners' sugar.

2 Trim the edges of the cake, then spread with the chocolate butter icing, reserving a tiny amount. Roll up the jelly roll, using the waxed paper as a guide, then cut in half widthwise.

3 ▲ To make the faces, cut the marzipan in half and roll each portion into a ball, then into a squat cone shape. Use a little of the reserved butter icing to stick the faces on to the bodies.

4 Place a few drops of green food coloring in a bowl with the shredded coconut. Add a few drops of water and stir until the coconut is flecked with green and white. Scatter it over the cake board, then position the two puppies a little apart on the board.

5 Cut off about 1 oz of the sugarpaste icing and set aside, wrapped in plastic wrap. Color half the remaining icing brown and half pink. Cut off about 2 oz from each color and wrap in plastic wrap.

6 ▲ Lightly dust the work surface with confectioners' sugar and then roll out the larger portions of brown and pink icings into 4 1/2 x 14 inch rectangles. Cut in half widthwise and trim the edges. Cover all four sections with plastic wrap and set aside.

7 ▲ Roll out the reserved pieces of brown and white icings, then use the small round cutter to stamp out several shapes. Gather up the icing trimmings and set aside, wrapped in plastic wrap. Stick the white rounds on to one of the brown rectangles, then the brown rounds on to one of the pink rectangles, using a little water. Use a rolling pin to press them in slightly.

8 Use a sharp knife to slash all four icing rectangles along the two short edges. Brush the body of each puppy with jam, then lay the brown icing without spots over one body, and the pink icing without spots over the other. Place a little water on the back of each, then put the brown spotted icing over the brown dog and the pink spotted icing over the pink dog.

9 ▲ Roll half of the reserved icings in your hands to make little tails. Stick them in place with a little reserved butter icing. Make a little fringe from the brown icing for the brown puppy, and tie a few strands of pink icing together with the ribbon to make a fringe for the pink puppy. Stick them in place with a little water.

10 Use the remaining pieces of sugarpaste icing to make the facial features for each puppy, choosing your own expressions, then stick them in place with some water. The little heart-shaped food bowl is an optional extra, or you can make a small bone, if you prefer.

Lion Cake

For an animal lover or a celebration cake for a Leo, this cake is quick and surprisingly easy to make.

INGREDIENTS
Serves 10–15
1½ x quantity Quick-Mix Sponge Cake mix
1 quantity orange-flavor Butter Icing
orange and red food colorings
1½ lb yellow marzipan
2 oz/¹⁄₆ quantity Sugarpaste Icing
red or orange liquorice strings
long and round marshmallows

MATERIALS AND EQUIPMENT
10 x 12 inch roasting pan
12 inch square cake board
cheese grater
small heart-shaped cutter

1 Preheat the oven to 350°F. Grease the roasting pan, line the base and sides with waxed paper and grease the paper. Spoon the cake mixture into the prepared pan and smooth the surface. Bake in the center of the oven for 45–50 minutes, or until a skewer inserted into the center of the cake comes out clean. Leave the cake in the pan for about 5 minutes, then turn out on to a wire rack, peel off the lining paper and leave to cool completely.

2 ▲ Place the cake, base side up, on the work surface. Use a small, sharp knife to cut around the edge of the cake in an uneven scallop design. You may need to do this several times in order to cut through to the bottom. Discard the excess cake from the edges. Turn the cake over and trim the top so that it sits squarely.

3 ▲ Place the cake on the cake board. Mix the orange-flavor butter icing in a bowl together with the orange food coloring. Spoon the butter icing on top of the cake and spread evenly over the surface and down the sides, using a small spatula.

4 On a work surface lightly dusted with confectioners' sugar, roll out about 4 oz of marzipan to a 6 inch square. Place the marzipan square in the center of the cake, gently pressing down to secure.

5 ▲ Grate the remaining marzipan on to a sheet of waxed paper. Use a spatula to lift the grated marzipan carefully on to the cake, evenly covering the sides and top up to the edges of the face panel.

6 ▲ Color the sugarpaste icing red, then roll out on a work surface dusted with confectioners' sugar. Use the heart-shaped cutter to stamp out the lion's nose and position on the cake, securing it with a little water. Take a little of the excess sugarpaste icing and use your fingers to roll out two thin strands for the mouth. Position on the cake, securing with water.

7 Cut the liquorice strings into graduated lengths, and place on the cake for the whiskers. For the eyes, flatten two round marshmallows and place on the cake, securing with water.

8 ▲ To make the eyebrows, cut the long marshmallows into 2 in lengths, and snip along one side. Place them on the cake, securing with water.

$\mathcal{P}$eepo Rabbits

*An easy cake to make for a chocoholic who loves rabbits.
All the fun is in the decorating.*

INGREDIENTS
Serves 6–8
For the Toadstools
2 large egg whites
2 tbsp superfine sugar

For the Cake
1 quantity Jelly Roll cake mix
1 quantity chocolate-flavor Butter Icing
2½ cups shredded coconut
3 tbsp cocoa powder, plus a little extra for dusting
8 oz/⅔ quantity Sugarpaste Icing pink, yellow, green and brown food colorings

MATERIALS AND EQUIPMENT
piping bag fitted with a small round nozzle
9 x 13 inch jelly roll pan
9 inch square cake board
small rabbit cutter
small butterfly cutter
1 toothpick
small leaf cutter

1 Preheat the oven to 275°F. To make the meringue toadstools, place a sheet of parchment paper on a baking sheet. Place the egg whites in a clean, dry mixing bowl and whisk until they hold soft peaks. Whisk in half of the sugar, then add the rest. Whisk until the mixture holds stiff peaks. Fill the piping bag with the meringue mixture and pipe several small rounds and several 1 inch stalks. Bake for about 1 hour, or until dry. Leave to cool completely.

2 ▲ To assemble the toadstools, gently press a stalk into a small meringue round. Set aside. Increase the oven temperature to 350°F.

3 Grease the pan, line the base and sides with waxed paper and grease the paper. Spoon the cake mixture into the pan and smooth the surface. Bake in the center of the oven for about 12 minutes, or until firm to the touch. Leave the cake in the pan, covered, to cool completely.

4 Lay a sheet of waxed paper on the work surface and sprinkle with confectioners' sugar. Tip the cake on to the waxed paper and remove the lining paper. Spread with about one-third of the butter icing and roll up. Cut off one-third of the roll and stand the larger section on the cake board, sticking it in place with a little butter icing.

5 ▲ Position the smaller log next to the larger one, then cover both in the remaining butter icing. Peak and swirl the icing quite unevenly to make it look like bark.

6 Place the coconut in a bowl and sift in the cocoa powder. Stir well until evenly blended. Spoon the coconut all around the cake.

7 ▲ Take half of the sugarpaste icing and divide into two portions. Color one portion pink. Roll out each piece on a work surface lightly dusted with confectioners' sugar until about ¼ inch thick. Stamp out two rabbits in each color. Use the pink and white trimmings to make tiny balls for the eyes, securing them in place with a little water. Place the rabbits on a baking sheet and leave until dry.

8 Cut off about one-quarter of the remaining sugarpaste icing and color it yellow. Roll out until about ¼ inch thick and stamp out a butterfly. Use the toothpick to indent the center of the butterfly gently and fold it a little. Press half of the toothpick through the base of the butterfly. Place the butterfly on the baking sheet with the rabbits, resting one wing on the edge of the baking sheet so that it dries in that position.

9 Cut off one-third of the remaining sugarpaste icing and color it green. Roll it out thinly, then cut it into strips using scissors and snip the strips into pointed sections to make the grass. Position the pieces of grass randomly in the coconut around the cake.

10 Color the remaining icing brown and roll out thinly. Cut out several leaf shapes, and then use a small, sharp knife to make the leaf indentations. Gently twist and bend the leaves a little, then place them in the coconut. Reserve the trimmings.

11 To assemble the rabbits, use a little of the reserved brown icing to stick them securely in place around the cake. Press the butterfly's toothpick into the back of the cake. Finally, position the meringue toadstools and dust them with a little cocoa powder.

Cat in a Basket

The pretty woven pattern of the basket is quite simple to do but is surprisingly realistic. The marzipan cat can be painted in appropriate colors to make it a portrait of your own family pet.

INGREDIENTS
Serves 8
7-inch round Madeira Cake
4 ounces/⅓ quantity Butter Icing
2 tablespoons apricot jam,
warmed and sieved
12 ounces pink marzipan
8 ounces green marzipan
8 ounces yellow marzipan
4 ounces/⅓ quantity
Sugar paste Icing (Fondant)
brown food coloring

MATERIALS AND EQUIPMENT
9-inch round cake board
fine paintbrush

1 ▲ Split the cake and fill with butter icing. Place on the cake board. Measure the circumference of the cake with string, fold in half and measure (this will give the length of the marzipan strips to be cut). Brush the cake with apricot jam.

2 Roll out the pink marzipan to a large rectangle. Cut into five ½-inch strips long enough to fit halfway around the cake. Roll out the green marzipan and cut into 3-inch lengths of the same width.

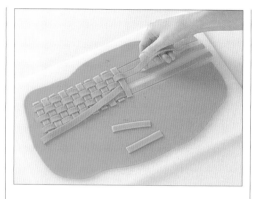

3 ▲ Fold back alternate pink strips and lay a green strip across widthwise. Fold back the pink strips over the green strip to form the weave, fold back the second set of pink strips and repeat the process. Press lightly to join.

4 ▲ Trim the basket weave and press onto the sides of the cake, joining the edges neatly.

5 ▲ Using the yellow marzipan, model a cat about 4 inches across. Allow to dry overnight.

6 Roll out the sugar paste icing, cut out a 9-inch-diameter circle and place on the cake, arranging it in folds to look like a blanket. Sit the cat in the center of the cake.

7 ▲ Roll any leftover pink and green marzipan into long ropes. Twist together and lay around the edge of the basket, then press on neatly. With a fine paintbrush and brown coloring, paint the face and markings on the cat.

$\mathcal{M}$ouse in Bed

This cake is suitable for a child of almost any age. The quilt and sheets may reflect a child's favorite color. Make the mouse well ahead to allow it time to dry.

INGREDIENTS
Serves 10
1½ x quantity Quick-mix Sponge
Cake baked in an 8-inch square pan
4 ounces/⅓ quantity Butter Icing
2 tablespoons apricot jam,
warmed and sieved
1 pound marzipan
1½ pounds/2 x quantity
Sugar paste Icing (Fondant)
blue and pink food coloring

MATERIALS AND EQUIPMENT
10-inch square cake board
flower cutter
pink and blue food-coloring pens

1 ▲ Split the cake and fill with butter icing. Cut 2 inches off one side and reserve; the cake should measure 8 x 6 inches. Place on the cake board and brush with apricot jam. Cover with marzipan. With the reserved cake, cut a pillow to fit the bed and cover with marzipan, pressing a hollow in the middle for the head. Cut a mound for the body and legs of the mouse and cover with marzipan. Allow to dry overnight.

2 ▲ Cover the cake and pillow with sugar paste icing. Lightly press a fork around the edge to make a frill around the pillow. Roll out one-half (12 ounces) sugar paste icing and cut into 3-inch-wide strips to make a valance. Attach to the side of the bed with a little water and arrange in drapes.

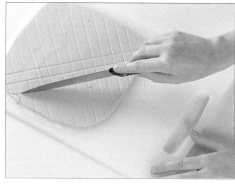

3 ▲ To make the top sheet and quilt, color 3 ounces sugar paste icing pale blue and roll out to a 7-inch square to cover the bed. Lightly mark a diamond pattern with the back of a knife and press a flower cutter into the diamonds to mark. Put the pillow and body on top of the cake and cover with the quilt.

4 ▲ Roll out a little white sugar paste and cut a 1 x 7½-inch strip for the sheet. Mark along one length to resemble a seam and place over the quilt, tucking it in at the top.

5 ▲ Color a little marzipan pink and make the head and paws.

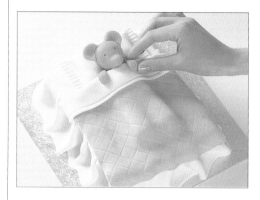

6 ▲ Put the mouse's paws over the edge of the sheet. Draw facial markings with food-coloring pens.

The Beehive

The perfect cake for an outdoors spring or summer party.
Take the bees along separately on their wires and
insert them into the cake at the picnic.

INGREDIENTS
Serves 8–10
1 quantity Quick-Mix Sponge
Cake mix
2 lb yellow marzipan
5 tbsp apricot jam, warmed and
sieved
black food coloring
25 g/1 oz Sugarpaste Icing

MATERIALS AND EQUIPMENT
2 qt Pyrex bowl
9 inch fluted or round cake board
8 inch square of rice paper
florists' wire covered in florists' tape

1 Preheat the oven to 350°F. Grease and flour the Pyrex bowl. Spoon in the cake mixture and smooth the surface. Bake in the center of the oven for 40–45 minutes or until a skewer inserted into the center of the cake comes out clean. Leave the cake in the bowl for about 5 minutes, then turn out on to a wire rack and leave to cool completely.

2 Cut off about 6 oz of marzipan and set aside, wrapped in plastic wrap. Knead the remainder on a work surface lightly dusted with confectioners' sugar, then roll it out into a long, thin sausage shape. If it breaks when it gets too long, start again. You may need to make more than one sausage. Place the cake, dome side up, on the cake board and brush evenly with apricot jam.

3 ▲ Starting at the back of the base, coil the marzipan sausage around the cake, keeping it neat and tight all the way to the top. Any joins that have to be made should be placed at the back of the cake.

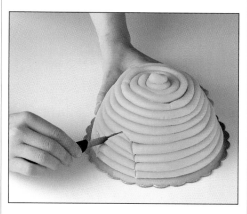

4 ▲ Using a small, sharp knife, cut an arched doorway at the front of the cake. Remove the cut-out section and cut away some of the inside cake to make a hollow. Brush the crumbs away from the doorway.

5 ▲ To make six bees, divide the reserved marzipan in half and color one portion black. Set aside a cherry-sized ball of black marzipan, and wrap in clear film. Divide both the black and the yellow marzipan into 12 small balls. To make a bee, pinch together two balls of each color, alternately placed. Stick them together with a little water, if necessary. Cut the rice paper into six pairs of rounded wings, then stick them to the bees with a tiny drop of water.

6 ▲ Use the reserved black marzipan and sugar-paste icing to make facial features. Then cut the florists' wire into various lengths, then use it to pierce the bees from underneath. Once secure, press the other end of the wire into the cake in various places. The wires must be removed before serving.

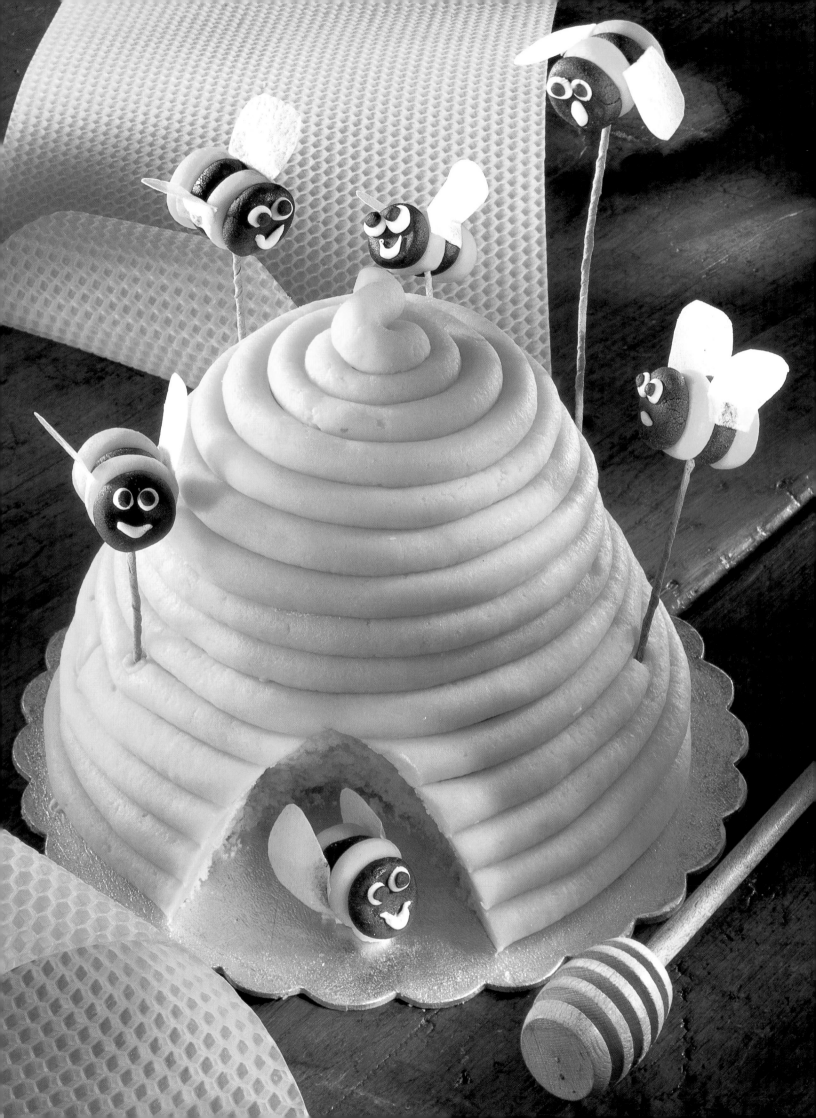

ℬumblebee

This friendly bee looks intricate, but is very quick and simple to construct. If time is short, you can decorate the board with ready-made sugar flowers instead of making them.

INGREDIENTS
Serves 10
1 quantity Quick-mix Sponge Cake
baked in an 8-inch round pan
4 ounces/⅓ quantity Butter Icing
2 tablespoons apricot jam,
warmed and sieved
12 ounces marzipan
1¼ pounds/1½ x quantity Sugar
paste Icing (Fondant)
yellow, black, blue, pink and green
food coloring
1 cup dried, shredded coconut
4 ounces/⅙ quantity
Royal Icing

MATERIALS AND EQUIPMENT
10-inch square cake board
paper doiley
tape
pipe cleaner

1 ▲ Split the cake and fill with butter icing. Cut in half, sandwich both halves together and stand upright on the cake board. Trim the ends to shape the head and tail. Brush with apricot jam and cover with marzipan. Color two-thirds of the sugar paste icing yellow, roll out and use to cover the cake. Reserve the trimmings.

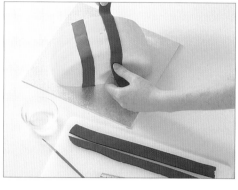

2 ▲ Color two-thirds of the remaining sugar paste icing black. Roll out and cut out three 1 x 10-inch stripes. Leave about 4 inches from the end of the cake for the head and position the stripes evenly spaced behind the head, attaching them with a little water. Roll out and cut eyes, mouth and daisies from the sugar paste icing. Color and stick on with a little water.

3 ▲ Put the coconut into a bowl and mix in a drop of green coloring. Cover the cake board with royal icing, then sprinkle the coconut over to look like grass. Place the daisies on the board. To make the wings, cut the doiley in half, wrap each half into a cone shape and stick together with tape. Cut the pipe cleaner in half and stick the pieces into the cake just behind the head. Place the wings over the pipe cleaners.

*T*eddy's Birthday

This is a perfect cake for anyone who loves teddy bears. To give the cake a really smooth, flat finish, use an icing smoother on the top.

INGREDIENTS
Serves 10
*1 quantity Quick-mix Sponge Cake baked in an 8-inch round pan
4 ounces/⅓ quantity Butter Icing
2 tablespoons apricot jam, warmed and sieved
12 ounces marzipan
1 pound/1⅓ x quantity
Sugar paste Icing (Fondant)
brown, red, blue and black food coloring
4 ounces/⅙ quantity Royal Icing
silver balls (dragées)*

MATERIALS AND EQUIPMENT
*10-inch round cake board
waxed or parchment paper
ribbon, 1 inch wide
waxed or parchment paper piping bag
No. 7 shell nozzle
No. 7 star nozzle
birthday cake candles*

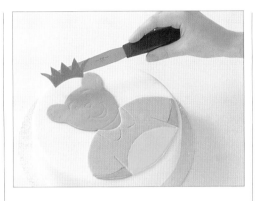

2 ▲ Color one-third of the remaining sugar paste icing pale brown. Color a piece pink, a piece red, some blue and a tiny piece black. Using the template, cut out the pieces and place in position on the cake. Stick down by lifting the edges carefully and brushing the undersides with a little water. Roll small ovals for the eyes and stick in place with the other face shapes.

3 ▲ Tie the ribbon round the cake. Color the royal icing blue and pipe the border around the base of the cake with the shell nozzle and tiny stars around the small cake with the star nozzle. Decorate the icing with silver balls. Put the candles on the cake.

1 ▲ Split the cake and fill with butter icing. Place on the cake board and brush with apricot jam. Cover with marzipan. Roll out two-thirds of the sugar paste icing and use to cover the cake. Make a template on waxed or parchment paper using the photograph as a guide, and mark the design on top of the cake.

Hickory Dickory Dock

This appealing cake is based on the nursery rhyme. Small children love the jolly clock face, and the sugar mouse can be given as a prize.

INGREDIENTS
Serves 12–15
2 x quantity Quick-mix Sponge
Cake baked in an 8-inch round pan
and a 6-inch square pan
8 ounces/⅔ quantity Butter Icing
3 tablespoons apricot jam,
warmed and sieved
1½ pounds marzipan
1¼ pound/1⅔ x quantity
Sugar paste Icing
brown, gold, red, blue and black
food coloring
2 silver balls
4 ounces/⅙ quantity Royal Icing

MATERIALS AND EQUIPMENT
10 x 14-inch cake board
paintbrush
plastic mouse mold
4-inch piece of string
waxed or parchment paper
waxed or parchment paper
piping bag
No. 1 writing nozzle

1 ▲ Split the cakes and fill with butter icing. Cut two wedges off one end of the square cake, 2½ inches from the corner.

2 ▲ Use a cake pan as a guide to cut a semicircle from the opposite end of the square cake to fit around the round cake. Place on the cake board and brush with apricot jam. Cover with marzipan. Color four-fifths of the sugar paste icing brown. Roll out and use to cover the cake. Reserve the trimmings.

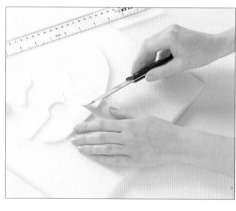

3 ▲ Roll out half the remaining sugar paste icing and cut a 6-inch circle for the face and a window for the pendulum. Cut out a 2-inch-long pendulum and 2-inch- and 2½-inch-long hands.

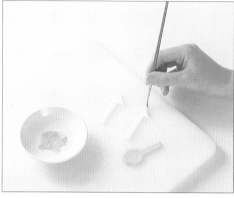

4 ▲ Paint the pendulum and hands gold and allow to dry overnight.

5 ▲ Color most of the remaining sugar paste icing pink and mold a mouse with a string tail and silver balls for eyes. Allow to dry overnight on waxed paper.

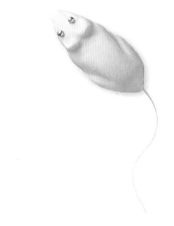

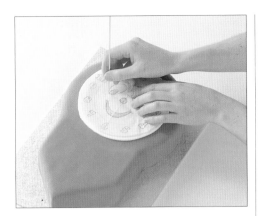

6 ▲ Stick on the clock face with a little water. Using a template, mark the numbers and face on the clock. Color the royal icing black and pipe the numbers with a No. 1 nozzle. Stick on the window with a little water. Roll out the excess brown sugar paste icing into long sausages and edge the face and the window. Color the remaining sugar paste icing blue, red and black. Roll out and cut the eyes, pupils, eyebrows, mouth and center. Stick on the hands, features and pendulum with a little water. Stick on the mouse.

𝒯ip

If you are making this cake for a children's party, you may want to model extra mice from pink sugar paste icing for the children to take home.

Noah's Ark

This charming cake is decorated with small plastic animals, about 1½ inches high, available at party and cake-decorating shops. Children will love to take home one of the novelties as a reminder of the party.

INGREDIENTS
Serves 10
1½ x quantity Quick-mix Sponge Cake baked in an 8-inch square cake pan
4 ounces/⅓ quantity Butter Icing
2 tablespoons apricot jam, warmed and sieved
1 pound marzipan
1 pound/1⅓ x quantity Sugar paste Icing (Fondant), colored light brown
4 ounces/⅙ quantity Royal Icing
yellow and blue food coloring
chocolate mint stick

MATERIALS AND EQUIPMENT
10-inch square cake board
rice paper
small animal cake ornaments

2 ▲ Cut a 4 x 2½-inch rectangle for the cabin and a triangular roof from the remaining piece of cake. Sandwich together with butter icing or apricot jam.

3 ▲ Brush the three pieces of cake with apricot jam and cover with marzipan, then cover the hull and cabin with brown sugar paste icing. Sandwich together with butter icing and place in position on the hull. Roll a long sausage from the remaining brown sugar paste icing and stick round the edge of the hull with a little water. Mark planks of wood with the back of a knife. Allow to dry overnight.

4 ▲ Color one-third of the royal icing yellow and spread over the roof with a spatula. Roughen it with a skewer to look like thatch.

5 ▲ Color the remaining royal icing pale blue and spread over the cake board, making rough waves. Stick a rice paper flag onto the chocolate mint stick and press on the back of the boat. Stick the small animals onto the deck with dabs of icing.

1 ▲ Split the cake and fill with butter icing. Cut a rectangle 8 x 5 inches and cut to shape the hull of the boat. Place diagonally on the cake board.

Magic Rabbit

This cheery rabbit bursting from a top hat is the perfect centerpiece for a party with a magic theme. For an extra surprise, cover the cake with a silk handkerchief, to be pulled away by the guest of honor.

INGREDIENTS
Serves 10
1½ x quantity Quick-mix
Sponge Cake baked in
6-inch round cake pans
8 ounces/⅔ quantity Butter Icing
4 ounces/⅙ quantity Royal Icing
3 tablespoons apricot jam,
warmed and sieved
1½ pounds marzipan
1½ pounds/2 x quantity Sugar paste
Icing (Fondant), colored gray
black and pink food coloring
silver balls (dragées)

MATERIALS AND EQUIPMENT
10-inch square cake board
wooden spoons
pink ribbon
waxed or parchment paper piping bag
small star nozzle
No. 1 writing nozzle

1 ▲ Split the cakes and fill with butter icing. Stick on the center of the cake board with a little royal icing. Brush with apricot jam. Cover with two-thirds of the marzipan. Roll out the gray icing and use about three-quarters to cover the cake. Roll out the remaining sugar paste icing to an 8-inch round. Cut a 6-inch circle from the center and lower the ring carefully over the cake. Shape the sides of the brim and hold in place to dry.

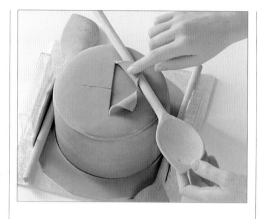

2 ▲ With the remaining gray sugar paste icing, roll out to a 6-inch circle, cut a cross in the center, place on the hat and curl triangles over a spoon handle to shape. Smooth the seam around the edge of the hat.

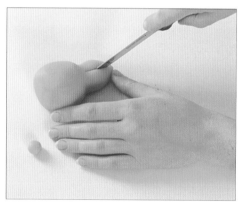

3 ▲ Color the remaining marzipan pink. Shape the rabbit's head about 2 inches in diameter, shaping a slightly pointed face. Mark the position of the eyes, nose and mouth. Shape the ears around the handle of a wooden spoon and allow to dry separately overnight.

4 ▲ Stick the rabbit in the center of the hat with a little royal icing. Tie the ribbon round the hat. Pipe a border of royal icing around the top and base of the hat and decorate with silver balls while the icing is still wet.

5 ▲ Color the remaining royal icing black and use to pipe two eyes and a smiling mouth.

Frog Prince

This smartly dressed frog, with his golden crown and happy smile, makes a perfect cake for a birthday princess.

INGREDIENTS
Serves 8
1 quantity Quick-mix Sponge Cake
baked in an 8-inch round
cake pan
4 ounces/⅓ quantity Butter Icing
2 tablespoons apricot jam,
warmed and sieved
1 pound marzipan
1¼ pound/1⅔ x quantity
Sugar paste Icing (Fondant)
4 ounces/⅙ quantity Royal Icing
green, red, black and gold
food coloring

MATERIALS AND EQUIPMENT
10-inch square cake board

1 ▲ Split the cake and fill with butter icing. Cut it in half and sandwich both halves together with apricot jam. Stand upright diagonally across the cake board.

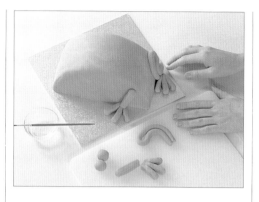

2 ▲ Brush the cake with apricot jam and cover with marzipan. Reserve one-third quantity of sugar paste icing and color the rest green. Cover the cake with the green sugar paste. To make the legs and feet, roll green sugar paste icing into 8-inch lengths about ½ inch in diameter. Fold in half for the back legs and stick on with a little water.

3 The front legs are rolled into 4-inch lengths, folded in half and pinched to taper to the foot end. The feet are made in the same way, cut to 1½-inch lengths and pinched together to tapered ends. Stick in place with a little royal icing. Roll balls for the eyes and stick in place on top of the cake.

4 ▲ Roll out the reserved sugar paste icing. Cut a 2 x 7½-inch strip and mark one edge at 1-inch intervals, then cut out triangles to make the crown shape. Wrap around a glass dusted with cornstarch and moisten the edges to join. Let stand to dry (this may take up to 2 days).

5 Cut a 4-inch circle for the white shirt. Stick in place and trim the edge level with the cake board. Cut white circles and stick to the eyes. Color a little sugar paste pink, roll into a sausage and stick on for the mouth. Color a little sugar paste black, roll out and cut pupils for the eyes and bow tie and stick in place.

6 ▲ Paint the crown gold and stick into position with royal icing.

Crazy Caterpillar

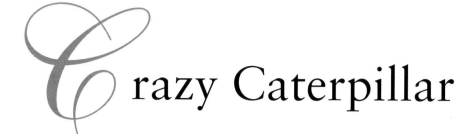

A no-bake cake made from sponge cake crumbs, home-made or bought. You can double the quantity for an extra-large party, but remember the cake is rich and heavy in texture so you only serve a small amount. One ball per person is more than enough!

INGREDIENTS
Serves 11
1 quantity Truffle Cake mix
1½ lb yellow marzipan
green, brown and orange food colorings
selection of colored liquorice sticks, or candies, for the feet
green-colored shredded coconut (see Puppies in Love, step 4), for the grass
small flowers, to decorate (optional)

MATERIALS AND EQUIPMENT
16 x 8 inch cake board (optional)
small round fluted cutter
round fluted aspic cutter

1 ▲ Using slightly damp hands, roll the truffle cake mixture into balls about the size of a large walnut. Place them on a cookie sheet as you make them, then cover with plastic wrap and set to one side.

2 ▲ Divide the marzipan into three equal portions, then color one portion green, one portion brown and the other portion orange. Remove a small amount of orange and green marzipan, to make the face features, and set aside, covered with plastic wrap.

3 ▲ Roll each color of marzipan into a sausage shape about 18 inches long on a work surface lightly dusted with confectioners' sugar. Make sure the sausage shape is even all the way along; if it breaks, compress the marzipan into a ball and start again.

4 ▲ Place the three long sausages side-by-side on the work surface. Starting at one end, hold them together firmly and start to turn them in a twisting motion — do not squeeze. Place the twist back on the work surface, then use a rolling pin to push and roll the twist gently until it is flat and the colors merge. It should be about 20 inches long.

5 Lay the truffle balls all along the length of the marzipan strip, then wrap the marzipan evenly around the balls, sealing the join by pinching the marzipan together. (An extra pair of hands is useful for this stage). Turn the caterpillar over so the join is underneath, tucking in and cutting off any excess marzipan from the ends. Lift the caterpillar on to the cake board, if using, otherwise position it on the table, curving it slightly.

6 Roll out the reserved orange and green marzipan thinly and use the fluted cutters to stamp out rounds for the eyes. Use a little water to stick the smaller green rounds on the orange rounds, then stick them on to one end of the caterpillar to make the face. Roll a tiny piece of orange marzipan into a little sausage, shape and stick it on to make the mouth. Cut the liquorice sticks into small pieces and position them along either side, to make the feet. Scatter the green-colored coconut all around. Add a few flowers, if you like.

Fun and Games

*Baking does not always have to be a serious business.
Celebrate any event with a novel cake design that will provide
an amusing twist to traditional occasions. Using a range of
colors and icing techniques, cakes can be fashioned into
almost any design you could dream of. From a pinball
machine to an army tank, from spaceships to circus clowns,
your imagination is really the only limit.*

Artist's Box and Palette

Making cakes is an art in itself, and this cake proves it.
It is the perfect celebration cake for artists of all ages.

INGREDIENTS
Serves 30
8 in square Rich Fruit Cake
3 tbsp apricot jam, warmed and
strained
1 lb marzipan
1³/₄ lb/2¹/₃ x quantity Sugarpaste
Icing
4 oz/¹/₆ quantity Royal Icing
brown, yellow, blue, black, silver,
orange, green, and purple food
colorings

MATERIALS AND EQUIPMENT
stiff paper for template
10 in square cake board
paintbrush

1 Brush the cake with the apricot jam. On a work surface lightly dusted with confectioner's sugar, roll out the marzipan and use to cover the cake. Allow to dry for 12 hours.

2 Make a template out of stiff paper in the shape of an artist's palette that will fit the top of the cake. Color just less than one-quarter of the sugarpaste icing a pale brown. On a work surface lightly dusted with confectioner's sugar, roll out to the size of the template and cut around the template to make the palette shape.

3 Color about two-thirds of the remaining sugarpaste icing brown. Roll out, brush the marzipanned cake with a little water and cover the cake with the icing. Place the cake on the cake board and then allow to dry for several hours.

4 ▲ With the remaining sugarpaste icing, leave half white and divide the remainder into seven equal portions. Color these yellow, blue, black, silver, orange, green, and purple. Shape the box handle with black icing and the box clips and paintbrush ferrules with silver icing. Shape the paintbrush bristles with orange icing and mark the hairs of the bristles with a knife. Shape the paintbrush handles in various colors and attach the handles, ferrules, and bristles with a little royal icing. Allow all the pieces to dry on wax paper for several hours.

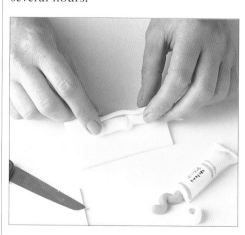

5 ▲ Make two paint tubes from some of the white icing. Roll out an oblong shape for each one and then wrap these around "sausages" of icing, sealing the edges with a little water. Paint markings on the tubes with food coloring.

6 ▲ Shape the squeezed-out paint in various colors and attach one to each of the paint tubes with a little royal icing. Allow all the pieces to dry on wax paper for several hours.

7 Using the remaining white sugarpaste icing, roll out two small rectangles to represent sheets of paper and brush on patterns with watered-down food coloring. Allow to dry on wax paper for several hours.

8 ▲ Paint wood markings on to the cake box with watered-down food coloring and allow to dry. To assemble the cake, attach the handles and clips to the front side of the box and the palette to the top of the cake with a little royal icing. Position the paintbrushes, paint tubes, squeezed-out paint, and the sheets of paper on the cake and around the cake board.

$\mathscr{S}$trawberry Cake

*A summer-time cake or for someone who's
simply mad about strawberries!*

INGREDIENTS
Serves 10–12
*1 quantity Quick-Mix Sponge
Cake mix
1 lb 7oz marzipan
green, red and yellow food
colorings
sugar, to dredge*

MATERIALS AND EQUIPMENT
*2 qt heart-shaped pan
12 inch round cake board
icing smoother*

$\mathscr{T}$ip

You can also sandwich the cake with a half quantity of strawberry-flavor Butter Icing before brushing it with apricot jam for extra flavor! Use a long, serrated knife and carefully cut the cake horizontally into two layers.

1 Preheat the oven to 350°F. Grease the heart-shaped pan, line the base with waxed paper and grease the paper. Spoon in the cake mixture and smooth the surface. Bake in the center of the oven for 35–40 minutes or until a skewer inserted into the center of the cake comes out clean.

2 Leave in the pan for about 5 minutes, then turn out on to a wire rack, peel off the lining paper and leave to cool completely.

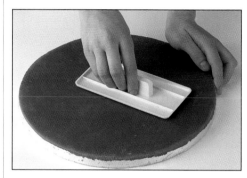

3 ▲ Cut off about 6 oz of the marzipan and color it green. Brush the cake board with a little apricot jam, then roll out the green marzipan on the work surface lightly dusted with confectioners' sugar and use to cover the cake board. Trim the edges. Use an icing smoother to make the marzipan as flat and as smooth as possible.

4 ▲ Evenly brush the remaining apricot jam over the top and sides of the cake. Position the cake on the cake board. Cut off about 10 oz of the remaining marzipan and color it red. Roll it out to about ¼ inch thick and use to cover the cake, smoothing down the sides and edges. Trim the edges. Use the handle of a teaspoon to indent the strawberry evenly and lightly all over.

5 To make the stalk, cut off another 6 oz of marzipan and color it bright green. Cut it in half and roll out one portion into a 4 x 6 inch rectangle. Use a sharp knife to cut 'V' shapes out of the rectangle, leaving a 1 inch border across the top, to form the calyx. Position this on the cake, curling and moving the sections to make them look more realistic.

6 ▲ Roll the other half of the green marzipan in your hands into a sausage shape about 5 inches long. Bend it slightly, then position it on the cake to form the stalk.

7 ▲ To make the strawberry seeds, color the remaining marzipan yellow. Pull off tiny pieces about the size of an apple pip and roll them into little tear-shaped seeds. Place them in the indentations all over the strawberry. Dust the cake with sifted sugar.

Sailing Boat

Make this cake for someone who loves sailing or is going on a journey—you can even personalize the cake with a rice-paper name-tag flag, written with a food-coloring pen.

INGREDIENTS
Serves 10–12
1½ x quantity Quick-mix Sponge Cake mix
4 tablespoons apricot jam, warmed and sieved
1 pound/1⅓ x quantity Sugar paste Icing (Fondant)
12 ounces/1 quantity Butter Icing colored blue
1 sheet of rice paper
1 grissini
1 black licorice wheel, with an orange candy in the center
1 white chocolate disk
9 short candy sticks
4 mint Lifesavers®
1 red licorice "shoelace"
1 black licorice "shoelace"

MATERIALS AND EQUIPMENT
9 x 5 x 3-inch loaf pan
waxed or parchment paper
13 x 7-inch cake board
toothpick
black food coloring pen

1 Preheat the oven to 350°F. Grease the loaf pan. Line the bottom and sides with waxed or parchment paper and grease the paper. Spoon the cake mixture into the prepared pan and smooth the top with a plastic spatula. Bake in the preheated oven for 55–60 minutes, or until a skewer inserted into the center of the cake comes out clean. Let stand for 5 minutes before turning out onto a wire rack to cool.

2 ▲ Slice a thin layer off the top of the cake to make it perfectly flat. Trim one end to make a pointed bow. Using a small sharp knife, cut a shallow hollow from the center of the cake, leaving a ½-inch border.

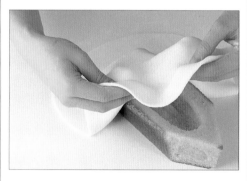

3 ▲ Brush the cake all over with the apricot jam. Roll out the sugar paste icing to a 14 x 9-inch rectangle and lay over the cake. Gently ease the sugar paste icing into the hollow middle and down the sides of the cake, until completely and evenly covered. Trim the edges at the base.

4 Cover the cake board with the blue butter icing, peaking it to resemble a rough sea. Position the cake on the iced board. Cut the rice paper into two tall triangular sails. Using a small brush, apply a little water along the length of the grissini and secure the rice paper sails to it. Insert the mast into the front of the hollowed compartment at the bow of the boat.

5 Cut a small flag shape from the remaining rice paper and personalize it with the recipient's name using the food coloring pen. Stick onto the toothpick using a little water and position the flag at the stern of the boat.

6 Uncoil the licorice wheel and remove the candy from the center. Use the licorice to make a fender all around the outside of the boat, securing it with a little water. Trim the excess and use the remainder to line the seating area in the same way. Position the candy from the center of the wheel to one side of the boat for the searchlight. Place the chocolate disk at the back of the seating area for the cushion.

7 ▲ Insert seven of the short candy sticks around the bow of the boat, leaving a little space between each one and allowing them to stand about 1 inch above the surface of the cake. Insert the remaining two short candy sticks at either side of the stern of the boat and hang two Lifesavers® on each, for the life preservers. Use the licorice shoelaces to tie loosely in and out of the candy sticks at the bow of the boat for the guard rail. Trim away any excess, if necessary.

Shirt and Tie Cake

Instead of buying the man in your life a shirt and tie for his birthday, make him a cake for a deliciously novel surprise.

INGREDIENTS
Serves 20–30
2 x quantity Quick-mix Sponge Cake mix
12 ounces/1 quantity coffee-flavor Butter Icing
6 tablespoons apricot jam, warmed and sieved
confectioners' sugar, for dusting
2¼ pounds/3 x quantity Sugar paste Icing (Fondant)
blue food coloring
1 cup confectioners' sugar, sifted
3–4 tablespoons water

MATERIALS AND EQUIPMENT
7½ x 10½-inch roasting pan
12 x 13-inch cake board
steel ruler
wooden skewer
waxed or parchment paper piping bag fitted with a small round nozzle
16 x 2-inch piece of flexible cardboard, the short ends cut at an angle, for the collar
paintbrush
"Happy Birthday" cake decoration
blue tissue paper

1 Preheat the oven to 350°F. Grease the roasting pan. Line the bottom and sides with waxed or parchment paper and grease the paper. Spoon the cake mixture into the pan and smooth the surface. Bake in the preheated oven for 1¼–1½ hours, or until a skewer inserted into the center of the cake comes out clean. Let stand for 5 minutes before turning out onto a wire rack to cool.

2 Cut the cake in half horizontally and spread with the butter icing. Sandwich together with the top half of the cake. Brush the cake evenly with apricot jam and lightly dust the work surface with confectioners' sugar.

3 Color 1½ pounds/2 x quantity sugar paste icing light blue. Roll out the light blue sugar paste icing to about ¼ inch thick and use to cover the cake, gently easing the sugar paste icing down the sides and corners. Trim away any excess icing. Place the cake on the cake board.

4 ▲ Using a steel ruler, make grooves down the length and sides of the cake in straight lines about 1 inch apart. Use a wooden skewer to re-indent the grooves, rolling the skewer slightly from side to side to make the channels deeper and slightly wider.

5 ▲ Mix the confectioners' sugar and water together in a small bowl to make a just-thick glacé icing and use to fill the piping bag fitted with the small round nozzle. Pipe lines of glacé icing into the grooves on the top and sides of the cake, moving slowly and evenly.

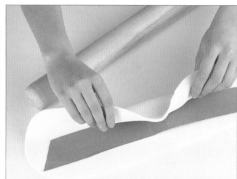

6 ▲ To make the collar, roll out ⅔ quantity (8 ounces) sugar paste icing on a work surface lightly dusted with confectioners' sugar to a 16½ x 4-inch rectangle. Lay the piece of cardboard for the collar on top, placing it along one edge of the sugar paste icing. Brush a little water around the edges of the sugar paste icing, then carefully lift the other edge of the sugar paste icing and fold over the card to encase it completely. Trim the two short ends to match the angles of the card. Carefully lift the collar, gently bend it around and position it on the cake, applying a little water to help secure it.

7 Color the remaining sugar paste icing dark blue. To make the tie, cut off one-third of the dark blue sugar paste icing and shape into a pyramid for the tie knot. Position the knot. Lightly dust the work surface with confectioners' sugar and roll out the remaining dark blue sugar paste icing to about ¼ inch thick.

8 Cut out a tie piece to fit under the knot and long enough to hang over the edge of the cake, making it slightly wider at the end where you cut a point. Position the tie piece, tucking it under the knot and applying a little water to secure it in place. Finish the cake with the "Happy Birthday" decoration and tissue paper.

Licorice Candy Cake

If licorice is a favorite, this is a cake to fantasize over. Larger than life, its base is a Madeira cake filled with butter icing, and it is topped with look-alike licorice candies.

INGREDIENTS
Serves 15–20
8-inch square Madeira cake
6-inch square Madeira cake
1½ pounds/2 x quantity
Butter Icing
3 tablespoons apricot jam,
warmed and sieved
12 ounces marzipan
1¾ pounds/2⅓ x quantity
Sugar paste Icing (Fondant)
egg-yellow, black, blue and
reddish-purple food coloring

MATERIALS AND EQUIPMENT
10-inch square cake board
1¾-inch round cutter

1 Cut both the cakes horizontally into three parts. Fill with the butter icing, reserving a little to coat the outsides of the smaller cake. Wrap and set aside the smaller cake.

2 Brush the 8-inch cake with the apricot jam. Roll out the marzipan and cover the cake. Position the cake on the cake board, securing underneath with a little butter icing. Let stand to dry for 12 hours.

3 Take 1 quantity sugar paste icing and color it yellow. Take ⅓ quantity sugar paste icing and color half black and leave the other half white. Brush the marzipanned cake lightly with water. Roll out the yellow icing; cover the top and down one-third of the sides of the cake.

4 ▲ Roll out the white icing and cut a strip wide and long enough to cover the sides of the bottom one-third of the cake. Position on the cake, securing the join with a little water. Roll out the black icing to a strip wide enough and long enough to fill the central third strip, between the yellow and white strips. Position on the cake.

5 Cut the 6-inch cake into three equal strips. Divide two of the strips each into three squares. From the remaining strip cut out two circles (about 1¾ inches), using a cutter as a guide.

6 Take another ⅓ quantity sugar paste icing and color it black. Take the remaining sugar paste icing and divide into four equal amounts: color blue, pink, yellow and leave one portion white.

7 Coat the outsides of the cut-out cake pieces with the reserved butter icing. Make the square licorice candies for the top of the cake using the colored icings, rolling out strips for the sides and squares to coat the tops. Secure any of the seams with a little water.

8 ▲ Make small balls of pink and blue icing for the round candies, attaching them by lightly pressing into the butter icing.

9 ▲ To make the small rolls for the edges of the cake, roll out any black sugar paste icing trimmings into a strip about 7 x 5 inches. With your fingers, roll out 7-inch long sausage shapes of yellow, pink, white and blue icing. Position one of the colors down the length of the black strip and roll over to form a filled roll, securing the seam underneath with water. Slice across into three pieces. Repeat with the remaining colors.

10 Arrange the smaller licorice candies in a pile on top and around the edges of the large cake.

Camping Tent

The perfect cake for a child who enjoys camping. You may find it easier to cover the sides of the cake first, and then the top, rather than all in one.

INGREDIENTS
Serves 8–10
1½ x quantity Quick-mix Sponge
Cake baked in an 8-inch square
cake pan
4 ounces/⅓ quantity Butter Icing
4 tablespoons apricot jam,
warmed and sieved
1 pound marzipan
1¼ pounds/1½ x quantity
Sugar paste Icing (Fondant)
brown, orange, green, red, yellow
and blue food coloring
4 ounces/⅙ quantity Royal Icing
2 ounces/1 cup dried coconut
chocolate matchsticks

MATERIALS AND EQUIPMENT
10-inch square cake board
wooden toothpicks
fine paintbrush
waxed or parchment paper piping bag
No. 1 writing nozzle
basket weave nozzle
toy soccer ball and mug

1 ▲ Split the cake and fill with a little butter icing. Cut the cake in half. Cut one half in two diagonally from the top right edge to the bottom left edge to form the roof of the tent.

2 ▲ Stick the two wedges back to back on top of the oblong with apricot jam to form the tent. Measure the height from the ground and trim off at 4 inches high. Use these trimmings on either side of the base. Place the cake diagonally and brush with apricot jam. Cover with marzipan, reserving one-eighth (2 ounces).

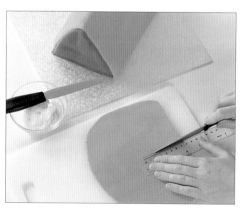

3 ▲ Color ⅙ quantity sugar paste icing brown and the remainder orange. Cover one end of the tent with brown sugar paste and the rest with orange. It is easier to cut the opening for the tent separately and then stick it on with a little water. Cut a 3-inch slit down the front of the tent, lay over the brown sugar paste, then trim off the excess and smooth the seams at the top. Fold back the sides and secure with royal icing. Allow to dry.

4 Stick halved toothpicks in the corners as pegs and in the ridge as poles.

5 ▲ Put the coconut in a bowl and mix in a little green coloring. Spread the cake board with a thin layer of royal icing and sprinkle with the coconut to look like grass.

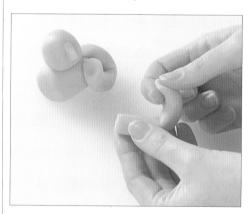

6 ▲ Color reserved marzipan flesh-color. Roll a ball for the head, a tiny wedge for the nose and shape the body and arms. Paint a blue T-shirt on the body and allow to dry. Color some of the royal icing brown and pipe on the hair with a basket weave nozzle. Pipe on the mouth and eyes. Make a bonfire beside the tent with broken chocolate matchsticks, and add the toy soccer ball and mug to complete the scene.

*D*art Board

Start the decoration several days before this cake is needed, as lots of patience and time are required. If the cake is well sealed to begin with, the decoration can be worked on in stages.

INGREDIENTS
Serves 10–12
1½ x quantity Quick-mix Sponge Cake baked in a 10-inch round cake pan
6 ounces/½ quantity Butter Icing
3 tablespoons apricot jam, warmed and sieved
1 pound marzipan
1¼ pounds/1⅔ x quantity Sugar paste Icing (Fondant)
black, yellow, red and silver food coloring
4 ounces/⅙ quantity Royal Icing

MATERIALS AND EQUIPMENT
12-inch round cake board
waxed or parchment paper
icing smoother
½-inch round cutter
waxed or parchment paper piping bag
No. 1 writing nozzle
fine paintbrush
candles

1 Split the cake and fill with butter icing. Place on the cake board and brush with apricot jam. Cover with marzipan. Color 1 pound/1⅓ x quantity sugar paste icing black. On a work surface lightly dusted with confectioners' sugar, roll out and use about three-quarters of the icing to cover the cake. Make a template to mark the board into equal sections.

2 Draw an 8-inch circle on a piece of waxed or parchment paper, cut out and fold in quarters. Divide each quarter into five equal portions and draw in lines to meet in the center. Place the template on the cake and mark the center and the edge of each wedge on the cake.

3 ▲ Mark the wedges on the top of the cake with a sharp knife. Color most of the remaining sugar paste icing yellow and roll out and cut out wedges, using the template as a guide. Place on alternate sections but do not stick in place yet. Repeat with the rest of the black sugar paste icing.

4 ▲ Carefully cut ⅛ inch off the wide end of each wedge and swap the colors. Mark a 5-inch circle in the center of the board and cut out ⅛ inch pieces to swap with adjoining colors. Stick in place and use an icing smoother to flatten.

5 ▲ Color the last piece of sugar paste icing red. Use the cutter to remove the center for the bull's eye. Cut out and stick on a red sugar paste bull's eye and surround with a thin strip of black sugar paste icing. Roll the remaining black icing into a long sausage to fit around the base of the cake and stick all the way around with a little water.

6 ▲ Mark numbers on the board and pipe on with royal icing using a No. 1 nozzle. Allow to dry, then paint the numbers with silver food coloring. Stick candles into the cake at an angle to resemble darts.

Spaceship

For this cake the triangles for the jets should be covered separately, then stuck into position after the cake is decorated.

INGREDIENTS
Serves 10–12
2 x quantity Quick-mix Sponge Cake baked in a 10-inch square cake pan
8 ounces/⅔ quantity Butter Icing
5 tablespoons apricot jam, warmed and sieved
12 ounces marzipan
1 pound/1⅓ x quantity Sugar paste Icing (Fondant)
blue, pink and black food coloring

MATERIALS AND EQUIPMENT
12-inch square cake board
1-inch plain round cutter
candles
gold paper stars

1 ▲ Split the cake and fill with a little butter icing. With a sharp serrated knife, cut a 4-inch piece diagonally across the middle of the cake and about 10 inches long.

2 ▲ Shape the nose and cut the remaining cake in to three 3-inch triangles for the sides and top of the ship. Cut two smaller triangles for the boosters and any remaining cake to fit down the middle of the spaceship. Assemble diagonally across the cake board and brush with apricot jam. Cover with a layer of marzipan.

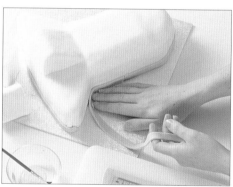

3 ▲ On a work surface dusted with confectioners' sugar, roll out about three-quarters of the sugar paste icing and use to cover the cake and the small triangles for the boosters. Color one-third of the remaining sugar paste icing blue, one-third pink and one-third black. Wrap each separately in plastic wrap. Roll out the blue and cut into ½-inch strips. Stick in a continuous line around the base of the cake with a little water and outline the triangles. Cut a 1-inch strip and stick down the center of the spaceship.

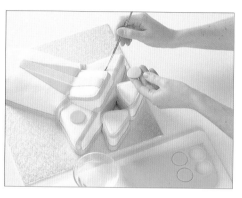

4 ▲ Roll out the pink sugar paste icing and cut out shapes to decorate the ship. Roll out the black sugar paste icing and cut out windows, circles, name and numbers. Stick in place with a little water.

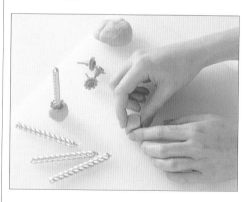

5 ▲ With any leftover sugar paste icing, make candle holders by shaping into small cubes. Stick the candles into them then, stick onto the board. Decorate the board with gold stars.

Chess Board

For this cake to look most effective, the squares have to have very sharp edges, so take care to neaten them as you stick them into position.

INGREDIENTS
Serves 12
1½ x quantity Quick-mix Sponge Cake baked in a 10-inch square cake pan
8 ounces/⅔ quantity Butter Icing
3 tablespoons apricot jam, warmed and sieved
1¼ pounds marzipan
1¼ pounds/1⅔ x quantity Sugar paste Icing (Fondant)
black and red food coloring
silver balls (dragées)
4 ounces/⅙ quantity Royal Icing

MATERIALS AND EQUIPMENT
12-inch square cake board
waxed or parchment paper piping bag
No. 8 star nozzle

1 ▲ Split the cake and fill with butter icing. Place on the cake board and brush with apricot jam. Roll out 1 pound marzipan and cover the cake. On a work surface dusted with confectioners' sugar, roll out 1 pound/1⅓ x quantity sugar paste icing and use to cover the cake. Allow to dry overnight.

2 ▲ Divide the remaining marzipan in half and color one half black and the other half red. To shape the chess pieces, work with one color at a time. Roll ¼ cup (2 ounces) marzipan into a sausage, cut into eight equal pieces, then shape into pawns. Divide ⅔ cup (3 ounces) marzipan into six equal pieces, then shape into two castles, two knights and two bishops. Divide 2 tablespoons (1 ounce) marzipan in half and shape a queen and a king. Decorate with silver balls. Allow to dry overnight.

3 ▲ Mark the cake into eight 1¼ inch squares along each side, leaving a border around the edge. Divide the board into 64 equal squares using a sharp knife.

4 ▲ Color the remaining sugar paste icing black, roll out and cut into 1¼-inch squares. Stick onto alternate squares on the board with a little water, starting with a black square in the bottom left-hand corner and finishing with another black square in the top right-hand corner.

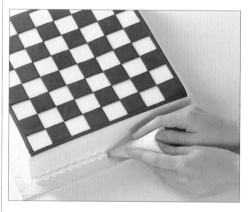

5 ▲ Cut ½-inch black strips to edge the board and stick in place with a little water. Pipe a border round the base of the cake with royal icing. Place the chess pieces in position.

Mobile Phone Cake

For the upwardly mobile man, this novel cake is the business!

INGREDIENTS
Serves 8–10
1 quantity Quick-Mix Sponge Cake mix
2 tbsp apricot jam, warmed and strained
12 oz/1 quantity Sugarpaste Icing
black food coloring
10 small square candies
1–2 striped liquorice candies
2–3 tbsp confectioner's sugar
1/2–1 tsp water

MATERIALS AND EQUIPMENT
2 lb loaf pan
9 x 7 in cake board
diamond-shaped cookie cutter
icing bag fitted with a small plain nozzle

ip

The dial pad is made from small candies. However, you could increase the quantity of sugarpaste icing slightly, color it as wished, then cut it to shape.

1 Preheat the oven to 350°F. Grease the pan, line with wax paper and grease the paper. Spoon the cake mixture into the prepared pan and smooth the surface. Bake in the center of the oven for 40–50 minutes, or until a skewer inserted into the center of the cake comes out clean. Leave the cake in the pan for 5 minutes, then turn out on to a wire rack, peel off the lining paper and allow to cool.

2 ▲ Turn the cake upside-down and starting about 1 in along the cake, slice into it, across and at an angle, about 1/2 in deep. Cut out this wedge and discard. Starting at the same position, slice horizontally along the length of the cake, stopping about 1 in away from the end. Withdraw the knife and re-insert it at the end of the cake. Slice vertically into the cake to meet up with the horizontal cut. Remove the inner piece of cake and discard.

3 ▲ Place the cake on the cake board and brush the cake evenly with the apricot jam. Color three-quarters of the sugarpaste icing black. On a work surface lightly dusted with confectioner's sugar, roll out to a 1/4 in thickness and use to cover the cake. Trim away any excess sugarpaste and reserve, wrapped in plastic wrap.

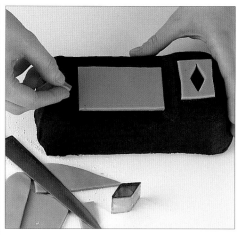

4 ▲ Color the remaining sugarpaste icing gray with a little black food coloring. On a work surface lightly dusted with confectioner's sugar, roll out to a 1/4 in thickness. Cut out an oblong to fit the center of the cake, leaving a 1/2 in border. Cut out another piece about 1 in square and stamp out the center of the square using the diamond-shaped cookie cutter. Stick all the pieces on the phone with a little water, placing the diamond at the bottom of the phone and the square at the top.

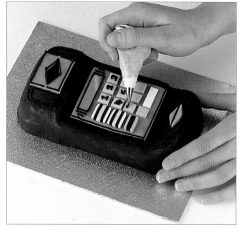

5 ▲ Position the candies and a strip of foil for the dial pad. To make the glacé icing, mix the confectioner's sugar with the water and black food coloring to a piping consistency. Fill the icing bag and pipe border lines around the edges of the phone and the gray pieces. Pipe the numbers on the keys.

6 Knead the reserved black sugarpaste icing and, with your hands, roll into a sausage shape for the aerial. Indent the top with a knife and position at the top of the phone to one side. Secure with a little water.

Personal Stereo

This loud cake in noisy colors will be a smash hit!
The cake board is optional.

INGREDIENTS
Serves 4–6
1 quantity chocolate-flavor Quick-
Mix Sponge Cake mix
¼ quantity chocolate-flavor
Butter Icing
4 tbsp apricot jam, warmed
and sieved
12 oz/1 quantity Sugarpaste Icing
orange, green, purple and black
food colorings
3 candies, for the buttons
2 liquorice candies, for the cassette
holes
2 long liquorice bootlaces
2 liquorice wheels

EQUIPMENT AND MATERIALS
8 x 5 inch shallow cake pan
edible black ink pen

1 Preheat the oven to 350°F. Grease the cake pan, line the base and sides with waxed paper and grease the paper. Spoon in the cake mixture and smooth the surface. Bake in the center of the oven for 35–40 minutes or until a skewer inserted into the center of the cake comes out clean. Turn out on to a wire rack, peel off the lining paper and leave to cool completely. Trim the top of the cake to make it perfectly flat, then cut horizontally in half.

2 ▲ Spread the chocolate butter icing over one half, then top with the other half. Brush the cake evenly with the apricot jam. Color about 9 oz of the sugarpaste icing orange. Lightly dust the work surface with confectioners' sugar and roll out the icing until it is large enough to cover the cake. Smooth and ease it over the sides and edges. Trim around the edges.

3 ▲ Color about 2 oz of the remaining sugarpaste icing green. Color all but a small ball of the remaining icing purple, then color the small ball black. Roll out the green and purple icings thinly. Cut the green icing into a rectangle about ½ inch smaller than the top surface of the cake. Stick it in place with a little water. Cut the purple icing into a 1 x 4 inch strip and stick it in place on top of the green rectangle with a little water.

4 Press the candies for the buttons into one side of the cake through the orange icing, then position the liquorice candies for the cassette holes, sticking them in place with a little water. Use the edible ink pen to draw tiny lines around the sweets.

5 Cut a few short pieces off the bootlace liquorice and stick on the personal stereo with a little water. Stick the reserved piece of black colored icing in place at the side of the cake with a little water.

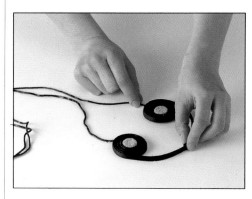

6 ▲ To make the headphones, unravel a little of each of the liquorice wheels and place in position on the table or board, if you are using. Overlap the unravelled ends of the liquorice wheels, sticking them together with a little water. Use a pin or thin metal skewer to make a small hole in the bottoms of the liquorice wheels, then press a liquorice bootlace into each one. Brush three-quarters of the liquorice bootlace with a little water and stick them together with your fingers, removing the excess water. Press the joined end into the black icing on the cake.

Hot Dog Cake

Make a meal of a cake! This hot dog tastes nothing like the real thing - it is much more delicious and looks very attractive when cut into slices.

INGREDIENTS
Serves 6–8
1 quantity Jelly Roll mix
confectioners' sugar, to dredge
½ quantity coffee-flavor Butter Icing
⅓ quantity Truffle Cake Mix
6 tbsp apricot jam, warmed and sieved
1 lb/1⅓ x quantity Sugarpaste Icing
brown and red food colorings
1–2 tbsp toasted sesame seeds
¼ quantity Glacé Icing

MATERIALS AND EQUIPMENT
9 x 13 inch jelly roll pan
2 small waxed paper piping bags

1 Preheat the oven to 350°F. Grease the pan, line the base and sides with waxed paper and grease the paper. Spoon the cake mixture into the pan and smooth the surface. Bake in the center of the oven for about 12 minutes or until springy to the touch. Cover and leave to cool.

2 Turn the cake out on to waxed paper dusted with confectioners' sugar and remove the lining paper. Spread over the butter icing, then roll the cake up using the waxed paper.

3 ▲ Shape the truffle cake mix into a sausage about 9 inches long.

4 Place the jelly roll on the work surface and slice along the middle lengthwise, almost through to the bottom. Ease the two halves apart to resemble a partially opened bun.

5 Color the sugarpaste icing brown, then cut off about 2 oz and set aside, wrapped in plastic wrap. Roll out the rest on a work surface lightly dusted with confectioners' sugar until about ¼ inch thick and use to cover the bun. Ease the icing into the center and down the sides of the cake.

6 ▲ Dilute a few drops of brown food coloring in a little water and paint the top of the bun very lightly to give a toasted effect. Dab on a little color, then rub it around gently with a finger until blended in. Carefully place the truffle cake sausage in position.

7 ▲ Divide the glacé icing between two small bowls. Color one half brown and the other red. Fill the piping bags with the icings and snip off the ends with scissors. Pipe red icing along the sausage for the ketchup, then overlay with brown icing for the mustard. Sprinkle the sesame seeds over the bun.

8 Roll out the reserved brown sugarpaste icing and cut thin strips to resemble onion rings. Place on the cake so that the joins lie under the sausage. Carefully place the cake on a napkin and serving plate, with a knife and fork.

Circus Cake

This design is very easy to achieve. The miniature circus ornaments measure 2 inches high and can be bought from party stores, although anything similar can be used.

INGREDIENTS
Serves 10–12
1 quantity Quick-mix Sponge Cake baked in an 8-inch round cake pan
4 ounces/⅓ x quantity Butter Icing
3 tablespoons apricot jam, warmed and sieved
1 pound marzipan
1 pound/1⅓ x quantity Sugar paste Icing (Fondant)
red and blue food coloring
4 ounces/¼ quantity Royal Icing
silver balls
3 digestive biscuits

MATERIALS AND EQUIPMENT
10-inch round cake board
waxed or parchment paper piping bag
No. 5 star nozzle
small plastic circus ornaments

1 ▲ Split the cake and fill with a little butter icing. Place on the cake board and brush with apricot jam. Cover with a layer of marzipan. Roll out half the sugar paste icing on a surface dusted with confectioners' sugar and use to cover the cake. Color ¾ cup (⅓ quantity) sugar paste icing pink, roll into a rope and stick around the top edge of the cake to make a wall.

2 ▲ Color half the remaining sugar paste red and the other half blue. Roll out each color and cut into twelve 1-inch squares. Stick alternately at an angle around the side of the cake with a little water. Pipe stars around the base of the cake with royal icing and stick in silver balls.

3 ▲ Crush the digestive biscuits by pressing through a sieve to make the sawdust. Scatter over the top of the cake and place small circus ornaments on top.

Clown Cake

Made in a clown-shaped pan, this is a quick and easy cake to make and decorate. Choose your own nozzle shapes for the designs, following the contours of the cake.

INGREDIENTS
Serves 10–15
1½ x quantity Quick-Mix Sponge
Cake mix
4 oz/⅓ quantity Sugarpaste
Icing
2 x quantity Butter Icing
yellow, red, pink and blue food
colorings
small colored candies, for the
features

MATERIALS AND EQUIPMENT
2 lb clown-shaped cake pan
10 x 12 inch cake board
waxed paper piping bags
small star, small plain
and large star nozzles
small party hat

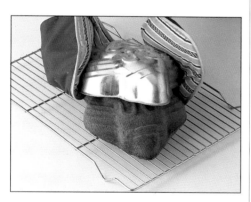

1 ▲ Preheat the oven to 350°F. Grease the cake pan generously. Spoon in the cake mixture and smooth the surface. Bake in the center of the oven for 45–50 minutes or until a skewer inserted into the center of the cake comes out clean. Leave for 5 minutes before turning out on to a wire rack.

2 ▲ To make a template for the clown's face, hold a piece of waxed paper firmly over the face on the cooled clown cake pan. Draw around the outline using a pen or pencil and cut around the shape.

3 ▲ On a work surface lightly dusted with confectioners' sugar, roll out the sugarpaste icing to about ¼ inch thick, then place the waxed paper template on top. Use a small, sharp knife to cut around the outline of the template. Place the cut-out sugarpaste on a cookie sheet and cover with plastic wrap.

4 To color the butter icing, place about one-third of the icing in a small mixing bowl and color it yellow. Place another third in another mixing bowl and color it red. Divide the remaining butter icing between two small bowls and color one pink and the other blue.

5 ▲ Place the cake on the cake board. Fit a small star nozzle in a paper piping bag and fill it with the yellow butter icing. Use to pipe along the contours of the hair on the clown's head. Place the cut-out sugarpaste template in position on the cake, then place a small plain nozzle in another piping bag and fill with the red butter icing. Use it to pipe decoratively around the neck and torso area of the clown. Pipe around the mouth, then change the nozzle to a large star shape and pipe in the nose.

6 Place a small star nozzle in another small piping bag and fill with the pink icing. Use to pipe a star border around the edges of the sugarpaste template. Place a large star nozzle in another piping bag and fill with the blue icing. Use to pipe in the buttons and the clown's eyes. Place the candies in the centers of the eyes, nose and buttons. Position the hat.

Magic Carpet Cake

The Master of the Lamp can also be made out of colored sugarpaste icing, instead of marzipan, if you prefer.

INGREDIENTS
Serves 8–10
*1 quantity Quick-Mix Sponge
Cake mix*
1½ lb/2 x quantity Sugarpaste Icing
*blue, brown, red, orange, yellow,
purple and black food colorings*
*4 x 1 oz squares milk or plain
chocolate, melted*
12 oz white marzipan
*small candy or diamond-shaped
cake decoration*
small brightly colored feather

MATERIALS AND EQUIPMENT
9 x 6 inch cake pan
13 inch round cake board
*1 inch and 2½ inch round fluted
pastry cutters*
small piece of yellow crepe paper

1 Preheat the oven to 350°F. Grease the cake pan, line the base and sides with waxed paper and grease the paper. Spoon in the cake mixture and smooth the surface. Bake in the center of the oven for 30–35 minutes or until a skewer inserted into the center of the cake comes out clean. Turn out on to a wire rack, peel off the lining paper and leave to cool completely.

2 Color 10 oz sugarpaste icing with blue food coloring. Remove a piece about the size of a walnut and set aside, wrapped in plastic wrap. Roll out the rest of the blue icing thinly on a surface dusted with confectioners' sugar into a round about the size of the cake board.

3 ▲ Roll out about 5 oz of white icing and cut out rounds using the pastry cutters. Arrange these on the blue icing to resemble clouds, then roll lightly into the icing. Brush the cake board lightly with water and cover with the blue and white icing, smoothing it with your hands to exclude air bubbles. Leave the icing draped over the edge of the board, if liked, or trim level with the edge of the board.

4 ▲ Color 6 oz sugarpaste icing dark brown, then roll it out thinly into an oblong large enough to cover the top and sides of the cake generously. Trim the edges. Knead the trimmings into a ball and set aside, wrapped in plastic wrap. Brush the cake with melted chocolate, then place on the cake board. Drape the brown icing over the top of the cake, being careful not to flatten it at the sides too much.

5 Divide 3 oz sugarpaste icing into two equal pieces. Color one piece red and the other orange. Then unwrap the reserved pieces of blue and brown sugarpaste icing.

6 Divide each of the four colors into three or four smaller pieces, then knead them together to make a marbled ball of icing. Roll it out into a rectangle slightly larger than the top of the cake. Trim the edges, then lay over the brown icing and stick into place with water.

7 ▲ Colour 3 oz marzipan yellow, then roll most of it into a long, thin sausage shape. Press it around the edge of the carpet to make a trim. Decorate with small balls of yellow marzipan. Snip pieces of yellow crepe paper with scissors to make tassels. Push into the small balls of icing.

8 ▲ To make the figure, roll about 3 oz of white marzipan into a pear shape, then cut in half to make two legs. Bend the legs into a sitting position. Color 2½ oz marzipan dark brown and shape into a head, body and arms. Make the eyes and mouth from tiny pieces of colored icing or marzipan and press on to the face. Press the head and body on to the legs. Color 1 oz of marzipan purple and use it to make the jacket. Press the arms on to the figure.

9 Color small pieces of marzipan black and deep red or purple and use to make hair and a hat respectively. Color the remaining marzipan bright orange. Roll a tiny piece into a ball and press on to the hat. Decorate with a tiny diamond-shaped candy or cake decoration and colored feather. Use the rest of the orange marzipan to make slippers and a lamp. Position the figure and the lamp on the carpet.

$\mathcal{J}$ack-in-the-Box Cake

An impressive, colorful cake which will delight a small party of young children. This cake does require a little extra time and patience, so be sure to start the cake well in advance and not on the morning of the party!

INGREDIENTS
Serves 6–8
1 quantity chocolate-flavor Quick-Mix Sponge Cake Mix
6 tbsp apricot jam, warmed and sieved
2¼ lb/3 x quantity Sugarpaste Icing
purple, yellow, orange and green food colorings
1 large round doughnut
1 small round doughnut
2 marshmallow candies, for the eyes
2 colored candies, for the buttons

MATERIALS AND EQUIPMENT
deep 4 inch square cake pan
7 inch cake board
3½ inch square piece of stiff cardboard
3 toothpicks
garlic press
ice-cream cone
balloon
small star cutter
butterfly cutter
wooden skewer

1 Preheat the oven to 350°F. Grease the cake pan, line the base and sides with waxed paper and grease the paper. Spoon the cake mixture into the prepared pan and smooth the surface. Bake in the center of the oven for 35–40 minutes, or until a skewer inserted into the center of the cake comes out clean. Leave the cake in the pan for about 5 minutes, then turn out on to a wire rack, peel off the lining paper and leave to cool completely.

2 ▲ Place the cake on the work surface and cut a 1 inch slice off the top for the lid. Use a small, sharp knife to hollow out the center of the box section of cake, leaving a ½ inch border. Spread a little apricot jam in the center of the cake board and some on the piece of cardboard. Place the bottom section of cake on the cake board and position the lid on the cardboard. Brush the box and lid with apricot jam.

3 ▲ Pull off a walnut-sized piece of sugarpaste icing, wrap in plastic wrap and set aside. Then take about half of the remaining sugarpaste icing and marble in the purple food coloring. Cut off one-quarter of the marbled icing and roll out on a surface lightly dusted with confectioners' sugar to a 6 inch square. Use to cover the lid section, wrapping the icing around the cardboard. Set aside, cardboard side down. Reserve the trimmings.

4 Roll out the remaining marbled icing and use to cover the box section of cake, lightly pressing the icing into the hollow. Reserve the trimmings.

5 Color about half of the remaining sugarpaste icing yellow and pull off two pieces, each the size of a cherry. Wrap these in plastic wrap and set aside. Cut a thin slice off the side of the large doughnut for the body to give it a flat base. Lay it down on the work surface and place the small doughnut above it for the head. Brush the head and body with jam. Roll out the large portion of yellow sugarpaste icing until about ¼ inch thick and use to cover the head and body of the clown. Wrap the icing around the back and then pinch it together to seal.

6 ▲ Pierce a toothpick into the base of the body, leaving about half of it exposed. Place the body in position on the box section of the cake, pressing the exposed toothpick into the cake for extra stability.

7 ▲ Cut off about half of the remaining sugarpaste icing and color it orange. Push about one-quarter of this through a garlic press on to a sheet of waxed paper for the hair. Stick it on to the clown's head with a little water. Use the remaining orange icing to make one hand, the nose, mouth and a few spots for the bow tie. Allow the hand to dry out on a baking sheet, but cover the other features with plastic wrap and set aside.

8 ▲ Color the remaining sugarpaste icing green. To make the hat, cut off about ½ oz of the green icing and roll out into a thin strip. Brush the pointed end of the ice-cream cone with a little apricot jam, then roll the strip of green sugarpaste icing around it, starting at the pointed end and working downwards. Use scissors to cut off the excess cone. Stick the hat in position on the clown's head with a little water. Reserve any trimmings.

9 Use the reserved piece of yellow sugarpaste icing to make two small ovals for the arms. Thread each one on to a toothpick and carefully press the hand on to one of them. Press the toothpicks into the body of the clown. Tie a slightly blown up balloon on to the arm without the hand.

10 Roll out the remaining piece of white sugarpaste icing and stamp out two small stars with the star cutter. Use a little water to stick them in place for the eyes. Stick the marshmallow candies on top.

11 Position the orange nose and mouth, sticking them in place with a little water. Roll out the remaining green icing to about 5mm/ ¼ inch thick and stamp out a butterfly and six small stars with the cutters. Stick the reserved red spots on to the butterfly bow tie, using a little water, then place the bow tie on the clown in the same way. Place the green stars around the edges of the cake board. Carefully stick the two colored candies in place for the clown's buttons, using a little more water.

12 To position the lid, carefully sit it, cardboard side out, on the back edge of the box section. Use the wooden skewer and the reserved icing trimmings to support the lid and hold it in place. This stage is best completed when the cake is in position on the table and unlikely to be moved again.

Happy Clown

This fun clown can be made with tiny edible flowers, or letters stuck onto the sides of the box.

INGREDIENTS
Serves 6–8
1 quantity Quick-mix Sponge Cake
baked in a 6-inch square cake pan
2 ounces/¹⁄₆ quantity Butter Icing
3 tablespoons apricot jam,
warmed and sieved
12 ounces marzipan
1 pound/1¹⁄₃ x quantity
Sugar paste Icing (Fondant)
ice cream cone
4 ounces/¹⁄₆ quantity Royal Icing
blue, black, green, red and yellow
food coloring
silver balls (dragées)

MATERIALS AND EQUIPMENT
8-inch round cake board
frill cutter
plain round cutter
wooden toothpick
cotton balls
No. 8 star nozzle

1 ▲ Split the cake and fill with butter icing. Cut a 2-inch rectangle from two sides of the cake to create a 4-inch square, a 2-inch square and two rectangles. Sandwich the rectangles together on top of the large square to make a cube. Place on the cake board and brush with apricot jam. Cover with a layer of marzipan.

2 On a work surface dusted with confectioners' sugar, roll out three-quarters of the sugar paste icing and use to cover the cake. Shape the remaining cube of cake into a ball for the head. Brush with apricot jam, cover with marzipan then with sugar paste icing. Allow to dry.

3 ▲ Cut the top off the ice cream cone. Stick the wide part of the cone in the center of the cake with a little royal icing, then stick on the head.

4 ▲ Color a small piece of sugar paste icing blue, roll out and cut a fluted circle with a small inner circle. (The depth of the frill will depend on the size of the central hole; the smaller the center, the wider the frill.) Cut one side and open out, then roll the fluted edge with a wooden toothpick to stretch it. Attach it to the neck with royal icing, carefully arranging the folds with a toothpick and supporting with cotton balls while they dry. Make a second frill in the same way.

5 ▲ Stick the ice cream cone hat on the head with a little royal icing. Cut eyes from blue sugar paste icing and stick on with a little water. Color pieces of sugar paste icing black, green and red and roll out. Cut and stick on black eyes. Cut a semicircle of green, stick around the back of the head and snip with sharp scissors to give spiky hair (or cut two short lengths). Cut out a red nose, a mouth and numbers for the sides of the box. Stick these on with a little water.

6 ▲ Color the remaining royal icing yellow and pipe stars around the edges of the cube and pompoms on the hat, sticking in silver balls as you go.

Treasure Chest

Allow yourself a few days before the party to make this cake. The lock and handles are made separately, then left to dry for 48 hours before sticking onto the cake.

INGREDIENTS
Serves 8–10
1½ x quantity Quick-mix Sponge
Cake baked in an 8-inch square
cake pan
4 ounces/⅓ quantity Butter Icing
4 tablespoons apricot jam,
warmed and sieved
12 ounces marzipan
12 ounces/1 quantity
Sugar paste Icing (Fondant)
brown, green and black
food coloring
1 cup dried coconut
4 ounces/⅙ quantity Royal Icing
edible gold dusting powder
silver balls (dragées)
chocolate coins

MATERIALS AND EQUIPMENT
12-inch round cake board
fine paintbrush

1 ▲ Split the cake and fill with butter icing. Cut the cake in half and sandwich the halves on top of each other. Place on the cake board.

2 ▲ Cut the top to shape the rounded lid and brush with apricot jam. Cover with a layer of marzipan. Color all but a small piece of the sugar paste icing brown. On a work surface dusted with confectioners' sugar, roll out the icing; use to cover the cake.

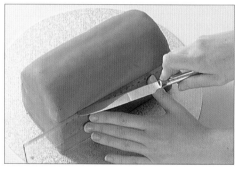

3 ▲ Mark the lid of the treasure chest with a sharp knife.

4 ▲ Roll out the trimmings of the brown sugar paste icing and stick on four ¼-inch wide strips with water.

5 ▲ Put the coconut in a bowl and mix in a few drops of green coloring. Spread a little royal icing over the cake board and press the coconut into it to look like grass.

6 ▲ From the remaining sugar paste icing, cut out the padlock and handles. Cut a keyhole shape from the padlock and shape the handles over a small box. Allow to dry. Stick the padlock and handles into place with royal icing. Paint them gold and stick silver balls on the handles and padlock with a little royal icing to look like nails. Arrange the chocolate money around the chest on the grass.

$\mathcal{S}$and Castle

Crushed graham crackers are used to cover this fun cake. It is ideal for children who do not like the richness of butter icing, as only a very small amount is used to sandwich the cake.

INGREDIENTS
Serves 8–10
1½ x quantity Quick-mix Sponge
Cake baked in 6-inch round
cake pans
4 ounces/⅓ quantity Butter Icing
4 tablespoons apricot jam,
warmed and sieved
4 ounces graham crackers
4 ounces/¹⁄₁₆ quantity Royal Icing
blue food coloring
candies

MATERIALS AND EQUIPMENT
10-inch square cake board
rice paper
plastic drinking straw
candles

2 ▲ Cut 1¼-inch cubes from the reserved piece and stick on for the turrets. Brush with apricot jam.

3 Crush the digestive biscuits and press through a sieve to make the sand.

4 ▲ Press on the crushed biscuits, using a baking spatula to get a smooth finish. Color some royal icing blue and spread around the sand castle on the board to make a moat. Spread a little royal icing around the board and sprinkle on sand. Make a flag with rice paper and half a straw and stick into the cake. Stick candles into each turret and arrange the candies on the board.

1 ▲ Split the cakes and sandwich all the layers together with butter icing. Place in the center of the cake board. Cut 1¼ inches off the top just above the filling and shape the rest of the cake with slightly sloping sides.

Ice-cream Cone Cakes

Individual cakes make a change for a party, the idea being that each guest has one to themselves. You could even put a candle in the special person's one.

INGREDIENTS
Makes 9
1 quantity Quick-Mix Sponge
Cake mix
9 ice-cream cones
1 quantity Butter Icing
red, green and brown food
colorings
selection of colored sprinkles,
wafers, chocolate sticks, etc.

MATERIALS AND EQUIPMENT
9 cup cake paper cases
muffin pan

4 ▲ Using a small spatula, spread each cake with some of one of the icings. Place in the ice-cream stand (see Tip). Continue coating the cones, making sure the icing isn't too smooth, so it looks like ice cream.

2 ▲ Gently press a cup cake into a cone, taking care not to damage the cone. If the bases of the cakes are a little large to insert into the cones, trim them down with a small, sharp knife. The cakes should feel quite secure once inserted into the cones.

3 Divide the butter icing into three small bowls and color one portion pale red, one portion green and one portion brown.

5 ▲ To insert a wafer or chocolate stick into an ice cream, use a small, sharp knife to make a hole or incision through the icing and into the cake, then insert the wafer or stick. Add the finishing touches by sprinkling over some colored sprinkles.

Tip

To have 3 sets of 3 ice-cream cakes placed on the table, you will need 3 egg cartons, which hold 12 eggs each. Place a ball of marzipan in 3 evenly spaced holes in the up-turned egg carton. Cover the box in foil, then pierce the foil and make a small hole with your finger where the marzipan balls are. Insert the iced ice-cream cones, pressing them in gently, so they stand securely.

1 Preheat the oven to 350°F. Place the paper cases in the muffin pan, then spoon in the cake mixture until they are all at least half full. Bake in the center of the oven for about 20 minutes or until the cakes have risen and are golden. Transfer the cakes to a wire rack to cool completely, and then remove the cases.

*P*izza Cake

*Quick, easy, and impressive – this deliciously sweet cake is a definite winner
for pizza fanatics everywhere. Serve in small wedges.*

INGREDIENTS
Serves 8–10
*1 quantity Quick-Mix Sponge Cake
mix*
1 quantity Butter Icing
6 oz yellow marzipan
1 tbsp shredded coconut
red and green food coloring
confectioner's sugar
1 oz Sugarpaste Icing

MATERIALS AND EQUIPMENT
9 in shallow, round cake pan
10 in pizza plate
cheese grater

*T*ip

This recipe can be adapted easily
for pepperoni pizza fanatics. You
will need an extra 6 oz/½ quantity
of sugarpaste icing. Color with
brown food coloring, then roll out
to a thick sausage shape with your
hands. Slice thinly and add to the
pizza cake as an extra topping.

1 Preheat the oven to 350°F. Grease
the pan, line the base with wax
paper and grease the paper. Spoon the
cake mixture into the prepared pan and
smooth the surface. Bake in the center
of the oven for 40–50 minutes, or until
a skewer inserted into the center of the
cake comes out clean. Leave the cake in
the pan for 5 minutes, then turn out on
to a wire rack, peel off the lining paper
and allow to cool.

2 ▲ Color the butter icing red. Place
the cake on the pizza plate and
spread evenly with the butter icing to
represent the tomato topping. Leave
a ½ in border around the edge of
the cake.

3 ▲ Knead the marzipan for a few
minutes to soften it slightly, then
grate it. Sprinkle over the red butter
icing to represent cheese.

4 ▲ Color the sugarpaste icing green.
On a work surface lightly dusted
with confectioner's sugar, roll out to
about a ¼ in thickness. Cut out two leaf
shapes freehand or cut around a real
leaf. Mark the veins with a knife and
add to the pizza cake for the garnish.

5 ▲ Place the shredded coconut in a
small bowl and color with green
food coloring. Sprinkle over the pizza
cake to represent chopped herbs.

Market Stall

An open-air market stall is the theme for this cake, bursting with colorful produce. Vary this design if you like, adding as wide a variety of fruit and vegetables as you can think of.

INGREDIENTS
Serves 30
8 in square Rich Fruit Cake
3 tbsp apricot jam, warmed and strained
2 lb marzipan
1lb/1¹/₃ x quantity Sugarpaste Icing
4 oz/¹/₆ quantity Royal Icing
brown, green, red, orange, yellow, peach, purple, pink, and black food colorings

MATERIALS AND EQUIPMENT
10 in square cake board
piping bag fitted with a small plain nozzle
paintbrush

1 Slice 1¹/₂ in off one side of the cake. Brush the cake pieces with the apricot jam. Take half of the marzipan and cut off about one-quarter. On a work surface lightly dusted with confectioner's sugar, roll out the small piece of marzipan and use to cover one long side, the top and the two short sides of the cake slice. Roll out the larger piece of marzipan and use to cover the large piece of cake. Allow to dry for 12 hours.

2 ▲ Color half of the sugarpaste icing brown and the other half green. Using three-quarters of the brown icing, cover three sides of the large cake (not the cut side), brushing the marzipan first with a little water. With the remaining brown icing, cover the marzipanned sides of the cake slice in the same way. With the brown trimmings, roll out and cut narrow dividers to fit the top of the cake. Allow to dry on wax paper for several hours.

3 ▲ Place the large piece of cake on the cake board, with the cake slice in front to form a step. Stick the cakes together and to the cake board with a little royal icing.

4 ▲ Measure the length and width of the cake, including the step. Roll out the green sugarpaste icing to about 1¹/₂ in wider and longer than the measured length. Brush the marzipan tops with a little water and cover the cakes loosely with the green icing. Let the icing fall naturally into folds over the edges of the cake. Allow to dry for several hours.

5 ▲ Take the remaining marzipan, reserve a little for the stall-holder, and color the rest red, orange, yellow, green, brown, peach, and purple. Use these colors to shape the fruits and vegetables. Add markings with a paintbrush and food coloring to the melons, peaches, and potatoes. For the front of the stall, shape baskets and a potato sack out of different shades of brown. For the stall-holder, color the reserved marzipan pink, purple, black, and pale peach and shape the head, body, and arms separately. Stick the figure together with a little royal icing. Make the hands, the facial features, and hair and press on with a little water. Place a melon in the stall-holder's arms. Allow all the marzipan shapes to dry on wax paper for several hours. Assemble on the cake just before serving, attaching the dividers, baskets and the stall-holder to the cake with royal icing.

Pinball Machine

The design of this machine is well suited to the clean, sharp lines of sugar paste icing (fondant).

INGREDIENTS
Serves 12
2 x quantity Quick-mix Sponge
Cake baked in a 10-inch square
cake pan
8 ounces/⅔ quantity Butter Icing
4 tablespoons apricot jam,
warmed and sieved
1 pound marzipan
4 ounces/¹⁄₁₆ quantity
Royal Icing
1 pound/1⅓ x quantity
Sugar paste Icing (Fondant)
yellow, blue, green and pink
food coloring
candies
2 ice cream fan wafers

MATERIALS AND EQUIPMENT
12-inch square cake board
8-inch cake pan
waxed or parchment paper
waxed or parchment paper piping bag
No. 1 writing nozzle

1 ▲ Split the cake and fill with butter icing. Cut off a 2-inch strip from one side and reserve.

2 ▲ Using a sharp serrated knife, cut a thin wedge off the top of the cake, diagonally along its length, to end just above the halfway mark. This will give a sloping top.

3 ▲ Using an 8-inch cake pan as a guide, cut an arched back from the reserved cake. Brush cakes with apricot jam. Cover separately with marzipan and place on the cake board, sticking together with royal icing. Allow to dry overnight.

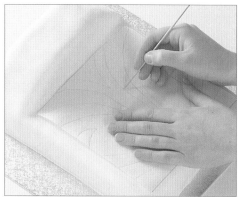

4 ▲ Roll out two-thirds of the sugar paste icing and use to cover the cake. Allow to dry. Using a template, mark out a design on top of the cake. Color the remaining sugar paste icing in different colors, roll out and cut to fit each section. Stick with water and smooth the seams carefully.

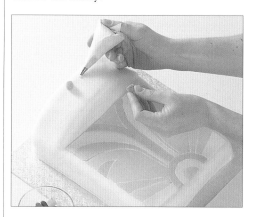

5 ▲ Use royal icing to stick different colored candies on the cake as buffers, flippers, lights and knobs. Roll some blue sugar paste icing into a long sausage and use to edge the pinball table and divider. Cut a zigzag design for the sides and a small screen for the back. Stick these on with a little water. Stick the ice cream fans at the back of the screen. Load the pinball candies. The name on the screen can be added with run-out letters or piping.

Computer Game

This is a small cake to give to a computer game fanatic. The fine rope is made by rolling the sugar paste (fondant) on a smooth surface with a plexiglass smoother to give a neat continuous finish.

INGREDIENTS
Serves 6
1 quantity Quick-mix Sponge Cake
baked in a 6-inch square cake pan
4 ounces/⅓ quantity Butter Icing
2 tablespoons apricot jam,
warmed and sieved
8 ounces marzipan
12 ounces/1 quantity
Sugar paste Icing (Fondant)
black, blue, red and yellow
food coloring
a little royal icing

MATERIALS AND EQUIPMENT
8-inch square cake board
toothpick
plexiglass icing smoother
fine paintbrush

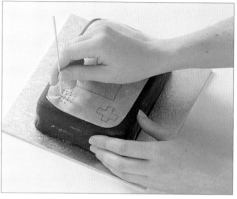

1 ▲ Split the cake and fill with butter icing. With a sharp serrated knife, cut 1 inch off one side of the cake and ½ inch off the other. Round the corners slightly. Place on the cake board and brush with apricot jam. Cover with marzipan.

2 ▲ Color two-thirds of the sugar paste icing black. Roll out on a work surface dusted with confectioners' sugar and use to cover the cake. With a toothpick, mark the speaker holes and position of the screen and knobs. Color half the remaining sugar paste icing pale blue, roll out and cut out a 2½-inch square for the screen. Stick it in the center of the game with a little water. Color a small piece of sugar paste icing red and the rest yellow. Cut out the start switch 1 inch long from the red and the controls from the yellow. Stick into position with a little water. Edge the screen and the base with the remaining black sugar paste.

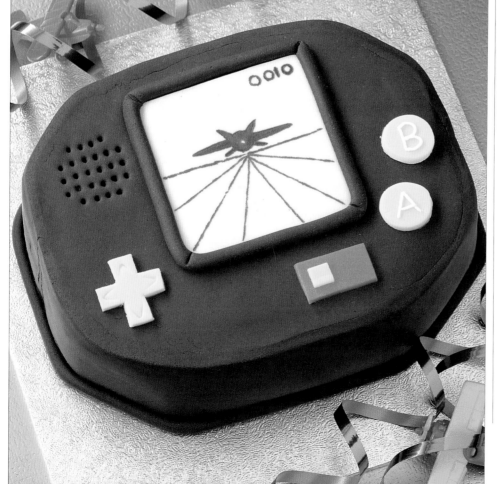

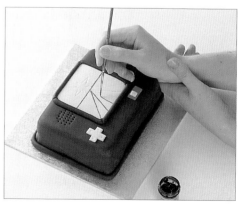

3 ▲ With a fine paintbrush, draw the game on the screen with a little blue color. Pipe letters onto the buttons with a little royal icing.

Sheet of Music

This cake is ideal for musicians young and old. As it requires very delicate piping, it is advisable to practice first before attempting the decoration.

INGREDIENTS
Serves 12
2 x quantity Quick-mix Sponge
Cake baked in a 10-inch square
cake pan
8 ounces/⅔ quantity Butter Icing
3 tablespoons apricot jam,
warmed and sieved
1 pound marzipan
1 pound/1⅓ x quantity
Sugar paste Icing (Fondant)
4 ounces/⅙ quantity Royal Icing
black food coloring

MATERIALS AND EQUIPMENT
10 x 12 inch
cake board
waxed or parchment paper
waxed or parchment paper piping bags
No. 0 writing nozzle
No. 7 shell nozzle
ribbon

2 ▲ With a template, mark out the sheet of music and the person's name on the top of the cake.

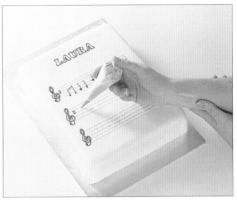

3 ▲ Pipe the staves and bars with white royal icing and a No. 0 nozzle, then color a little of the remaining royal icing black and pipe the clefs, name and notes. Pipe a royal icing border around the base with the shell nozzle and tie a ribbon around the sides.

1 ▲ Split the cake and fill with a little butter icing. Cut 2 inches off one side of the cake so that it measures 8 x 10 inches. Place on the cake board and brush with apricot jam. Cover with a layer of marzipan. On a work surface dusted with confectioners' sugar, roll out the sugar paste icing and use to cover the cake. Allow to dry overnight.

Banjo Cake

The perfect cake for the musician in the family. It can be set on a
tray or you could cut out cardboard for a template to support it.

INGREDIENTS
Serves 15–20
2 x quantity Quick-Mix Sponge
Cake mix
6 tbsp seedless raspberry jam,
warmed
2 lb/2²/₃ x quantity Sugarpaste Icing
lime green food coloring
2 colored liquorice sticks
4 round lollipops
4 tbsp colored jimmies
piece of flat green liquorice
2 long red liquorice strings
4 long green liquorice strings
sugarpaste stars, or other decoration

MATERIALS AND EQUIPMENT
8 inch round cake pan
7 inch square cake pan
21 inch stiff cardboard
2 inch round cutter
ribbon and 2 pins, for the strap

1 Preheat the oven to 350°F. Grease
the pans, line the bases with waxed
paper and grease the paper. Divide the
cake mixture between the two pans and
smooth the surfaces. Bake for 35–40
minutes, or until firm to the touch.
Turn out on to a wire rack, peel off
the lining paper and then leave to
cool completely.

2 ▲ Cut off the dome from the round
cake and place bottom side up on
the work surface. Cut the dome off the
square cake, then cut in half down the
middle. Place the cakes together to form
the banjo shape, then draw around
them on to stiff cardboard. Cut out the
shape to make the reinforcing template.

3 ▲ Use the cutter to stamp out a
shallow hollow from the center of
the round cake. Place both cakes on the
cardboard base and brush with the
raspberry jam. Color the sugarpaste
icing with the lime green food coloring
and roll out on a work surface lightly
dusted with confectioners' sugar to
about a 25 x 10 inch rectangle. Use to
cover the banjo in one piece, easing the
icing into the hollow and down the
sides. Make finger indentations along
the length of the neck of the banjo.

4 Cut off four ½ inch pieces from
one of the liquorice sticks and press
into the cake at the top end of the neck
to resemble stays for the strings. Place
the remains of the liquorice stick with
the other one at the base of the banjo,
next to the hollow. Dip the lollipops in
water, then in the colored jimmies to
coat. Press the lollipops into the sides
of the neck end so that they line up
with the pieces of liquorice stick
forming the stays.

5 Place the two flat pieces of liquorice
side by side at the base, securing
with a little water. Cut the red liquorice
strings into about 2 inch lengths and
position them along the length of the
banjo neck, in the indentations. Use a
little water to stick them securely in
place, if necessary.

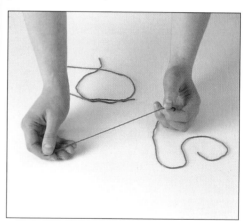

6 ▲ Dip the green liquorice strings
in hot water, then stretch and
smooth each one until perfectly straight.
Wrap one end of the banjo strings
around the liquorice sticks at the top of
the neck end and bring the other ends
down so they meet together on the flat
liquorice at the rounded end. Secure the
ribbon strap with pins pushed through
each end and into the cake. Decorate
the banjo with sugarpaste stars and
more colored jimmies, if wished. The
pins *must* be removed from the cake
before serving.

$\mathcal{D}$rum Cake

The ropes can be made by rolling by hand on a smooth work surface, but a plexiglass icing smoother gives a much better result.

INGREDIENTS
Serves 8
*1 quantity Quick-mix Sponge Cake
baked in a deep 6-inch round
cake pan
2 ounces/¹⁄₁₆ quantity Butter Icing
2 tablespoons apricot jam,
warmed and sieved
12 ounces marzipan
1 pound/1¹⁄₃ x quantity
Sugar paste Icing (Fondant)
red, blue and yellow
food coloring*

MATERIALS AND EQUIPMENT
8-inch round cake board

1 ▲ Split the cake and fill with a little butter icing. Place on the cake board and brush with apricot jam. Cover with a layer of marzipan and allow to dry overnight. Color half the sugar paste icing red. Roll out to 10 x 12 inches and cut in half. Stick to the sides of the cake with water.

2 Roll out a circle of white sugar paste icing to fit the top of the cake and divide the rest in half. Color one half blue and the other yellow. Divide the blue into four equal pieces and roll each piece into a sausage long enough to go halfway round the cake. Stick around the base and the top of the cake with a little water.

3 ▲ Mark the cake into six pieces around the top and bottom using a disk of waxed paper folded into six wedges.

4 ▲ Roll the yellow sugar paste icing into strands long enough to cross diagonally from top to bottom to form the drum strings. Roll the rest of the yellow sugar paste icing into 12 small balls and stick where the strings join the drum. Using red and white sugar paste icing, knead together until streaky and roll two balls and sticks 6 inches long. Dry overnight. Stick together with royal icing to make the drumsticks and place on top of the drum.

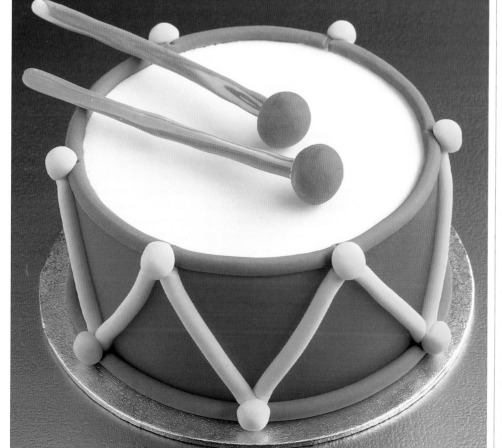

Army Tank

Create an authentic camouflaged tank by combining green and brown sugar paste icing (fondant).

INGREDIENTS
Serves 12
*2 x quantity Quick-mix Sponge
Cake baked in a 10-inch square
cake pan
8 ounces/⅔ quantity Butter Icing
4 tablespoons apricot jam,
warmed and sieved
1 pound marzipan
1 pound/1⅓ x quantity
Sugar paste Icing (Fondant)
green and brown food coloring
chocolate twig or Tootsie Roll
licorice wheels
4 ounces/⅙ quantity Royal Icing
round cookies
sweets*

MATERIALS AND EQUIPMENT
10 x 14-inch cake board

1 Split the cake and fill with butter
icing. Cut off a 6-inch rectangle
from one side of the cake. Cut a
smaller rectangle 6 x 3 inches and stick
on the top.

2 ▲ Using a sharp serrated knife, shape
the sloping top and cut a 1-inch piece
from both ends between the tracks.
Shape the rounded ends for the wheels
and tracks. Assemble the cake on the
cake board and brush with apricot jam.
Cover with a layer of marzipan.

3 Color 1 quantity sugar paste icing
green and the remainder brown. On
a work surface dusted with
confectioners' sugar, roll out the green
sugar paste icing to about a 10-inch
square. Break small pieces of brown
icing and place all over the green.
Flatten and roll out together to give the
camouflage effect.

4 Turn the icing over, brush off the
excess confectioners' sugar and
repeat on the underside. Continue to
roll out until the sugar paste icing is
about ⅛ inch thick. Lay it over the
cake, gently pressing over the turret
and down the sides of the tracks on
both sides.

5 ▲ Carefully mold over the tracks,
cutting away the excess. Cut a piece
into a 2½-inch disk and stick on with a
little water for the hatch on top. Cut a
small hole for the gun and stick the
chocolate twig in for the gun. Unroll
some licorice wheels and stick on the
strips for the tracks, using a little royal
icing. Stick on cookies for the wheels
and candies for the lights and portholes.

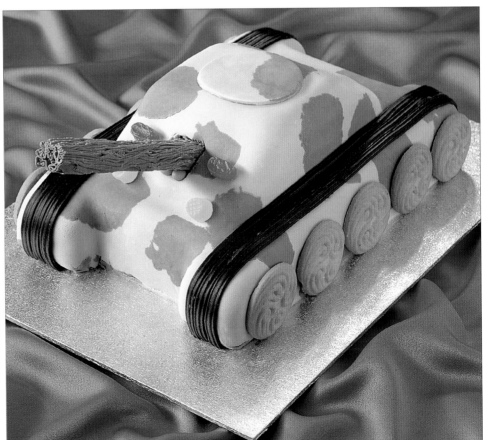

Box of Chocolates

This sophisticated-looking cake is perfect for an older child's birthday and will delight all chocolate lovers. For a younger child you could adapt the idea and fill the box with the birthday person's favorite candies.

INGREDIENTS
Serves 6–8
1 quantity chocolate-flavor Quick-mix Sponge Cake baked in a 6-inch square cake pan
2 ounces/¹⁄₆ quantity Butter Icing
3 tablespoons apricot jam, warmed and sieved
12 ounces marzipan
12 ounces/1 quantity Sugar paste Icing (Fondant)
red food coloring
chocolates

MATERIALS AND EQUIPMENT
8-inch square cake board
small paper candy cups
gold and red ribbon, 1½ inches wide

1 ▲ Split the cake and fill with a little butter icing. With a sharp knife, cut a shallow square from the top of the cake, leaving a ½-inch border around the edge. Place on the cake board and brush with apricot jam. Cover with a layer of marzipan.

2 ▲ Color two-thirds of the sugar paste icing red and set aside. Roll out the remainder on a work surface dusted with confectioners' sugar and cut into a 7-inch square. Lay it in the hollow dip and trim off the excess. Roll out the red sugar paste icing and cover the sides.

3 ▲ Put the chocolates into paper cups and arrange in the box. Tie the ribbon around the sides and tie a big bow.

Gift-wrapped Package

If you do not have a tiny flower cutter for the design on the wrapping paper, you could press a small decorative button into the sugar paste icing (fondant) while still soft to create a pattern.

INGREDIENTS
Serves 6–8
*1 quantity Quick-mix Sponge Cake
baked in a 6-inch square cake pan
2 ounces/⅛ quantity Butter Icing
3 tablespoons apricot jam,
warmed and sieved
1 pound marzipan
12 ounces/1 quantity
Sugar paste Icing (Fondant)
yellow, red and green food coloring
4 ounces/⅛ quantity Royal Icing*

MATERIALS AND EQUIPMENT
*8-inch square cake board
small flower cutter
wooden spoon
waxed or parchment paper
piping bag
No. 1 writing nozzle*

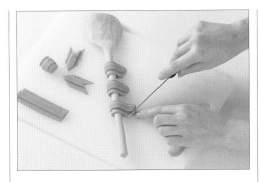

3 ▲ Cut the rest of the green into 1 x 3-inch lengths and the pink into ½ x 3-inch lengths. Center the pink on top of the green, fold in half, stick the ends together and slip over the handle of a wooden spoon, dusted with cornflour. Allow to dry overnight. Cut the ends in V shapes to fit neatly together. Cut a piece for the seam in the center, and fold in half with the seam at the bottom.

4 ▲ Carefully remove the bows from the wooden spoon and stick in position with royal icing.

1 Split the cake and fill with butter icing. Place on the cake board and brush with apricot jam. Cover with half the marzipan. Color the sugar paste icing pale yellow and roll out on a work surface dusted with confectioners' sugar. Use to cover the cake, turning in the corners neatly to look like wrapping paper. Mark the paper with a small flower cutter.

2 Divide the remaining marzipan in half, color one half pink and the other pale green. Roll out the pink marzipan and cut into four 1 x 7-inch strips. Roll out the green marzipan and cut into four ½-inch strips the same length. Center the green strips on top of the pink strips and stick on to the cake with a little water. Cut two 2-inch strips from each color and cut a V from the ends to form the ends of the ribbon. Stick in place and allow to dry overnight.

Children's Party Cakes

There can be no better way to celebrate a child's birthday than with a special cake. An imaginative design can provide a focal point for a party theme, and this chapter should give inspiration to any parent. The cake-decorating ideas here range from pirate hats and monsters from outer space to fairy castles and ballerinas. Easy-to-follow instructions ensure that you achieve the cake of your choice with minimum fuss, and guarantee your child's party will be a hit!

Flickering Birthday Candle Cake

Striped icing candles are flickering and ready to blow out on this birthday celebration cake for all ages.

INGREDIENTS
Serves 15–20
8 inch square Madeira Cake
1 quantity Butter Icing
3 tbsp apricot jam, warmed and sieved
1³/₄ lb/2¹/₃ x quantity Sugarpaste Icing
pink, yellow, purple and jade food colorings
edible silver balls, to decorate

MATERIALS AND EQUIPMENT
9 inch square cake board
leaf cutter
small round cutter
pink and purple food coloring pens
¹/₄ inch wide jade-colored ribbon

1 Cut the cake horizontally into three layers, using a long serrated knife. Sandwich the layers together with the butter icing and brush the cake with the apricot jam. Roll out 1¹/₄ lb of the sugarpaste icing on a work surface lightly dusted with confectioners' sugar and use to cover the cake. Position on the cake board.

2 Divide the remaining sugarpaste into four portions and color one portion pink, one portion yellow, one portion pale purple and one portion jade. Roll out the jade icing and cut into six ¹/₂ inch wide strips of slightly different lengths, but each long enough to go over the side and on to the top of the cake. Make a diagonal cut at one end of each strip.

3 ▲ Roll out the yellow icing and cut out six candle flames with the leaf cutter. Place a silver ball in each flame. Set aside the remaining yellow icing, wrapped in plastic wrap. Arrange the candles on top of the cake, securing them with a little water. Mold small strips, fractionally longer than the width of each candle, from the yellow and purple icings. Arrange alternate colors on the candles at a slight angle, securing with water. Position the flames at the end of each jade strip, also securing with water.

4 ▲ Roll out the pink and remaining purple icings, then cut out wavy pieces with a sharp knife. Attach to the cake, above the candles, with a little water. Gather together the pink icing trimmings and roll into a ball.

5 ▲ Using the leftover yellow and pink icings, make the decorations for the sides of the cake. Roll out the yellow icing and cut out circles with the small round cutter or the end of a piping nozzle. Make small balls from the pink icing and attach to the yellow circles with a little water. Press a silver ball in the center of each pink ball.

6 Arrange the decorations around the bottom edge of the cake, securing with water.

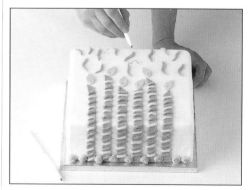

7 ▲ Using food coloring pens, draw wavy lines and dots coming from the purple and pink wavy icings. Decorate the sides of the cake board with the ribbon, securing at the back with a little softened sugarpaste.

Birthday Balloons

A colorful cake for a child's birthday party, made using either a sponge cake or fruit cake base.

INGREDIENTS
Serves 10–12
8-inch round *Quick-mix Sponge
Cake* or *Light Fruit Cake*, covered
with 1¾ pounds marzipan, if liked
2 pounds/2⅔ x quantity
Sugar paste Icing
red, green and yellow
food coloring
3 eggs
2 egg whites
4 cups confectioners' sugar

MATERIALS AND EQUIPMENT
*10-inch round cake board
3 bamboo skewers, 10 inches,
9½ inches and 9 inches long
small star cutter
baking parchment
waxed or parchment paper
piping bags
fine writing nozzle
narrow ribbon
candles*

1 Place the cake on the cake board. Color 2 ounces/⅙ quantity sugar paste icing red, 2 ounces/⅙ quantity green and 4 ounces/⅓ quantity yellow. Roll out the remaining icing on a surface dusted with confectioners' sugar and use to cover the cake. Use half the yellow icing to cover the cake board.

2 Using the tip of a skewer or the end of a paintbrush, make a small hole in the pointed end of one egg. Stir the egg lightly inside, then tip out into a bowl. Repeat with the remaining eggs. Carefully wash and dry the shells. (The eggs should be strained before using.)

3 ▲ Roll out the red sugar paste icing to about 4½ inches diameter and use to cover one of the eggshells, trimming off any excess around the pointed ends. Keep smoothing the icing in the palms of the hands. Push a bamboo skewer up through the hole and rest in a tall glass to harden. Repeat on the other eggshells with the green and yellow sugar paste icing.

4 ▲ Roll out the red, green and yellow trimmings and cut out a small star shape from each. Dampen lightly, then thread onto the skewers and secure to the bases of the balloons, matching the colors, for the knots on each balloon.

5 Draw 16 balloon shapes on a large sheet of baking parchment. Beat the egg whites with the confectioners' sugar until smooth and divide among four bowls. Add red coloring to one bowl, green to the second and yellow to the third, leaving the last white. Cover each with plastic wrap to prevent a crust from forming.

6 ▲ Place the white icing in a piping bag fitted with a plain writing nozzle and use to pipe over the traced outlines. Allow to harden slightly. Thin the green icing with a little water to the consistency of cream. Place in a waxed or parchment paper piping bag and snip off the end. Use to fill a third of the balloon shapes. Repeat with the red and yellow icings. Allow the run-outs at least 24 hours to harden.

7 Carefully peel the balloons off the baking parchment and secure around the sides of the cake. Pipe narrow strings for the balloons with white icing.

8 ▲ Press the large balloons into the top of the cake and decorate with the ribbon. Press the candles into the icing around the top edge.

Candle Cake

Marbled icing is so effective that little other decoration is required. This design combines blue and orange, but any other strong color combination is equally effective. It makes a lovely cake for a child's first birthday.

INGREDIENTS
Serves 20
8-inch round Rich Fruit Cake,
covered with 1¼ pounds marzipan
2 pounds/2⅔ x quantity
Sugar paste Icing (Fondant)
orange, blue and green
food coloring

MATERIALS AND EQUIPMENT
10-inch round silver
cake board
1 bamboo skewer
2 household candles
plastic wrap

1 Place the cake on the cake board. Color 4 ounces/⅓ quantity of the sugar paste icing orange and reserve. Reserve another 4 ounces/⅓ quantity of white sugar paste icing. Divide the remaining icing into three parts. Knead the orange coloring into one piece until deep orange but still streaked with color. Knead a mixture of blue- and green-colored icing into another piece until streaky. Leave the remaining piece white.

2 ▲ Lightly dust the work surface with confectioners' sugar. Roll long sausages of icing in the three colors and lay on the work surface.

3 ▲ Twist the colors together and knead for several seconds, until the strips of color are secured together but retain their individual colors.

4 Roll out the marbled icing and use to cover the cake, trimming off the excess around the base.

5 ▲ Take a small piece of the reserved orange sugar paste icing, about the size of a large grape, and shape into a candle flame. Thread onto the end of a bamboo skewer. Thinly roll the remaining orange sugar paste icing and use to cover the board around cake. Re-roll the trimmings and cut another strip, ½ inch wide. Secure over the orange icing around the cake. Cut another strip, ¼ inch wide, and use to complete the border.

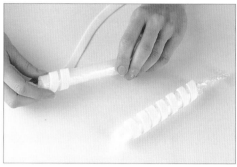

6 ▲ Wrap the candles in plastic wrap, twisting the ends together. (One candle is prepared as a spare.) Roll the reserved white sugar paste icing to a long thin strip cut vertically into two sections, each about ¼ inch wide. Starting from one end of a covered candle, coil the icing around the candle, trimming off any excess icing at the end. Set aside for at least 48 hours to harden completely.

7 To release the icing, untwist the plastic wrap and gently push out the candle inside. Carefully peel away the plastic wrap.

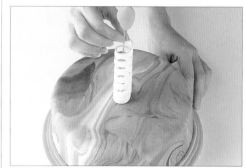

8 ▲ Place a dot of white icing in the center of the cake and use to secure the icing candle. Push the bamboo skewer down through the center of the cake to finish.

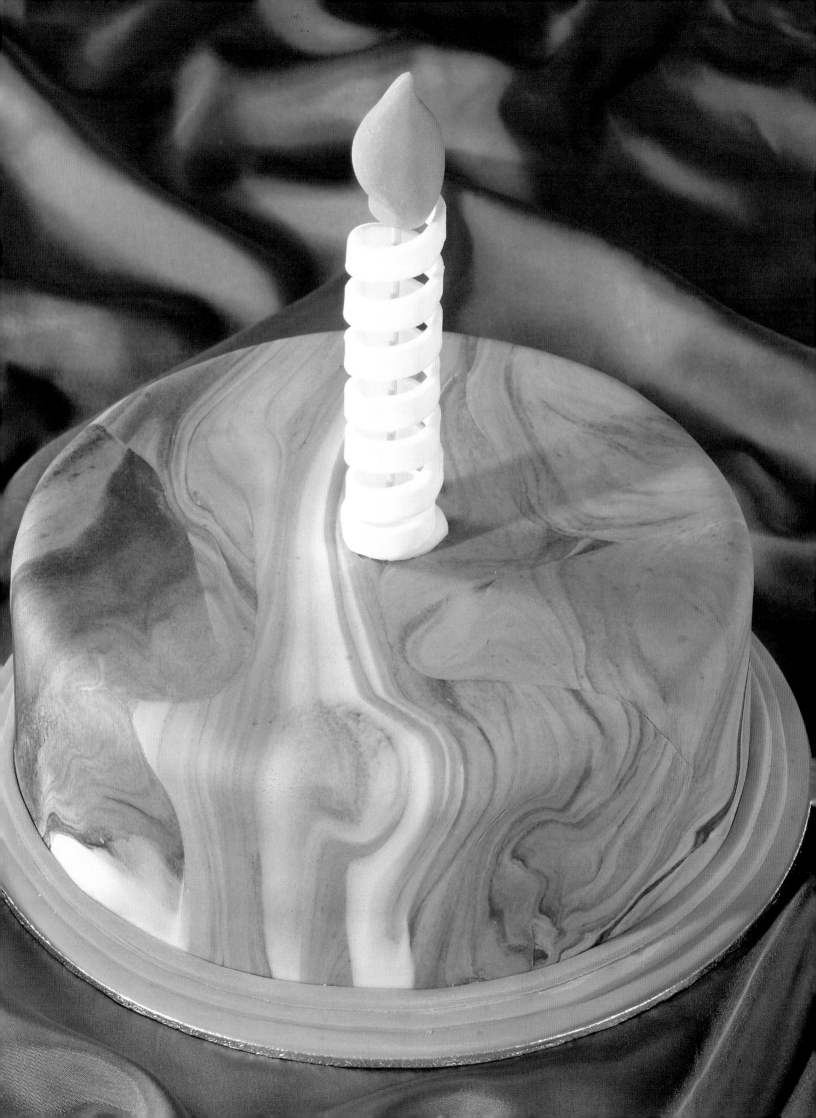

 An Apple Tree

For this unusual centerpiece, choose whichever fruit you prefer. You could make the apples green instead of red, or have a mixture of red and green apples or golden pears.

INGREDIENTS
Serves 10–12
1 quantity chocolate-flavor Quick-Mix Sponge Cake mix
1 quantity chocolate-flavor Jelly Roll, baked and rolled with
¼ quantity chocolate-flavor Butter Icing
¼ quantity chocolate-flavor Butter Icing
½ quantity Butter Icing, colored green with food coloring
8 oz marzipan
red and green food colorings
green-colored shredded coconut (see Puppies in Love, step 4)
tiny fresh flowers, to decorate (optional)

MATERIALS AND EQUIPMENT
1 qt fluted round cake pan or Pyrex bowl
6 inch round cake board
wooden toothpick
2 x 12 inch lengths of florists' wire
florists' tape
waxed paper piping bag
leaf nozzle

Tip

To stand the tree up at a slight angle, you can cut out a template of thick card from around the un-iced cake. Then decorate the cake on the card and prop it up on a small block of wood. Alternatively, decorate the cake flat on a cake board.

1 Preheat the oven to 350°F. Grease and flour the pan or bowl. Spoon in the cake mixture and smooth the surface. Bake in the center of the oven for 35–40 minutes or until a skewer inserted into the center of the cake comes out clean. Leave in the pan for about 5 minutes, then turn out on to a wire rack and leave to cool.

2 ▲ Arrange the jelly roll on the card template or cake board (see Tip), trimming it, if necessary. Spread the chocolate butter icing over the tree trunk, making swirls. Use about three-quarters of the green butter icing for the top of the tree, making it peak and swirl. Position on top of the tree trunk.

3 ▲ Color about 1 oz of the marzipan green. Color the remainder red, then roll it into cherry-size balls. Roll the green marzipan into tiny sausage shapes to make the stalks and leaves. Use the toothpick to make tiny holes in the tops of the apples, and then insert the stalks and leaves.

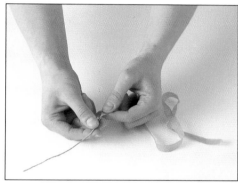

4 ▲ Twist the florists' tape around the florists' wire, then cut it into 3 inch lengths. Press the lengths of wire through the apples, bending the ends so the apples cannot fall off when hanging. Press the hanging apples into the tree, reserving the extra apples to scatter around the bottom.

5 ▲ Use the remaining green butter icing to fill the piping bag. Practice piping the leaves on a piece of waxed paper before piping leaves all over the tree top. Scatter the green shredded coconut around the base of the tree and pipe a few extra leaves. Add a few tiny fresh flowers for effect, if liked. The wires must be removed from the cake before serving.

A Basket of Flowers

This attractive arrangement of flowers looks very impressive, yet none of the stages are very difficult to do.

INGREDIENTS
Serves 10–12
1½ x quantity orange-flavor Quick-Mix Sponge Cake mix
2 x quantity orange-flavor Butter Icing
orange, yellow, pink, red, black and green food colorings
2 lb/2⅔ x quantity Sugarpaste Icing

MATERIALS AND EQUIPMENT
deep 8 inch round cake pan
8 inch oval cake board
3 waxed paper piping bags
small round nozzle
small straight serrated nozzle
selection of small flower and leaf cutters
12 inch piece of strong wire, bent to a curve with the two ends about 8 inch apart
plasticine

1 Preheat the oven to 350°F. Grease the cake pan, line the base with waxed paper and grease the paper. Spoon the cake mixture into the prepared pan and smooth the surface. Bake in the center of the oven for 45–50 minutes or until a skewer inserted into the center of the cake comes out clean. Turn out on to a wire rack, carefully peel off the lining paper and leave the cake to cool completely.

2 Place the butter icing in a bowl and beat in a few drops of orange food coloring. Cut the cake in half down the middle and spread the bottom of one half with a little of the butter icing. Sandwich with the other half of the cake, base to base.

3 Cut a thin slice from the bottom of the sandwiched cake. Place a little butter icing on the cake board and position the cake on top, with the large flat surface facing upwards.

4 ▲ Spread more of the butter icing over the cut surface of the cake, covering right up to the edges.

5 Place about 4 tbsp of the butter icing in a small bowl and color it with a little more orange food coloring to make it a slightly deeper color. Fit a paper piping bag with the small round nozzle and fill with the deeper orange butter icing. Pipe a decorative border around the top edge of the basket.

6 Fit the clean round nozzle into a fresh paper piping bag and fill with the lighter orange butter icing. Pipe vertical lines about 1 inch apart all around the sides of the cake. Fit a fresh paper piping bag with the serrated nozzle and fill with more orange butter icing. Starting at the top of the cake pipe short lines alternately crossing over, then stopping at the vertical lines to give a basket-weave effect.

7 Divide the sugarpaste icing into two. Cut one of the portions in half and color one half pale orange and the other half darker orange. Wrap these separately in plastic wrap and set aside. Divide the other portion of sugarpaste icing into five equal amounts. Color these yellow, pink, red, black and green.

8 ▲ Roll out the yellow, pink and red portions on a work surface lightly dusted with confectioners' sugar and use the flower cutters to stamp out the flower shapes. Place some of the flowers in an egg carton so they dry curved and place others on a baking sheet so they dry flat. Leave the flowers for at least 2 hours to dry out.

9 Use a little of the orange, yellow and black sugarpaste icings to roll into tiny balls to make the centers of the flowers, sticking them in place with a little water.

10 Roll out the green icing and use a leaf-shaped cutter to stamp out leaves, indenting them with a small, sharp knife and curling them slightly to give them more interest. Place them on the baking sheet to dry out.

11 When dry, arrange the flowers and leaves attractively on top of the basket and the cake board.

12 ▲ To make the handle for the basket, roll the two shades of orange sugarpaste icing into balls about the size of small marbles. Thread these alternately on to the curved piece of wire, leaving about 1 inch of wire exposed at each end. Stand the handle in two pieces of plasticine stuck to the work surface or a baking sheet, supported by a dish towel pushed under the handle to keep it from falling over. Leave to dry for at least 2 hours. To finish, gently press the handle into the cake, pushing it in until secure.

Telephone Cake

A great idea for a first or second birthday, as the telephone is an endless source of amusement for many toddlers.

INGREDIENTS
Serves 8–10
1 quantity chocolate-flavor Quick-Mix Sponge Cake mix
6 tbsp apricot jam, warmed and sieved
1¼ lb/1⅔ x quantity Sugarpaste Icing
1 quantity Butter Icing
red, blue, yellow and green food colorings
black liquorice ribbon

MATERIALS AND EQUIPMENT
7 inch square cake pan
8 inch square cake board
3 waxed paper piping bags
small round cutter

1 Preheat the oven to 350°F. Grease the pan, line with waxed paper and grease the paper. Spoon the mixture into the pan and smooth the surface. Bake in the center of the oven for 35 – 40 minutes or until firm. Turn out and leave to cool.

2 ▲ Cut off a 1½ inch strip for the receiver. Cut the main body of the telephone in half. Cut about one-quarter off the top half of the main body of the telephone for the receiver rest.

3 ▲ Brush the center of the main cake with apricot jam and reposition the top of the cake, leaving space to replace the receiver rest.

4 ▲ To shape the receiver rest, cut a ½ inch cross out of the center of this portion, then cut away the four end corners. Brush the base with apricot jam and position on the cake.

5 ▲ Brush the top surface of the cake evenly with apricot jam. On a work surface lightly dusted with confectioners' sugar, roll out 12 oz of the sugarpaste icing to a 12 inch square and use to cover the telephone cake. Place the cake on the cake board.

6 ▲ Divide the butter icing into three separate bowls, coloring one red, one blue and one yellow. Fill the piping bags with the colored butter icings and snip the end off each one to make a small hole. Pipe spots in all three colors evenly over the cake.

7 Color 6 oz of the remaining sugarpaste icing green. Cut off about 1 oz and set aside, wrapped in plastic wrap. Brush the receiver piece of cake with a little apricot jam, then roll out the larger piece of green sugarpaste icing and use to cover the receiver. Position the receiver on the cake.

8 Take a small piece of the remaining green sugarpaste icing and roll it into a ball. Stick it on to the side of the receiver with a little water.

9 Roll out the remaining green sugarpaste icing and cut out a flower pot shape, measuring approximately 3 inches across the top. Place this on the front of the telephone, sticking it down with a little water. To make the dial, color the remaining sugarpaste icing red and roll out to a 3 inch round, or stamp it out using a cutter. Use a tiny round cutter to stamp out the finger holes, then position the dial on the cake with a little water. Use any remaining butter cream to pipe in the numbers.

10 To make the telephone cord, twist the piece of liquorice around a pencil until tightly coiled and leave it for about 10 minutes. Carefully remove the pencil, and press one end of the liquorice into the ball of green sugarpaste icing on the receiver and the other end into the back of the cake.

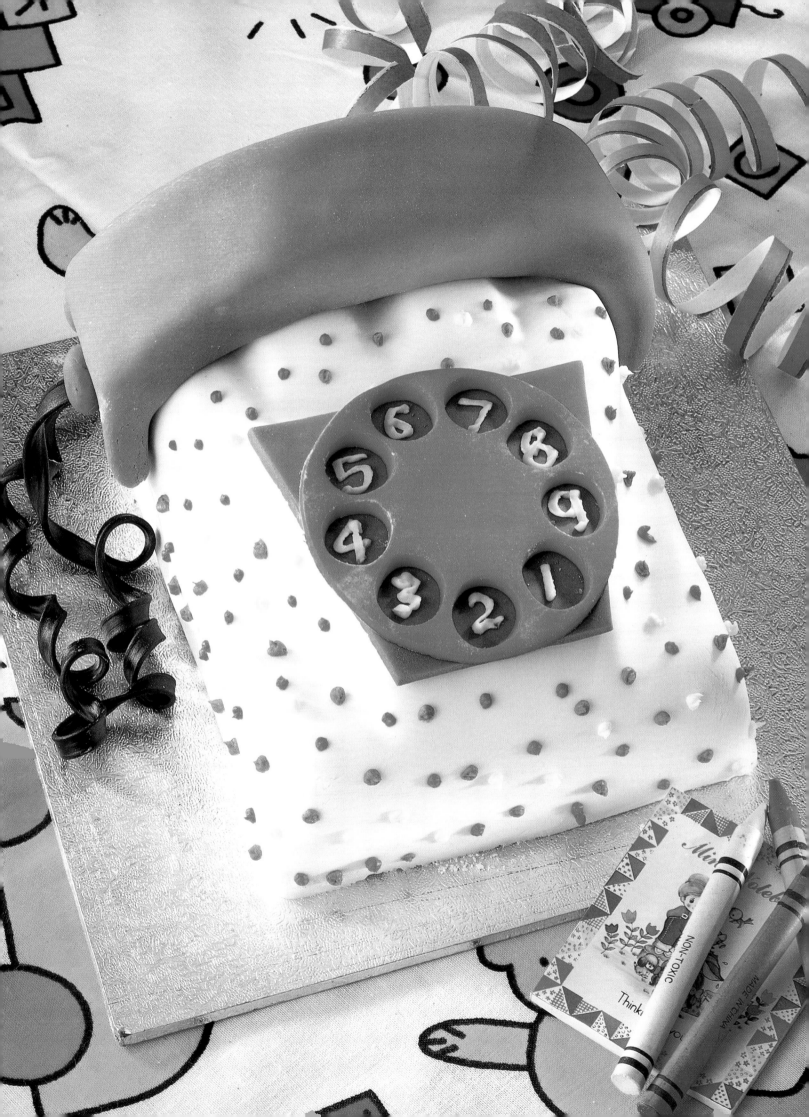

ump Truck

Any large, round cookies will work well for the wheels, and all sorts of colored candies can go in the truck.

INGREDIENTS
Serves 8–10
1½ x quantity Quick-Mix Sponge
Cake mix
6 tbsp apricot jam, warmed and
sieved
2 lb/2⅔ x quantity Sugarpaste Icing
yellow, red and blue food colorings
confectioners' sugar, to dredge
sandwich wafer cookies
4 coconut swirl cookies
4 oz colored candies
2 inch piece blue liquorice stick
raw sugar, for the sand

MATERIALS AND EQUIPMENT
2 lb loaf pan
12 x 7 inch cake board
7 x 3 inch piece of cake cardboard,
brushed with apricot jam
small crescent-shaped cutter

1 Preheat the oven to 350°F. Grease the pan, line the base and sides with waxed paper and grease the paper. Spoon the cake mixture into the pan and smooth the surface. Bake in the center of the oven for 40–45 minutes or until a skewer inserted into the center of the cake comes out clean. Turn out on to a wire rack, peel off the lining paper and leave the cake to cool completely.

2 Using a large, sharp knife, cut off the top of the cake to make a flat surface. Then cut off one-third of the cake to make the cabin of the truck.

3 ▲ Take the larger piece of cake, and, with the cut side up, cut a hollow in the center, leaving a ½ inch border. Brush the hollowed cake evenly with apricot jam.

4 ▲ Color 12 oz of the sugarpaste icing yellow and remove a piece about the size of a walnut. Set aside, wrapped in plastic wrap. Roll out the remainder on a work surface lightly dusted with confectioners' sugar until about ¼ inch thick. Use to cover the hollowed-out piece of cake, carefully pressing it into the hollow. Trim the bottom edges and then set aside.

5 Color 12 oz of the sugarpaste icing red. Cut off one-third of this and set aside, wrapped in plastic wrap. Roll out the rest on a work surface dusted with confectioners' sugar until about ¼ inch thick. Use to cover the remaining piece of cake and trim the edges.

6 Take the reserved red icing, break off a piece the size of a walnut and wrap in plastic wrap. Roll out the rest and use to cover the cake cardboard.

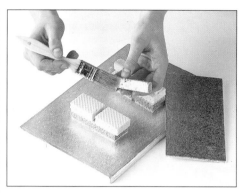

7 ▲ Brush the wafers with a little apricot jam and stick them together in two equal piles. Place the piles on the cake board, about 3 inches apart. Place the red-covered cake cardboard on top of the wafers. Place a little of the remaining white sugarpaste icing about half way along the covered cardboard in order to tip the bed part of the truck slightly. Place the bed on top, with the cabin in front. Stand the coconut cookies in position for the wheels.

8 ▲ Roll out the reserved piece of yellow sugarpaste icing to make a 2 x 1 inch rectangle. Color the remaining white sugarpaste icing with blue food coloring and roll out thinly. Use the crescent-shaped cutter to stamp out the eyes. Either make simple ones, or overlay them with white crescent shapes for detail.

9 Roll out the reserved red sugarpaste icing thinly and stamp out a mouth shape with an appropriate cutter. Use a little water to stick the yellow panel on to the front of the truck, then stick on the features in the same way.

10 To finish, fill the bed part of the truck with brightly colored candies and push a piece of colored liquorice into the top of the cabin. Scatter the sugar around the base of the dump truck to resemble sand.

Train Cake

This quick-and-easy train cake is made in a shaped pan, so all you need to do is decorate it!

INGREDIENTS
Serves 8–10
1½ x quantity Quick-Mix Sponge
Cake mix
yellow food coloring
2 x quantity Butter Icing
red liquorice strings
6–8 tbsp colored jimmies
4 liquorice wheels

MATERIALS AND EQUIPMENT
train-shaped cake pan
10 x 15 inch cake board
2 fabric piping bags
small round and small star nozzles
pink and white cotton wool balls

Tip

When applying butter icing to a cake, it is a good idea to have a small bowl of very hot water at the ready to dip your spatula into. This will ensure that you get a really smooth finish on the cake.

1 Preheat the oven to 350°F. Grease and flour the cake pan and stand firmly on a greased baking sheet. Grease some strips of foil and press along the edges of the cake pan to prevent the cake mixture escaping. Spoon the cake mixture into the prepared pan and smooth the surface. Bake in the center of the oven for 40–45 minutes or until a skewer inserted into the center of the cake comes out clean. Leave the cake to cool in the pan.

2 ▲ Slice off the top surface of the cake to make it perfectly flat. Run a knife around the edges of the cake to release it from the pan, then turn out the cake and place on the cake board.

3 ▲ Add a few drops of yellow food coloring to the butter icing and beat well until evenly blended.

4 ▲ Using a spatula, cover the cake smoothly with about half of the butter icing.

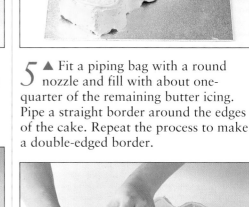

5 ▲ Fit a piping bag with a round nozzle and fill with about one-quarter of the remaining butter icing. Pipe a straight border around the edges of the cake. Repeat the process to make a double-edged border.

6 ▲ Position the red liquorice strings around the edge of the cake, on top of the piped border. Snip the strings with scissors as you bend them around the curves on the train.

7 Fit a piping bag with a small star nozzle and fill with the remaining butter icing. Pipe small stars evenly over the top of the cake. Add extra details to the train with the liquorice, or by piping, if you like. Use a spatula to press on the colored jimmies all around the sides of the cake.

8 Pull a few balls of cotton wool apart for the steam and stick in position with a little butter icing. Press the liquorice wheels in place.

Merry-go-round Cake

Choose your own figures to sit on the merry-go-round, from chocolate animals to jelly bears. Remember to position the top of the cake at the last minute for the best results.

INGREDIENTS
Serves 16–20
1½ x quantity lemon-flavor
Quick-mix Sponge Cake mix
4 tablespoons apricot jam,
warmed and sieved
1¼ pounds/1⅔ x quantity
Sugar paste Icing
orange and yellow food coloring
7-inch-long candy sticks
candy figures

MATERIALS AND EQUIPMENT
8-inch round layer cake pans
9-inch round scalloped
cake board
7-inch round piece of
card stock
toothpick
star-shaped cookie cutters in 2 sizes

1 Preheat the oven to 350°F. Grease the pans. Line the bottoms with waxed or parchment paper and grease the paper. Spoon two-thirds of the mixture into one pan and the other third into the other pan. Smooth the surfaces with a plastic spatula. Bake for 55–60 minutes, or until a skewer inserted into the center of each cake comes out clean. Let stand for 5 minutes before turning out onto a wire rack to cool.

2 ▲ Place the larger cake, upside down, on the scalloped cake board to make the base of the merry-go-round, and place the smaller cake, right side up, on the piece of card stock. Brush both cakes evenly with apricot jam and set aside. Lightly dust the work surface with confectioners' sugar and place 1 pound/1⅓ x quantity sugar paste icing on it. Using the toothpick, apply a few spots of orange food coloring to the sugar paste icing.

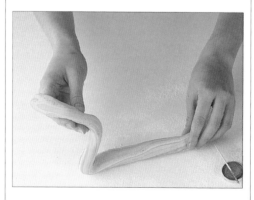

3 ▲ To achieve the marbled effect in the sugar paste icing, roll into a sausage shape on the work surface. Fold the sausage shape in half and continue to roll out until it reaches its original length. Fold over again and roll out again into a sausage shape. Continue this process until the sugar paste is streaked with the orange color.

4 Divide the marbled sugar paste icing into two thirds and one third. Roll out the larger portion on the work surface lightly dusted with confectioners' sugar and use to cover the larger cake. Repeat with the smaller portion of marbled sugar paste icing and use to cover the smaller cake. Trim away any excess sugar paste icing and reserve, wrapped in plastic wrap.

5 ▲ Using one of the candy sticks, make eight holes, evenly spaced, around the edge of the larger cake, leaving about a ¾-inch border. Push the upright stick through the cake to the board.

6 Knead the reserved marbled sugar paste icing until the orange color is evenly blended, then roll out on the work surface lightly dusted with confectioners' sugar. Using the smaller star cutter, cut out nine stars. Cover with plastic wrap and set aside. Color 4 ounces/⅓ quantity sugar paste icing yellow. Roll out on a surface lightly dusted with confectioners' sugar and cut out nine stars with the larger star cutter. Sit the smaller cake on an upturned bowl and stick eight large and eight small stars around the edge of the cake, using a little water to secure. Stick the remaining stars on top of the cake.

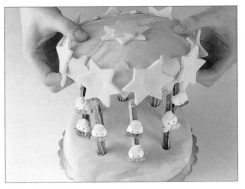

7 ▲ To secure the candy figures to the candy sticks, stick tiny balls of the excess sugar paste icing behind the figures and then lightly press onto the sticks. Allow to set for about 30 minutes. Place the candy sticks in the holes on the larger cake.

8 ▲ To assemble the cake, carefully lift the smaller cake, with its card stock base, onto the candy sticks, making sure it balances before letting go.

$\mathcal{R}$acing Circuit

A simple ring cake makes the perfect base for this teddy-bear racing track. Choose the flattest and widest side of the cake for the top (this will depend on the shape of your ring mold), so there's plenty of room for the icing cars to race around on.

INGREDIENTS
Serves 12
1 quantity Quick-mix Sponge Cake mix
12 ounces/1 quantity Butter Icing
1¼ pound/1½ x quantity Sugar paste Icing (Fondant)
black, blue, yellow, green, orange, red and purple food coloring
4 ounces/⅙ quantity Royal Icing, for fixing
selection of miniature licorice candies, licorice all-sorts and teddy bears
4 ounces licorice wheels

MATERIALS AND EQUIPMENT
8-inch ring mold
10-inch round cake board
wooden skewer
fine paintbrush
waxed paper

1 Preheat the oven to 325°F. Spoon the cake mixture into a greased ring mold. Bake for 35–40 minutes. Turn out and cool on a wire rack.

2 ▲ Cut the cake in half horizontally and fill with some of the butter icing. Cover the outside of the cake with the remaining butter icing, having the widest part of the cake on top.

3 Cut 12 ounces/1 quantity of the sugar paste icing in half. To coat the inside of the ring, cut one half of the icing in half again and roll out to the measured circumference and height (reserve the other piece for the top). Press in position over the butter icing. Roll out the reserved piece for the top to the measured diameter and width (you may find this easier to do in two halves), pressing in position and easing into shape over the butter icing.

4 ▲ Take the half piece of icing reserved for coating the outside and roll out to the measured circumference and height. Press in position around the outside of the cake, reserving the trimmings. Place the cake on the cake board.

5 ▲ Take the reserved white icing trimmings and roll out to an oblong for the flag. Cut the wooden skewer to a height of about 5 inches and fold one end of the flag around it, securing with a little water. With black food coloring and a fine paintbrush, paint on a checkered pattern. Color a small piece of icing black, make into a ball and stick on top of the skewer. Create a few folds in the flag and allow to dry on waxed paper.

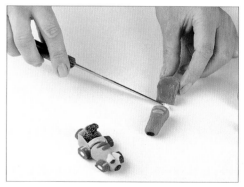

6 ▲ Color the remaining sugar paste icing blue, yellow, green, orange, red and a very small amount purple. Shape each car in two pieces, attaching in the center with royal icing where the seat joins the body of the car. Add decorations and headlights and attach licorice all-sorts wheels with royal icing. Place a candy teddy bear in each car and allow to set.

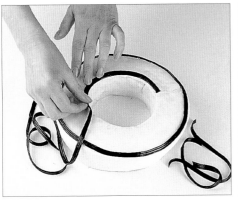

7 ◀ Unwind the licorice wheels, removing the center sweets. Lay the licorice around the top of the cake to represent the track, leaving a gap in the middle and securing the strips with royal icing. Secure one strip around the bottom of the cake also.

8 Cut some of the licorice into small strips and attach round the middle of the outside of the cake with some royal icing.

9 Arrange small licorice candies around the bottom of the cake. Position the cars on top of the cake on the tracks and attach the flag to the outside with royal icing.

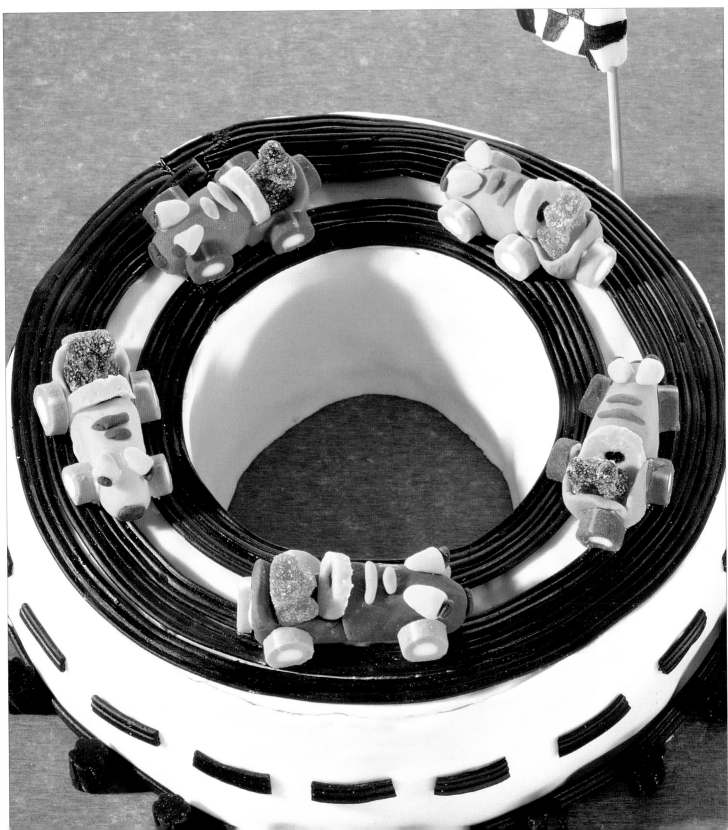

Balloons

This is a simple yet effective design that can be adapted to any age.

INGREDIENTS
Serves 8
*1 quantity Quick-mix Sponge Cake
baked in an 8-inch round
cake pan
4 ounces/⅓ quantity Butter Icing
3 tablespoons apricot jam,
warmed and sieved
1 pound marzipan
1 pound/1⅓ x quantity
Sugar paste Icing (Fondant)
pink, blue, green and yellow
food coloring
4 ounces/⅙ quantity Royal Icing*

*MATERIALS AND EQUIPMENT
10-inch cake board
ribbon
waxed or parchment paper piping bag
No. 2 writing nozzle
No. 7 star nozzle
candles*

1 Split the cake and fill with butter icing. Place on the cake board and brush with apricot jam. Cover with a layer of marzipan. On a work surface dusted with confectioners' sugar, roll out 12 ounces/1 quantity sugar paste icing and use to cover the cake.

2 ▲ Divide the remaining sugar paste icing into three pieces; color one pink, one blue and the other green. Roll out and, using a template, cut out a balloon from each color. Stick onto the cake with a little water, rubbing the edges gently with a finger to round off straight edges.

3 ▲ Tie the ribbon around the cake. With yellow icing and a No. 2 writing nozzle, pipe on the strings, attaching them to the balloons. Using the star nozzle, pipe a border around the base of the cake.

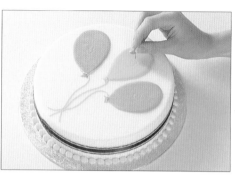

4 ▲ Pipe a number onto each balloon. Place the candles on the cake.

Treasure Map

Allow several days to paint the map, because each color must dry completely before adding another. Use a fairly dry paintbrush to apply the color.

INGREDIENTS
Serves 12
2 x quantity Quick-mix Sponge Cake baked in a 10-inch square cake pan
8 ounces/⅔ quantity Butter Icing
4 tablespoons apricot jam, warmed and sieved
1 pound marzipan
1½ pounds/2 x quantity Sugar paste Icing
yellow, brown, orange, green, blue, red and black food coloring
4 ounces/⅙ quantity Royal Icing

MATERIALS AND EQUIPMENT
10 x 14-inch cake board
fine paintbrush
waxed or parchment paper
waxed or parchment paper piping bag
No. 7 shell nozzle
No. 1 writing nozzle

1 ▲ Split the cake and fill with butter icing. Cut into an 8 x 10-inch rectangle and place on the cake board. Brush with apricot jam. Cover with a layer of marzipan. On a work surface dusted with confectioners' sugar, roll out 1 pound/1⅓ quantity sugar paste icing and use to cover the cake. Color the remaining sugar paste icing yellow and roll out. Mark out the island, river, lake, mountains and trees on top of the cake.

2 ▲ With brown and orange colors and a fine paintbrush, paint the edges of the map to look old and smudge the colors together with paper towels. Paint the island pale green and the water around the island, river and lake pale blue. Dry overnight before painting on other details, otherwise the colors will run.

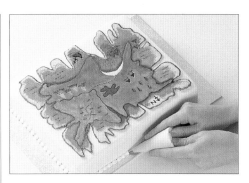

3 ▲ Pipe a border of royal icing around the base of the cake with a shell nozzle. Color a little royal icing red and, using a No. 1 nozzle, pipe the path to the treasure, finishing with the letter X. Color some icing green and pipe on grass and trees. Color some icing black and pipe on a North sign.

Pirate's Hat

Pirates are an enduringly popular theme for children's parties, and this cake will be much admired. Surround it with lots of stolen treasures.

INGREDIENTS
Serves 12
2 x quantity Quick-mix Sponge
Cake baked in a 10-inch round
cake pan
8 ounces/²⁄₃ quantity Butter Icing
4 tablespoons apricot jam,
warmed and sieved
1 pound marzipan
1¼ pound/1²⁄₃ x quantity
Sugar paste Icing (Fondant)
black and gold food coloring
chocolate coins
jewel candies

MATERIALS AND EQUIPMENT
12-inch square cake board
waxed paper
fine paintbrush

1 ▲ Split the cake and fill with butter icing. Cut in half and sandwich the halves together. Stand upright diagonally across the cake board and use a template to cut shallow dips to create the crown of the hat. Brush with apricot jam.

2 Cut a strip of marzipan to lay over the top of the cake to neaten the seams. Cover the whole cake with a layer of marzipan. Color 1 pound/1¹⁄₃ quantity sugar paste icing black. On a work surface dusted with confectioners' sugar, roll out the sugar paste icing and use to cover the cake.

3 ▲ Roll out the remaining sugar paste icing, cut ½-inch strips and stick in place around the brim of the hat with a little water.

4 ▲ Mark the strip with a fork to look like braid. Using the template, mark the skull and crossbones on the hat. Cut the shapes out of the white sugar paste and stick in place with a little water. Paint the braid strip around the hat gold and arrange the chocolate coins and candies around the board.

Number 6 Cake

Use the round pan as a guide to cut the square cake to fit neatly around the round cake.

INGREDIENTS
Serves 12
*2 x quantity Quick-mix Sponge
Cake baked in a 6-inch round and a
6-inch square cake pan
4 ounces/⅓ quantity Butter Icing
5 tablespoons apricot jam,
warmed and sieved
1 pound marzipan
1¼ pounds/1½ x quantity
Sugar paste Icing (Fondant)
yellow and green food coloring
4 ounces/⅙ quantity Royal Icing*

MATERIALS AND EQUIPMENT
*10 x 14-inch cake board
3-inch fluted cutter
waxed or parchment paper
piping bags
No. 1 writing nozzle
No. 8 star nozzle
plastic train set with 6 candles*

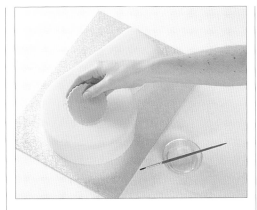

3 ▲ Color most of the sugar paste icing pale yellow. On a work surface dusted with confectioners' sugar, roll out and use to cover the cake. Mark a 3-inch circle in the center of the round cake. Color the reserved sugar paste icing pale green, roll out and cut out a fluted circle. Stick in place with water and allow to dry overnight.

4 Mark the track ¾ inch wide (or the width of the train). Color the royal icing yellow and pipe the track with a No. 1 writing nozzle.

5 Using a star nozzle, pipe a border around the base and top of the cake. Pipe the name on the green circle and attach the train with royal icing.

1 ▲ Split the cake and fill with a little butter icing. Cut the square cake in half and cut a rounded end from one oblong to fit neatly around the round cake. Trim the cakes to the same depth and assemble on the cake board as shown. Brush with apricot jam.

2 Cover with a thin layer of marzipan. Smooth any seams and make sure surface is flat.

Clown Face

Children love this happy clown. His frilly collar is quite easy to make, but you do have to work quickly before the sugar paste icing (fondant) dries.

INGREDIENTS
Serves 10
1 quantity Quick-mix Sponge Cake
baked in an 8-inch round cake pan
4 ounces/⅓ quantity Butter Icing
3 tablespoons apricot jam,
warmed and sieved
1 pound marzipan
1 pound/1⅓ x quantity
Sugar paste Icing (Fondant)
4 ounces/⅙ quantity Royal Icing
silver balls (dragées)
pink, red, green, blue and black
food coloring

MATERIALS AND EQUIPMENT
10-inch round cake board
waxed or parchment paper piping bag
No. 8 star nozzle
frill cutter
toothpick
small round cutter
cotton balls
candles

1 ▲ Split the cake and fill with butter icing. Place in the center of the cake board and brush with apricot jam. Cover with a thin layer of marzipan. On a work surface lightly dusted with confectioners' sugar, roll out about half the sugar paste icing and use to cover the cake. Mark the position of the features on the top of the cake. Pipe stars around the base of the cake with royal icing, placing silver balls as you work, and allow to dry overnight.

2 ▲ Color half the remaining sugar paste icing pale pink, roll out and, with the use of a template, cut out the shape of the face. Lay on the cake with the top of the head touching one edge.

3 ▲ Color the remaining pink sugar paste icing red, roll out and cut out the nose. Roll out some of the white sugar paste icing, cut out the eyes and mouth and stick on the face with the nose, using a little water. Roll a little of the red sugar paste icing into a thin sausage and cut to fit the mouth. Stick in place with a little water.

4 ▲ Roll out the rest of the red sugar paste icing, cut into thin strands for hair and stick in place with water.

5 ▲ Color most of the remaining sugar paste icing pale green and roll out thinly. Cut out a frill using a frill cutter. Cut through one side and roll along the fluted edge with a toothpick to stretch it. Stick on the cake with a little water and arrange the frills. Repeat to make three layers of frills, holding them in place with cotton balls until dry.

6 Color a little sugar paste icing blue, roll and cut out eyes and stick in place with a little water. Color the rest of the sugar paste icing black, roll and cut out the eyes and eyebrows, then stick in position. Place the candles at the top of the head.

Kite Cake

This cheerful kite has a bright and happy clown's face, and is a great favorite with children of all ages.

INGREDIENTS
Serves 10
1½ x quantity Quick-mix Sponge Cake baked in a 10-inch square cake pan
8 ounces/⅔ quantity Butter Icing
3 tablespoons apricot jam, warmed and sieved
1 pound marzipan
1½ pounds/2 x quantity Sugar paste Icing (Fondant)
yellow, red, green, blue and black food coloring
4 ounces/⅙ quantity Royal Icing

MATERIALS AND EQUIPMENT
12-inch square cake board
waxed or parchment paper
piping bag
No. 8 star nozzle

1 ▲ Split the cake and fill with butter icing. Mark 6 inches from one corner down two sides and, using a ruler, from this point cut down to the opposite corner on both sides to make the kite shape. Place diagonally on the cake board and brush with apricot jam. Cover with marzipan.

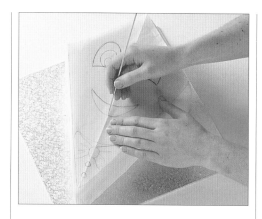

2 ▲ Color 1 pound/1⅓ quantity sugar paste icing pale yellow. Roll out and use to cover the cake. Using a template, mark the face on the kite. Divide the remaining sugar paste icing into four pieces and color them red, green, blue and black. Wrap each separately in plastic wrap. Using royal icing, pipe a border of shells around the base of the cake.

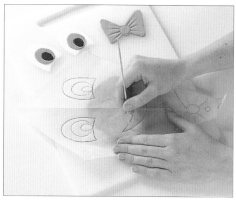

3 ▲ Using a template, cut out the face, bow tie and buttons and stick in place with a little water.

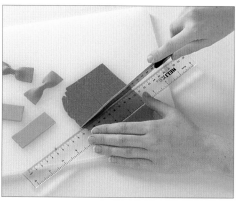

4 ▲ To make the kite's tail, roll out each color separately and cut two 1½ x ½-inch lengths from the blue, red and green sugar paste icing. Pinch them to shape into bows.

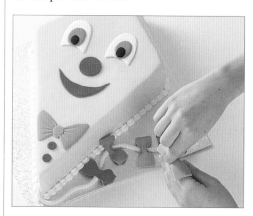

5 ▲ Roll the yellow sugar paste icing into a long rope, lay it on the board in a wavy line from the narrow end of the kite and stick the bows in place with water. Roll balls of yellow sugar paste icing, stick to the board with a little royal icing and press in the candles.

Fairy Castle

Allow plenty of time to cover the cake with royal icing, as it is quite a delicate job. If the icing dries too quickly, dip the spatula into hot water to help smooth the surface.

INGREDIENTS
Serves 10–12
1 quantity Quick-mix Sponge Cake
baked in an 8-inch round
cake pan
4 ounces/⅓ quantity Butter Icing
6 tablespoons apricot jam,
warmed and sieved
1½ pounds marzipan
8 Ding Dongs®
1½ pounds/1 quantity
Royal Icing
pink, blue and green
food coloring
jelly diamonds
4 ice cream cones
2 ice cream wafers
2 ounces/1 cup dried coconut
marshmallows

MATERIALS AND EQUIPMENT
12-inch square cake board
toothpick

2 ▲ Color two-thirds of the royal icing pale pink and spread evenly over the cake. Cover the extra pieces of Ding Dongs® with icing and stick around the top of the cake. Using a toothpick, score the walls with brick patterns and stick jelly diamonds on the corner towers as windows. Cut the ice cream cones to fit the turrets and stick them in place. Allow to dry overnight.

4 ▲ Cut the wafers to shape for the gates, stick to the cake and cover with blue icing, marking planks with the back of a knife.

5 ▲ Put the coconut in a bowl and mix in a few drops of green coloring. Spread the board with the remaining royal icing and sprinkle the coconut over. Stick the marshmallows on the small turrets with royal icing.

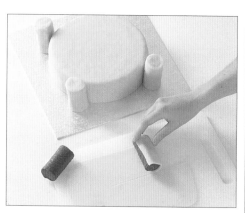

1 ▲ Split the cake and fill with butter icing. Place in the center of the board and brush with apricot jam. Cover with a layer of marzipan. Cover the Ding Dongs® separately with marzipan. Stick four at regular intervals around the cake. Cut the remaining rolls in half.

3 ▲ Color half the remaining royal icing pale blue and spread thinly over the cones, using a fork to pattern the icing.

Fire Engine

This jolly fire engine is simplicity itself, as the decorations are mainly bought candies and novelties.

Ingredients
Serves 8–10
1½ x quantity Quick-mix Sponge
Cake baked in an 8-inch square
cake pan
4 ounces/⅓ quantity Butter Icing
3 tablespoons apricot jam,
warmed and sieved
12 ounces marzipan
1 pound/1⅓ x quantity
Sugar paste Icing (Fondant)
red, black and green
food coloring
licorice wheels
4 ounces/⅙ quantity Royal Icing
candies
1 cup dried coconut

MATERIALS AND EQUIPMENT
10-inch round cake board
waxed or parchment paper piping bag
No. 2 writing nozzle
2 silver bells
candles

1 ▲ Split the cake and fill with a little butter icing. Cut in half and sandwich one half on top of the other. Place on the cake board.

2 ▲ Trim a thin wedge off the front edge to make a sloping windshield. Brush the cake with apricot jam and cover with marzipan. Color 12 ounces/1 quantity sugar paste icing bright red. Roll out on a work surface dusted with confectioners' sugar and use to cover the cake.

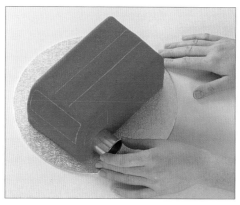

3 ▲ Mark the positions of the windows, ladder and wheels.

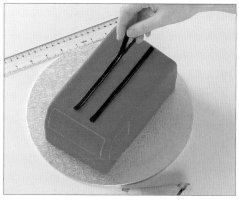

4 ▲ To make the ladder, unwind some licorice wheels and cut the licorice into two strips and short pieces for the rungs. Color half the royal icing black and stick the ladder to the top of the cake with royal icing. Roll out the remaining sugar paste icing, cut out and stick on the windows with a little water.

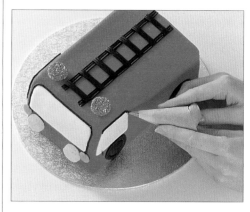

5 ▲ Pipe around the windows in black royal icing. Stick candies in place for headlights and wheels and stick the silver bells on the roof. Put the coconut in a bowl and mix in a few drops of green food coloring. Spread a little white royal icing over the cake board and sprinkle with coconut. Stick candies to the board with royal icing and press in the candles.

Baby's First Cake

This delicately decorated cake would be a lovely centerpiece for a party to welcome a new baby. Sugar paste icing (fondant) twists will dry quickly, so have the cake marked out in sections before you attempt to make the swags around the sides.

INGREDIENTS
Serves 8–10

1 quantity Quick-mix Sponge Cake
baked in an 8-inch round
cake pan
4 ounces/⅓ quantity Butter Icing
3 tablespoons apricot jam,
warmed and sieved
1 pound marzipan
1¼ pounds/1⅔ x quantity
Sugar paste Icing (Fondant)
yellow and blue food coloring
4 ounces/⅙ quantity Royal Icing
pink dusting powder

MATERIALS AND EQUIPMENT
10-inch round cake board
waxed or parchment paper piping bag
No. 1 writing nozzle
6 small blue bows

2 ▲ Color 1½ ounces/3 tablespoons of the remaining sugar paste pale blue and roll out thinly. Wet a paintbrush with water, remove excess on paper towels and brush lightly over the sugar paste icing. Roll out thinly the same quantity of white sugar paste icing, lay this on top and press together. Roll out together to an 8-inch square.

4 ▲ Using a template, mark the knitting in the center of the cake. Cut out the sweater from white sugar paste icing and stick into place with a little water.

5 Roll a little white sugar paste into a ball and color another amount blue. Roll into two tapering 3-inch-long needles with a small ball for the end of each. Dry overnight.

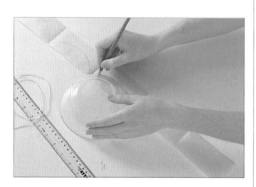

1 ▲ Split the cake and fill with butter icing. Place on the board and brush with apricot jam. Cover with a thin layer of marzipan. Color 1 pound/1⅓ x quantity sugar paste icing pale yellow. On a work surface dusted with confectioners' sugar, roll it out and use to cover the cake, extending it over the board. Measure the circumference of the cake with a piece of string and cut a strip of paper of the same length and depth as the cake. Fold the paper into six sections, mark with a deep scallop and cut in the top edge. Use to mark the swags on the side of the cake with a sharp needle.

3 ▲ Cut ¼-inch strips, carefully twist each one, moisten the swag marks with water and stick in place.

Tip

The powder tints should be mixed with a drop of vodka or gin, as they evaporate more quickly than water and do not have a chance to dissolve the delicate icing.

6 ▲ Stick the needles and ball in position and, with royal icing and a No. 1 writing nozzle, pipe knitting and stitches over the needles and a trail of wool to the ball. Pipe wool over the ball. Pipe a border around the base of the cake. Stick small bows around the edge of the cake with a little royal icing and carefully brush the knitting with powder tints.

Tablecloth Cake

This beautiful cake for an older child uses the elegant draping qualities of sugar paste icing (fondant) to make a covering that looks like an embroidered tablecloth.

INGREDIENTS
Serves 8–10
1 quantity Quick-mix Sponge Cake baked in an 8-inch round cake pan
4 ounces/⅓ quantity Butter Icing
3 tablespoons apricot jam, warmed and sieved
1 pound marzipan
1½ pounds/2 x quantity Sugar paste Icing (Fondant)
red food coloring
4 ounces/⅙ quantity Royal Icing candies

MATERIALS AND EQUIPMENT
10-inch round cake board
decorative teaspoon
8 wooden toothpicks
knitting needle or skewer
waxed or parchment paper piping bags
No. 0 writing nozzle
No. 2 writing nozzle
No. 1 writing nozzle
8 small red bows

1 Split the cake and fill with butter icing. Place on the board and brush with apricot jam. Cover with a layer of marzipan. Color two-thirds of the sugar paste icing red. On a work surface dusted with confectioners' sugar, roll the red sugar paste out and use to cover the cake, extending it over the board. Reserve a little for the base of the cake. Brush the lower edge of the cake with a thin band of water.

2 ▲ Roll the reserved red sugar paste into a thin rope long enough to go around the cake. Lay it neatly around the base of the cake and cut off the excess. Mark with the decorative handle of a spoon. Allow to dry overnight.

3 ▲ Roll out the white sugar paste icing to a 10-inch circle, place over the cake and quickly form drapes over wooden toothpicks at eight equal positions around the cake.

4 Mark a 4-inch circle in the center of the cake. Make a template of the small flower design and transfer to the cake with a needle. Press a fine knitting needle or skewer into the sugar paste icing to make the flowers. The red color should show through—do not press quite so deeply for the stems and leaves.

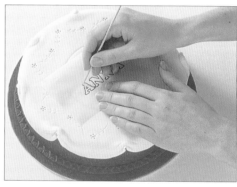

5 ▲ Mark the child's name in the center. Color a little royal icing with red food coloring and pipe with a No. 0 writing nozzle.

6 ▲ Stick on the bows with a dab of royal icing. With a No. 2 writing nozzle and white royal icing, pipe around the circle in the center. With a No. 1 writing nozzle, pipe small dots around the edge of the cloth to finish.

*N*umber 7 Cake

Any combination of colors works well for this marbled cake.

INGREDIENTS
Serves 8–10
1½ x quantity Quick-Mix Sponge
Cake mix
1 quantity orange-flavor
Butter Icing
4 tbsp apricot jam, warmed and
sieved
1½ lb/2 x quantity Sugarpaste Icing
green and blue food colorings

MATERIALS AND EQUIPMENT
9 x 12 inch roasting pan
10 x 13 inch cake board
small No 7 cutter

*T*ip

If you feel unsure about shaping the number seven cake freehand, you can purchase or rent shaped cake pans from specialist cake decorating shops.

1 Preheat the oven to 350°F. Grease the roasting pan, line the base and sides with waxed paper and grease the paper. Spoon the cake mixture into the prepared pan and smooth the surface. Bake in the center of the oven for 45–50 minutes, or until a skewer inserted into the center of the cake comes out clean. Leave the cake in the pan for about 5 minutes, then turn out on to a wire rack, peel off the lining paper and leave to cool completely.

2 ▲ Working with the cake flat side up, lightly mark out the shape of the number seven on the cake. Cut through the cake, starting at the bottom end and working up.

3 ▲ Slice through the cake horizontally, then carefully lift off the top layer and place on the work surface. Place the bottom layer of cake on the cake board and spread with the butter icing. Reassemble the cake.

4 Brush the cake evenly with apricot jam. Divide the sugarpaste icing into three equal portions. Leave one portion white, color one blue and the last green. Cut off about 2 oz from each of the blue and green icings, wrap each separately in plastic wrap and set aside. Marble the remaining blue and green sugarpaste icing with the white portion of icing.

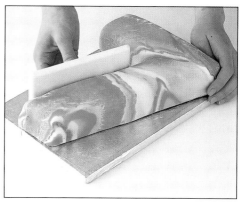

5 ▲ Roll out the marbled icing on a work surface lightly dusted with confectioners' sugar to a rectangle of 14 x 11 inches and use to cover the number seven. Smooth the icing with a cake smoother or with your hands.

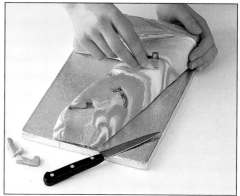

6 ▲ Use the cutter to cut random shapes out of the covered cake. Press the cutter into the icing carefully, but firmly. Remove the cutter and the shape should be wedged in the cutter. Poke out the shape with a toothpick and discard. This stage needs to be done immediately after the cake has been covered, or the sugarpaste icing will start drying out.

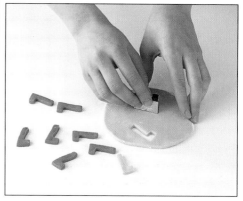

7 ▲ Roll out the reserved blue and green colored sugarpaste icing and then use the cutter to stamp out a combination of blue and green shapes. Use these to replace the stamped out shapes from the cake, pressing them in gently to fill the holes.

Wading Pool

This fun cake will need at least a day's preparation before the party; the bather, boat and duck are modeled from marzipan and sugarpaste and allowed to dry overnight before arranging them in partly dried royal icing.

INGREDIENTS
Serves 8–10
1 quantity Quick-mix Sponge Cake baked in a deep 6-inch round cake pan
2 ounces/¹⁄₆ quantity Butter Icing
3 tablespoons apricot jam, warmed and sieved
12 ounces marzipan
1 pound/1¹⁄₃ x quantity Sugar paste Icing (Fondant)
blue, red, yellow, green and brown food coloring
4 ounces/¹⁄₆ quantity Royal Icing

MATERIALS AND EQUIPMENT
8-inch round cake board
drinking straw
sheet of rice paper
waxed or parchment paper piping bag
basket weave nozzle
No. 1 writing nozzle

1 Split the cake and fill with a little butter icing. Place in the center of the cake board and brush with apricot glaze. Cover with a layer of marzipan. Roll out about three-quarters of the sugarpaste icing on a work surface dusted with confectioners' sugar and use to cover the cake. Divide the remaining sugar paste icing into four pieces and color them blue, red, yellow and green. Shape a small duck from the yellow, a 1½-inch rubber ring from the red and a boat from the green. Roll the remains of each color into two sausages long enough to go halfway around the cake. Stick to the sides of the cake with a little water, flattening slightly and smoothing the seams so the stripes come to the top of the cake.

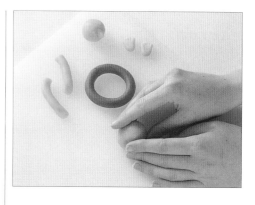

2 ▲ Color 2 ounces marzipan flesh color and shape into a small child with a head, half a body, arms and feet. Place in the rubber ring and allow to dry overnight. Cut a mast for the boat from a drinking straw and thread on a square rice-paper sail.

3 ▲ Color two-thirds of the royal icing blue and spread on top of the cake to resemble water, placing the child, duck and boat in the water. Color a little royal icing brown and pipe on the child's hair using a basket weave pipe. Pipe the eyes and mouth.

*T*oy Car

This little car can be made for any age. You could add a personalized license plate with the child's name and age to the back of the car.

INGREDIENTS
Serves 8–10
1 quantity Quick-mix Sponge Cake baked in an 8-inch round cake pan
4 ounces/⅓ quantity Butter Icing
3 tablespoons apricot jam, warmed and sieved
1 pound marzipan
1¼ pounds/1⅔ x quantity Sugar paste Icing (Fondant)
red, yellow and black food coloring
4 ounces/⅙ quantity Royal Icing candies

MATERIALS AND EQUIPMENT
10-inch round cake board
1½-inch plain round cutter
¾-inch plain round cutter
waxed or parchment paper piping bag
No. 1 writing nozzle
candles

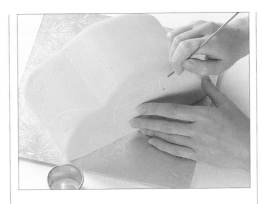

2 ▲ Color a small piece of sugar paste icing red and the rest yellow. Roll out the yellow icing on a work surface dusted with confectioners' sugar and use to cover the cake. Mark the doors and windows on the car with a sharp skewer.

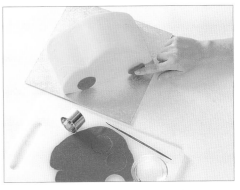

3 ▲ Roll out the red sugar paste icing and cut out four 1½-inch wheels with a cutter. Stick in place with water. Mark the center of each wheel with a smaller cutter. Color the royal icing black and pipe around the doors and windows. Stick on candies for headlights with a little royal icing. Stick the candles into candies with royal icing.

1 ▲ Split the cake and fill with a little butter icing. Cut in half and sandwich the halves upright together. With a sharp serrated knife, cut a shallow dip to create the windshield and to shape the hood. Place on the cake board and brush with apricot jam. Cut a strip of marzipan to cover the top of the cake to level the seams. Then cover the whole cake with an even layer of marzipan.

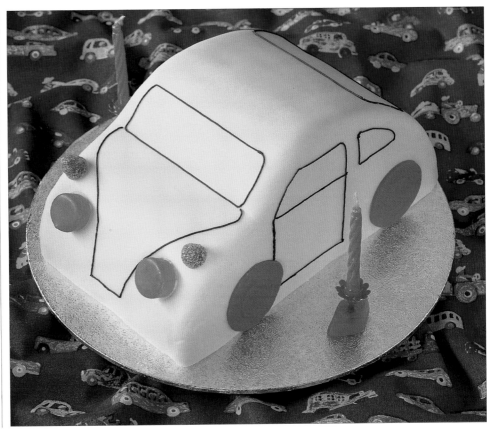

*N*urse's Kit

This is a simple cake to make. Any toy medical equipment is suitable to use, but make sure it doesn't get confused with the edible bits!

INGREDIENTS
Serves 12–15
1½ x quantity chocolate-flavor
Quick-Mix Sponge Cake mix
8 tbsp apricot jam, warmed and
sieved
1½ lb/2 x quantity Sugarpaste Icing
pink and red food colorings

MATERIALS AND EQUIPMENT
14 x 8 inch roasting pan
10 inch square cake board
selection of toy medical equipment

1 Preheat the oven to 350°F. Grease the roasting pan, line the base and sides with waxed paper and grease the paper. Spoon in the cake mixture and smooth the surface. Bake in the center of the oven for 45–50 minutes or until a skewer inserted into the center of the cake comes out clean. Leave the cake in the pan for about 5 minutes, then turn out on to a wire rack, peel off the lining paper and leave to cool completely.

2 ▲ Place the cake, dome side down, and cut in half widthways.

3 ▲ Turn one half of the cake dome side up, then use a small, sharp knife to indent a border about ½ inch in from the edge and about the same measurement deep, around the three uncut edges. Cut out the center in strips, keeping the edges neat. Brush the tops and sides of both halves of the cake with the apricot jam.

4 Cut off about 5 oz of the sugarpaste icing and color it deep pink. Cut off about ½ oz from this and shape into a small handle for the box. Carefully wrap in plastic wrap and set aside. Lightly dust the work surface with confectioners' sugar, then roll out the remaining pink icing and use to cover the cake board. Trim the edges. Cut off about ½ oz from the remaining white icing and color it red. Cover with plastic wrap and set aside. Color the remaining icing light pink and then divide it into two portions, one slightly bigger than the other.

5 Roll out the slightly bigger portion of light pink icing and use to cover the base of the nurse's box, gently easing it into the hollow and along the edges. Trim the edges, then position the covered cake on the cake board.

6 ▲ Roll out the other portion of light pink icing and use to cover the lid of the box, using your hands to ease it over the edges. Trim the edges. Place on top of the other cake, back a little and slightly turned to an angle.

7 ▲ Stick the handle on to the bottom section of the box, using a little water. Roll out the red icing and cut out a small cross. Use a little water to stick the cross on the lid of the box. Carefully insert a few toy items into the box, allowing them to hang over the edges a little. Arrange any other items of toy medical equipment around the board and cake when it is positioned on the table.

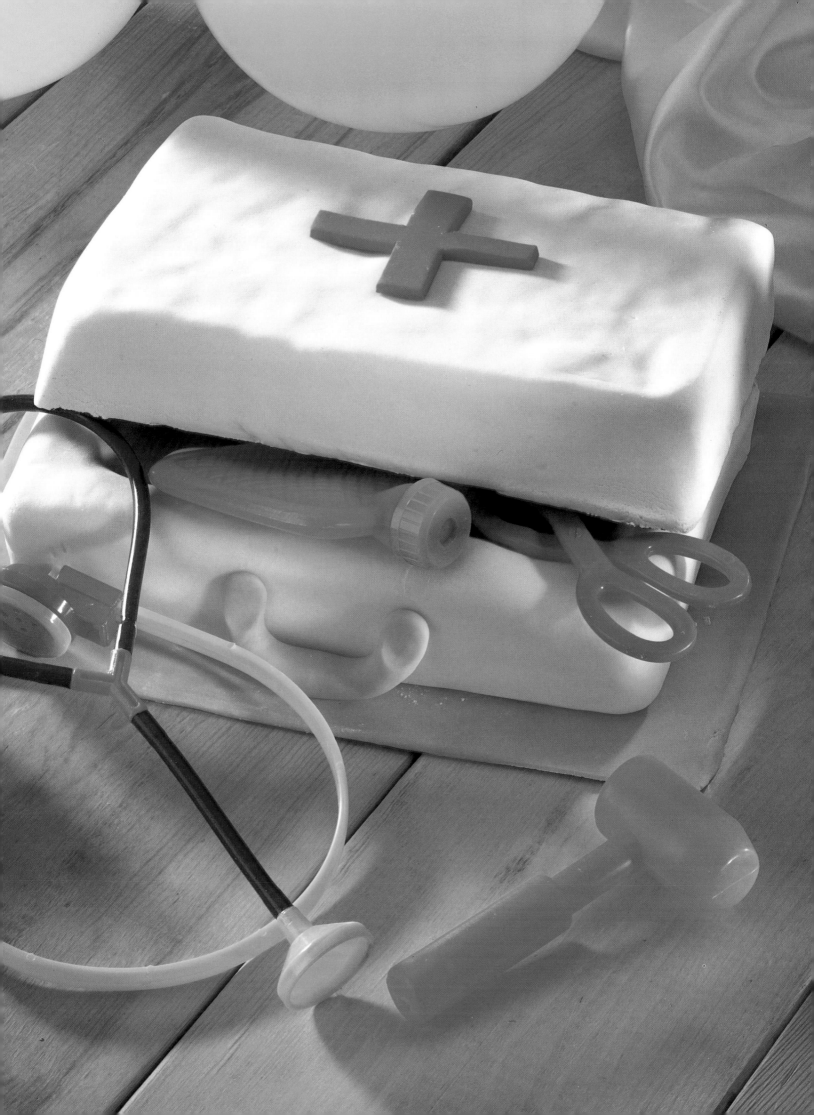

Mermaid Cake

Pretty, elegant and chocolatey! Every little girl's dream.

INGREDIENTS
Serves 6–8
1 quantity chocolate-flavor Quick-Mix Sponge Cake mix
1 lb plain chocolate
3 cups unsalted, unflavored popcorn
1 lb/1⅓ x quantity Sugarpaste Icing
lilac and pink food colorings
3 tbsp apricot jam, warmed and sieved
1 egg white, lightly beaten
raw sugar, for the sand

MATERIALS AND EQUIPMENT
2 lb loaf pan
12 x 6 inch cake board
doll, similar in dimensions to a "Barbie" or "Sindy" doll
small crescent-shaped cutter
small fluted round cutter
6 inch piece of thin lilac ribbon

Tip

For an even more chocolatey version of this cake, cut the sponge into three horizontally and use 1 quantity chocolate-flavor Butter Icing to spread between the layers. Reassemble the cake and then cover with chocolate popcorn.

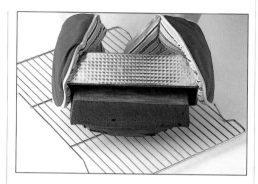

1 ▲ Preheat the oven to 350°F. Grease the pan, line the base and sides with waxed paper and grease the paper. Spoon the cake mixture into the prepared pan and smooth the surface. Bake in the center of the oven for 35–40 minutes, or until a skewer inserted into the center of the cake comes out clean. Leave the cake in the pan for about 5 minutes, then turn out on to a wire rack, peel off the lining paper and leave to cool.

2 ▲ Turn the cake dome side up and place on the cake board. Melt the chocolate in a bowl placed over hot water. Add the popcorn and stir until evenly coated. Spoon the popcorn around the sides of the cake and on the cake board. Spread any remaining melted chocolate over the top of the cake until evenly covered. Set aside at room temperature.

3 Cut off about one-quarter of the sugarpaste icing. Color the larger piece lilac and the smaller piece pink. Cut off about one-third of the lilac icing, wrap this and the pink icing separately in plastic wrap and set aside.

4 ▲ On a work surface lightly dusted with confectioners' sugar, roll out the larger portion of lilac sugarpaste icing to an oblong shape wide enough to wrap around the doll's legs and about 2 inches longer. Brush the doll from the waist down with the apricot jam, then wrap her in the sugarpaste icing, lightly pinching and squeezing it around her legs to make it stick. Working downwards towards her feet, pinch the end of the tail to form a fin shape, curling the ends slightly.

5 ▲ Position the mermaid on the cake, moving her slightly until she feels secure and then pressing down firmly. Roll out the reserved lilac and pink sugarpaste icing and use the crescent-shaped cutter to stamp out the scales. Cover the scales and the reserved trimmings with plastic wrap to prevent them drying out. Starting at the fin end of the tail, brush the scales with a tiny amount of egg white and stick on to the tail, overlapping all the time, until the tail is completely covered.

6 Re-roll the reserved icing trimmings and use the small fluted cutter to stamp out a shell-shaped bra top for the mermaid. Make indentations on the top with the back of a knife, then stick in place with a little extra apricot jam. Use the ribbon to tie up the mermaid's hair.

7 Position the cake on the serving table or large board, then scatter the raw sugar around the base of the cake for the sand and add a few real shells, if you like. Remove the doll before serving the cake.

Helicopter Cake

Perfect for a party of boys or girls who are partial to helicopters. The cake involves a little creative use of non-edible items which must be removed before eating.

INGREDIENTS
Serves 6–8
1 quantity Quick-Mix Sponge Cake mix
2 fan wafers
6–8 tbsp apricot jam, warmed and sieved
12 oz/1 quantity Sugarpaste Icing
red, blue and black food colorings
small round candy
¼ quantity Butter Icing
2 candies, for the headlights
2 x 6 inch pieces of flat liquorice
4 x 1 inch pieces of liquorice sticks
1 cup shredded coconut, toasted

MATERIALS AND EQUIPMENT
2 lb loaf pan
small round cutter
2 wooden skewers
wood glue
small wooden block, to raise helicopter
7 inch square cake board
5 inch piece of white ribbon
piping bag fitted with a small plain nozzle

1 Preheat the oven to 350°F. Grease the pan, line with waxed paper and grease the paper. Spoon the cake mixture into the prepared pan and smooth the surface. Bake in the center of the oven for 35–40 minutes, or until a skewer inserted into the center of the cake comes out clean. Turn out on to a wire rack, peel off the lining paper and leave to cool.

2 ▲ To shape the cake, stand it flat side down and use a large, sharp knife to cut it into the shape of a teardrop. Trim the sides from top to bottom so that the top is wider than the bottom. Turn the cake on its side, and cut a wedge shape out of the back part.

3 ▲ Invert the cake so that the flat side is uppermost. Use the round cutter to stamp out a hole for the cockpit, indenting about 1 inch. Remove the round piece and reserve.

4 Cut a thin slice from each of the wafers, reserve one for the tail fin and discard the other slice. Cut each wafer in half lengthwise. Measure the long side of one of the wafers and then cut the wooden skewers double that length. Glue the skewers together in the center to form a cross and set aside.

5 Remove a small piece of sugarpaste icing. Take another piece of icing about the size of an egg and color it deep blue. Wrap these pieces in plastic wrap and set aside.

6 Color the remaining sugarpaste icing pale blue. Remove an egg-sized piece, wrap in plastic wrap and set aside. Brush the cake with jam. Roll out the pale blue sugarpaste on a work surface dusted with confectioners' sugar and use to cover the helicopter. Position the covered cake on the small block of wood on the cake board.

7 To make the propeller support, brush the reserved piece of round cake cut out for the pilot's cockpit with apricot jam. Roll out the reserved pale blue sugarpaste icing and cover the round cake. Reserve the trimmings. Position the propeller support on the helicopter, half way between the cockpit and the tail, sticking it in place with a dab of jam. Place the crossed skewers on top of the propeller support and secure them in place with a little of the pale blue icing. Place the wafers over the skewers, securing them underneath with more icing. Place the small round candy on top.

8 ▲ To make the pilot, shape the dark blue sugarpaste icing into a small head and body to fit into the cockpit. Color a little of the reserved white icing red for the nose and mouth and use white icing for the buttons. Stick the details in place with a little water. Shape some of the reserved pale blue icing into the pilot's hat and place on his head, securing with a little water if necessary. Sit the pilot in his seat and tie the ribbon scarf around his neck.

9 Color the butter icing black and fill the piping bag. First pipe in the pilot's eyes, then pipe the zigzag and straight borders around the helicopter. Stick the headlight candies in position with a little of the remaining butter icing and stick the tail fin on in the same way. To make the landing feet, smooth out the flat pieces of liquorice and fold in half lengthwise. Position on the cake board, wedged in with the liquorice sticks. Scatter the shredded coconut around the cake board.

Doll's House

Little children love this cake. You can pipe their age on the door and the same number of candles can be added to the cake if you wish.

INGREDIENTS
Serves 10–12
2 x quantity Quick-mix Sponge Cake baked in a 10-inch square cake pan
8 ounces/⅔ quantity Butter Icing
4 tablespoons apricot jam, warmed and sieved
1 pound marzipan
1 pound/1⅓ x quantity Sugar paste Icing (Fondant)
red, yellow, blue, black, green and gold food coloring
4 ounces/¼ quantity Royal Icing

MATERIALS AND EQUIPMENT
12-inch square cake board
paintbrush
waxed or parchment paper piping bag
No. 2 writing nozzle
flower decorations

1 ▲ Split the cake and fill with butter icing. Cut 2½-inch triangles off two corners, then use these pieces to make a chimney. Shape the top of the roof. Place on the cake board and brush with apricot jam. Cover with a layer of marzipan.

2 ▲ On a work surface dusted with confectioners' sugar, roll out three-quarters of the sugar paste icing and use to cover the house. Using a pastry wheel, mark the roof to look like thatch. Mark the chimney with the back of a knife to look like bricks.

3 ▲ Paint the chimney red and the roof yellow.

4 ▲ Mark the door 3 x 4½ inches and the windows 2½ inches square. Color 2 tablespoons of sugar paste icing with red food coloring, cut out and stick on the door with a little water. Color a small piece blue, cut out and stick on for the top fanlight. Paint on the curtains with blue food coloring. Color half the royal icing black and pipe the window frames and panes, around the door and the fanlight.

5 ▲ Color the remaining royal icing green. Pipe the flower stems under the windows and the climbing vine up the wall and onto the roof. Stick the flowers in place with a little icing and pipe green flower centers. Pipe the knocker, the handle and the age of the child on the door. Allow to dry for 1 hour. Paint the knocker, handle and number with gold food coloring.

Fairy Cake

This is one of the more advanced cakes and requires a lot of skill and patience. Allow yourself plenty of time if you are attempting the techniques for the first time.

INGREDIENTS
Serves 8–10
1 quantity Quick-mix Sponge Cake baked in an 8-inch round cake pan
4 ounces/⅓ quantity Butter Icing
3 tablespoons apricot jam, warmed and sieved
1 pound marzipan
1 pound/1⅓ x quantity Sugar paste Icing (Fondant)
blue, pink, yellow and gold food coloring
4 ounces/⅙ quantity Royal Icing silver balls (dragées)

MATERIALS AND EQUIPMENT
10-inch round cake board
waxed or parchment paper
piping bags
No. 1 writing nozzle
fine paintbrush
pink sparkle luster powder
frill cutter
small round cutter
wooden toothpick
cotton balls
No. 7 star nozzle
silver ribbon

1 Split the cake and fill with butter icing. Place on the board and brush with apricot jam. Cover with a thin layer of marzipan. Color most of the sugar paste icing pale blue and roll out on a surface dusted with confectioners' sugar to cover the cake. Dry overnight. Using a template, carefully mark the position of the fairy on the cake. As royal icing dries quickly, work only on about 1-inch sections of the fairy's wings at a time. Fill a piping bag with a No. 1 writing nozzle with white royal icing and carefully pipe over the outline of each wing section.

2 ▲ Pipe a second line just inside that and, with a damp paintbrush, brush long strokes from the edges toward the center, leaving more icing at the edges and fading away to a thin film near the base of the wings. Allow to dry for 1 hour. Brush with dry luster powder (not dissolved in alcohol).

3 ▲ Color a little sugar paste icing flesh color, roll and cut out the body. Lay carefully in position. Dampen a paintbrush, remove the excess water on paper towels and carefully brush under the arms, legs and head to stick. Round off any sharp edges by rubbing gently with a finger. Cut out the bodice and shoes from white sugar paste and stick in place. Cut out a wand and star and allow to dry.

4 Work quickly to make the tutu, as thin sugar paste dries quickly and will crack easily. Each frill must be made separately. Roll out a small piece of sugar paste to ⅛ inch thick and cut out a fluted circle with a small plain inner circle. (The depth of the frill will be determined by the size of the central hole; the smaller the central hole, the wider the frill.)

5 ▲ Cut into quarters and, with a wooden toothpick, roll along the fluted edge to stretch it and give fullness.

6 Attach the frills to the waist with a little water. Repeat with the other layers, tucking the sides under neatly. Use a wooden toothpick to arrange the frills and small pieces of cotton wool to hold the folds of the skirt in place until dry. Allow to dry overnight. Brush a little luster powder over the edge of the tutu. Paint on the hair and face, stick on the wand and star and paint the star gold. Pipe a border of royal icing round the edge of the board with a star nozzle and place a silver ball on each point. Allow to dry. Color a little royal icing yellow and pipe over the hair. Paint with a touch of gold coloring.

Ballerina Cake

This cake shows how you can adapt the design of the Fairy Cake to make a ballerina. The delicate pink flowers look especially pretty against the white icing background.

INGREDIENTS
Serves 8–10
1 quantity Quick-mix Sponge Cake
baked in an 8-inch round
cake pan
4 ounces/⅓ quantity Butter Icing
3 tablespoons apricot jam,
warmed and sieved
1 pound marzipan
1 pound/1⅓ x quantity
Sugar paste Icing (Fondant)
pink, yellow, green and
blue food coloring
4 ounces/⅙ quantity Royal Icing

MATERIALS AND EQUIPMENT
10-inch round cake board
plunger blossom cutters
frill cutter
small round cutter
wooden toothpick
cotton balls
waxed or parchment paper piping bag
No. 1 writing nozzle
fine paintbrush
No. 7 shell nozzle
ribbon

1 Split the cake and fill with butter icing. Place on the board and brush with apricot jam. Cover with a layer of marzipan. On a work surface dusted with confectioners' sugar, roll out three-quarters of the sugar paste icing and use to cover the cake. Allow to dry overnight. Divide the remaining sugar paste icing into three pieces; color one flesh tone and the other two contrasting pinks for the tutu and flowers. Roll out each color separately and cut out twelve flowers and three tiny flowers from the paler pink sugar paste icing for the headdress. Allow to dry.

2 ▲ Make a template for the ballerina and carefully mark her position on the cake. Cut out the body from flesh-colored sugar paste icing and stick into position with a little water. Round off the edges by rubbing gently with a finger. Cut out a bodice from the darker pink sugar paste icing and stick in place.

3 To make the tutu, work quickly, as the thin sugar paste dries quickly and will crack. Roll out the darker pink sugar paste icing to ⅛ inch thick and cut out a fluted circle with a small plain inner circle.

4 ▲ Cut the circle into quarters and, with a wooden toothpick, roll along the fluted edge to stretch it and give fullness.

5 ▲ Attach the frills to the waist with a little water. Repeat with two more layers, using a toothpick to shape the frills and cotton balls to hold them in place until dry. For the final layer, use the paler pink and cover with a short dark frill, as the bodice extension. Allow to dry overnight.

6 ▲ Attach flowers to make a hoop. Color a little royal icing green and pipe tiny leaves in between. Paint on the face and hair. Color a little royal icing yellow and pipe over the hair. Stick three tiny flowers in place around the head. Cut pale pink sugar paste shoes and stick in place with water, and paint ribbons. Color a little royal icing dark pink and pipe the flower centers on the hoop and headdress. Pipe white royal icing around the base of the cake with the shell nozzle and tie the ribbon around it.

Royal Crown

The most difficult part of this cake is supporting the covered ice cream wafers with toothpicks while they dry in place. Plenty of royal icing can be used to smooth the seams and help to support the pieces.

INGREDIENTS
Serves 12–14
2 x quantity Quick-mix Sponge
Cake baked in an 8-inch round cake
pan and a 6-inch round cake pan
6 ounces/½ quantity Butter Icing
5 tablespoons apricot jam,
warmed and sieved
1 pound marzipan
1¼ pound/1⅔ x quantity
Sugar paste Icing (Fondant)
red food coloring
1 pound/⅔ quantity Royal Icing
small black jelly candies
4 ice cream fan wafers
silver balls (dragées)
jewel candies

MATERIALS AND EQUIPMENT
*12-inch square cake board
wooden toothpicks*

1 ▲ Split the cakes and fill with a little butter icing. Sandwich one on top of the other and place on the board. Shape the top cake into a dome. Brush with apricot jam and cover with a layer of marzipan. On a work surface dusted with confectioners' sugar, roll out three-quarters of the sugar paste icing and use to cover the cake.

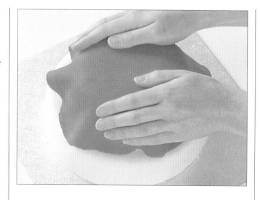

2 ▲ Color the remaining sugar paste icing red and use to cover the dome of the cake. Trim away the excess with a knife.

3 ▲ Spoon rough mounds of royal icing around the base of the cake and stick a black jelly candy on each mound.

4 ▲ Cut the ice cream wafers in half with a sharp knife.

5 ▲ Spread both sides of the wafers with royal icing and stick to the cake, smoothing the icing level with the sides of the cake. Use toothpicks to support until dry. Put a silver ball on top of each point and jewel candies around the sides of the crown, sticking in place with a little royal icing.

*M*onsters on the Moon

A great cake for little monsters!
This cake is best eaten the day it is made.

INGREDIENTS
Serves 12–15
1 quantity Quick-Mix Sponge
Cake mix
4 oz/¹/₃ quantity Sugarpaste Icing
edible silver glitter powder
(optional)

For the Icing
1³/₄ cups plus 2 tbsp sugar
2 large egg whites
4 tbsp water

MATERIALS AND EQUIPMENT
ovenproof wok
various sizes of plain round cutters
12 inch round cake board
several small monster toys

1 ▲ Preheat the oven to 350°F. Grease the wok, line the base with waxed paper and grease the paper. Spoon in the cake mixture and smooth the surface. Bake in the center of the oven for 35–40 minutes or until a skewer inserted into the center of the cake comes out clean. Leave the cake in the wok for about 5 minutes, then turn out on to a wire rack, peel off the lining paper and leave to cool completely.

2 ▲ With the cake dome side up, use the round cutters to cut out craters. Press in a cutter about 1 inch deep, then remove and use a knife to cut out the cake to make a crater.

3 ▲ Pull off small pieces of the sugarpaste icing and press them into uneven strips which can be moulded around the edges of the craters. Make one of the craters especially deep by adding an extra-wide sugarpaste strip to make the edges higher.

4 Place the cake on the cake board. To make the icing, place all the ingredients in a heatproof bowl, then sit the bowl over a saucepan of simmering water. Beat until thick and peaked. Spoon the icing over the cake, swirling it into the craters and peaking it unevenly. Sprinkle over the silver glitter powder, if using, then position the monsters on the cake.

*T*ip

To cover the cake board, roll out 1 lb of black sugarpaste icing. Trim the edges. Using various sizes of star-shaped cutters, stamp out stars from the black icing. Roll out 8 oz of yellow marzipan thinly and use the star-shaped cutters to stamp out replacement stars. Dust with a little extra silver powder.

Rosette Cake

This lovely cake is actually very quick to decorate. If the icing becomes too soft, put it in the refrigerator to stiffen. If you make a mistake, you can always try again until you get a good finish.

INGREDIENTS
Serves 10
1½ x quantity Quick-mix Sponge
Cake baked in an 8-inch square
cake pan
12 ounces/1 quantity Butter Icing
3 tablespoons apricot jam,
warmed and sieved
dark red food coloring
crystallized violets

MATERIALS AND EQUIPMENT
10-inch square cake board
cake comb
piping bag
No. 8 star nozzle
candles

2 ▲ Hold the cake comb against the cake and move it from side to side across the top to create the impression of waves.

3 ▲ Put the rest of the butter icing into a piping bag fitted with a star nozzle. Mark a 6-inch circle on the top of the cake and pipe stars around it and around the base of the cake. Place the candles and flowers in the corners.

1 ▲ Split the cake and fill with a little butter icing. Place in the center of the cake board and brush with apricot jam. Color the remaining butter icing dark pink. Spread the top and sides with butter icing. Hold the comb against the side of the cake, resting the flat edge on the board, and draw along to give straight ridges along each side.

Index

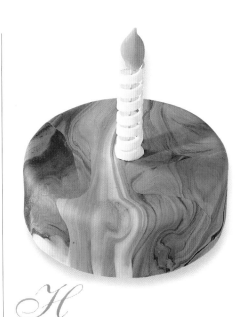

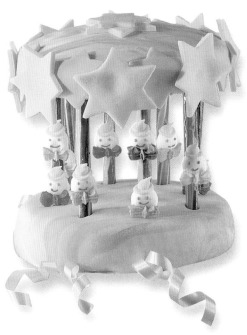

Acknowledgments

The publisher and authors would like to thank the following for supplying props and
equipment for photography: Scenics Cakes Boards, Colours Direct (0181 441 3082),
the Cloth Store (01293 560 943), Cake Fayre (0243 771 857), Jean Ainger, Braun and Kenwood.
Thanks also to Stork Cookery Service for the Rich Fruit Cake chart,
and Jackie Mason, Mavis Giles and Teresa Goldfinch for their help.